ADVANCED JAVA PROGRAMMING:

OBJECTS, DATA STRUCTURES AND CONCURRENCY

ADVANCED JAVA PROGRAMMING:

OBJECTS, DATA STRUCTURES AND CONCURRENCY

Kagiso Molefe
Nchimunya Phiri

Kruger Brentt
Publishers

2026

Kruger Brentt Publishers UK. LTD.
Company Number 9728962

Regd. Office: 68 St Margarets Road, Edgware, Middlesex HA8 9UU

ISBN: 978-1-78715-672-2

For information on all our publications visit our website at http://krugerbrentt.com/

PREFACE

The landscape of software development has undergone tremendous transformation over the past few decades, with Java remaining one of the most resilient and adaptable programming languages in this journey. Since its inception, Java has evolved from a simple object-oriented language to a powerful ecosystem capable of supporting enterprise applications, distributed systems, cloud-native solutions, and high-performance computing. This book, Advanced Java Programming, has been crafted with the aim of helping readers bridge the gap between foundational Java knowledge and the advanced skills required in modern development environments.

As applications grow more complex, developers are expected to work with sophisticated programming constructs, optimized data structures, and concurrent processing models. This text has been structured around these essential pillars—Object-Oriented Design, Data Structures, and Concurrency—to offer an in-depth understanding of how Java leverages these concepts to build efficient and scalable systems. Each chapter progresses systematically from conceptual explanations to implementation strategies, allowing readers to strengthen both theoretical and practical competencies.

A major emphasis of this book is on writing clean, maintainable, and reusable code using advanced Java features such as generics, functional programming, collections framework, multithreading, parallel streams, and modern JVM capabilities. Real-world examples, case studies, and code snippets have been integrated throughout the book to demonstrate how these features can be effectively applied to solve programming challenges. Furthermore, the text explores best practices in software design, including modular architecture, design patterns, and performance optimization techniques, which are indispensable for professional software development.

This book is intended for undergraduate and postgraduate students, software practitioners, educators, and anyone aspiring to elevate their Java proficiency beyond the basics. Whether you are preparing for competitive examinations, tackling industry-level coding assignments, or contributing to large-scale software projects, the concepts presented here will support your learning and professional growth. The content aims not only to enhance technical capability but also to inspire readers to think critically, design thoughtfully, and develop solutions that stand the test of time.

We sincerely hope that this book becomes a valuable companion in your journey toward mastering advanced Java concepts. As with all technology, Java will continue to evolve, and it is my belief that the knowledge gained through this text will equip you to adapt confidently to future developments. Your dedication to learning and improving your craft is commendable, and we trust that the insights contained within these pages will play a meaningful role in your success as a Java developer.

Kagiso Molefe

Nchimunya Phiri

CONTENTS

Chapter 1 ADVANCED PROGRAMMING IN THE LARGE: OBJECTS AND CLASSES

1.1 PROGRAMMING EXAMPLE: CARD, HAND, DECK

In this section, we look at some specific examples of object-oriented design in a domain that is simple enough that we have a chance of coming up with something reasonably reusable. Consider card games that are played with a standard deck of playing cards (a so-called "poker" deck, since it is used in the game of poker).

1.1.1 Designing the classes

In a typical card game, each player gets a hand of cards. The deck is shuffled and cards are dealt one at a time from the deck and added to the players' hands. In some games, cards can be removed from a hand, and new cards can be added. The game is won or lost depending on the value (ace, 2, 3, . . . , king) and suit (spades, diamonds, clubs, hearts) of the cards that a player receives. If we look for nouns in this description, there are several candidates for objects: game, player, hand, card, deck, value, and suit. Of these, the value and the suit of a card are simple values, and they might just be represented as instance variables in a *Card* object. In a complete program, the other five nouns might be represented by classes. But let's work on the ones that are most obviously reusable: *card*, *hand*, and *deck*.

If we look for verbs in the description of a card game, we see that we can *shuffle* a deck and *deal* a card from a deck. This gives use us two candidates for instance methods in a *Deck* class: shuffle() and dealCard(). Cards can be added to and removed from hands. This gives two candidates for instance methods in a *Hand* class: addCard() and removeCard(). Cards are relatively passive things, but we at least need to be able to determine their suits and values. We will discover more instance methods as we go along.

First, we'll design the deck class in detail. When a deck of cards is first created, it contains 52 cards in some standard order. The *Deck* class will need a constructor to create a new deck. The constructor needs no parameters because any new deck is the same as any other. There will be an instance method called shuffle() that will rearrange the 52 cards into a random order.

The dealCard() instance method will get the next card from the deck. This will be a function with a return type of Card, since the caller needs to know what card is being dealt. It has no parameters—when you deal the next card from the deck, you don't provide any information to the deck; you just get the next card, whatever it is. What will happen if there are no more cards in the deck when its dealCard() method is called? It should probably be considered an error to try to deal a card from an empty deck, so the deck can throw an exception in that case. But this raises another question: How will the rest of the program know whether the deck is empty? Of course, the program could keep track of how many cards it has used. But the deck itself should know how many cards it has left, so the program should just be able to ask the deck object. We can make this possible by specifying another instance method, cardsLeft(), that returns the number of cards remaining in the deck. This leads to a full specification of all the subroutines in the *Deck* class:

Constructor and instance methods in class Deck:

```
    /**
    * Constructor.    Create an unshuffled deck of cards.
    */
    public Deck()
    /**
    Put all the used cards back into the deck,
    and shuffle it into a random order.
    */
public void shuffle()
    /**
    As cards are dealt from the deck, the number of
    cards left decreases.      This function returns the
    number of cards that are still left in the deck.
    */
public int cardsLeft()
    /**
    Deals one card from the deck and returns it.
    @throws IllegalStateException if no more cards are left.
    */
public Card dealCard()
```

This is everything you need to know in order to use the Deck class. Of course, it doesn't tell us how to write the class. This has been an exercise in design, not in coding. You can look at the source code, Deck.java, if you want. It should not be a surprise that the class includes an array of *Cards* as an instance variable, but there are a few things you might not understand at this point. Of course, you can use the class in your programs as a black box, without understanding the implementation.

We can do a similar analysis for the *Hand* class. When a hand object is first created, it has no cards in it. An addCard() instance method will add a card to the hand. This method needs a parameter of type *Card* to specify which card is being added. For the removeCard() method, a parameter is needed to specify which card to remove. But should we specify the card itself ("Remove the ace of spades"), or should we specify the card by its position in the hand ("Remove the third card in the hand")? Actually, we don't have to decide, since we can allow for both options. We'll have two removeCard() instance methods, one with a parameter of type *Card* specifying the card to be removed and one with a parameter of type int specifying the position of the card in the hand. (Remember that you can have two methods in a class with the same name, provided they have different numbers or types of parameters.) Since a hand can contain a variable number of cards, it's convenient to be able to ask a hand object how many cards it contains. So, we need an instance method getCardCount() that returns the number of cards in the hand. When I play cards, I like to arrange the cards in my hand so that cards of the same value are next to each other. Since this is a generally useful thing to be able to do, we can provide instance methods for sorting the cards in the hand. Here is a full specification for a reusable *Hand* class:

Constructor and instance methods in class Hand:

```
    /**
    * Constructor. Create a Hand object that is initially empty.
    */
public Hand()
    /**
    * Discard all cards from the hand, making the hand empty.
    */
public void clear()
    /**
    Add the card c to the hand.        c should be non-null.
    @throws NullPointerException if c is null.
```

```
    */
public void addCard(Card c)
    /**
    If the specified card is in the hand, it is removed.
    */
public void removeCard(Card c)
    /**
    Remove the card in the specified position from the
    hand.   Cards are numbered counting from zero.
    @throws IllegalArgumentException if the specified
    position does not exist in the hand.
    */
public void removeCard(int position)
    /**
    Return the number of cards in the hand.
    */
public int getCardCount()
    /**
    Get the card from the hand in given position, where
    positions are numbered starting from 0.
    @throws IllegalArgumentException if the specified
    position does not exist in the hand.
    */
public Card getCard(int position)
    /**
    Sorts the cards in the hand so that cards of the same
    suit are grouped together, and within a suit the cards
    are sorted by value.
    */
public void sortBySuit()
    /**
    Sorts the cards in the hand so that cards are sorted into
```

```
    order of increasing value.        Cards with the same value
    are sorted by suit. Note that aces are considered
    to have the lowest value.
    */
public void sortByValue()
```

Again, there are a few things in the implementation of the class that you won't understand at this point, but that doesn't stop you from using the class in your projects. The source code can be found in the file Hand.java

1.1.2 The Card Class

We will look at the design and implementation of a *Card* class in full detail. The class will have a constructor that specifies the value and suit of the card that is being created. There are four suits, which can be represented by the integers 0, 1, 2, and 3. It would be tough to remember which number represents which suit, so I've defined named constants in the *Card* class to represent the four possibilities. For example, Card.SPADES is a constant that represents the suit, "spades." (These constants are declared to be public final static ints. It might be better to use an enumerated type, but I will stick here to integer-valued constants.) The possible values of a card are the numbers 1, 2, . . . , 13, with 1 standing for an ace, 11 for a jack, 12 for a queen, and 13 for a king. Again, I've defined some named constants to represent the values of aces and face cards. (When you read the *Card* class, you'll see that I've also added support for Jokers.)

A *Card* object can be constructed knowing the value and the suit of the card. For example, we can call the constructor with statements such as:

```
card1 = new Card( Card.ACE, Card.SPADES );  // Construct ace of spades.
card2 = new Card( 10, Card.DIAMONDS );      // Construct 10 of diamonds.
card3 = new Card( v, s );     // This is OK, as long as v and s
                              //      are integer expressions.
```

A *Card* object needs instance variables to represent its value and suit. I've made these private so that they cannot be changed from outside the class, and I've provided getter methods getSuit() and getValue() so that it will be possible to discover the suit and value from outside the class. The instance variables are initialized in the constructor, and are never changed after that. In fact, I've declared the instance variables suit and value to be final, since they are never changed after they are initialized. An instance variable can be declared final provided it is either given an initial value in its declaration or is initialized in every constructor in the class. Since all its instance variables are final, a *Card* is an immutable object.

Finally, I've added a few convenience methods to the class to make it easier to print out cards in a human-readable form. For example, I want to be able to print out the suit of a card as the word "Diamonds", rather than as the meaningless code number 2, which is used in the class to represent diamonds. Since this is something that I'll probably have to do in many programs, it makes sense to include support for it in the class. So, I've provided instance methods getSuitAsString() and getValueAsString() to return string representations of the suit and value of a card. Finally, I've defined the instance method toString() to return a string with both the value and suit, such as "Queen of Hearts". Recall that this method will be used automatically whenever a *Card* needs to be converted into a *String*, such as when the card is concatenated onto a string with the + operator. Thus, the statement

```
System.out.println( "Your card is the " + card );
```

is equivalent to

```
System.out.println( "Your card is the " + card.toString() );
```

If the card is the queen of hearts, either of these will print out "Your card is the Queen of Hearts".

Here is the complete *Card* class, which can also be found in Card.java. This class is general enough to be highly reusable, so the work that went into designing, writing, and testing it pays off handsomely in the long run.

```
/**
An object of type Card represents a playing card from a
standard Poker deck, including Jokers.          The card has a suit, which
can be spades, hearts, diamonds, clubs, or joker.          A spade, heart,
diamond, or club has one of the 13 values: ace, 2, 3, 4, 5, 6, 7,
8, 9, 10, jack, queen, or king.   Note that "ace" is considered to be
the smallest value.    A joker can also have an associated value;
this value can be anything and can be used to keep track of several
different jokers.
*/
public class Card {
    public final static int SPADES = 0;// Codes for the 4 suits, plus Joker.
    public final static int HEARTS = 1;
    public final static int DIAMONDS = 2;
    public final static int CLUBS = 3; public final static int JOKER = 4;
```

```
public final static int ACE = 1;      // Codes for the non-numeric cards.
public final static int JACK = 11;   //      Cards 2 through 10 have their
public final static int QUEEN = 12;           //      numerical values for their codes.
public final static int KING = 13;
/**
This card's suit, one of the constants SPADES, HEARTS, DIAMONDS,
CLUBS, or JOKER.          The suit cannot be changed after the card is
constructed.
*/
private final int suit;
/**
The card's value.           For a normal card, this is one of the values
1 through 13, with 1 representing ACE.      For a JOKER, the value
can be anything.The value cannot be changed after the card
is constructed.
*/
private final int value;
/**
Creates a Joker, with 1 as the associated value.      (Note that
"new Card()" is equivalent to "new Card(1,Card.JOKER)".)
*/
public Card() {
        suit = JOKER;
        value = 1;
}
/**
Creates a card with a specified suit and value.
@param theValue the value of the new card.       For a regular card (non-joker),
the value must be in the range 1 through 13, with 1 representing an Ace.
You can use the constants Card.ACE, Card.JACK, Card.QUEEN, and Card.KING.
For a Joker, the value can be anything.
@param theSuit the suit of the new card.  This must be one of the values
```

```
Card.SPADES, Card.HEARTS, Card.DIAMONDS, Card.CLUBS, or Card.JOKER.
@throws IllegalArgumentException if the parameter values are not in the
permissible ranges
*/
public Card(int theValue, int theSuit) {
        if (theSuit != SPADES && theSuit != HEARTS && theSuit != DIAMONDS &&
                        theSuit != CLUBS && theSuit != JOKER)
                throw new IllegalArgumentException("Illegal playing card suit");
        if (theSuit != JOKER && (theValue < 1 || theValue > 13))
                throw new IllegalArgumentException("Illegal playing card value");
        value = theValue;
        suit = theSuit;
}
/**
Returns the suit of this card.
@returns the suit, which is one of the constants Card.SPADES,
Card.HEARTS, Card.DIAMONDS, Card.CLUBS, or Card.JOKER
*/
public int getSuit() {
        return suit;
}
/**
Returns the value of this card.
@return the value, which is one of the numbers 1 through 13, inclusive for
a regular card, and which can be any value for a Joker.
*/
public int getValue() {
        return value;
}
/**
Returns a String representation of the card's suit.
```

```
    @return one of the strings "Spades", "Hearts", "Diamonds", "Clubs"
    or "Joker".
    */
    public String getSuitAsString() {
            switch ( suit ) {
            case SPADES:    return "Spades";
            case HEARTS:    return "Hearts";
            case DIAMONDS: return "Diamonds";
            case CLUBS:     return "Clubs";
            default: return "Joker";
            }
    }
/**
    Returns a String representation of the card's value.
    @return for a regular card, one of the strings "Ace", "2",
    "3", ..., "10", "Jack", "Queen", or "King".   For a Joker, the
    string is always numerical.
    */
    public String getValueAsString() {
            if (suit == JOKER)
                    return "" + value;
            else { // (Note use of traditional syntax for the switch statement.)
                    switch ( value ) {
                    case    1:      return  "Ace";
                    case    2:      return  "2";
                    case    3:      return  "3";
                    case    4:      return  "4";
                    case    5:      return  "5";
                    case    6:      return  "6";
                    case    7:      return  "7";
                    case    8:      return  "8";
```

```
                case    9:      return  "9";
                case    10:     return  "10";
                case    11:     return  "Jack";
                case    12:     return  "Queen";
                default: return "King";
                }
            }
        }
        /**
        Returns a string representation of this card, including both
        its suit and its value (except that for a Joker with value 1,
        the return value is just "Joker").  Sample return values
        are: "Queen of Hearts", "10 of Diamonds", "Ace of Spades",
        "Joker", "Joker #2"
        */
    public String toString() {
        if (suit == JOKER) {
        if (value == 1) return "Joker";
        else
            return "Joker #" + value;
        }
        else
            return getValueAsString() + " of " + getSuitAsString();
        }
    } // end class Card
```

1.1.3 Example: A Simple Card Game

I will finish this section by presenting a complete program that uses the *Card* and *Deck* classes. The program lets the user play a very simple card game called HighLow. A deck of cards is shuffled, and one card is dealt from the deck and shown to the user. The user predicts whether the next card from the deck will be higher or lower than the current card. If the user predicts correctly, then the next card from the deck becomes the current card, and the user makes another prediction.

This continues until the user makes an incorrect prediction. The number of correct predictions is the user's score.

My program has a static method that plays one game of HighLow. The main() routine lets the user play several games of HighLow. At the end, it reports the user's average score.

I won't go through the development of the algorithms used in this program, but I encourage you to read it carefully and make sure that you understand how it works. Note in particular that the subroutine that plays one game of HighLow returns the user's score in the game as its return value. This gets the score back to the main program, where it is needed. Here is the program:

```
import textio.TextIO;

/**

This program lets the user play HighLow, a simple card game

that is described in the output statement at the beginning of

the main() routine.    After the user plays several games,

the user's average score is reported.

*/

public class HighLow {

    public static void main(String[] args) {

            System.out.println("""

                    This program lets you play the simple card game, HighLow. A card
                    is dealt from a deck of cards. You have to predict whether the next
                    card will be higher or lower.        Your score in the game is the
                    number of correct predictions you make before you guess wrong. """);

            int gamesPlayed = 0;        // Number of games user has played.

            int sumOfScores = 0;        // The sum of all the scores from

                                        //        all the games played.

            double averageScore;        // Average score, computed by dividing

                                        //        sumOfScores by gamesPlayed.

            boolean playAgain;          // Record user's response when user is

                                        //        asked whether he wants to play

                                        //        another game.

            do {
```

```
            int scoreThisGame;         // Score for one game.
            scoreThisGame = play();  // Play the game and get the score.
            sumOfScores += scoreThisGame;
            gamesPlayed++;
            System.out.print("Play again? ");
            playAgain = TextIO.getlnBoolean();
        } while (playAgain);
        averageScore = ((double)sumOfScores) / gamesPlayed;
        System.out.println();
        System.out.println("You played " + gamesPlayed + " games.");
        System.out.printf("Your average score was %1.3f.\n", averageScore);
}       // end main()
/**
Lets the user play one game of HighLow, and returns the
user's score in that game.          The score is the number of
correct guesses that the user makes.
*/
private static int play() {
        Deck deck = new Deck();  // Get a new deck of cards, and
                                 //         store a reference to it in
                                 //         the variable, deck.
        Card currentCard;        // The current card, which the user sees.
        Card nextCard;           // The next card in the deck.        The user tries
                                 //         to predict whether this is higher or lower
                                 //         than the current card.
        int correctGuesses ;     // The number of correct predictions the
                                 //         user has made.   At the end of the game,
                                 //         this will be the user's score.
        char guess;              // The user's guess. 'H' if the user predicts that
                                 //         the next card will be higher, 'L' if the user
                                 //         predicts that it will be lower.
```

```
deck.shuffle();              // Shuffle the deck into a random order before
                             //        starting the game.
correctGuesses = 0;
currentCard = deck.dealCard();
System.out.println("The first card is the " + currentCard);
while (true) {      // Loop ends when user's prediction is wrong.
        /* Get the user's prediction, 'H' or 'L' (or 'h' or 'l'). */
        System.out.print("Will the next card be higher (H) or lower (L)?
        "); do {
                guess  =  TextIO.getlnChar();
                guess = Character.toUpperCase(guess);
                if (guess != 'H' && guess != 'L')
                        System.out.print("Please respond with H or L: ");
        } while (guess != 'H' && guess != 'L');
        /* Get the next card and show it to the user. */
        nextCard = deck.dealCard();
        System.out.println("The next card is " + nextCard);
        /* Check the user's prediction. */
        if (nextCard.getValue() == currentCard.getValue()) {
        System.out.println("The value is the same as the previous card.")
        System.out.println("You lose on ties.        Sorry!");
        break;   // End the game.
}
else if (nextCard.getValue() > currentCard.getValue()) {
        if (guess == 'H') {
                System.out.println("Your prediction was correct.");
                correctGuesses++;
        }
        else {
                System.out.println("Your prediction was incorrect.");
                break;    // End the game.
```

```
                }
            }
            else {    // nextCard is lower
            if (guess == 'L') {
                    System.out.println("Your prediction was correct.");
                    correctGuesses++;
            }
            else {
                    System.out.println("Your prediction was incorrect.");
                    break;   // End the game.
            }
        }
        /* To set up for the next iteration of the loop, the nextCard becomes the currentCard,
        since the currentCard has to be the card that the user sees, and the nextCard will be
        set to the next card in the deck after the user makes his prediction. */
            currentCard = nextCard;
            System.out.println();
            System.out.println("The card is " + currentCard);
        } // end of while loop
        System.out.println();
        System.out.println("The game is over.");
        System.out.println("You  made  "  + correctGuesses
                                          + " correct predictions.");
        System.out.println();
        return correctGuesses;
        }         // end play()
    } // end class HighLow
```

1.2 INHERITANCE, POLYMORPHISM, AND ABSTRACT CLASSES

A class represents a set of objects which share the same structure and behaviors. The class determines the structure of objects by specifying variables that are contained in each instance of the class, and it determines behavior by providing the instance methods that express the behavior of the objects. This is a powerful idea. However, something like this can be done in most programming languages. The central new idea in object-oriented programming—the idea that really distinguishes it from traditional programming—is to allow classes to express the similarities among objects that share some, but not all, of their structure and behavior. Such similarities can be expressed using *inheritance* and *polymorphism* .

1.2.1 Extending Existing Classes

Any programmer should know what is meant by subclass, inheritance, and polymorphism. However, it will probably be a while before you actually do anything with inheritance except for extending classes that already exist. In the first part of this section, we look at how that is done.

In day-to-day programming, especially for programmers who are just beginning to work with objects, subclassing is used mainly in one situation: There is an existing class that can be adapted with a few changes or additions. This is much more common than designing groups of classes and subclasses from scratch. The existing class can be *extended* to make a subclass.

The syntax for this is

```
public class (subclass-name ) extends (existing-class-name ) {
.
    .        // Changes and additions.
    .
}
```

As an example, suppose you want to write a program that plays the card game, Blackjack. You can use the *Card*, *Hand*, and *Deck* classes developed in Section 1.1. However, a hand in the game of Blackjack is a little different from a hand of cards in general, since it must be possible to compute the "value" of a Blackjack hand according to the rules of the game. The rules are as follows: The value of a hand is obtained by adding up the values of the cards in the hand. The value of a numeric card such as a three or a ten is its numerical value. The value of a Jack, Queen, or King is 10. The value of an Ace can be either 1 or 11. An Ace should be counted as 11 unless doing so would put the total value of the hand over 21. Note that this means that the second, third, or fourth Ace in the hand will always be counted as 1.

One way to handle this is to extend the existing *Hand* class by adding a method that computes the Blackjack value of the hand. Here's the definition of such a class:

```
public class BlackjackHand extends Hand {
/**
Computes and returns the value of this hand in the game
```

```
of Blackjack.
*/
public int getBlackjackValue() {
    int val; // The value computed for the hand.
    boolean ace;      // This will be set to true if the
                      //        hand contains an ace.
    int cards;        // Number of cards in the hand.
    val = 0;
    ace = false;
    cards = getCardCount();  // (method defined in class Hand.)
    for ( int i = 0;    i < cards;        i++ ) {
                      // Add the value of the i-th card in the hand.
        Card card;          // The i-th card;
        int cardVal;        // The blackjack value of the i-th card.
        card = getCard(i);
        cardVal = card.getValue();          // The normal value, 1 to 13.
        if (cardVal > 10) {
            cardVal = 10;     // For a Jack, Queen, or King.
        }
        if (cardVal == 1) {
            ace = true;       // There is at least one ace.
        }
        val = val + cardVal;
        }
        // Now, val is the value of the hand, counting any ace as 1.
        // If there is an ace, and if changing its value from 1 to
        // 11 would leave the score less than or equal to 21,
        // then do so by adding the extra 10 points to val.
        if ( ace == true    &&      val + 10 <= 21 )
            val = val + 10;
        return val;
```

```
        }        // end getBlackjackValue()
    } // end class BlackjackHand
```

Since *BlackjackHand* is a subclass of *Hand*, an object of type *BlackjackHand* contains all the instance variables and instance methods defined in *Hand*, plus the new in- stance method named getBlackjackValue(). For example, if bjh is a variable of type BlackjackHand, then the following are all legal: bjh.getCardCount(), bjh. removeCard(0), and bjh.getBlackjackValue(). The first two methods are defined in *Hand*, but are inherited by *BlackjackHand*.

Variables and methods from the *Hand* class are inherited by *BlackjackHand*, and they can be used in the definition of *BlackjackHand* just as if they were actually defined in that class— except for any that are declared to be private, which prevents access even by subclasses. The statement "cards = getCardCount();" in the above definition of getBlackjackValue() calls the instance method getCardCount(), which was defined in *Hand*.

Extending existing classes is an easy way to build on previous work. We'll see that many standard classes have been written specifically to be used as the basis for making subclasses.

Access modifiers such as public and private are used to control access to members of a class. There is one more access modifier, *protected* , that comes into the picture when subclasses are taken into consideration. When protected is applied as an access modifier to a method or member variable in a class, that member can be used in subclasses—direct or indirect—of the class in which it is defined, but it cannot be used in non-subclasses. (There is an exception: A protected member can also be accessed by any class in the same package as the class that contains the protected member. Recall that using no access modifier makes a member accessible to classes in the same package, and nowhere else. Using the protected modifier is strictly more liberal than using no modifier at all: It allows access from classes in the same package and from subclasses that are not in the same package.)

When you declare a method or member variable to be protected, you are saying that it is part of the implementation of the class, rather than part of the public interface of the class. However, you are allowing subclasses to use and modify that part of the implementation.

For example, consider a *PairOfDice* class that has instance variables die1 and die2 to represent the numbers appearing on the two dice. We could make those variables private to make it impossible to change their values from outside the class, while still allowing read access through getter methods. However, if we think it possible that *PairOfDice* will be used to create subclasses, we might want to make it possible for subclasses to change the numbers on the dice. For example, a *GraphicalDice* subclass that draws the dice might want to change the numbers at other times besides when the dice are rolled. In that case, we could make die1 and die2 protected, which would allow the subclass to change their values without making them public to the rest of the world. (An even better idea would be to define protected setter methods for the variables. A setter method could, for example, ensure that the value that is being assigned to the variable is in the legal range 1 through 6.)

1.2.2 Inheritance and Class Hierarchy

The term *inheritance* refers to the fact that one class can inherit part or all of its structure and behavior from another class. The class that does the inheriting is said to be a *subclass* of the class from which it inherits. If class B is a subclass of class A, we also say that class A is a *superclass* of class B. (Sometimes the terms *derived class* and *base class* are used instead of subclass and superclass; this is the common terminology in C++.) A subclass can add to the structure and behavior that it inherits. It can also replace or modify inherited behavior (though not inherited structure). The relationship between subclass and superclass is sometimes shown by a diagram in which the subclass is shown below, and connected to, its superclass, as shown on the left below:

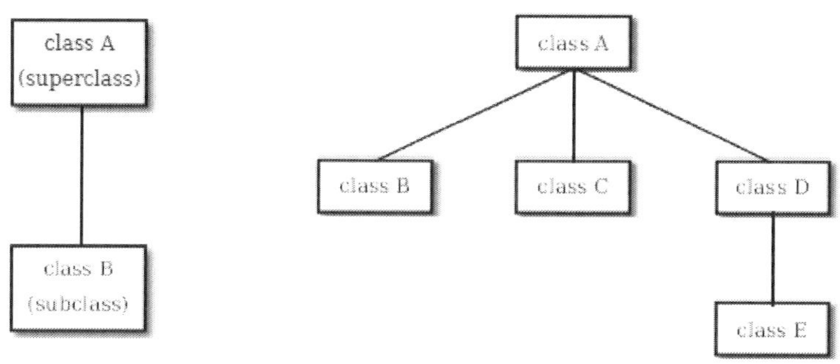

In Java, to create a class named "B" as a subclass of a class named "A", you would write

```
class B extends A {
    .
    .        // additions to, and modifications of,
    .        // stuff inherited from class A
    .
}
```

Several classes can be declared as subclasses of the same superclass. The subclasses, which might be referred to as "sibling classes," share some structures and behaviors—namely, the ones they inherit from their common superclass. The superclass expresses these shared structures and behaviors. In the diagram shown on the right above, classes B, C, and D are sibling classes. Inheritance can also extend over several "generations" of classes. This is shown in the diagram, where class E is a subclass of class D which is itself a subclass of class A. In this case, class E is considered to be a subclass of class A, even though it is not a direct subclass. This whole set of classes forms a small *class hierarchy* .

1.2.3 Example: Vehicles

Let's look at an example. Suppose that a program has to deal with motor vehicles, including cars, trucks, and motorcycles. (This might be a program used by a Department of Motor Vehicles to keep track of registrations.) The program could use a class named *Vehicle* to represent all types of vehicles. Since cars, trucks, and motorcycles are types of vehicles, they would be represented by subclasses of the *Vehicle* class, as shown in this class hierarchy diagram:

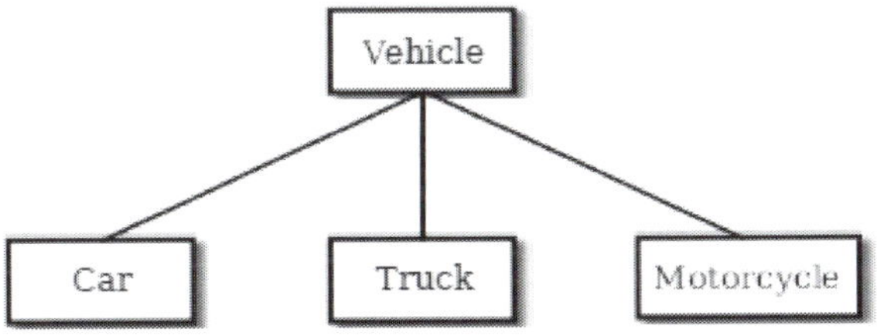

The *Vehicle* class would include instance variables such as registrationNumber and owner and instance methods such as transferOwnership(). These are variables and methods common to all vehicles. The three subclasses of *Vehicle*—*Car*, *Truck*, and *Motorcycle*—could then be used to hold variables and methods specific to particular types of vehicles. The *Car* class might add an instance variable numberOfDoors, the *Truck* class might have numberOfAxles, and the *Motorcycle* class could have a boolean variable hasSidecar. (Well, it could in theory at least, even if it might give a chuckle to the people at the Department of Motor Vehicles.) The declarations of these classes in a Java program would look, in outline, like this (although they are likely to be defined in separate files and declared as public classes):

```
class Vehicle {
    int registrationNumber;
    Person owner;    // (Assuming that a Person class has been defined!)
    void transferOwnership(Person newOwner) {
    . . .
    }
```

```
   ...
}
class Car extends Vehicle {
        int numberOfDoors;
   ...
}
class Truck extends Vehicle {
        int numberOfAxles;
   ...
}
class Motorcycle extends Vehicle {
        boolean hasSidecar;
   ...
}
```

Suppose that myCar is a variable of type *Car* that has been declared and initialized with the statement

```
Car myCar = new Car();
```

Given this declaration, a program could refer to myCar.numberOfDoors, since numberOfDoors is an instance variable in the class Car. But since class *Car* extends class *Vehicle*, a car also has all the structure and behavior of a vehicle. This means that myCar.registrationNumber, myCar.owner, and myCar.transferOwnership() also exist.

Now, in the real world, cars, trucks, and motorcycles are in fact vehicles. The same is true in a program. That is, an object of type *Car* or *Truck* or *Motorcycle* is automatically an object of type *Vehicle* too. This brings us to the following Important Fact:

A variable that can hold a reference to an object of class A can also hold a reference to an object belonging to any subclass of A.

The practical effect of this in our example is that an object of type *Car* can be assigned to a variable of type *Vehicle*. That is, it would be legal to say

```
Vehicle myVehicle = myCar;
```

or even

```
Vehicle myVehicle = new Car();
```

After either of these statements, the variable myVehicle holds a reference to a *Vehicle* object that happens to be an instance of the subclass, *Car*. The object "remembers" that it is in fact a *Car*, and not just a *Vehicle*. Information about the actual class of an object is stored as part of that object. It is even possible to test whether a given object belongs to a given class, using the instanceof operator. The test:

```
if (myVehicle instanceof Car) ...
```

determines whether the object referred to by myVehicle is in fact a car.

On the other hand, the assignment statement

```
myCar = myVehicle; // ERROR!
```

would be illegal because myVehicle could potentially refer to other types of vehicles that are not cars. The computer will not allow you to assign an int value to a variable of type short, because not every int is a short. Similarly, it will not allow you to assign a value of type *Vehicle* to a variable of type *Car* because not every vehicle is a car. As in the case of ints and shorts, the solution here is to use type-casting. If, for some reason, you happen to know that myVehicle does in fact refer to a *Car*, you can use the type cast (Car)myVehicle to tell the computer to treat myVehicle as if it were actually of type *Car*. So, you could say

```
myCar = (Car)myVehicle;
```

and you could even refer to ((Car)myVehicle).numberOfDoors. (The parentheses are necessary because of precedence. The "." has higher precedence than the type-cast, so (Car)myVehicle.numberOfDoors would be read as (Car)(myVehicle.numberOfDoors), an attempt to type-cast the int myVehicle.numberOfDoors into a *Vehicle*, which is impossible.)

As an example of how this could be used in a program, suppose that you want to print out relevant data about the *Vehicle* referred to by myVehicle. If it's a *Car*, you will want to print out the car's numberOfDoors, but you can't say myVehicle.numberOfDoors, since there is no numberOfDoors in the *Vehicle* class. But you could say:

```
System.out.println("Vehicle Data:");
System.out.println("Registration number:     "
                        + myVehicle.registrationNumber);
if (myVehicle instanceof Car) {
    System.out.println("Type of vehicle:     Car");
    Car myCar;
```

```
        myCar = (Car)myVehicle;// Type-cast to get access to numberOfDoors!
        System.out.println("Number of doors:      " + myCar.numberOfDoors);
    }
    else if (myVehicle instanceof Truck) {
        System.out.println("Type of vehicle:      Truck");
        Truck myTruck;
        myTruck = (Truck)myVehicle;     // Type-cast to get access to numberOfAxles!
        System.out.println("Number of axles:      " + myTruck.numberOfAxles);
    }
    else if (myVehicle instanceof Motorcycle) { System.out.println("Type of vehicle: 
    Motorcycle"); Motorcycle myCycle;
    myCycle = (Motorcycle)myVehicle;     // Type-cast to get access to hasSidecar! System.
    out.println("Has a sidecar:    " + myCycle.hasSidecar);
    }
```

Note that for object types, when the computer executes a program, it checks whether type-casts are valid. So, for example, if myVehicle refers to an object of type *Truck*, then the type cast (Car)myVehicle would be an error. When this happens, an exception of type *ClassCastException* is thrown. This check is done at run time, not compile time, because the actual type of the object referred to by myVehicle is not known when the program is compiled. The code above avoids *ClassCastExceptions* by using instanceof to test the type of the variable before doing a type cast.

In Java 17, the previous example can also be written using one of the more obscure new language features, known as *pattern matching* for instanceof. Pattern matching makes it possible to include declaration and initialization of a variable in an instanceof test. For example,

```
    if (myVehicle instanceof Car myCar) {
        System.out.println("Type of vehicle: Car");
        System.out.println(Number of doors: " + myCar.numberOfDoors);
    }
```

If the test succeeds, then the variable myCar is created and automatically assigned the value (Car)myVehicle. The scope of the variable is limited to the body of the if statement.

1.2.4 Polymorphism

As another example, consider a program that deals with shapes drawn on the screen. Let's say that the shapes include rectangles, ovals, and roundrects of various colors. (A "roundrect" is just a rectangle with rounded corners.)

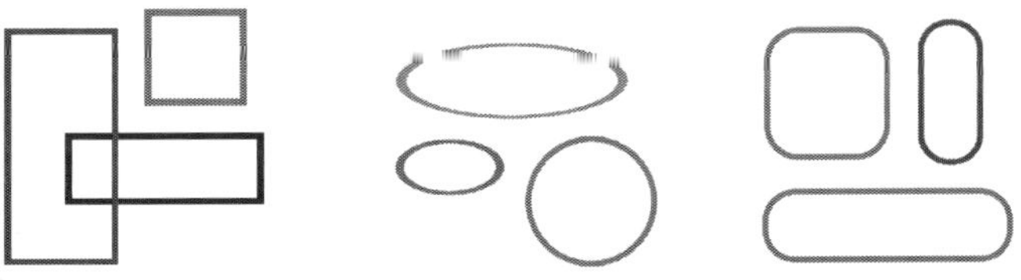

Three classes, *Rectangle*, *Oval*, and *RoundRect*, could be used to represent the three types of shapes. These three classes would have a common superclass, *Shape*, to represent features that all three shapes have in common. The *Shape* class could include instance variables to represent the color, position, and size of a shape, and it could include instance methods for changing the values of those properties. Changing the color, for example, might involve changing the value of an instance variable, and then redrawing the shape in its new color:

```
class Shape {
    Color color; // (must be imported from package javafx.scene.paint)
    void setColor(Color newColor) {
            // Method to change the color of the shape.
            color = newColor; // change value of instance variable
            redraw(); // redraw shape, which will appear in new color
    }
    void redraw() {
                // method for drawing the shape
            ? ? ?   // what commands should go here?
    }
    . . .   // more instance variables and methods
} // end of class Shape
```

Now, you might see a problem here with the method redraw(). The problem is that each different type of shape is drawn differently. The method setColor() can be called for any type of shape. How does the computer know which shape to draw when it executes the redraw() command in the setColor() method? Informally, we can answer the question like this: The computer executes redraw() by asking the shape to redraw itself. Every shape object knows what it has to do to redraw itself.

In practice, this means that each of the specific shape classes has its own redraw() method:

```
class Rectangle extends Shape {
    void redraw() {
            . . .      // commands for drawing a rectangle
    }
    . . . // possibly, more methods and variables
}
class Oval extends Shape {
    void redraw() {
    . . .      // commands for drawing an oval
    }
    . . . // possibly, more methods and variables
    }
class RoundRect extends Shape {
    void redraw() {
    . . .      // commands for drawing a rounded rectangle
    }
    . . . // possibly, more methods and variables
}
```

Suppose that someShape is a variable of type *Shape*. Then it could refer to an object of any of the types *Rectangle*, *Oval*, or *RoundRect*. As a program executes, and the value of someShape changes, it could even refer to objects of different types at different times! Whenever the statement

```
someShape.redraw();
```

is executed, the redraw method that is actually called is the one appropriate for the type of object to which someShape actually refers. There may be no way of telling, from looking at the text of the program, what shape this statement will draw, since it depends on the value that someShape happens to have when the program is executed. Even more is true. Suppose the statement is in a loop and gets executed many times. If the value of someShape changes as the loop is executed, it is possible that the very same statement "someShape.redraw();" will call different methods and draw different kinds of shapes as it is executed several times. We say that the redraw() method is *polymorphic*. A method is polymorphic if the action performed by the method depends on the actual type of the object to which the method is applied at run time. Polymorphism is one of the major distinguishing features of object-oriented programming. This can be seen most vividly, perhaps, if we have an array of shapes. Suppose that shapelist is a variable of type Shape[ ], and that the array has already been created and filled with data. Some of the elements in the array might be *Rectangles*, some might be *Ovals*, and some might be *RoundRects*. We can draw all the shapes in the array by saying

```
for (int i = 0; i < shapelist.length; i++ ) {
    Shape shape = shapelist[i];
    shape.redraw();
}
```

As the computer goes through this loop, the statement shape.redraw() will sometimes draw a rectangle, sometimes an oval, and sometimes a roundrect, depending on the type of object to which array element number i refers.

Perhaps this becomes more understandable if we change our terminology a bit: In object-oriented programming, calling a method is often referred to as sending a *message* to an object. The object responds to the message by executing the appropriate method. The statement "someShape.redraw();" is a message to the object referred to by someShape. Since that object knows what type of object it is, it knows how it should respond to the message. From this point of view, the computer always executes "someShape.redraw();" in the same way: by sending a message. The response to the message depends, naturally, on who receives it. From this point of view, objects are active entities that send and receive messages, and polymorphism is a natural, even necessary, part of this view. Polymorphism just means that different objects can respond to the same message in different ways.

One of the most beautiful things about polymorphism is that it lets code that you write do things that you didn't even conceive of, at the time you wrote it. Suppose that I decide to add beveled rectangles to the types of shapes my program can deal with. A beveled rectangle has a triangle cut off each corner:

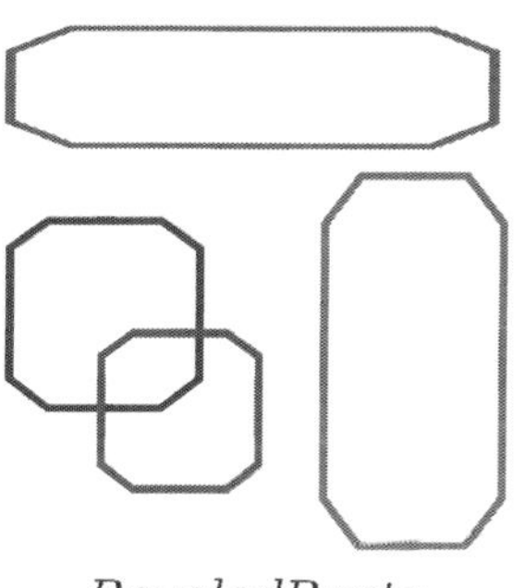

BeveledRects

To implement beveled rectangles, I can write a new subclass, *BeveledRect*, of class *Shape* and give it its own redraw() method. Automatically, code that I wrote previously—such as the statement someShape.redraw()—can now suddenly start drawing beveled rectangles, even though the beveled rectangle class didn't exist when I wrote the statement!

In the statement "someShape.redraw();", the redraw message is sent to the object someShape. Look back at the method in the *Shape* class for changing the color of a shape:

```
void setColor(Color newColor) {
    color = newColor; // change value of instance variable redraw(); //
    redraw shape, which will appear in new color
}
```

A redraw message is sent here, but which object is it sent to? Well, the setColor method is itself a message that was sent to some object. The answer is that the redraw message is sent to that same object, the one that received the setColor message. If that object is a rectangle, then it contains a redraw() method for drawing rectangles, and that is the one that is executed. If the object is an oval, then the redraw() method from the *Oval* class is executed. This is what you should expect, but it means that the "redraw();" statement in the setColor() method does not necessarily call the redraw() method in the *Shape* class! The redraw() method that is executed could be in any subclass of *Shape*. This is just another case of polymorphism.

1.2.5 Abstract Classes

Whenever a *Rectangle*, *Oval*, or *RoundRect* object has to draw itself, it is the redraw() method in the appropriate class that is executed. This leaves open the question, What does the redraw() method in the *Shape* class do? How should it be defined?

The answer may be surprising: We should leave it blank! The fact is that the class *Shape* represents the abstract idea of a shape, and there is no way to draw such a thing. Only particular, concrete shapes like rectangles and ovals can be drawn. So, why should there even be a redraw() method in the *Shape* class? Well, it has to be there, or it would be illegal to call it in the setColor() method of the *Shape* class, and it would be illegal to write "someShape.redraw();". The compiler would complain that someShape is a variable of type *Shape* and there's no redraw() method in the *Shape* class.

Nevertheless the version of redraw() in the *Shape* class itself will never actually be called. In fact, if you think about it, there can never be any reason to construct an actual object of type *Shape*! You can have variables of type *Shape*, but the objects they refer to will always belong to one of the subclasses of *Shape*. We say that *Shape* is an *abstract class*. An abstract class is one that is not used to construct objects, but only as a basis for making subclasses. An abstract class exists only to express the common properties of all its subclasses. A class that is not abstract is said to be *concrete*. You can create objects belonging to a concrete class, but not to an abstract class. A variable whose type is given by an abstract class can only refer to objects that belong to concrete subclasses of the abstract class.

Similarly, we say that the redraw() method in class *Shape* is an *abstract method* , since it is never meant to be called. In fact, there is nothing for it to do—any actual redrawing is done by redraw() methods in the subclasses of *Shape*. The redraw() method in *Shape* has to be there. But it is there only to tell the computer that all Shapes understand the redraw message. As an abstract method, it exists merely to specify the common interface of all the actual, concrete versions of redraw() in the subclasses. There is no reason for the abstract redraw() in class *Shape* to contain any code at all.

Shape and its redraw() method are semantically abstract. You can also tell the computer, syntactically, that they are abstract by adding the modifier “abstract” to their definitions.

For an abstract method, the block of code that gives the implementation of an ordinary method is replaced by a semicolon. An implementation must then be provided for the abstract method in any concrete subclass of the abstract class. Here’s what the *Shape* class would look like as an abstract class:

```
public abstract class Shape {
    Color color;        // color of shape.
    void setColor(Color newColor) {
            // method to change the color of the shape
            color = newColor; // change value of instance variable
            redraw(); // redraw shape, which will appear in new color
    }
    abstract void redraw();
            // abstract method---must be defined in
            // concrete subclasses
    . . .   // more instance variables and methods
} // end of class Shape
```

Once you have declared the class to be abstract, it becomes illegal to try to create actual objects of type *Shape*, and the computer will report a syntax error if you try to do so.

Note, by the way, that the *Vehicle* class discussed above would probably also be an abstract class. There is no way to own a vehicle as such—the actual vehicle has to be a car or a truck or a motorcycle, or some other "concrete" type of vehicle.

Recall from a class that is not explicitly declared to be a subclass of some other class is automatically made a subclass of the standard class *Object*. That is, a class declaration with no "extends" part such as

public class myClass {. . .

is exactly equivalent to

public class myClass extends Object {. . .

This means that class *Object* is at the top of a huge class hierarchy that includes every other class. (Semantically, *Object* is an abstract class, in fact the most abstract class of all. Curiously, however, it is not declared to be abstract syntactically, which means that you can create objects of type *Object*. However, there is not much that you can do with them.)

Since every class is a subclass of *Object*, a variable of type *Object* can refer to any object whatsoever, of any type. Similarly, an array of type Object[ ] can hold objects of any type.

The sample source code file ShapeDraw.java uses an abstract *Shape* class and an array of type Shape[ ] to hold a list of shapes. You might want to look at this file, even though you won't be able to understand all of it at this time. Even the definitions of the shape classes are somewhat different from those that I have described in this section. (For example, the draw() method has a parameter of type *GraphicsContext*>. This parameter is required because all drawing in Java requires a graphics context.) I'll return to similar examples in later chapters when you know more about GUI programming. However, it would still be worthwhile to look at the definition of the *Shape* class and its subclasses in the source code. You might also check how an array is used to hold the list of shapes. Here is a scaled-down screenshot from the program:

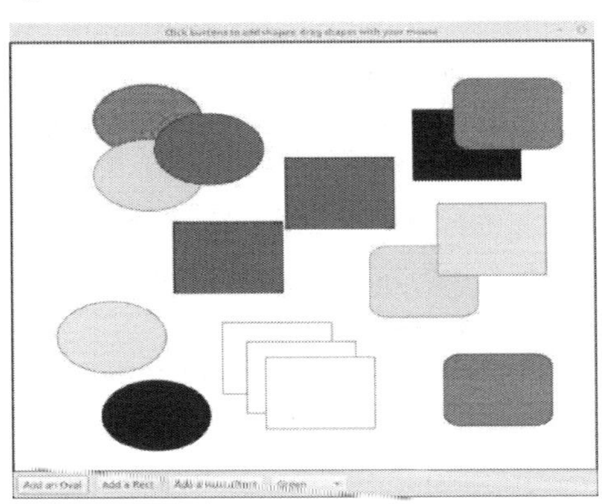

If you run the ShapeDraw program, you can click one of the buttons along the bottom to add a shape to the picture. The new shape will appear in the upper left corner of the drawing area. The color of the shape is given by the "pop-up menu" of colors below the drawing area. Once a shape is on the screen, you can drag it around with the mouse. A shape will maintain the same front-to-back order with respect to other shapes on the screen, even while you are dragging it. However, you can move a shape out in front of all the other shapes if you hold down the shift key as you click on it.

In the program, the only time when the actual class of a shape is used is when that shape is added to the screen. Once the shape has been created, it is manipulated entirely as an abstract shape. The routine that implements dragging, for example, works with variables of type *Shape* and makes no reference to any of its subclasses. As the shape is being dragged, the dragging routine just calls the shape's draw method each time the shape has to be drawn, so it doesn't have to know how to draw the shape or even what type of shape it is. The object is responsible for drawing itself. If I wanted to add a new type of shape to the program, I would define a new subclass of *Shape*, add another button, and program the button to add the correct type of shape to the screen. No other changes in the programming would be necessary.

1.2.6 Final Methods and Classes

We have seen how the final modifier applies to variables: It makes it impossible to assign a new value to the variable after it has been initialized. (For a final instance variable, the initialization can take place in the constructors for the class that contains the variable.) However, the final modifier can also be applied to classes and to method definitions.

A final class cannot be used be used as a basis for making subclasses. That is, if a class is defined as "final class A...", then it is a syntax error to try to extend *A* with "class B extends A. . . ".

If a method is declared final in a class, then it is not possible for a subclass to contain a method with the same signature. That is, the method cannot be "overridden". This is true both for static methods and for instance methods. Note that in a final class, all methods are implicitly final since it is not even possible to make a subclass of that class.

The idea is that a final class or method is in its final form—it cannot be modified or replaced by a subclass. With final, it is possible to make a guarantee about the behavior of a method. For example, suppose that a *Rectangle* class has an instance method draw() that draws a rectangle, and that rect is a variable of type *Rectangle*. If draw() is a final method, then we are guaranteed that a call to rect.draw() will draw a rectangle. But if draw() is not final, then it could draw anything, or nothing! The problem is that rect could actually refer to an object belonging to some subclass of *Rectangle*, and that subclass could define its own draw() method that overrides the draw() method from class *Rectangle*. Using final can make it easier to reason about the behavior of a program.

1.3 THIS AND SUPER

Although the basic ideas of object-oriented programming are reasonably simple and clear, they are subtle, and they take time to get used to. And unfortunately, beyond the basic ideas there are a lot of details. The rest of this chapter covers more of those annoying details. Remember that you don't need to master everything in this chapter the first time through. In this section, we'll look at two variables, this and super, that are automatically defined in any instance method or constructor.

1.3.1 The Special Variable this

What does it mean when you use a simple identifier such as amount or process() to refer to a variable or method? The answer depends on scope rules that tell where and how each declared variable and method can be accessed in a program. Inside the definition of a method, a simple variable name might refer to a local variable or parameter, if there is one "in scope," that is, one whose declaration is in effect at the point in the source code where the reference occurs. If not, it must refer to a member variable of the class in which the reference occurs. Similarly, a simple method name must refer to a method in the same class.

A static member of a class has a simple name that can only be used inside the class definition; for use outside the class, it has a full name of the form (*class-name*).(*simple-name*). For example, "Math.PI" is a static member variable with simple name "PI" in the class "*Math*". It's always legal to use the full name of a static member, even within the class where it's defined.

Sometimes it's even necessary, as when the simple name of a static member variable is hidden by a local variable or parameter of the same name.

Instance variables and instance methods also have simple names. The simple name of such an instance member can be used in instance methods in the class where the instance member is defined (but not in static methods). Instance members also have full names—but remember that an instance variable or instance method is actually contained in an object rather than in a class, and each object has its own version. A full name of an instance member starts with a reference to the object that contains the instance member. For example, if std is a variable that refers to an object of type *Student*, then std.test1 could be a full name for an instance variable named test1 that is contained in that object.

But when we are working inside a class and use a simple name to refer to an instance variable like test1, where is the object that contains the variable? The solution to this riddle is simple: Suppose that a reference to "test1" occurs in the definition of some instance method. The method is part of some particular object of type *Student*. When that method gets executed, the occurrence of the name "test1" refers to the test1 variable in that same object. (This is why simple names of instance members cannot be used in static methods– when a static method is executed, it is not part of an object, and hence there are no instance members in sight!)

This leaves open the question of full names for instance members inside the same class where they are defined. We need a way to refer to "the object that contains this method." Java defines a special variable named *this* for just this purpose. The variable this can be used in the source code of an instance method to refer to the object that contains the method. This intent of the name, "this," is to refer to "this object," the one right here that this very method is in. If var is an instance variable in the same object as the method, then "this.var" is a full name for that variable. If otherMethod() is an instance method in the same object, then this.otherMethod() could be used to call that method. Whenever the computer executes an instance method, it automatically sets the variable this to refer to the object that contains the method.

(Some object oriented languages use the name "self" instead of "this." Here, an object is seen as an entity that receives messages and responds by performing some action. From the point of view of that entity, an instance variable such as self.name refers to the entity's own name, something that is part of the entity itself. Calling an instance method such as self.redraw() is like saying "message to self: redraw!")

One common use of this is in constructors. For example:

```
public class Student {
    private String name;      // Name of the student.
    public Student(String name) {
                    // Constructor.  Create a student with specified name.
        this.name = name;
}
    .
    .       // More variables and methods.
    .
}
```

In the constructor, the instance variable called name is hidden by a formal parameter that is also called "name." However, the instance variable can still be referred to by its full name, which is this.name. In the assignment statement "this. name = name", the "name" on the right is the formal parameter, and the value of that formal parameter is being assigned to the instance variable, this.name. This is considered to be acceptable style: There is no need to dream up cute new names for formal parameters that are just used to initialize instance variables. You can use the same name for the parameter as for the instance variable.

There are other uses for this. Sometimes, when you are writing an instance method, you need to pass the object that contains the method to a subroutine, as an actual parameter. In that case, you can use this as the actual parameter. For example, if you wanted to print out a string representation of the object, you could say "System.out.println(this);". Or you could assign the value of this to another variable in an assignment statement. You can store it in an array. In fact, you can do anything with this that you could do with any other variable, except change its value. (Consider it to be a final variable.)

1.3.2 The Special Variable super

Java also defines another special variable, named "super", for use in the definitions of instance methods. The variable super is for use in a subclass. Like this, super refers to the object that contains the method. But it's forgetful. It forgets that the object belongs to the class you are writing, and it remembers only that it belongs to the superclass of that class. The point is that the class can contain additions and modifications to the superclass. super doesn't know about any of those additions and modifications; it can only be used to refer to methods and variables in the superclass.

Let's say that you use a method call super.doSomething() in a class that you are writing. Now, super doesn't know anything about any doSomething() method in the same class. It only knows about things in the superclass of that class, so super. doSomething() represents an attempt to execute a method named doSomething() from the superclass. If there is no such method in the superclass, you'll get a syntax error—even if there is a doSomething() method in the class that you are writing.

The reason super exists is so you can get access to things in the superclass that are hidden by things in the subclass. For example, super.var always refers to an instance variable named var in the superclass. This can be useful for the following reason: If a class contains an instance variable with the same name as an instance variable in its superclass, then an object of that class will actually contain two variables with the same name: one defined as part of the class itself and one defined as part of the superclass. The variable in the subclass does not replace the variable of the same name in the superclass; it merely hides it. The variable from the superclass can still be accessed, using super.

When a subclass contains an instance method that has the same signature as a method in its superclass, the method from the superclass is hidden in the same way. We say that the method in the subclass *overrides* the method from the superclass. Again, however, super can be used to access the method from the superclass.

The major use of super is to override a method with a new method that extends the behavior of the inherited method, instead of replacing that behavior entirely. The new method can use super to call the method from the superclass, and then it can add additional code to provide additional behavior. As an example, suppose you have a *PairOfDice* class that includes a roll() method. Suppose that you want a subclass, *GraphicalDice*, to represent a pair of dice drawn on the computer screen. The roll() method in the *GraphicalDice* class should do everything that the roll() method in the *PairOfDice* class does. We can express this with a call to super.roll(), which calls the method in the superclass. But in addition to that, the roll() method for a *GraphicalDice* object has to redraw the dice to show the new values. The *GraphicalDice* class might look something like this:

```
public class GraphicalDice extends PairOfDice {
    public void roll() {
                    // Roll the dice, and redraw them.
            super.roll();     // Call the roll method from PairOfDice.
            redraw();         // Call a method to draw the dice.
    }
            .
            .       // More stuff, including definition of redraw().
            .
}
```

Note that this allows you to extend the behavior of the roll() method even if you don't know how the method is implemented in the superclass!

1.3.3 super and this As Constructors

Constructors are not inherited. That is, if you extend an existing class to make a subclass, the constructors in the superclass do not become part of the subclass. If you want constructors in the subclass, you have to define new ones from scratch. If you don't define any constructors in the subclass, then the computer will make up a default constructor, with no parameters, for you.

This could be a problem, if there is a constructor in the superclass that does a lot of necessary work. It looks like you might have to repeat all that work in the subclass! This could be a real problem if you don't have the source code to the superclass, and don't even know how it is implemented. It might look like an impossible problem, if the constructor in the superclass uses private member variables that you don't even have access to in the subclass!

Obviously, there has to be some fix for this, and there is. It involves the special variable, super. As the very first statement in a constructor, you can use super to call a constructor from the superclass. The notation for this is a bit ugly and misleading, and it can only be used in this one particular circumstance: It looks like you are calling super as a subroutine (even though super is not a subroutine and you can't call constructors the same way you call other subroutines anyway). As an example, assume that the *PairOfDice* class has a constructor that takes two integers as parameters. Consider a subclass:

```
public class GraphicalDice extends PairOfDice {
    public GraphicalDice() {  // Constructor for this class.
            super(3,4);          // Call the constructor from the
                                 //      PairOfDice class, with parameters 3, 4.
            initializeGraphics();    // Do some initialization specific
                                     //      to the GraphicalDice class.
    }
            .
            .       // More constructors, methods, variables...
            .
    }
```

The statement "super(3,4);" calls the constructor from the superclass. This call must be the first line of the constructor in the subclass. Note that if you don't explicitly call a constructor from the superclass in this way, then the default constructor from the superclass, the one with no parameters, will be called automatically. (And if no such constructor exists in the superclass, the compiler will consider it to be a syntax error.)

You can use the special variable this in exactly the same way to call another constructor in the same class. That is, the very first line of a constructor can look like a subroutine call with "this" as the name of the subroutine. The result is that the body of another constructor in the same class is executed. This can be very useful since it can save you from repeating the same code in several different constructors. A *MosaicCanvas* represents a grid of colored rectangles. It has a constructor with four parameters:

```
public MosaicCanvas(int rows, int columns,
        int preferredBlockWidth, int preferredBlockHeight)
```

This constructor provides several options and does a lot of initialization. I wanted to provide easier-to-use constructors with fewer options, but all the initialization still has to be done. The class also contains these constructors:

```
public MosaicCanvas() {
        this(42,42);
}
public MosaicCanvas(int rows, int columns) {
        this(rows,columns,16,16);
}
```

Each of these constructors exists just to call another constructor, while providing constant values for some of the parameters. For example, this(42,42) calls the second constructor listed here, while that constructor in turn calls the main, four-parameter constructor. That main constructor is eventually called in all cases, so that all the essential initialization gets done in every case.

1.4 INTERFACES

Some object-oriented programming languages, such as C++, allow a class to extend two or more superclasses. This is called *multiple inheritance*. In the illustration below, for example, class E is shown as having both class A and class B as direct superclasses, while class F has three direct superclasses.

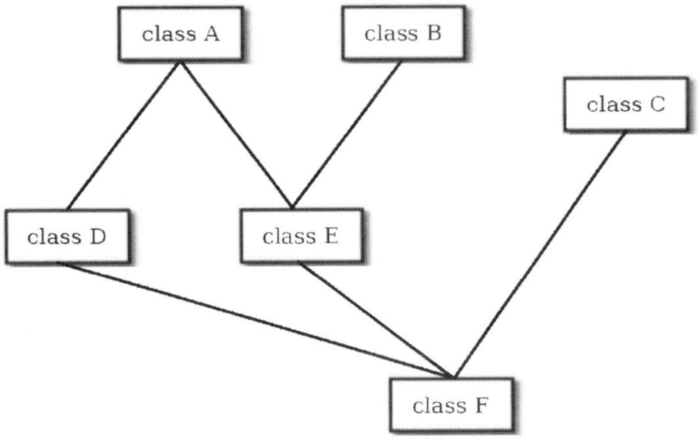

Multiple inheritance (NOT allowed in Java)

Such multiple inheritance is not allowed in Java. The designers of Java wanted to keep the language reasonably simple, and felt that the benefits of multiple inheritance were not worth the cost in increased complexity. However, Java does have a feature that can be used to accomplish many of the same goals as multiple inheritance: *interfaces*. A functional interface specifies a single method. However, interfaces can be much more complicated than that, and they have many other uses.

You are not likely to need to write your own interfaces until you get to the point of writing fairly complex programs. However, there are several interfaces that are used in important ways in Java's standard packages, and you will need to learn how to use them.

1.4.1 Defining and Implementing Interfaces

We encountered the term "interface" in other contexts, in connection with black boxes in general and subroutines in particular. The interface of a subroutine consists of the name of the subroutine, its return type, and the number and types of its parameters. This is the information you need to know if you want to call the subroutine. A subroutine also has an implementation: the block of code which defines it and which is executed when the subroutine is called.

In Java, interface is a reserved word with an additional, technical meaning. An "interface" in this sense consists of a set of instance method interfaces, without any associated implementations. (Actually, a Java interface can contain other things as well, as we'll see later.) A class can *implement* an interface by providing an implementation for each of the methods specified by the interface. Here is an example of a very simple Java interface:

```
public interface Strokeable {
    public void stroke(GraphicsContext g);
}
```

This looks much like a class definition, except that the implementation of the stroke() method is omitted. A class that implements the interface *Strokeable* must provide an implementation for stroke(). Of course, the class can also include other methods and variables. For example,

```
public class Line implements Strokeable {
    public void stroke(GraphicsContext g) {
            . . . // do something---presumably, draw a line
    }
    . . . // other methods, variables, and constructors
```

```
}
```

Note that to implement an interface, a class must do more than simply provide an implementation for each method in the interface; it must also state that it implements the interface, using the reserved word implements as in this example: "public class Line implements Strokeable". Any concrete class that implements the *Strokeable* interface must define a stroke() instance method. Any object created from such a class includes a stroke() method. We say that an object implements an interface if it belongs to a class that implements the interface. For example, any object of type *Line* implements the *Strokeable* interface.

While a class can extend only one other class, it can implement any number of interfaces. In fact, a class can both extend one other class and implement one or more interfaces. So, we can have things like

```
class FilledCircle extends Circle
    implements Strokeable, Fillable {
...
}
```

The point of all this is that, although interfaces are not classes, they are something very similar. An interface is very much like an abstract class, that is, a class that can never be used for constructing objects, but can be used as a basis for making subclasses. The subroutines in an interface are abstract methods, which must be implemented in any concrete class that implements the interface. You can compare the *Strokeable* interface with the abstract class

```
public abstract class AbstractStrokeable {
    public abstract void stroke(GraphicsContext g);
}
```

The main difference is that a class that extends *AbstractStrokeable* cannot extend any other class, while a class that implements *Strokeable* can also extend some class, as well as implement other interfaces. Of course, an abstract class can contain non-abstract methods as well as abstract methods. An interface is like a "pure" abstract class, which contains only abstract methods.

Note that the methods declared in an interface must be public and abstract. In fact, since that is the only option, it is not necessary to specify either of these modifiers in the declaration. In addition to method declarations, an interface can also include variable declarations. The variables must be "public static final" and effectively become public static final variables in every class that implements the interface. In fact, since the variables can only be public and static and final, specifying the modifiers is optional. For example,

```
public interface ConversionFactors {
    int INCHES PER FOOT = 12;
    int FEET PER YARD = 3;
    int YARDS PER MILE = 1760;
}
```

This is a convenient way to define named constants that can be used in several classes. A class that implements *ConversionFactors* can use the constants defined in the interface as if they were defined in the class.

Note in particular that any variable that is defined in an interface is a constant. It's not really a variable at all. An interface cannot add instance variables to the classes that implement it.

An interface can extend one or more other interfaces. For example, if *Strokeable* is the interface given above and *Fillable* is an interface that defines a method fill(g), then we could define

```
public interface Drawable extends Strokeable, Fillable {
    // (more methods/constants could be defined here)
}
```

A concrete class that implements *Drawable* must then provide implementations for the stroke() method from *Strokeable* and the fill() method from *Fillable*, as well as for any abstract methods specified directly in the *Drawable* interface.

An interface is usually defined in its own .java file, whose name must match the name of the interface. For example, *Strokeable* would be defined in a file named Strokeable.java. Just like a class, an interface can be in a package and can import things from other packages.

This discussion has been about the syntax rules for interfaces. But of course, an interface also has a semantic component. That is, the person who creates the interface intends for the methods that it defines to have some specific meaning. The interface definition should include comments to express that meaning, and classes that implement the interface should take that meaning into account. The Java compiler, however, can only check the syntax; it can't enforce the meaning. For example, the stroke() method in an object that implements *Strokeable* is presumably meant to draw a graphical representation of the object by stroking it, but the compiler can only check that the stroke() method exists in the object.

1.4.2 Default Methods

Starting in Java 8, interfaces can contain *default methods.* Unlike the usual abstract methods in interfaces, a default method has an implementation. When a class implements the interface, it does not have to provide an implementation for the default method—although it can do so if it wants to provide a different implementation. Essentially, default methods are inherited from interfaces in much the same way that ordinary methods are inherited from classes. This moves Java partway towards supporting multiple inheritance. It's not true multiple inheritance, however, since interfaces still cannot define instance variables. Default methods can call abstract methods that are defined in the same interface, but they cannot refer to any instance variables.

Note that a functional interface can include default methods in addition to the single abstract method that it specifies.

A default method in an interface must be marked with the modifier default. It can optionally be marked public but, as for everything else in interfaces, default methods are automatically public and the public modifier can be omitted. Here is an example:

```
public interface Readable { // represents a source of input
    public char readChar();  // read the next character from the input
    default public String readLine() { // read up to the next line feed
            StringBuilder line = new StringBuilder();
            char ch = readChar();
            while (ch != '\n') {
                    line.append(ch);
                    ch = readChar();
            }
            return line.toString();
    }
}
```

A concrete class that implements this interface must provide an implementation for readChar(). It will inherit a definition for readLine() from the interface, but can provide a new definition if necessary. When a class includes an implementation for a default method, the implementation given in the class overrides the default method from the interface.

Note that the default readLine() calls the abstract method readChar(), whose definition will only be provided in an implementing class. The reference to readChar() in the definition is polymorphic. The default implementation of readLine() is one that would make sense in almost any class that implements *Readable*. Here's a rather silly example of a class that implements *Readable*, including a main() routine that tests the class. Can you figure out what it does?

```
public class Stars implements Readable {
    public char readChar() {
        if (Math.random() > 0.02)
            return '*';
        else
            return '\n';
    }
    public static void main(String[] args) {
        Stars stars = new Stars();
        for (int i = 0 ; i < 10; i++ ) {
            String line = stars.readLine();     // Calls the default method!
            System.out.println( line );
        }
    }
}
```

Default methods provide Java with a capability similar to something called a "mixin" in other programming languages, namely the ability to mix functionality from another source into a class. Since a class can implement several interfaces, it is possible to mix in functionality from several different sources.

1.4.3 Interfaces as Types

As with abstract classes, even though you can't construct an object from an interface, you can declare a variable whose type is given by the interface. For example, if *Strokeable* is the interface given above, and if *Line* and *Circle* are classes that implement *Strokeable*, as above, then you could say:

```
Strokeable figure;  // Declare a variable of type Strokeable.  It
                    //     can refer to any object that implements the
                    //     Strokeable interface.
figure = new Line(); // figure now refers to an object of class Line figure.stroke(g);
                    // calls stroke() method from class Line
figure = new Circle();// Now, figure refers to an object
                    //     of class Circle.
figure.stroke(g);   // calls stroke() method from class Circle
```

A variable of type *Strokeable* can refer to any object of any class that implements the *Strokeable* interface. A statement like figure.stroke(g), above, is legal because figure is of type *Strokeable*, and any *Strokeable* object has a stroke() method. So, whatever object figure refers to, that object must have a stroke() method.

Note that a *type* is something that can be used to declare variables. A type can also be used to specify the type of a parameter in a subroutine, or the return type of a function. In Java, a type can be either a class, an interface, or one of the eight built-in primitive types. These are the only possibilities (given a few special cases, such as an enum, which is considered to be a special kind of class). Of these, however, only classes can be used to construct new objects.

An interface can also be the base type of an array. For example, we can use an array type Strokeable[ ] to declare variables and create arrays. The elements of the array can refer to any objects that implement the *Strokeable* interface:

```
Strokeable[] listOfFigures;
listOfFigures = new Strokeable[10];
listOfFigures[0] = new Line();
listOfFigures[1] = new Circle();
listOfFigures[2] = new Line();
    .
    .
    .
```

Every element of the array will then have a stroke() method, so that we can say things like listOfFigures[i].stroke(g).

1.5 NESTED CLASSES

A class seems like it should be a pretty important thing. A class is a high-level building block of a program, representing a potentially complex idea and its associated data and behaviors. I've always felt a bit silly writing tiny little classes that exist only to group a few scraps of data together. However, such trivial classes are often useful and even essential. Fortunately, in Java, I can ease the embarrassment, because one class can be nested inside another class. My trivial little class doesn't have to stand on its own. It becomes part of a larger more respectable class. This is particularly useful when you want to create a little class specifically to support the work of a larger class. And, more seriously, there are other good reasons for nesting the definition of one class inside another class.

In Java, a *nested class* is any class whose definition is inside the definition of another class. (In fact, a class can even be nested inside a method, which must, of course, itself be inside a class.) Nested classes can be either *named* or *anonymous.* I will come back to the topic of anonymous classes later in this section. A named nested class, like most other things that occur in classes, can be either static or non-static. Interfaces, like classes, can be nested inside class definitions and can be either static or non-static. (In fact, interface definitions can contain static nested classes and interfaces, but that is not something that you will see in this textbook.)

1.5.1 Static Nested Classes

The definition of a static nested class looks just like the definition of any other class, except that it is nested inside another class and it has the modifier static as part of its declaration. A static nested class is part of the static structure of the containing class. It can be used inside that class to create objects in the usual way. If it is used outside the containing class, its name must indicate its membership in the containing class. That is, the full name of the static nested class consists of the name of the class in which it is nested, followed by a period, followed by the name of the nested class. This is similar to other static components of a class: A static nested class is part of the class itself in the same way that static member variables are parts of the class itself.

For example, suppose a class named *WireFrameModel* represents a set of lines in three- dimensional space. (Such models are used to represent three-dimensional objects in graphics programs.) Suppose that the *WireFrameModel* class contains a static nested class, *Line*, that represents a single line. The definition of the *WireFrameModel* class with its nested *Line* class would look, in outline, like this:

```
public class WireFrameModel {
    . . . // other members of the WireFrameModel class
    static public class Line {
                // Represents a line from the point (x1,y1,z1)
                // to the point (x2,y2,z2) in 3-dimensional space.
        double x1, y1, z1;
        double x2, y2, z2;
    } // end class Line
    . . . // other members of the WireFrameModel class
} // end WireFrameModel
```

The full name of the nested class is *WireFrameModel.Line*. That name can be used, for example, to declare variables. Inside the *WireFrameModel* class, a *Line* object would be created with the constructor "new Line()". Outside the class, "new WireFrameModel.Line()" would be used. A static nested class has full access to the static members of the containing class, even to the private members. Similarly, the containing class has full access to the members of the nested class, even if they are marked private. This can be another motivation for declaring a nested class, since it lets you give one class access to the private members of another class without making those members generally available to other classes. Note also that a nested class can itself be private, meaning that it can only be used inside the class in which it is nested.

When you compile the above class definition, two class files will be created. Even though the definition of *Line* is nested inside *WireFrameModel*, the compiled *Line* class is stored in a separate file. The name of the class file for *Line* will be WireFrameModel Line.class.

1.5.2 Inner Classes

Non-static nested classes are referred to as *inner classes*. Inner classes are not, in practice, very different from static nested classes, but a non-static nested class is actually associated with an object rather than with the class in which its definition is nested. This can take some getting used to.

Any non-static member of a class is not really part of the class itself (although its source code is contained in the class definition). This is true for inner classes, just as it is for any other non-static part of a class. The non-static members of a class specify what will be contained in objects that are created from that class. The same is true—at least logically—for inner classes.

It's as if each object that belongs to the containing class has its own copy of the nested class (although it does not literally contain a copy of the compiled code for the nested class). This copy has access to all the instance methods and instance variables of the object, even to those that are declared private. The two copies of the inner class in two different objects differ because the instance variables and methods they refer to are in different objects. In fact, the rule for deciding whether a nested class should be static or non-static is simple: If the nested class needs to use any instance variable or instance method from the containing class, make the nested class non-static. Otherwise, it might as well be static.

In most cases, an inner class is used only within the class where it is defined. When that is true, using the inner class is really not much different from using any other class. You can create variables and declare objects using the simple name of the inner class in the usual way (although you can only do that in the non-static part of the class).

From outside the containing class, however, an inner class has to be referred to using a name of the form (*variableName*).(*NestedClassName*), where (*variableName*) is a variable that refers to the object that contains the inner class. In order to create an object that belongs to an inner class, you must first have an object that belongs to the containing class. (When working inside the class, the object "this" is used implicitly.)

Looking at an example will help, and will hopefully convince you that inner classes are really very natural. Consider a class that represents poker games. This class might include a nested class to represent the players of the game. The structure of the *PokerGame* class could be:

```
public class PokerGame {      // Represents a game of poker.
    class Player {     // Represents one of the players in this game.
            .
            .
            .
    } // end class Player
    private Deck deck;          // A deck of cards for playing the game.
    private int pot;  // The amount of money that has been bet.
    .
    .
    .
} // end class PokerGame
```

If game is a variable of type *PokerGame*, then, conceptually, game contains its own copy of the *Player* class. In an instance method of a *PokerGame* object, a new *Player* object would be created by saying "new Player()", just as for any other class. (A *Player* object could be created outside the *PokerGame* class with an expression such as "game.new Player()". Again, however, this is rare.) The *Player* object will have access to the deck and pot instance variables in the *PokerGame* object. Each PokerGame object has its own deck and pot and Players. Players of that poker game use the deck and pot for that game; players of another poker game use the other game's deck and pot. That's the effect of making the *Player* class non-static: it associates any *Player* object with some particular *PokerGame* object and gives it access to the instance variables for that particular game. This is the most natural way for players to behave. A *Player* object represents a player of one particular poker game. If *Player* were an independent class or a static nested class, on the other hand, it would represent the general idea of a poker player, independent of a particular poker game.

1.5.3 Anonymous Inner Classes

In some cases, you might find yourself writing an inner class and then using that class in just a single line of your program. Is it worth creating such a class? Indeed, it can be, but for cases like this you have the option of using an *anonymous inner class*. An anonymous class is created with a variation of the new operator that has the form

```
new(superclass-or-interface ) ( (parameter-list ) ) {
    (methods-and-variables )
}
```

This constructor defines a new class, without giving it a name. At run time, it creates an object that belongs to that class. This form of the new operator can be used in any statement where a regular "new" could be used. The intention of this expression is to create: "a new object belonging to a class that is the same as (*superclass-or-interface*) but with these (*methods-and- variables*) added." The effect is to create a uniquely customized object, just at the point in the program where you need it. Note that it is possible to base an anonymous class on an interface, rather than a class. In this case, the anonymous class must implement the interface by defining all the methods that are declared in the interface. If an interface is used as a base, the (*parameter-list*) must be empty. Otherwise, it can contain parameters for a constructor in the (*superclass*).

For now, we will look at one not-very-plausible example. Suppose that *Drawable* is an interface defined as:

```
public interface Drawable {
    public void draw(GraphicsContext g);
}
```

Suppose that we want a *Drawable* object that draws a filled, red, 100-pixel square. Rather than defining a new, separate class and then using that class to create the object, we can use an anonymous class to create the object in one statement:

```
Drawable redSquare = new Drawable() {
    public void draw(GraphicsContext g) {
            g.setFill(Color.RED);
            g.fillRect(10,10,100,100);
    }
};
```

Then redSquare refers to an object that implements *Drawable* and that draws a red square when its draw() method is called. By the way, the semicolon at the end of the statement is not part of the class definition; it's the semicolon that is required at the end of every declaration statement.

Anonymous classes are often used for actual parameters. For example, consider the following simple method, which draws a *Drawable* in two different graphics contexts:

```
void drawTwice( GraphicsContext g1, GraphicsContext g2, Drawable figure ) {
    figure.draw(g1);
    figure.draw(g2);
}
```

When calling this method, the third parameter can be created using an anonymous inner class. For example:

```
drawTwice( firstG, secondG, new  Drawable()  {
            void draw(GraphicsContext g) {
                  g.fillOval(10,10,100,100);
            }
    } );
```

When a Java class is compiled, each anonymous nested class will produce a separate class file. If the name of the main class is MainClass, for example, then the names of the class files for the anonymous nested classes will be MainClass 1.class, MainClass 2.class, MainClass 3.class, and so on.

Of course, in this example, *Drawable* is a functional interface, and we could use lambda expressions instead of anonymous classes. The last example could then be written simply

```
drawTwice( firstG, secondG, g -> g.fillOval(10,10,100,100) );
```

and redSquare could be defined as

```
Drawable redSquare = g -> {
    g.setFill(Color.RED);
    g.fillRect(10,10,100,100);
};
```

This approach has the advantage that it does not create an extra .class file. However, lambda expressions can only be used with functional interfaces, while anonymous classes can be used with any interface or class.

1.5.4 Local Classes and Lambda Expressions

A class can be defined inside a subroutine definition. Such classes are called *local classes.* A local class can only be used inside the subroutine where it is defined. However, an object that is defined by a local class can be used outside that subroutine. It can be returned as the value of the subroutine, or it can be passed as a parameter to another subroutine. This is possible because an object belonging to some class *B* can be assigned to a variable of type *A*, as long as *B* is a subclass of *A* or, if *A* is an interface, as long as class *B* implements interface *A*. For example, if a subroutine takes a parameter of type *Drawable*, where *Drawable* is the interface defined above, then any object that implements *Drawable* can be passed as a parameter to that subroutine. And that object can be defined by a local class.

In an example earlier in this section, we passed a customized object of type *Drawable* to the drawTwice() method, which takes a parameter of type *Drawable.* In that example, the class was an anonymous inner class. Local classes are often anonymous, but that is not required. It is also true that anonymous classes are often local classes, but that is also not required. For example, an anonymous class could be used to define the initial value of a global variable. In that case, the anonymous class is not enclosed in any subroutine and therefore is not local.

The definition of a local class can use local variables from the subroutine where it is defined. It can also use parameters to that subroutine. However, there is a restriction on the use of such variables and parameters in a local class: The local variable or parameter must be declared to be final or, if it is not explicitly declared final, then it must be "effectively final." A parameter is effectively final if its value is not changed inside the subroutine (including in any local class that references the parameter). A local variable is effectively final if its value is never changed after it is initialized. Note that there is no such restriction on global variables that are used in the definition of a local class.

The same restriction on the use of local variables also applies to lambda expressions, which are very similar to anonymous classes. Here is an example using the *FunctionR2R* functional in- terface, which defines the single method "double valueAt(double x))". This code segment creates an array of *FunctionR2R* objects, where multpliers[i] is a function that multiplies its parameter by i:

```
FunctionR2R[] multipliers = new FunctionR2R[100];
    for (int i = 0; i < 100; i++) {
            int n = i;
            multipliers[i]  =  z -> n * z;
}
```

The local variable n is effectively final and therefore can be used in the lambda expression. On the other hand, it would have been illegal to use the variable i directly in the lambda expression, since i is not effectively final; its value is changed when i++ is executed. Note also that this example could be written using an anonymous class instead of a lambda expression:

```
FunctionR2R[] multipliers = new FunctionR2R[100];
for (int i = 0; i < 100; i++) {
    int n = i;
    multipliers[i] =  new FunctionR2R() {
            public double valueAt(double x) {
                    return n * x;
            }
    };
}
```

Chapter 2 ADVANCED GUI PROGRAMMING: AN INTRODUCTION

2.1 BASIC CONTROLS

In preceding sections, you've seen how to use a graphics context to draw on the screen and how to handle mouse events and keyboard events. In one sense, that's all there is to GUI programming. If you're willing to program all the drawing and handle all the mouse and keyboard events, you have nothing more to learn. However, you would either be doing a lot more work than you need to do, or you would be limiting yourself to very simple user interfaces. A typical user interface uses standard GUI components such as buttons, scroll bars, text-input boxes, and menus. These components have already been written for you, so you don't have to duplicate the work involved in developing them. They know how to draw themselves, and they can handle the details of processing the mouse and keyboard events that concern them.

Consider one of the simplest user interface components, a push button. The button has a border, and it displays some text. This text can be changed. Sometimes the button is disabled, so that clicking on it doesn't have any effect. When it is disabled, its appearance changes. When the user clicks on the button, it changes appearance when the mouse button is pressed and changes back when the mouse button is released. In fact, it's more complicated than that. If the user moves the mouse outside the push button before releasing the mouse button, the button changes to its regular appearance, and releasing the mouse at that time will not trigger the button. To implement this, it is necessary to respond to mouse exit or mouse drag events. Furthermore, on many platforms, a button can receive the input focus. The button changes appearance when it has the focus. If the button has the focus and the user presses the space bar, the button is triggered. This means that the button must respond to keyboard and focus events as well.

Fortunately, you don't have to program any of this, provided you use an object belonging to the standard class javafx.scene.control.Button. A *Button* object draws itself and processes mouse, keyboard, and focus events on its own. You only hear from the *Button* when the user triggers it by clicking on it or pressing the space bar while the button has the input focus. When this happens, the *Button* object creates an event object belonging to the class javafx.event.ActionEvent. The event object is sent to any registered listener to tell it that the button has been pushed. Your program gets only the information it needs—the fact that a button was pushed.

Many standard components that are defined as part of the JavaFX graphical user interface API are defined by subclasses of the class *Control*, from package javafx.scene.control. Controls (with just a couple of exceptions) can be manipulated by the user to generate input and events for the program. A number of useful methods are defined for controls. I begin by mentioning three methods that can be used with any *Control* control:

- control.setDisable(true) can be called to disable the control. The control can be re- enabled with control.setDisable(false). When a control is disabled, its appearance might change, and it cannot be the target of mouse or key events. This function can actually be called with any scene graph node, not just controls; when you disable a node, any nodes contained inside that node are also disabled. There is a boolean-valued function, control.isDisabled() that you can call to discover whether the control is disabled, either because it was explicitly disabled or because it is inside a container node that was explicitly disabled.
- control.setTooltip(new Tooltip(string)) sets the specified string as a "tool tip" for the control. The tool tip is displayed if the mouse cursor is inside the control and the mouse is not moved for a few seconds. The tool tip should give some information about the meaning of the control or how to use it.
- control.setStyle(cssString) sets the CSS style of the control. CSS was discussed in Subsection 6.2.5.

Note that using a control, or any scene graph node, is a multi-step process. The component object must be created with a constructor. It must be added to a container. In many cases, a listener must be registered to respond to events from the component. And in some cases, a reference to the component must be saved in an instance variable so that the component can be manipulated by the program after it has been created. In this section, we will look at a few of the basic standard control components that are available in JavaFX. They are all defined by classes in the package *javafx.scene.control*. In the next section we will consider the problem of laying out components in containers.

2.1.1 ImageView

But before we turn to controls, I want to mention one other node type: *ImageView* from package javafx.scene.image. Recall from Subsection 6.2.3 that an *Image* object represents a picture, and that images can be loaded from resource files. An *Image* can be drawn on a *Canvas*, but an *Image* is not a *Node*. That is, it can't be part of a scene graph.

An *ImageView* is a scene graph node that is a simple wrapper for an image. Its purpose is simply to display the image. It makes it possible to add the image to a scene graph without having to draw the image on a canvas. The image can be specified as a parameter to the *ImageView* constructor. For example, suppose that "icons/tux.png" is the path to an image resource file. Then an *ImageView* can be created to display the image like this:

```
Image tux = new Image("icons/tux.png");
ImageView tuxIcon = new ImageView( tux );
```

In this case, I am thinking of the image as an "icon," that is, a small image that is typically used on a button, label, or menu item to add a graphical element to the usual plain text. In fact, we'll see that you can do exactly that in JavaFX.

2.1.2 Label and Button

The first four controls that we will look at have something in common: They all display a string of text to the user, which the user can view but not edit. Furthermore they can all display a graphical element in addition to or instead of the text. The graphic can be any *Node* but is usually a small icon, implemented as an object of type *ImageView*. In fact, all four types of controls inherit their behavior from a common superclass named *Labeled*. In Subsection 2.6.2, we look at menu items, which also inherit from *Labeled*. That class defines a number of instance methods that can be used with labels, buttons, and other labeled controls. Those methods include:

- setText(string) for setting the text that is displayed on the control. The text can be multi-line. The new line character, "\n", in the string represents a line break.
- setGraphic(node) for setting the control's graphical element.
- setFont(font) for setting the font that is used for the text.
- setTextFill(color) for setting the paint that is used for drawing the text.
- setGraphicTextGap(size) for setting the amount of space that is put between the text and the graphic. The parameter is of type double.
- setContentDisplay(displayCode) for setting where the graphic should be placed with respect to the text. The parameter is a constant from an enum, *ContentDis- play*, such as ContentDisplay.LEFT, ContentDisplay.RIGHT, ContentDisplay.TOP or ContentDisplay.BOTTOM.

All of these setter methods have corresponding getters, such as getText() and getFont(). I have not listed a setter method for the background color. It is possible to set a background color, but it's cumbersome. (Setting the background color of a control, c, to white looks like this:

```
c.setBackground(new Background(new BackgroundFill(Color.WHITE,null,null)));
```

where *Background* and *BackgroundFill* are in package javafx.scene.layout.) It is more easily done by setting the CSS style of the control with the setStyle() method. CSS is also useful for setting the border and for setting padding (the amount of empty space left around the content).

A *Label* is certainly the simplest type of control. It adds almost nothing to the *Labeled* class. Its purpose is simply to display some unedited text and/or a graphic to the user. The label class has two constructors. The first has one parameter of type *String* specifying the text for the label. The second adds a parameter of type *Node* specifying a graphic for the label. For example, assuming that tuxIcon is the *ImageView* object from the previous subsection,

```
Label message = new Label("Hello World");
Label linuxAd = new Label("Choose Linux First!", tuxIcon);
```

The default background of a label is completely transparent, and the label has no border or padding by default. Often I would like to add at least some padding. Here is an example of setting all three properties using CSS:

```
message.setStyle("-fx-border-color: blue; -fx-border-width: 2px; " +
                        "-fx-background-color: white; -fx-padding: 6px");
```

You've already seen buttons used in Section 2.1. A *Button*, like a *Label*, displays some text and/or a graphic to the user, and the *Button* class, like the *Label* class, has two constructors:

```
Button stopButton = new Button("Stop");
Button linuxButton = new Button("Get Linux", tuxIcon);
```

When the user clicks a button, an event of type *ActionEvent* is generated. You can register an event handler for the action with the button's setOnAction method. For example,

```
stopButton.setOnAction( e -> animator.stop() );
```

In addition to the methods inherited from *Labeled*, a button has the instance methods setDisable(boolean) and setToolTip(string) that were mentioned at the beginning of this section. The setDisable() and setText() methods are particularly useful for giving the user information about what is going on in the program. A disabled button is better than a button that gives an obnoxious error message such as "Sorry, you can't click on me now!" For example, suppose that we want to use two buttons to start and stop an *AnimationTimer*, animator. When the animation is running, the start button should be disabled, and when the animation is paused, the stop button should be disabled. The code for this might look like:

```
Button startButton = new Button("Run Animation");
```

```
Button stopButton = new Button("Stop Animation");
stopButton.setDisable(true); // Stop button is initially disabled.
startButton.setOnAction( e -> {
    animator.start();
    startButton.setDisable(true);\
    stopButton.setDisable(false);
} );
stopButton.setOnAction( e -> {
    animator.stop();
    startButton.setDisable(false);
    stopButton.setDisable(true);
} );
```

This ensures that the user can't try to start the animation when it is already started or stop it when it is already stopped.

Often, there is a button that triggers some default action in a program. For example, the user might enter data into some text input boxes and then click a "Compute" button to process the data. It would be nice if the user could just press Return when done typing, instead of having to click the button. In JavaFX, you can make a *Button*, button, into the default button for the window that contains it by calling

```
button.setDefaultButton(true);
```

When a window has a default button, then pressing the Return (or Enter) key on the keyboard is equivalent to clicking the default button, unless the key event generated by the Return key is consumed by another component. This can be very convenient for the user.

2.1.3 CheckBox and RadioButton

A *CheckBox* is a component that has two states: selected or unselected. (Being "selected" means that the checkbox is checked.) The user can change the state of a check box by clicking on it. The state of a checkbox is represented by a boolean value that is true if the box is selected and is false if the box is unselected. A checkbox has a label, which is specified when the box is constructed:

```
CheckBox showTime = new CheckBox("Show Current Time");
```

CheckBox is a subclass of *Labeled*, so a checkbox can also have a graphic, and all the instance methods from the *Labeled* class can also be used with checkboxes. (There is no constructor that specifies a graphic for the checkbox; any graphic has to be set by calling setGraphic(node).)

Usually, it's the user who sets the state of a *CheckBox* by clicking on it, but you can also set the state programmatically. The current state of a checkbox is set using its setSelected(boolean) method. For example, if you want the checkbox showTime to be checked, you would say "showTime.setSelected(true)". To uncheck the box, say "showTime.setSelected(false)". You can determine the current state of a checkbox by calling its isSelected() method, which returns a boolean value.

In many cases, you don't need to worry about events from checkboxes. Your program can just check the state whenever it needs to know it by calling the isSelected() method. However, a checkbox does generate an event when its state is changed by the user, and you can detect this event and respond to it if you want something to happen at the moment the state changes. When the state of a checkbox is changed by the user, it generates an event of type *ActionEvent*. If you want something to happen when the user changes the state, you must register a handler with the checkbox by calling its setOnAction() method. (Note that if you change the state by calling the setSelected() method, no *ActionEvent* is generated. However, there is another method in the *CheckBox* class, fire(), which simulates a user click on the checkbox and does generate an *ActionEvent*.)

It is actually possible for a checkbox to be in a third state, called "indeterminate," although that possibility is turned off by default. See the API documentation for details.

Closely related to checkboxes are *radio buttons*. Like a checkbox, a radio button can be either selected or not. However, radio buttons are expected to occur in groups, where at most one radio button in a given group can be selected at any given time. Radio button groups let the user select one choice among several alternatives. In JavaFX, a radio button is represented by an object of type *RadioButton*. When used in isolation, a *RadioButton* acts just like a *CheckBox*, and it has the same constructor, methods, and events, including methods inherited from *Labeled*. Ordinarily, however, a *RadioButton* is used in a group. A group of radio buttons is represented by an object belonging to the class *ToggleGroup*. A *ToggleGroup* is not a component and does not itself have a visible representation on the screen. A *ToggleGroup* works behind the scenes to organize a group of radio buttons, to ensure that at most one button in the group can be selected at any given time.

To use a group of radio buttons, you must create a *RadioButton* object for each button in the group, and you must create one object of type *ToggleGroup* to organize the individual buttons into a group. Each *RadioButton* must be added individually to the scene graph, so that it will appear on the screen. (A *ToggleGroup* plays no role in the placement of the buttons on the screen.) Each *RadioButton* must also be added to the *ToggleGroup*. You do that by calling the radio button's setToggleGroup(group) instance method. If you want one of the buttons to be selected initially, you can call setSelected(true) for that button. If you don't do this, then none of the buttons will be selected until the user clicks on one of them.

As an example, here is how you could set up a group of radio buttons that can be used to select a color:

```
RadioButton redRadio, blueRadio, greenRadio, yellowRadio;
                    // Variables to represent the radio buttons.
                    // These might be instance variables, so that
                    // they can be used throughout the program.
ToggleGroup colorGroup = new ToggleGroup();
redRadio = new RadioButton("Red");  // Create a button.
redRadio.setToggleGroup(colorGroup); // Add it to the ToggleGroup.
blueRadio = new RadioButton("Blue");
blueRadio.setToggleGroup(colorGroup);
greenRadio = new RadioButton("Green");
greenRadio.setToggleGroup(colorGroup);
yellowRadio = new RadioButton("Yellow");
yellowRadio.setToggleGroup(colorGroup);
redRadio.setSelected(true);   // Make an initial selection.
```

As an alternative to calling redRadio.setSelected(true), you can use the selectToggle() instance method in the *ToggleGroup* class to select the radio button:

```
colorGroup.selectToggle( redRadio );
```

Just as for checkboxes, it is not always necessary to register listeners for radio buttons. You can test the state of an individual *RadioButton* by calling its isSelected() method, or you can call the toggle group's getSelectedToggle() method. The return type of this method is *Toggle*, which is an interface implemented by *RadioButton*. For example:

```
Toggle selection = colorGroup.getSelectedToggle();
if (selection == redRadio) {
    color = Color.RED;
}
else if (selection == greenRadio){
    .
```

•

•

Here's what these radio buttons look like, lined up vertically in a container:

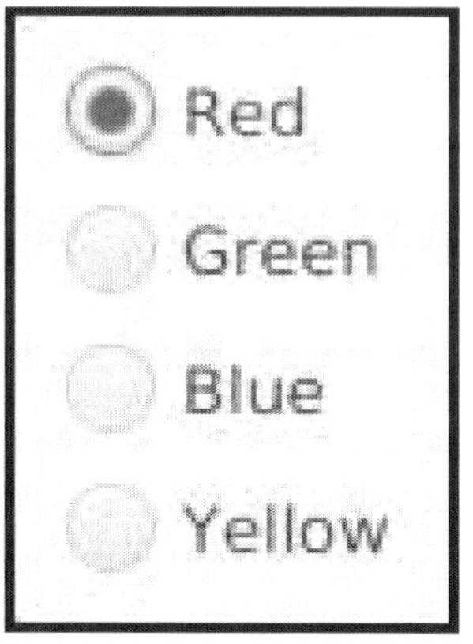

2.1.4 TextField and TextArea

The *TextField* and *TextArea* classes represent components that contain text that can be edited by the user. A *TextField* holds a single line of text, while a *TextArea* can hold multiple lines. It is also possible to set a *TextField* or *TextArea* to be read-only so that the user can read the text that it contains but cannot edit the text. Both classes are subclasses of an abstract class, *TextInputControl*, which defines their common properties.

TextField and *TextArea* have many methods in common. The instance method setText(text), which takes a parameter of type *String*, can be used to change the text that is displayed in an input component. The contents of the component can be retrieved by calling its getText() instance method, which returns a value of type *String*. You can add a *String* of text onto the end of the text that is already in the component by calling the instance method appendText(text). The text in the setText() and appendText() methods can include "\n" characters to represent line breaks; in a *TextField* they will be ignored. The instance method setFont(font) can be used to change the font that is used in the text component.

If you want to stop the user from modifying the text, you can call setEditable(false). Call the same method with parameter true to make the input component user-editable again.

The user can only type into a text component when it has the input focus. The user can give the input focus to a text component by clicking it with the mouse, but sometimes it is useful to give the input focus to a text field programmatically. You can do this by calling its requestFocus() method.

A substring of the text in a text component can be "selected." The selected text is highlighted and can be cut or copied from the text component. (The user can right-click in the component to bring up a pop-up menu of editing commands.) *TextInputComponent* has several instance methods for working with the text selection, but I only mention one of them: selectAll(), which selects the entire string of text in the text component.

For example, when I discover an error in the user's input in a *TextField*, input, I usually call both input.requestFocus() and input.selectAll(). This helps the user see where the error occurred and lets the user start typing the correction immediately. If the user starts typing, the old text in the input box, which is highlighted, will automatically be deleted.

Both the *TextField* class and the *TextArea* class have two constructors. One of the constructors has no parameter and makes an initially empty text input box. The second constructor takes a parameter of type *String*, specifying the initial content of the box.

A *TextField* has a preferred number of columns, which by default is 12. This determines the preferred width of the text field, that is, the size that is used if the size is not reset by the program or when the text field is laid out by a container. The preferred number of columns for a *TextField*, input, can be changed by calling input.setPrefColumnCount(n), where n is a positive integer.

Similarly, a *TextArea* has both a preferred number of columns and a preferred number of rows, which by default are 40 and 10. The value can be changed using the *TextArea* instance methods setPrefColumnCount(n) and setPrefRowCount(n).

The *TextArea* class adds a few useful methods to those inherited from *TextInputControl*, including some methods for getting and setting the amount by which the text has been scrolled.

Most important is setWrapText(wrap), where wrap is of type boolean. This method says what should happen when a line of text is too long to be displayed in the text area. If wrap is true, then any line that is too long will be "wrapped" onto the next line, with the line break occurring between words if possible; if wrap is false, the line will simply extend outside the text area, and the user will have to scroll the text area horizontally to see the entire line. The default value of wrap is false.

Since it might be necessary to scroll a text area to see all the text that it contains, a *TextArea* comes with scroll bars. The scroll bars are visible only when they are needed because the text cannot fit in the available space.

See the sample program TextInputDemo.java for a short example of using a text field and a text area. Here is the window from that program, after the text has been edited and scrolled down a few lines:

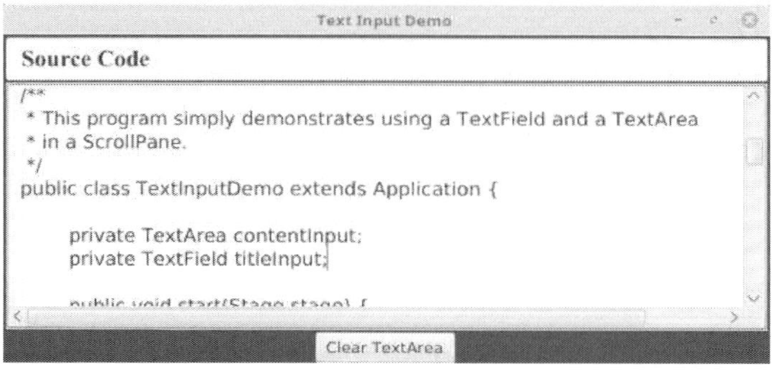

(I pasted the source code of the program into the text area!)

2.1.5 Slider

A *Slider* provides a way for the user to select an integer value from a range of possible values. The user does this by dragging a "knob" along a bar, or by clicking at some point along the bar. A slider can, optionally, be decorated with tick marks and with labels. This picture, from the sample program SliderDemo.java, shows three sliders with different decorations and with different ranges of values:

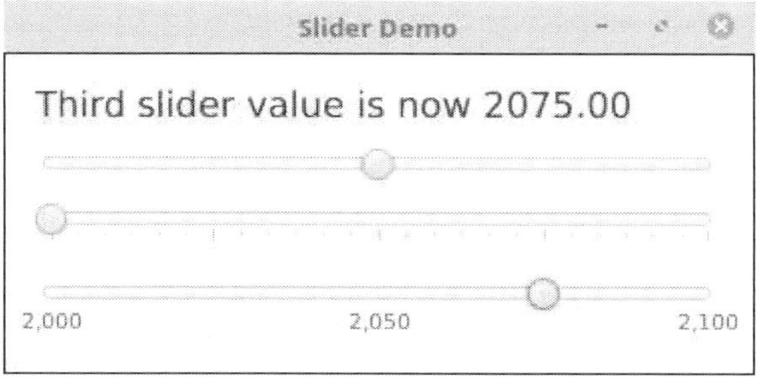

Here, the second slider is decorated with tick marks, and the third one is decorated with labels. It's possible for a single slider to have both types of decorations.

The most commonly used constructor for *Sliders* specifies the start and end of the range of values for the slider and its initial value when it first appears on the screen:

public Slider(double minimum, double maximum, double value)

If the parameters are omitted, the values 0, 100, and 0 are used. By default, a slider is horizontal, but you can make it vertical by calling its method setOrientation(Orientation.VERTICAL). *Orientation* is an enum from package javafx.geometry.

The current value of a *Slider* can be read at any time with its getValue() method, which returns a value of type double. If you want to change the value programmatically, you can do so with the method setValue(val), which takes a parameter of type double. If the specified value is not between the minimum and maximum slider values, it is adjusted to lie in that range.

If you want to respond immediately when the user changes the value of a slider, you can register a listener with the slider. *Sliders*, unlike other components we have seen, do not generate ActionEvents. Instead, they have an observable property of type Double that represents the value. (See Subsection 2.3.7.) You can access the value property of a *Slider*, slider, by calling slider.valueProperty(), and you can add a listener to the property that will be called whenever the value changes. For example, in the sample program, I add listeners to the sliders with commands such as

slider1.valueProperty().addListener(e -> sliderValueChanged(slider1));

The listener will be called whenever the value changes, either because the user is dragging the knob on the slider or because the program calls setValue(). If you want to know whether the user generated the event by dragging the slider's knob, call the slider's boolean-valued isValueChanging() method, which returns true if the user is dragging the knob.

Using tick marks on a slider is a two-step process: Specify the interval between the tick marks, and tell the slider that the tick marks should be displayed. There are actually two types of tick marks, "major" tick marks and "minor" tick marks. You can have one or the other or both. Major tick marks are a bit longer than minor tick marks. The method setMajorTickSpacing(x) indicates that there should be a major tick mark every x units along the slider. The parameter is of type double. (The spacing is in terms of values on the slider, not pixels.) To control the minor tick marks, you can call setMinorTickCount(n). The parameter is an int that specifies how many minor tick marks are placed between consecutive major tick marks. The default value is 4. If you don't want minor tick marks, set the count to zero. Calling these methods is not enough to make the tick marks appear. You also have to call setShowTickMarks(true). For example, the second slider in the sample program was created and configured using the commands:

slider2 = new Slider();   // Use default values (0,100,0)

slider2.setMajorTickUnit(25); // space between big tick marks

slider2.setMinorTickCount(5); // 5 small tick marks between big tick marks.

slider2.setShowTickMarks(true);

Labels on a slider are handled similarly. A label will be placed at every major tick mark, but some labels will be omitted if they would overlap. To see the labels, you need to call setShowTickLabels(true). For example, the third slider in the above illustration was created and configured to show labels with the commands:

slider3 = new Slider(2000,2100,2022);

slider3.setMajorTickUnit(50); // tick marks are not shown!

slider3.setShowTickLabels(true)

The value of a slider is of type double. You might want to restrict the value to be an integer, or to be some multiple of a given value. What you can do is call slider.setSnapToTicks(true). After the user finishes dragging the slider's knob, the value will be moved to the value at the nearest major or minor tick mark, even if the tick marks are not visible. The value will not be restricted while the user is dragging the knob; the value is just adjusted at the end of the drag. The value set by calling setValue(x) is also not restricted, but there is another method, adjustValue(x), that will set the value to the value at the tick mark nearest to x. For example, if you want a slider to snap to integral values in the range 0 to 10, you could say:

```
Slider sldr = new Slider(0,10,0);
sldr.setMajorTickUnit(1);      // major ticks 1 unit apart
sldr.setMinorTickCount(0); // no minor tick marks
sldr.setSnapToTicks(true);
```

In the sample program, the third slider has been configured to snap to an integer value at the end of a drag operation.

2.2 BASIC LAYOUT

Components are the fundamental building blocks of a graphical user interface. But you have to do more with components besides create them. Another aspect of GUI programming is *laying out* components on the screen, that is, deciding where they are placed and how big they are. You have probably noticed that computing coordinates can be a difficult problem, especially if you don't assume a fixed size for the drawing area. Java has a solution for this, as well.

Components are the visible objects that make up a GUI. Some components are *containers*, which can hold other components. In JavaFX terms, a container is a scene graph node that can contain other scene graph nodes as "children." The children of a container must be "laid out," which means setting their sizes and positions. It is possible for you to program the layout yourself, but layout is usually done automatically by the container. Different kinds of containers implement different policies for laying out their child nodes. In this section, we will cover some common types of JavaFX containers and their layout policies. In this section and the next, we will look at several programming examples that use components and layout.

Because a container is itself a scene graph node, you can add a container as a child of another container. This makes complex nesting of components possible, as shown in this illustration:

In this picture, a large container holds two smaller containers. Each of the two smaller containers in turn holds three components.

Every scene graph node has a minimum width and height, a maximum width and height, and a preferred width and height. A container consults these values when it is deciding how to lay out its children. (Some nodes, however, are not resizable, meaning not meant to be resized by a container during layout; for such components, the minimum, maximum, and preferred width and height are effectively equal to the component's actual size. *Canvas* and *ImageView* are examples of non-resizable components.) In general, a container will compute its own preferred size based on the components that it contains. The container's preferred size will allow each component that it contains to have at least its preferred size. The container will compute its own minimum and maximum sizes in a similar way, based on the minimum and maximum sizes of its children.

When setting the size of a child while doing layout, most containers will not set the width of the child to be less than the child's minimum width or greater than the child's maximum width, and the same for the child's height. This will be true even if it means that the child will overlap other components or will extend outside the container. (The part outside the container might or might not be shown, depending on the container.) This can also leave empty space in the container.

Resizable nodes, which includes controls and most containers, have instance methods for setting the minimum, preferred, and maximim width: setMinWidth(w), setPrefWidth(w), and setMaxWidth(w), where the parameter is of type double, with similar instance methods for the height. You can also set width and height values simultaneously with methods such as setMaxSize(w,h) and setPrefSize(w,h). For a container, the values set by these methods will override the values that would have been computed by the container based the children that it contains.

In JavaFX, containers that do layout are defined by the class *Pane* and its subclasses. (*Pane* and its subclasses are in package javafx.scene.layout.) Here, we look at a few of these layout classes, starting with using *Pane* directly.

2.2.1 Do Your Own Layout

Sometimes, you would like to do your own layout, instead of letting it up to one of the standard container classes. You can get complete control of the size and location of a node by setting it to be "unmanaged":

node.setManaged(false);

When you do that, any container that contains node as a child will completely ignore node, as far as layout is concerned. It is your responsibility to set its location and (for resizable nodes) size. Note that an unmanaged node must still be placed inside a container for it to appear on the screen.

For our first layout example, we'll look at using the *Pane* class itself for the container. The *Pane* will manage the size, but not the location, of the managed nodes that it contains. That is, by using a *Pane* as container, you assume responsibility for setting the positions of the child nodes. The *Pane* will, by default, resize each child to its preferred size; if you want to take over that job too, you need to make the child unmanaged.

If node is any scene graph node that is unmanaged or is in a container that does not set the location of its child nodes, then you can set the location by calling

node.relocate(x, y);

This puts the top left corner of the node at the point (x,y), measured in the coordinate system of the container that contains the node. Similarly, you can set the size of node, when that is allowed, by calling

node.resize(width, height)

The width and height are measured in pixels.

We will look at an example that contains four components: two buttons, a label, and a canvas that displays a checkerboard pattern:

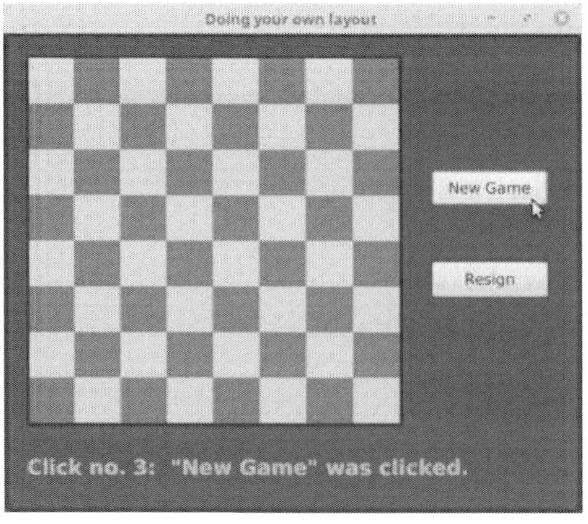

The program is just an example of layout; it doesn't do anything, except that clicking the buttons changes the text of the label.

This example uses a *Pane* as the root node of the scene and as the container for the four components. This means that the program is responsible for setting the locations of the components, by calling their relocate() method. (Without that, they will all appear with their top left corners at the default location, (0,0)!) After looking at the result, I decided that I wanted the two buttons to have the same size and to be larger than their preferred sizes. For that to work, the buttons had to be made unmanaged. (Otherwise, calling their resize() method would have no effect because the pane would set them back to their preferred size.) Here is the code from the application's start() method that creates the four components and configures them, including setting their locations and sizes:

```
/* Create the child nodes. */
board = new Checkerboard(); // a nested subclass of Canvas
board.draw();          // draws the content of the checkerboard
newGameButton = new Button("New Game");
newGameButton.setOnAction( e -> doNewGame() );
resignButton = new Button("Resign");
resignButton.setOnAction( e -> doResign() );
message = new Label("Click \"New Game\" to begin.");
message.setTextFill( Color.rgb(100,255,100) ); // Light green.
message.setFont( Font.font(null, FontWeight.BOLD, 18) );
/* Set the location of each child by calling its relocate() method */
board.relocate(20,20);
newGameButton.relocate(370, 120);
resignButton.relocate(370, 200);
message.relocate(20, 370);
/* Set the sizes of the buttons. For this to have an effect, make
the butons "unmanaged."    If they are managed, the Pane will set
their sizes. */
resignButton.setManaged(false);
resignButton.resize(100,30);
newGameButton.setManaged(false);
newGameButton.resize(100,30);
```

The *Pane* that holds the components is the root node of the scene. The window for the program will be sized to be just large enough to hold the *Pane* at its preferred size. By default, a *Pane* computes its preferred size to be just large enough to show all of its managed children. Since I made the buttons unmanaged, they would not be included in the preferred size. To make the window large enough to include them (and to allow more empty space below the label), the program sets the preferred width and height of the pane:

```
Pane root = new Pane();
root.setPrefWidth(500);
root.setPrefHeight(420);
```

The buttons, label, and board must still be added as children of the pane, to make them appear on the screen. This is done with the command:

```
root.getChildren().addAll(board, newGameButton, resignButton, message);
```

Alternatively, they could have been added one by one using statements such as

```
root.getChildren().add(board);
```

or the child nodes could have been given as parameters to the constructor:

```
Pane root = new Pane(board, newGameButton, resignButton, message);
```

The pane still has to be made the root of the scene, the scene has to be placed in the stage, and the stage has to be configured and shown on the screen. See the source code, OwnLayoutDemo.java, for the complete story.

It's fairly easy in this case to get a reasonable layout. It's much more difficult to do your own layout if you want to allow for changes in the size of the window. To do that, you would probably write your own subclass of *Pane* (or of its superclass, *Region*), and override the layoutChildren() method, which is called by the system when a container needs to do layout, including when the container is resized. However, my real advice is that if you want to allow for changes in the container's size, try to find a standard container that will do the layout work for you.

2.2.2 BorderPane

A *BorderPane* is a subclass of *Pane* that is designed to display one large, central component, with up to four smaller components arranged around the edges of the central component. The five positions are referred to as center, top, right, bottom, and left. The meaning of the five positions is shown in this diagram:

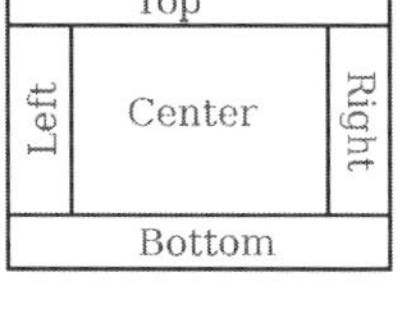

Note that a border layout can contain fewer than five components, so that not all five of the possible positions need to be filled. It would be very unusual, however, to have no center component.

The *BorderPane* class has two constructors, one with no parameters and one that takes a single parameter giving the center child of the pane. Child nodes can be added to a *BorderPane*, pane, using the methods

pane.setCenter(node);

pane.setTop(node);

pane.setRight(node);

pane.setBottom(node);

pane.setLeft(node);

Calling one of these methods with parameter null will remove the child from that position in the pane.

A *BorderPane* sets the sizes of its child nodes as follows, except that the width and height of a component is always restricted to lie between the minimum and maximum width and height of that component: The top and bottom components (if present) are shown at their preferred heights, but their width is set equal to the full width of the container. The left and right components are shown at their preferred widths, but their height is set to the height of the container, minus the space occupied by the top and bottom components. Finally, the center component takes up any remaining space.

The default preferred size of *BorderPane* is set just big enough to accommodate the preferred sizes of its (managed) children. The minimum size is computed in a similar way. The default maximum size of a *BorderPane* is unlimited.

For some subclasses of *Pane*, it is possible to tweak the layout of the children by applying things called *layout constraints*. For example, what happens in a *BorderPane* if a child cannot be resized to exactly fit the available space? In that case, the child has a default position within the available space. The center child is centered within the center space of the pane, the bottom child is placed at the bottom left corner of the bottom space in the pane, and so on. You can change this default placement using a static method from the *BorderPane* class:

BorderPane.setAlignment(child, position);

where child is the child node whose position you want to tweak and position is one of the constants from the enumerated type *Pos*, from package javafx.geometry. Possible positions include Pos.CENTER, POS.TOP LEFT, Pos.BOTTOM RIGHT, and so on. (I find it strange that the alignment is set using a static method, but that's the way layout constraints work in JavaFX.) You can also set a *margin* for any child of a

BorderPane. A margin is empty space around the child. The background color of the pane will show in the margin. A margin is specified as a value of type *Insets*, from package javafx.geometry. An object of type *Insets* has four double properties, top, right, bottom, and left, which can be specified in the constructor:

new Insets(top,right,bottom,left)

There is also a constructor that takes a single parameter, which is used as the value for all four properties. When used as a margin for a child node, the properties specify the width of the margin along the top, right, bottom, and left edges of the child. The margin can be specified using another static method:

BorderPane.setMargin(child, insets);

For example,

BorderPane.setMargin(topchild, new Insets(2,5,2,5));

Remember that you can also tweak the appearance of a container using CSS (Subsec- tion 6.2.5), which is the easiest way to set a border or background color for the container.

2.2.3 HBox and VBox

It is common to want to lay out a set of components in a horizontal row or in a vertical column. For that, the classes *HBox* and *VBox* can be used. *HBox* is a subclass of *Pane* that lays out its children next to each other, in a horizontal row. *VBox* is a subclass of *Pane* that lays out its children in vertical column. An *HBox* might be used as the bottom component in a *BorderPane*, making it possible to line up several components along the bottom of the border pane. Similarly, a *VBox* might be used as the left or right component of a *BorderPane*. Here, I will only discuss *HBox*, but *VBox* is used in an entirely analogous way.

An *HBox*, hbox, can be configured to leave a gap between each child and the next. The amount of the gap is given by a value of type double, which can be set by calling

hbox.setSpacing(gapAmount);

The default value is zero. Children can be added to hbox in the same way as for *Pane*, that is, by calling hbox.getChildren().add(child) or hbox.getChildren(). addAll(child1,child2,...). The *HBox* class has a constructor with no parameters, as well as one that takes the size of the gap as its first parameter, optionally followed by child nodes to be added to the box.

By default, an *HBox* will resize its children to their preferred widths, possibly leaving some blank extra space on the right. (The blank space would be there because the width of the *HBox* has been set to be larger than its preferred width.) If using the children's preferred widths would make the total width greater than the actual width of the *HBox*, it will shrink the children, within the limit of their minimum widths. The height of the children will be set to the full available height in the *HBox*, but, as always, within the limits set by their minimum and maximum heights.

Perhaps you would like the children to grow beyond their preferred widths, to fill the available space in an *HBox*. To make that happen, you need to set a layout constraint on each child that you want to grow, using a static method:

HBox.setHgrow(child, priority);

The second parameter is a constant of the enumerated type *Priority*, from package javafx.scene.layout. The value will likely be Priority.ALWAYS, which means that the child will always get a share of the extra space. The child's width will still be limited by its maximum width, so you might need to increase that maximum to get the child to grow to the extent that you want.

As an example, suppose that an *HBox* contains three *Buttons*, but1, but2, and but3, and that you would like them to grow to fill the entire *HBox*. You need to set the HGrow constraint on each button. Furthermore, since the maximum width of a button is equal to its preferred width, you need to increase each button's maximum width. Here, I set the maximum width to be Double.POSITIVE INFINITY, which means that the button can grow without any limit:

HBox.setHgrow(but1, Priority.ALWAYS);

HBox.setHgrow(but2, Priority.ALWAYS);

HBox.setHgrow(but3, Priority.ALWAYS);

but1.setMaxWidth(Double.POSITIVE INFINITY);

but2.setMaxWidth(Double.POSITIVE INFINITY);

but3.setMaxWidth(Double.POSITIVE INFINITY);

Any extra space will be distributed equally to the three buttons and added on to their preferred widths. This does not mean that they will all have the same width, because their original, preferred widths might not be equal. For a sample program in the next section, I wanted the three buttons in an *HBox* to be the same size. To accomplish that, I simply gave all three buttons the same large preferred width:

but1.setPrefWidth(1000);

but2.setPrefWidth(1000);

but3.setPrefWidth(1000);

The *HBox* will then shrink the buttons proportionately to fit in the available space, and they all end up with the same width.

There are other ways to tweak the layout in an *HBox*. You can add a margin around any child using a static method similar to the one that is used for the same purpose in a *BorderPane*. You can set the *HBox* to use the preferred heights of its children, instead of stretching them to fit the height of the hbox by calling hbox.setFillHeight(false). You can say where in the hbox the children are placed, when they do not fill the entire hbox by calling hbox.setAlignment(position); the parameter is of type *Pos* with a default of Pos.TOP LEFT. And, of course, you can apply CSS style properties.

As an example, we look at a GUI built entirely using *HBox* and *VBox*. The complete program can be found in SimpleCalc.java. The program has two *TextFields* where the user can enter numbers, four *Buttons* that the user can click to add, subtract, multiply, or divide the two numbers, and a *Label* that displays the result of the operation. Here is a picture of the program's window:

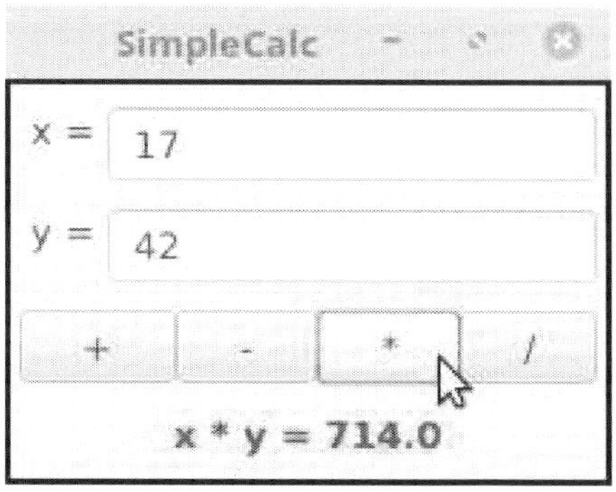

The root node for the window is a *VBox* containing four items, where the first three items are *HBoxes*. The first *HBox* contains two components, a *Label* displaying the text "x =" and a *TextField*. It is created with the commands

xInput = new TextField("0"); // Text input box initially containing "0" HBox xPane = new HBox(new Label(" x = "), xInput);

and it is later added as the first child of the *VBox* Note that the label is simply created with a constructor and added to the *HBox*, since there is no need to keep a reference to it.

The third *HBox* contains the four buttons. The buttons' default widths would be rather small. To make them fill the entire *HBox*, I add an hgrow constraint to each button and increase its maximum width. Here is how it's done:

/ Create the four buttons and an HBox to hold them. */*

Button plus = new Button("+");

plus.setOnAction(e -> doOperation('+'));

Button minus = new Button("-");

minus.setOnAction(e -> doOperation('-'));

Button times = new Button("");*

```
times.setOnAction( e -> doOperation('*') );
Button divide = new Button("/");
divide.setOnAction( e -> doOperation('/') );
HBox buttonPane = new HBox( plus, minus, times, divide );
/* The four buttons need to be tweaked so that they will fill the entire buttonPane.
This can be done by giving each button a large maximum width and setting an hgrow
constraint for the button. */
HBox.setHgrow(plus, Priority.ALWAYS);
plus.setMaxWidth(Double.POSITIVE INFINITY);
HBox.setHgrow(minus, Priority.ALWAYS);
minus.setMaxWidth(Double.POSITIVE INFINITY);
HBox.setHgrow(times, Priority.ALWAYS);
times.setMaxWidth(Double.POSITIVE INFINITY);
HBox.setHgrow(divide, Priority.ALWAYS);
divide.setMaxWidth(Double.POSITIVE INFINITY);
```

The last position in the *VBox* is occupied by a *Label*. Since there is only one component, it is added directly to the *VBox* ; there is no need to wrap it in an *HBox*. However, in order to get the text in the label to appear in the center instead of at the left edge of the window, I needed to increase the maximum width of the label (so that the *VBox* will set its width to fill the entire available space). Furthermore, I had to set the alignment property of the label, to tell the label to place its text in the center of the label and not at the left:

```
answer.setMaxWidth(Double.POSITIVE INFINITY);
answer.setAlignment(Pos.CENTER);
```

One point of interest in this example, aside from the layout, is the doOperation() method that is called when the user clicks one of the buttons. This method must retrieve the user's numbers from the text fields, perform the appropriate arithmetic operation on them (depending on which button was clicked), and set the text of the *Label* to represent the result. However, the contents of the text fields can only be retrieved as strings, and these strings must be converted into numbers. If the conversion fails, the label is set to display an error message:

```
private void doOperation( char op ) {
    double x, y;        // The numbers from the input boxes.
    try {     // Get x from the first input box.
```

```
        String xStr = xInput.getText();
        x = Double.parseDouble(xStr);
}
catch (NumberFormatException e) {
                // The string xStr was not a legal number.
                // Show an error message, move the input focus
                // to xInput and select all the text in that box.
        answer.setText("Illegal data for x.");
        xInput.requestFocus();
        xInput.selectAll();
        return; // stop processing when an error occurs!
}
try {   // Get a number from the second input box.
        String yStr = yInput.getText();
        y = Double.parseDouble(yStr);
}
catch (NumberFormatException e) {
        answer.setText("Illegal data for y.");
        yInput.requestFocus();
        yInput.selectAll();
        return;
}
/* Perform the operation based on the parameter, op. */
if (op == '+')
        answer.setText( "x + y = " + (x+y) );
else if (op == '-')
        answer.setText( "x - y = " + (x-y) );
else if (op == '*')
        answer.setText( "x * y = " + (x*y) );
else if (op == '/') {
        if (y == 0) {       // Can't divide by zero! Show an error message.
        answer.setText("Can't divide by zero!");
```

```
            yInput.requestFocus();
            yInput.selectAll();
      }
      else {
            answer.setText( "x / y = " + (x/y) );
            }
      }
   } // end doOperation()
```

The complete source code for this example can be found in SimpleCalc.java.

2.2.4 GridPane and TilePane

Next, we consider *GridPane*, a subclass of *Pane* that lays out its children in rows and columns. Rows and columns are numbered, starting from zero. Here is an illustration of a typical grid with 4 rows and 5 columns:

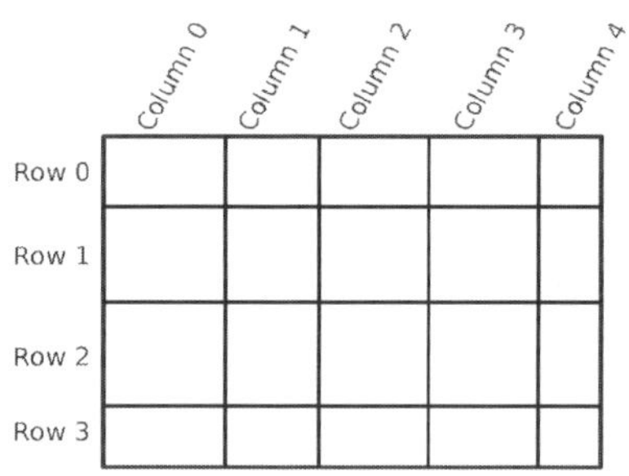

Note that the rows are not necessarily all the same height, and columns are not necessarily all the same width.

It is possible to leave gaps between rows or between columns, where the background of the *GridPane* will show. If grid is the *GridPane*, set the size of the gaps by calling

```
grid.setHGap( gapSize );      // gap between columns
gris.setVGap( gapSize );      // gap between rows
```

You can specify the row and column where a child is to be placed when you add the child to the *GridPane*:

```
grid.add( child, column, row );
```

(Note that the column number is specified first.) In fact, it is possible for a child to span several rows or several columns in the grid. The number of columns and number of rows that the child should occupy can be given as additional parameters to the add() method:

```
grid.add( child, column, row, columnCount, rowCount );
```

The number of rows and number of columns in the grid are determined by the positions of the children that have been added to it.

A *GridPane* will resize each child to fill the position or positions that it occupies in the grid (within minimum and maximum size limits). The preferred width of a column will be just large enough to accommodate the preferred widths of all the children in that column, and similarly for the preferred height. There are several ways to tweak this behavior, but here I will only mention that the actual column width and row height can be controlled.

A *GridPane* can have a set of *column constraints* and a set of *row constraints* that determine how the column width and row height are computed. The width of a column can be computed based on the widths of its children (the default), it can be set to a constant value, or it can be computed as a percentage of available space. Computation of row height is similar. Here is how to set constant row heights for a gridpane that has four rows:

```
gridpane.getRowConstraints().addAll(
    new RowConstraints(100), // row 0 has height 100 pixels
    new RowConstraints(150), // row 1 has height 150 pixels
    new RowConstraints(100), // row 2 has height 100 pixels
    new RowConstraints(200), // row 3 has height 200 pixels
);
```

In this case, the total height of the gridpane is the same, no matter how much space is available for it.

When percentages are used, the grid pane will expand to fill available space, and the row height or column width will be computed from the percentages. For example, to force a five- column gridpane to fill the available width and to force all columns to have the same size:

```
for (int i = 0; i < 5; i++) {
    ColumnConstraints constraints = new ColumnConstraints();
    constraints.setPercentWidth(20); // (there is no constructor that does this)
    gridpane.getColumnConstraints().add(constraints);
}
```

If the percentages add up to more than 100, then they will be decreased proportionately. In the example, setting all five percentages to be 50 would have the same effect as setting them all to be 20. Things can get more complicated than this, but these are probably the most common cases.

For an example of using a *GridPane* see the source code of SimpleColorChooser.java from Subsection 2.2.1. You should now be able to read and understand the entire program.

If you would like a grid in which all the rectangles are the same size, you can use a *TilePane*. A *TilePane* arranges equal-size "tiles" in rows and columns. Each tile holds one of the child nodes; there is no way to spread out a child over several tiles.

A *TilePane*, tpane, has a preferred number of rows and a preferred number of columns, which you should set by calling

tpane.setPrefColumns(cols);

The preferred number of columns will be used if the *TilePane* is shown at its preferred size, which is the usual case. However, that is not necessarily true if it is shown at a different size; in that case, the number of columns will be determined by the width of the available space. The number of rows will be determined by the number of child nodes that are added to the *TilePane*. The children will be laid out in order, filling the first row from left to right, then the second row, and so on. It is not required that the last row be completely filled. (All of this is true if the "orientation" of the *TilePane* is horizontal. It is possible to change the orientation to vertical. In that case, the number of preferred rows is specified instead of the number of columns. However, I have found little reason to do that.)

It's very common to have a *TilePane* in which the number of preferred columns is one. In that case, it is similar to a *VBox*. It is also common for the number of columns to be equal to the number of child nodes, and in that case, it is similar to an *HBox*.

At its preferred size, the width of each tile is equal to the largest preferred width of any child node, and similarly for the height. The *TilePane* will resize each child to completely fill its tile, except that it will not make a child larger than its maximum width and height.

There is a *TilePane* constructor with no parameters and one that takes a list of any number of children to be added to the pane. You can also add children later using one of

tpane.getChildren().add(child);

tpane.getChildren().addAll(child1, child2, ...);

You can specify the size of a horizontal gap that will be placed between columns and of a vertical gap that will be placed between rows. The background of the pane will show through the gaps. The gap amounts can be specified in the constructor (optionally followed by a list of children):

TilePane tpane = new TilePane(hgapAmount, vgapAmount);

or they can be specified later with tpane.setHgap(h) and tpane.setVgap(v). For an example that uses *TilePanes* for layout, see the solution to Exercise 6.7.

2.3 COMPLETE PROGRAMS

In this chapter, we have covered many of the basic aspects of GUI programming. There is still a lot more to learn, But you already know enough to write some interesting programs. In this section, we look at two complete programs that use what you have learned about GUI programming in this chapter, as well as what you learned about programming in general in earlier chapters. Along the way, we will also encounter a few new ideas.

2.3.1 A Little Card Game

The first program that we will consider is a GUI version of the command-line card game HighLow.java from Subsection 1.4.3. In the new version, HighLowGUI.java, you look at a playing card and try to predict whether the next card will be higher or lower in value. (Aces have the lowest value in this game.) In this GUI version of the program, you click on a button to make your prediction. If you predict wrong, you lose. If you make three correct predictions, you win. After completing a game, you can click "New Game" to start another game. Here is what the program looks like in the middle of a game:

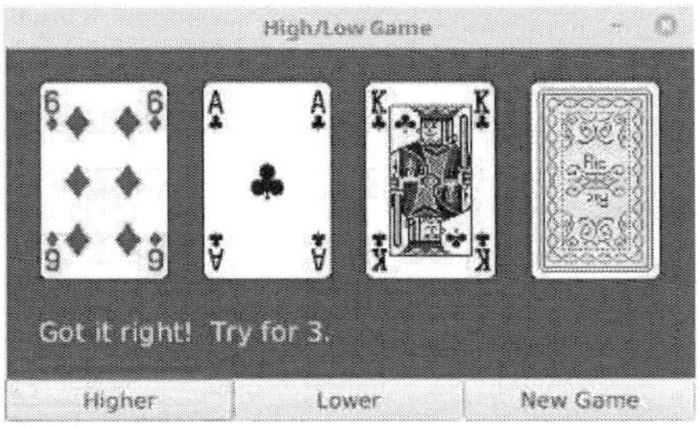

The complete source code for the program can be found in the file HighLowGUI.java. I encourage you to compile and run it. Note that the program also requires Card.java, Deck.java, and Hand.java, from Section 1.4, since they define classes that are used in the program. And it requires the file of card images, cards.png, that was used in RandomCards.java from Subsection 2.2.4.

The layout of the program should be easy to guess: HighLowGUI uses a *BorderPane* as the root of the scene graph. The center position is occupied by a *Canvas* on which the cards and a message are drawn. The bottom position contains an *HBox* that in turn contains three *Buttons*. In order to make the buttons fill the *HBox*, I set them all to have the same width, as discussed in Subsection 2.5.3. You can see all this in the start() method from the program:

```
public void start(Stage stage) {
    cardImages = new Image("cards.png");     // Load card images.
    board = new Canvas(4*99 + 20, 123 + 80); // Space for 4 cards.
```

```
    Button higher = new Button("Higher");    // Create the buttons, and
    higher.setOnAction( e -> doHigher() );   //    install event handlers.
    Button lower = new Button("Lower");
    lower.setOnAction( e -> doLower() );
    Button newGame = new Button("New Game");
    newGame.setOnAction( e -> doNewGame() );
    HBox buttonBar = new HBox( higher, lower, newGame );
    higher.setPrefWidth(board.getWidth()/3.0); // Make each button fill
    lower.setPrefWidth(board.getWidth()/3.0); // 1/3 of the width.
    newGame.setPrefWidth(board.getWidth()/3.0);
    BorderPane root = new BorderPane();      // Create the scene graph root node.
    root.setCenter(board);
    root.setBottom(buttonBar);
    doNewGame();  // set up for the first game
    Scene scene = new Scene(root);   // Finish setting up the scene and stage.
    stage.setScene(scene);
    stage.setTitle("High/Low Game");
    stage.setResizable(false);
    stage.show();
}  // end start()
```

Note that the event handlers call methods such as doNewGame() that are defined elsewhere in the program. The programming of those methods is a nice example of thinking in terms of a state machine. (See Subsection 2.3.6.) It is important to think in terms of the states that the game can be in, how the state can change, and how the response to events can depend on the state. The approach that produced the original, text-oriented game in Subsection 1.4.3 is not appropriate here. Trying to think about the game in terms of a process that goes step-by-step from beginning to end is more likely to confuse you than to help you.

The state of the game includes the cards and the message. The cards are stored in an object of type *Hand*. The message is a *String*. These values are stored in instance variables. There is also another, less obvious aspect of the state: Sometimes a game is in progress, and the user is supposed to make a prediction about the next card. Sometimes we are between games, and the user is supposed to click the "New Game" button. It's a good idea to keep track of this basic difference in state. The program uses a boolean instance variable named gameInProgress for this purpose.

The state of the game can change whenever the user clicks on a button. The program has three methods to respond to button clicks: doHigher(), doLower(), and newGame(). It's in these three event-handling methods that the action of the game takes place.

We don't want to let the user start a new game if a game is currently in progress. That would be cheating. So, the response in the newGame() method is different depending on whether the state variable gameInProgress is true or false. If a game is in progress, the message instance variable should be set to be an error message. If a game is not in progress, then all the state variables should be set to appropriate values for the beginning of a new game. In any case, the board must be redrawn so that the user can see that the state has changed. The complete newGame() method is as follows:

```
/**
Called by the start() method, and called by an event handler if
the user clicks the "New Game" button.        Start a new game.
*/
private void doNewGame() {
    if (gameInProgress) {
                // If the current game is not over, it is an error to try
                // to start a new game.
            message = "You still have to finish this game!";
            drawBoard();
            return;
    }
    deck = new Deck();       // Create the deck and hand to use for this game.
    hand = new Hand();
    deck.shuffle();
    hand.addCard( deck.dealCard() ); // Deal the first card into the hand.
    message = "Is the next card higher or lower?";
    gameInProgress = true;
    drawBoard();
} // end doNewGame()
```

The doHigher() and doLower() methods are almost identical to each other (and could probably have been combined into one method with a parameter, if I were more clever). Let's look at the doHigher() routine. This is called when the user clicks the "Higher" button. This only makes sense if a game is in progress, so the first thing doHigher() should do is check the value of the state variable gameInProgress. If the value is false, then doHigher() should just set up an error message. If a game is in progress, a new card should be added to the hand and the user's prediction should be tested. The user might win or lose at this time. If so, the value of the state variable gameInProgress must be set to false because the game is over. In any case, the board is redrawn to show the new state. Here is the doHigher() method:

```
/**
Called by an event handler when user clicks "Higher" button.
Check the user's prediction.   Game ends if user guessed
wrong or if the user has made three correct predictions.
*/
private void doHigher() {
    if (gameInProgress == false) {
            // If the game has ended, it was an error to click "Higher",
            // So set up an error message and abort processing.
    message = "Click \"New Game\" to start a new game!";
    drawBoard();
    return;
}
hand.addCard( deck.dealCard() );      // Deal a card to the hand.
int cardCt = hand.getCardCount();
Card thisCard = hand.getCard( cardCt - 1 );     // Card just dealt.
Card prevCard = hand.getCard( cardCt - 2 );    // The previous card.
if ( thisCard.getValue() < prevCard.getValue() ) {
    gameInProgress = false;
    message = "Too bad! You lose.";
}
else if ( thisCard.getValue() == prevCard.getValue() ) {
    gameInProgress = false;
    message = "Too bad!      You lose on ties.";
}
```

```
else if ( cardCt == 4) {
    gameInProgress = false;
    message = "You win!    You made three correct guesses.";
}
else {
    message = "Got it right!  Try for " + cardCt + ".";
    }
    drawBoard();
} // end doHigher()
```

The drawBoard() method, which is responsible for drawing the content of the canvas, uses the values in the state variables to decide what to show. It displays the string stored in the message variable. It draws each of the cards in the hand. There is one little tricky bit: If a game is in progress, it draws an extra face-down card, which is not in the hand, to represent the next card in the deck. The technique for drawing the individual cards was explained in Section 2.2. See the source code for the method definition.

2.3.2 Menus and Menubars

Our second example program, "MosaicDraw," is a kind of drawing program. The source code for the program is in the file MosaicDraw.java. The program also requires MosaicCanvas.java. Here is a half-size screenshot showing a sample drawing made with the program:

As the user clicks-and-drags the mouse in the large drawing area of this program, it leaves a trail of little colored squares. There is some random variation in the color of the squares. (This is meant to make the picture look a little more like a real mosaic, which is a picture made out of small colored stones in which there would be some natural color variation.) The program has one feature that we have not encountered before: There is a menu bar above the drawing area. The "Control" menu contains commands for filling and clearing the drawing area, along with a few options that affect the appearance of the picture. The "Color" menu lets the user select the color that will be used when the user draws. The "Tools" menu affects the behavior of the mouse. Using the default "Draw" tool, the mouse leaves a trail of single squares. Usingthe "Draw 3x3" tool, the mouse leaves a swatch of colored squares that is three squares wide. There are also "Erase" tools, which let the user set squares back to their default black color.

The drawing area of the program is a panel that belongs to the *MosaicCanvas* class, a subclass of *Canvas* that is defined in MosaicCanvas.java. *MosaicCanvas* is a highly reusable class for representing mosaics of colored rectangles. It was also used behind the scenes in the sample program. The *MosaicCanvas* class does not directly support drawing on the mosaic, but it does support setting the color of each individual square. The MosaicDraw program installs mouse handlers on the canvas. The handlers respond to MousePressed and MouseDragged events on the canvas by applying the currently selected tool to the canvas at the square that contains the mouse position. This is a nice example of applying event listeners to an object to do something that was not programmed into the object itself.

I urge you to study MosaicDraw.java. I will not be discussing all aspects of the code here, but you should be able to understand it all after reading this section. As for MosaicCanvas.java, it uses some techniques that you would not understand at this point, but I encourage you to at least read the comments in that file to learn about the API for *MosaicCanvas*.

MosaicDraw is the first example that we have seen that uses a menu bar. Fortunately, menus are very easy to use in JavaFX. The items in a menu are represented by objects belonging to class *MenuItem* or to one of its subclasses. (*MenuItem* and other menu-related classes are in package javafx.scene.control.) Menu items are used in almost exactly the same way as buttons. In particular, a *MenuItem* can be created using a constructor that specifies the text of the menu item, such as:

MenuItem fillCommand = new MenuItem("Fill");

Menu items, like buttons, can have a graphic as well as text, and there is a second constructor that allows you to specify both text and graphic. When the user selects a *MenuItem* from a menu, an *ActionEvent* is generated. Just as for a button, you can add an action event listener to the menu item using its setOnAction(handler) method. A menu item has a setDisable(disabled) method that can be used to enable and disable the item. And it has a setText() method for changing the text that is displayed in the item.

The main difference between a menu item and a button, of course, is that a menu item is meant to appear in a menu. (Actually, a menu item is a *Node* that can appear anywhere in a scene graph, but the usual place for it is in a menu.) A menu in JavaFX is represented by the class *Menu*. (In fact, *Menu* is actually a subclass of *MenuItem*, which means that you can add a menu as an item in another menu. The menu that you add becomes a submenu of the menu that you add it to.) A *Menu* has a name, which is specified in the constructor. It has an instance method getItems() that returns a list of menu items contained in the menu. To add items to the menu, you need to add them to that list:

```
Menu sampleMenu = new Menu("Sample");
sampleMenu.getItems().add( menuItem );      // Add one menu item to the menu.
sampleMenu.getItems().addAll( item1, item2, item3 );  // Add multiple items.
```

Once a menu has been created, it can be added to a menu bar. A menu bar is represented by the class *MenuBar*. A menu bar is just a container for menus. It does not have a name. The *MenuBar* constructor can be called with no parameters, or it can have a parameter list containing *Menus* to be added to the menu bar. The instance method getMenus() returns a list of menus, with methods add() and addAll() for adding menus to the menu bar. For example, the MosaicDraw program uses three menus, controlMenu, colorMenu, and toolMenu. We could create a menu bar and add the menus to it with the statements:

```
MenuBar menuBar = new MenuBar();
menuBar.getMenus().addAll(controlMenu,  colorMenu,  toolMenu);
```

Or we could list the menus in the menu bar constructor:

```
MenuBar menuBar = new MenuBar(controlMenu, colorMenu, toolMenu);
```

The final step in using menus is to add the menu bar to the program's scene graph. The menu bar could actually appear anywhere, but typically, it should be at the top of the window. A program that has a menu bar will usually use a *BorderPane* as the root of its scene graph, and it will add the menu bar as the top component in that root pane. The rest of the GUI for the program can be placed in the other four positions of the border pane.

So using menus generally follows the same pattern: Create a menu bar. Create menus and add them to the menu bar. Create menu items and add them to the menus (and set up listening to handle action events from the menu items). Place the menu bar at the top of a *BorderPane*, which is the root of the scene graph.

There are other kinds of menu items, defined by subclasses of *MenuItem*, that can be added to menus. A very simple example is *SeparatorMenuItem*, which appears in a menu as a line between other menu items. You can see an example in the "Control" menu of *MosaicDraw*. To add a separator to a *Menu*, menu, you just need to say

```
menu.getItems().add( new SeparatorMenuItem() );
```

Much more interesting are the subclasses *CheckMenuItem* and *RadioMenuItem*.

A *CheckMenuItem* represents a menu item that can be in one of two states, selected or not selected. The state is changed when the user selects the item from the menu that contains it. A *CheckMenuItem* has the same functionality and is used in the same way as a *CheckBox* (see Subsection 2.4.3). Three *CheckMenuItems* are used in the "Control" menu of the MosaicDraw program. One is used to turn the random color variation of the squares on and off. Another turns a symmetry feature on and off; when symmetry is turned on, the user's drawing is reflected horizontally and vertically to produce a symmetric pattern. And the third *CheckMenuItem* shows and hides "grouting" in the mosaic (grouting consists of gray lines drawn around each of the little squares in the mosaic). The *CheckMenuItem* that corresponds to the "Use Randomness" option in the "Control" menu could be set up with the statements:

```
useRandomness = new CheckMenuItem("Use Randomness");
useRandomness.setSelected(true); // Randomness is initially turned on.
controlMenu.getMenus().add(useRandomness); // Add menu item to the menu.
```

No *ActionEvent* handler is added to useRandomness; the program simply checks its state by calling useRandomness.isSelected() whenever it is coloring a square, to decide whether to add some random variation to the color. On the other hand, when the user selects the "Use Grouting" check box from the menu, the canvas must immediately be redrawn to reflect the new state. A handler is added to the *CheckMenuItem* to take care of that by calling an appropriate method:

```
useGrouting.setOnAction( e -> doUseGrouting(useGrouting.isSelected()) );
```

The "Color" and "Tools" menus contain items of type *RadioMenuItem*, which are used in the same way as the *RadioButtons* that were discussed in Subsection 2.4.3: A *RadioMenuItem*, like a check box, can be either selected or unselected, but when several *RadioMenuItems* are added to a *ToggleGroup*, then at most one of the group members can be selected. In the program, the user selects the tool that they want to use from the "Tools" menu. Only one tool can be selected at a time, so it makes sense to use *RadioMenuItems* to represent the available tools, and to put all of those items into the same *ToggleGroup*. The currently selected option in the "Tools" menu will be marked as selected; when the user chooses a new tool, the mark is moved. This gives the user some visible feedback about which tool is currently selected for use. Furthermore, the *ToggleGroup* has an observable property representing the currently selected option (see Subsection 2.3.7). The program adds a listener to that property with an event handler that will be called whenever the user selects a new tool. Here is the code that creates the "Tools" menu:

```
Menu toolMenu = new Menu("Tools");
ToggleGroup toolGroup = new ToggleGroup();
toolGroup.selectedToggleProperty().addListener(
                    e -> doToolChoice(toolGroup.getSelectedToggle()) );
addRadioMenuItem(toolMenu,"Draw",toolGroup, true);
addRadioMenuItem(toolMenu,"Erase",toolGroup, false);
addRadioMenuItem(toolMenu,"Draw 3x3",toolGroup, false);
addRadioMenuItem(toolMenu,"Erase 3x3",toolGroup, false);
```

The addRadioMenuItem method that is used in this code is a utility method that is defined elsewhere in the program:

```
/**
Utility method to create a radio menu item, add it
to a ToggleGroup, and add it to a menu.
*/
private void addRadioMenuItem(Menu menu, String command,
            ToggleGroup group, boolean selected) {
    RadioMenuItem menuItem = new RadioMenuItem(command);
    menuItem.setToggleGroup(group);
    menu.getItems().add(menuItem);
    if (selected) {
            menuItem.setSelected(true);
    }
}
```

The complete code for creating the menu bar in MosaicDraw can be found in a method createMenuBar(). Again, I encourage you to study the source code.

2.3.3 Scene and Stage

Before ending this brief introduction to GUI programming, we look at two fundamental classes in a little more detail: *Scene*, from package javafx.scene, and *Stage*, from package javafx.stage.

A *Scene* represents the content area of a window (that is, not including the window's border and title bar), and it serves as a holder for the root of the scene graph. The *Scene* class has several constructors, but they all require the root of the scene graph as one of the parameters, and the root cannot be null. Perhaps the most common constructor is the one that has only the root as parameter: new Scene(root).

A scene has a width and a height, which can be specified as parameters to the constructor: new Scene(root,width,height). In the typical case where the root is a *Pane*, the size of the pane will be set to match the size of the scene, and the pane will lay out its contents based on that size. If the size of the scene is not specified in the constructor, then the size of the scene will be set to the preferred size of the pane. It is not possible for a program to set the width or height of a *Scene* after it has been created, but if the size of the stage that contains a scene is changed, then the size of the scene is automatically changed to match the new size of the stage's content area, and the root node of the scene (if it is a *Pane*) will be resized as well.

A *Scene* can have a background fill *color* (actually a *Paint*), which can be specified in the constructor. Generally, the scene's background is not seen, since it is covered by the background of the root node. The default style sets the background of the root to be light gray. However, you can set the background color of the root to be transparent if you want to see the scene background instead.

A *Stage*, from package javafx.stage, represents a window on the computer's screen. Any JavaFX *Application* has at least one stage, called the primary stage, which is created by the system and passed as a parameter to the application's start() method. Although we have not seen any examples so far in this textbook, many programs use more than one window. It is possible for a program to create new *Stage* objects; we will see how to do that in Chapter 13. A stage contains a scene, which fills its content area. The scene is installed in the stage by calling the instance method stage.setScene(scene). It is possible to show a stage that does not contain a scene, but its content area will just be a blank rectangle.

In addition to a content area, a stage has a title bar above the content. The title bar contains a title for the window and some "decorations"—little controls that the user can click to do things like close and maximize the window. The title bar is provided by the operating system, not by Java, and its style is set by the operating system. The instance method stage.setTitle(string) sets the text that is shown in the title bar. The title can be changed at any time.

By default a stage is resizable. That is, the size of the window can be changed by the user, by dragging its borders or corners. To prevent the user from changing the window size, you can call stage.setResizable(false). However, a program can change the size of a stage with the instance methods stage.setWidth(w) and stage.setHeight(h), and this can be done even if the stage has been made non-resizable. Usually, the initial size of a stage is determined by the size of the scene that it contains, but it is also possible to set the initial size before showing the window using setWidth() and setHeight().

By default, when a stage is resizable, the user can make the window arbitrarily small and arbitrarily large. It is possible to put limits on the resizability of a window with the instance methods stage.setMinWidth(w), stage.setMaxWidth(w), stage.setMinHeight(h), and stage.setMaxHeight(h). The size limits apply only to what the user can do by dragging the borders or corners of the window.

It is also possible to change the position of a stage on the screen, using the instance methods stage.setX(x) and stage.setY(y). The x and y coordinates specify the position of the top left corner of the window, in the coordinate system of the screen. Typically, you would do this before showing the stage.

Finally, for now, remember that a stage is not visible on the screen until you show it by calling the instance method stage.show(). Showing the primary stage is typically the last thing that you do in a application's start() method.

2.3.4 Creating Jar Files

Java classes and resource files are often distributed in jar ("java archive") files. For a program that consists of multiple files, it can make sense to pack them into a single jar file. As the last topic for this chapter, we look at how to do that. The program can be run directly from the jar file, without unpacking it. However, for JavaFX programs, the user will still need access to the JavaFX SDK. A jar file can be "executable," meaning that it specifies the class that contains the main() routine that will be run when the jar file is executed. If you have an executable jar file that does not require JavaFX or other external resources, you can run it on the command line using a command of the form:

java -jar JarFileName.jar

and you might even be able to run the jar file by double-clicking its icon in a file browser window. If an executable jar file requires JavaFX, you will need to add the same options to the java command that were discussed. For example,

java -p /opt/jfx17/lib --add-modules=ALL-MODULE-PATH JarFileName.jar

The question, then, is how to create a jar file. The answer depends on what programming environment you are using. The two basic types of programming environment—command line and IDE. Any IDE (Integrated Development Environment) for Java should have a command for creating jar files. In the Eclipse IDE, for example, it can be done as follows: In the Package Explorer pane, select the programming project (or just all the individual source and resource files that you want to include). Right-click on the selection, and choose "Export" from the menu that pops up. In the window that appears, select "JAR file" and click "Next". In the window that appears next, enter a full path name for the jar file in the box labeled "JAR file". (Click the "Browse" button next to this box to select the file name using a file dialog box.) The name of the file should end with ".jar". If you are creating a regular jar file, not an executable one, you can hit "Finish" at this point, and the jar file will be created. To create an executable file, hit the "Next" button *twice* to get to the "Jar Manifest Specification" screen. At the bottom of this screen is an input box labeled "Main class". You have to enter the name of the class that contains the main() routine that will be run when the jar file is executed. If you hit the "Browse" button next to the "Main class" box, you can select the class from a list of classes that contain main() routines. Once you've selected the main class, you can click the "Finish" button to create the executable jar file.

It is also possible to create jar files on the command line. The Java Development Kit includes a command-line program named jar that can be used to create jar files. If all your classes are in the default package (like most of the examples in this book), then the jar command is easy to use. To create a non-executable jar file on the command line, change to the directory that contains the class files that you want to include in the jar. Then give the command

*jar -c -f JarFileName.jar *.class*

where JarFileName can be any name that you want to use for the jar file. The -c option is used to create a jar file. The -f is followed by the name of the jar file that is to be created. The "*" in "*.class" is a wildcard that makes *.class match every class file in the current directory. This means that all the class files in the directory will be included in the jar file. If you want to include only certain class files, you can name them individually, separated by spaces. You can also list the class file names separately. If the program uses resource files, such as images, they should also be listed in the command. (Things get more complicated if your classes and resources are not in the default package. In that case, the files must be in subdirectories of the directory in which you issue the jar command, and you have to include the path to the file in the name. For example: textio/TextIO.class on MacOS and Linux, or textio\TextIO.class on Windows.)

Making an executable jar file on the command line is only a little more complicated. There has to be some way of specifying which class contains the main() routine. This can be done by adding the -e option to the command, with a value giving the full name of the class that is to be executed when the jar file is run. For example, if the name of the class is *MyMainClass*, then the jar file could be created with:

*jar -c -f JarFileName.jar -e MyMainClass *.class*

For a program defined in two packages, grapher.ui and grapher.util, with a main class defined in the file Main.java in package grapher.ui, the command would become

jar -c -f Grapher.jar -e grapher.ui.Main grapher/ui/.class grapher/util/*.class*

except that on Windows, the slashes would be replaced by backslashes. (The options -c, -f, and -e are abbreviations for the longer forms --create, --file, and --main-class, and you can use the longer forms, if you prefer clarity to brevity.)

2.3.5 jpackage

You can collect the class files and resource files for a program into a jar file, and you can give that jar file to someone who would like to use your program. However, that person will still need to have Java installed on their computer—something that is really not very likely these days, unless that person is a Java developer. A possible solution is to bundle a Java virtual machine along with your program. The Java Development Kit includes the jpackage command to make that possible.

The jpackage command can create an installer that will install your program along with as much Java support as is needed to run it. It has some significant limitations. It can only make an installer for the type of computer and operating system that you are using; for example, it is not possible to use jpackage on Linux to make an installer for Windows. And the files that it makes are very large, since they have to include large parts of a Java execution environment. So jpackage is really meant for packaging large, serious applications. But if you want to try it, here is a basic example, using only a few of the options that are available for jpackage. For the example, I made an installer for the network poker game. This might also help you understand how to work with packages in general.

To apply jpackage to a program that uses JavaFX, you have to make Java packages available to the jpackage command. For this purpose, you can't use the JavaFX SDK. Instead, you need the JavaFX "jmods". A discussion of the JavaFX SDK. For jpackage, you will need to download the jmods for your operating system from https://gluonhq.com/products/javafx/. For my computer, I extracted the downloaded file into /opt/javafx-jmods-17.0.2. (The jmods are required because they include specific operating system support that is not in the SDK jar files.)

To use jpackage, you need a jar file that contains the classes and resource files for your program. The poker game uses classes from the packages netgame.common and netgame.fivecarddraw, plus a resource image file cards.png in netgame.fivecarddraw. To make the jar file, I first compiled the Java files for the program. Since the poker game uses JavaFX, I included the necessary options in the javac command. I used the following command in the directory that contained the netgame directory, *typed all on one line:*

javac --module-path /opt/jfx17/lib --add-modules=ALL-MODULE-PATH netgame/common/.javanetgame/fivecarddraw/*.java*

I then created a jar file, Poker.jar, with this command, *typed all on one line*:

jar -c -f Poker.jar netgame/common/.class netgame/fivecarddraw/*.class netgame/fivecarddraw/cards.png*

It is important to include the image resource file along with the class files. (Note that on Windows, the slashes, "/", would be replaced by backslashes, "\".)

I moved Poker.jar to a new directory. Working in that new directory, I used the following very long jpackage command, again *typed all on one line*:

jpackage --input . --main-jar Poker.jar

--main-class netgame.fivecarddraw.Main --name NetPoker

--module-path /opt/javafx-jmods-17.0.2

--add-modules javafx.base,javafx.controls,javafx.graphics

The value for the --input option is a period, which represents the current working directory; it could be replaced by a path to the directory that contains Poker.jar. The value for the --main-class option is the full name of the class that contains the main program; this option is not needed if the jar file is executable. The value of the --name option is used to name the installer and to name the executable file that it will install. The --module-path refers to the directory that contains the JavaFX jmods. And the added modules are just those JavaFX modules that are needed for this program.

When used on my computer, running Linux Mint, this produced a file named netpoker 1.0-1 amd64.deb that I could then install in the usual way. It installed the poker executable as /opt/netpoker/bin/NetPoker.

On MacOS 10.15, using the JDK from adoptium.net, I found that jpackage was installed as part of the JDK, but it was not made available on the command-line. I was able to define it myself as an alias:

alias jpackage=

"/Library/Java/JavaVirtualMachines/temurin-17.jdk/Contents/Home/bin/jpackage"

Again, type this all on one line. With that done, I used the same commands as given above, with appropriate directory names for the JavaFX SDK and jmods. The result was a .dmg file containing a program, netpoker.app, that could be run by double-clicking. (The jpackage command might be properly set up in newer versions of MacOS.)

The jpackage command should also work on Windows, but it requires something called the "WiX toolset" in addition to the JDK. I have not tried it.

Chapter 3 ARRAYS, ARRAYLISTS, AND RECORDS

Computers derive significant power from their utilization of data structures. A data structure is a systematic arrangement of interconnected data. An object is a data structure, typically accompanied by methods; nonetheless, this particular data structure—comprising a limited number of named instance variables—is merely the initial stage. Programmers often construct intricate data structures manually by interconnecting things. Chapter 5 will examine these custom-built data structures. This chapter examines fundamental data structures. An essential and fundamental data structure, the array, is integrated into every programming language.

This chapter continues the examination of arrays, incorporating fresh insights into their application and various strategies for array processing. Specifically, we shall examine the significant subject of algorithms for searching and sorting an array in Section 3.5.

An array possesses a fixed size that cannot be altered post-creation. In numerous instances, it is advantageous to own a data structure that may expand and contract as required. In Section 3.3, we will examine the ArrayList class, which exemplifies this data structure.

An array is a sequential collection of elements, all of identical kind. A record constitutes an alternative form of standard data structure. A record, akin to an array, comprises a sequence of things; however, in a record, the elements are identified by name rather than by index, and they may vary in type. In Java, any object can be conceptualized as a record; however, Java 17 officially established records as a distinct class type with specific limitations. Section 3.4 will examine record classes.

3.1 ARRAY DETAILS

Array basics have been discussed in previous chapters, but there are still details of Java syntax to be filled in, and there is a lot more to say about using arrays. This section looks at some of the syntactic details, with more information about array processing to come in the rest of the chapter.

To briefly review some of the basics...... An array is a numbered sequence of *elements*, and each element acts like a separate variable. All of the elements are of the same type, which is called the *base type* of the array. The array as a whole also has a type. If the base type is *btype*, then the array is of type btype[ ]. Each element in the array has an *index*, which is just its numerical position in the sequence of elements with numbering starting from zero. If the array is A, then element number i of the array is A[i]. The number of elements in an array is called its *length*. The length of an array A is A.length. The length of an array can't be changed after the array is created. The elements of the array A are A[0], A[1], . . . , A[A.length-1]. An attempt to refer to an array element with an index outside the range from zero to A.length-1 causes an *ArrayIndexOutOfBoundsException*.

Arrays in Java are objects, so an array variable can only refer to an array; it does not contain the array. The value of an array variable can also be null. In that case, it does not refer to any array, and an attempt to refer to an array element such as A[i] will cause a *NullPointerException*. Arrays are created using a special form of the new operator. For example,

```
int[] A = new int[10];
```

creates a new array with base type int and length 10, and it sets the variable A to refer to the newly created array.

3.1.1 For-each Loops

Arrays are often processed using for loops. A for loop makes it easy to process each element in an array from beginning to end. For example, if namelist is an array of *Strings*, then all the values in the list can be printed using

```
for (int i = 0; i < namelist.length; i++) {
    System.out.println( namelist[i] );
}
```

This type of processing is so common that there is an alternative form of the for loop that makes it easier to write. The alternative is called a *for-each loop*. It is probably easiest to start with an example. Here is a for-each loop for printing all the values in an array of *Strings*:

```
for ( String name : namelist ) {
    System.out.println( name );
}
```

The meaning of "for (String name : namelist)" is "for each String, name, in the array, namelist, do the following". The effect is that the variable name takes on each of the values in namelist in turn, and the body of the loop is executed for each of those values. Note that there is no array index in the loop. The loop control variable, name, represents one of the values in the array, not the index of one of the values.

The for-each loop is meant specifically for processing all the values in a data structure, and we will see in Section 7.3 and Chapter 10 that it applies to other data structures besides arrays. The for-each loop makes it possible to process the values in a data structure without even knowing the details of how the data is structured. In the case of arrays, it lets you avoid the complications of using array indices.

A for-each loop will perform the same operation for each value that is stored in an array. If itemArray is an array of type BaseType[ ], then a for-each loop for itemArray has the form:

```
for ( BaseType item : itemArray ) {
    .
    .        // process the item
    .
}
```

As usual, the braces are optional if there is only one statement inside the loop. In this loop, item is the loop control variable. It is declared as a variable of type *BaseType*, where *BaseType* is the base type of the array. (In a for-each loop, the loop control variable must be declared in the loop; it cannot be a variable that already exists outside the loop.) When this loop is executed, each value from the array is assigned to item in turn and the body of the loop is executed for each value. Thus, the above loop is exactly equivalent to:

```
for ( int index = 0; index < itemArray.length; index++ ) {
    BaseType item;
    item = itemArray[index]; // Get one of the values from the array
    .
    .        // process the item
    .
}
```

For example, if A is an array of type int[ ], then we could print all the values from A with the for-each loop:

```
for ( int item : A )
    System.out.println( item );
```

and we could add up all the positive integers in A with:

```
int sum = 0; // This will be the sum of all the positive numbers in A.
for ( int item : A ) {
```

```
        if (item > 0)
                sum = sum + item;
    }
```

I also note that the use of var for declaring local variables applies to the loop control variable in a for-each loop. So, instead of "for (BaseType item : itemArray)", we could write "for (var item : itemArray)". The type of the variable is deduced from the base type of the array. This syntax becomes more useful when dealing with more complicated types.

The for-each loop is not always appropriate. For example, there is no simple way to use it to process the items in just a part of an array, or to process the elements in reverse order. However, it does make the code a little simpler when you do want to process all the values, in order. since it eliminates any need to use array indices.

But it's important to note that a for-each loop processes the values in the array, not the elements (where an element means the actual memory location that is part of the array and that holds the value). For example, consider the following incorrect attempt to fill an array of integers with 17's:

```
int[] intList = new int[10];
for ( int item : intList ) {       // INCORRECT! DOES NOT MODIFY THE ARRAY!
    item = 17;
}
```

The assignment statement item = 17 assigns the value 17 to the loop control variable, item. However, this has nothing to do with the array. When the body of the loop is executed, the value from one of the elements of the array is copied into item. The statement item = 17 replaces that copied value but has no effect on the array element from which it was copied; the value in the array is not changed. The loop is equivalent to

```
int[] intList = new int[10];
for ( int i = 0; i < intList.length; i++ ) {
    int item = intList[i];
    item = 17;
}
```

which certainly does not change the value of any element in the array.

3.1.2 Variable Arity Methods

Before Java 5, every method in Java had a fixed arity. (The *arity* of a method is defined as the number of parameters in a call to the method.) In a fixed arity method, the number of parameters must be the same in every call to the method and must be the same as the number of formal parameters in the method's definition. Java 5 introduced *variable arity methods*. In a variable arity method, different calls to the method can have different numbers of parameters. For example, the formatted output method System.out.printf is a variable arity method. The first parameter of System.out.printf must be a *String*, but it can have any number of additional parameters, of any types.

Calling a variable arity method is no different from calling any other sort of method, but writing one requires some new syntax. As an example, consider a method that can compute the average of any number of values of type double. The definition of such a method could begin with:

```
public static double average( double...numbers ) {
```

Here, the ... after the type name, double, is what makes this a variable arity method. It indicates that any number of values of type double can be provided when the subroutine is called, so that for example average(1,4,9,16), average(3.14,2.17), average(0.375), and even average() are all legal calls to this method. Note that actual parameters of type int can be passed to average. The integers will, as usual, be automatically converted to real numbers. When the method is called, the values of all the actual parameters that correspond to the variable arity parameter are placed into an array, and it is this array that is actually passed to the method. That is, in the body of a method, a variable arity parameter of type *T* actually looks like an ordinary parameter of type T[ ]. The length of the array tells you how many actual parameters were provided in the method call. In the average example, the body of the method would see an array named numbers of type double[ ]. The number of actual parameters in the method call would be numbers.length, and the values of the actual parameters would be numbers[0], numbers[1], and so on. A complete definition of the method would be:

```
public static double average( double... numbers ) {
                    // Inside this method, numbers is of type double[].
    double sum;     // The sum of all the actual parameters.
    double average; // The average of all the actual parameters.
    sum = 0;
    for (int i = 0; i < numbers.length; i++) {
        sum = sum + numbers[i]; // Add one of the actual parameters to the sum.
    }
    average = sum / numbers.length;
```

```
        return average; // (Will be Double.NaN if numbers.length is zero.)
    }
```

By the way, it is possible to pass a single array to a variable arity method, instead of a list of individual values. For example, suppose that salesData is a variable of type double[ ]. Then it would be legal to call average(salesData), and this would compute the average of all the numbers in the array.

The formal parameter list in the definition of a variable-arity method can include more than one parameter, but the ... can only be applied to the very last formal parameter.

As an example, consider a method that can draw a polygon through any number of points. The points are given as values of type *Point*, where an object of type *Point* has two instance variables, x and y, of type double. In this case, the method has one ordinary parameter— the graphics context that will be used to draw the polygon— in addition to the variable arity parameter. Remember that inside the definition of the method, the parameter points becomes an array of *Points*:

```
    public static void drawPolygon(GraphicsContext g, Point... points) {
        if (points.length > 1) {    // (Need at least 2 points to draw anything.)
                for (int i = 0; i < points.length - 1; i++) {
                        // Draw a line from i-th point to (i+1)-th point
                        g.strokeLine( points[i].x, points[i].y, points[i+1].x, points[i+1].y );
                }
                // Now, draw a line back to the starting point.
                g.strokeLine( points[points.length-1].x, points[points.length-1].y,
                points[0].x, points[0].y );
        }
    }
```

When this method is called, the subroutine call statement must have one actual parameter of type *GraphicsContext*, which can be followed by any number of actual parameters of type *Point*.

For a final example, let's look at a method that strings together all of the values in a list of strings into a single, long string. This example uses a for-each loop to process the array:

```
    public static String concat( String... values ) {
        StringBuilder buffer;      // Use StringBuilder for more efficient concatenation.
        buffer = new StringBuilder();      // Start with an empty StringBuilder.
```

```
    for ( String str : values ) { // A "for each" loop for processing the values.
            buffer.append(str); // Add string to the buffer.
    }
    return buffer.toString(); // return the contents of the buffer
}
```

Given this method definition, the method call concat("Hello", "World") would return the string "HelloWorld", and concat() would return an empty string. Since a variable arity method can also accept an array as actual parameter, we could also call concat(lines) where lines is of type String[ ]. This would concatenate all the elements of the array into a single string.

3.1.3 Array Literals

We have seen that it is possible to initialize an array variable with a list of values at the time it is declared. For example,

```
int[] squares = { 1, 4, 9, 16, 25, 36, 49 };
```

This initializes squares to refer to a newly created array that contains the seven values in the list.

A list initializer of this form can be used only in a declaration statement, where it gives an initial value to a newly declared array variable. It cannot be used in an assignment statement to assign a value to a variable that already existed. However, there is another, similar notation for creating a new array that can be used in other places. The notation uses another form of the new operator to both create a new array object and fill it with values. (The rather odd syntax is similar to the syntax for anonymous inner classes, which were discussed in Subsection 1.8.3.) As an example, to assign a new value to an array variable, cubes, of type int[ ], you could use:

```
cubes = new int[] { 1, 8, 27, 64, 125, 216, 343 };
```

This is an assignment statement rather than a declaration, so the array initializer syntax, without "new int[]," would not be legal here. The general syntax for this form of the new operator is

new (base-type) [ ] { (list-of-values) }

This is actually an expression whose value is a reference to a newly created array object. In this sense, it is an "array literal," since it is something that you can type in a program to represent a value. This means that it can be used in any context where an object of type (*base-type*)[] is legal. For example, you could pass the newly created array as an actual parameter to a subroutine. Consider the following utility method for creating a menu from an array of strings.

```
/**
Creates a Menu.       The names for the MenuItems in the menu are
    given as an array of Strings.
@param menuName the name for the Menu that is to be created.
@param itemNames an array holding the text that appears in each
    MenuItem.       If a null value appears in the array, the corresponding
    item in the menu will be a separator rather than a MenuItem.
@return     the menu that has been created and filled with items.
*/
public static Menu createMenu( String menuName, String[] itemNames ) {
    Menu menu = new Menu(menuName);
    for ( String itemName : itemNames ) {
            if ( itemName == null ) {
                    menu.getItems().add( new SeparatorMenuItem() );
            }
            else {
                    MenuItem item = new MenuItem(itemName);
                    menu.getItems().add(item);
            }
    }
    return menu;
}
```

The second parameter in a call to createMenu is an array of strings. The array that is passed as an actual parameter could be created in place, using the new operator. For example, we can use the following statement to create an entire File menu:

```
Menu fileMenu = createMenu( “File”,
    new String[] { “New”, “Open”, “Close”, null, “Quit” } );
```

This should convince you that being able to create and use an array “in place” in this way can be very convenient, in the same way that anonymous inner classes are convenient. (However, this example could have been done even more conveniently if createMenu() had been written as a variable arity method!)

By the way, it is perfectly legal to use the “new BaseType[] { ... }” syntax instead of the array initializer syntax in the declaration of an array variable. For example, instead of saying:

int[] primes = { 2, 3, 5, 7, 11, 13, 17, 19 };

you can say, equivalently,

int[] primes = new int[] { 2, 3, 5, 7, 11, 17, 19 };

In fact, rather than use a special notation that works only in the context of declaration statements, I sometimes prefer to use the second form.

One final note: For historical reasons, an array declaration such as

int[] list;

can also be written as

int list[];

which is a syntax used in the languages C and C++. However, this alternative syntax does not really make much sense in the context of Java, and it is probably best avoided. After all, the intent is to declare a variable of a certain type, and the name of that type is "int[ ]". It makes sense to follow the "(*type-name*) (*variable-name*);" syntax for such declarations.

3.2 ARRAY PROCESSING

Most examples of array processing that we have looked at have actually been fairly straightforward: processing the elements of the array in order from beginning to end, or random access to an arbitrary element of the array. In this section and later in the chapter, you'll see some of the more interesting things that you can do with arrays.

3.2.1 Some Processing Examples

To begin, here's an example to remind you to be careful about avoiding array indices outside the legal range. Suppose that lines is an array of type String[], and we want to know whether lines contains any duplicate elements in consecutive locations. That is, we want to know whether lines[i].equals(lines[i+1]) for any index i. Here is a failed attempt to check that condition:

```
boolean dupp = false;// Assume there are no duplicates
    for ( int i = 0; i < list.length; i++ ) {
            if ( lines[i].equals(lines[i+1]) ) { // THERE IS AN ERROR HERE!
                    dupp = true;      // we have found a duplicate!
                    break;
            }
    }
```

This for loop looks like many others that we have written, so what's the problem? The error occurs when i takes on its final value in the loop, when i is equal to lines.length-1. In that case, i+1 is equal to lines.length. But the last element in the array has index lines.length-1, so lines.length is not a legal index. This means that the reference to lines[i+1] causes an ArrayIndexOutOfBoundsException. This is easy to fix; we just need to stop the loop before i+1 goes out of range:

```
boolean dupp = false;// Assume there are no duplicates
for ( int i = 0; i < list.length - 1 ; i++ ) {
    if ( lines[i].equals(lines[i+1]) ) {
            dupp = true;      // we have found a duplicate!
            break;
    }
}
```

This type of error can be even more insidious when working with partially full arrays, where usually only part of the array is in use, and a counter is used to keep track of how many spaces in the array are used. With a partially full array, the problem is not looking beyond the end of the array, but looking beyond *the part of the array that is in use*. When your program tries to look beyond the end of an array, at least the program will crash to let you know that there is a problem. With a partially full array, the problem can go undetected.

For the next example, let's continue with partially full arrays. We have seen how to add an item to a partially full array, but suppose that we also want to be able to remove items? Suppose that you write a game program, and that players can join the game and leave the game as it progresses. As a good object-oriented programmer, you probably have a class named *Player* to represent the individual players in the game. A list of all players who are currently in the game could be stored in an array, playerList, of type Player[ ]. Since the number of players can change, you will follow the partially full array pattern, and you will need a variable, playerCt, to record the number of players currently in the game. Assuming that there will never be more than 10 players in the game, you could declare the variables as:

```
Player[] playerList = new Player[10];  // Up to 10 players.
int  playerCt = 0;      // At the start, there are no players.
```

After some players have joined the game, playerCt will be greater than 0, and the player objects representing the players will be stored in the array elements playerList[0], playerList[1], . . . , playerList[playerCt-1]. Note that the array element playerList[playerCt] is not in use: Besides being the number of items in the array, playerCt is also the index of the next open spot in the array. The procedure for adding a new player, newPlayer, to the game is simple:

```
playerList[playerCt] = newPlayer; // Put new player in next
                                   //        available spot.
playerCt++; // And increment playerCt to count the new player.
```

But deleting a player from the game is a little harder, since you don't want to leave a "hole" in the array where the deleted player used to be. Suppose you want to delete the player at index k in playerList. The number of players goes down by one, so one fewer space is used in the array. If you are not worried about keeping the players in any particular order, then one way to delete player number k is to move the player from the last occupied position in the array into position k and then to decrement the value of playerCt:

```
playerList[k] = playerList[playerCt - 1];
playerCt--;
```

The player previously in position k has been replaced and is no longer in the array, so we have deleted that player from the list. The player previously in position playerCt - 1 is now in the array twice. But it's only in the occupied or valid part of the array once, since playerCt has decreased by one. Remember that every element of the array has to hold some value, but only the values in positions 0 through playerCt - 1 will be looked at or processed in any way. You can set playerList[playerCt] = null, which could free up the deleted *Player* objectfor garbage collection, but that is not necessary to correctly delete the player from the list of (active) players. (By the way, you should think about what happens if the player that is being deleted is in the last position in the list. The code does still work in this case. What exactly happens?)

Suppose that when deleting the player in position k, you'd like to keep the remaining players in the same order. (Maybe because they take turns in the order in which they are stored in the array.) To do this, all the players in positions k+1 and following must move up one position in the array. Player k+1 replaces player k, who is out of the game. Player k+2 fills the spot left open when player k+1 is moved. And so on. The code for this is

```
for (int i = k+1; i < playerCt; i++) {
    playerList[i-1] = playerList[i];
}
playerCt--;
```

Here is an illustration of the two ways of deleting an item from a partially full array. Here, player "C" is being deleted:

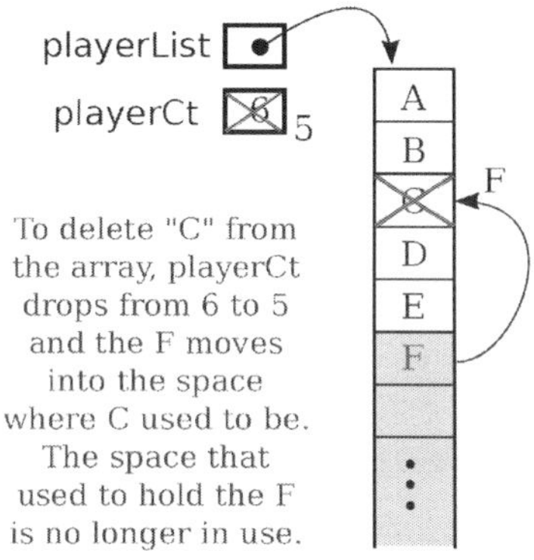

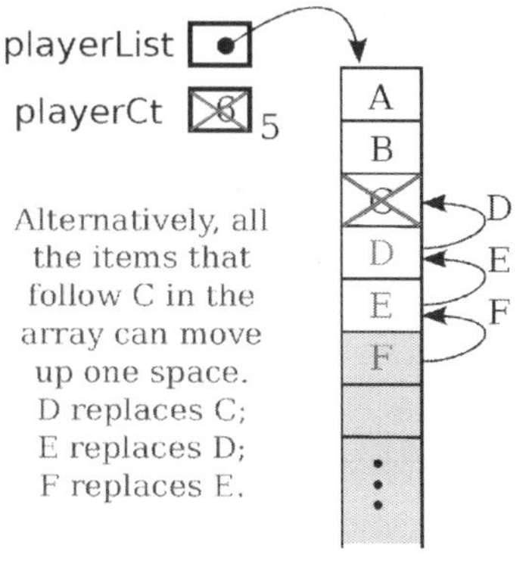

This leaves open the question of what happens when a partially full array becomes full, but you still want to add more items to it? We can't change the size of the array—but we can make a new, bigger array and copy the data from the old array into the new array. But what does it mean to copy an array in the first place?

Suppose that A and B are array variables, with the same base type, and that A already refers to an array. Suppose that we want B to refer to a copy of A. The first thing to note is that the assignment statement

```
B = A;
```

does not make a copy of A. Arrays are objects, and an array variable can only hold a pointer to an array. The assignment statement copies the pointer from A into B, and the result is that A and B now point to the same array. For example, A[0] and B[0] are just different names for exactly the same array element. To make B refer to a copy of A, we need to make an entirely new array and copy all the items from A into B. Let's say that A and B are of type double[ ].

Then to make a copy of A, we can say

```
double[] B;
B = new double[A.length];     // Make a new array with the same length as A.
for ( int i = 0; i < A.length; i++ ) {
    B[i] = A[i];
}
```

To solve the problem of adding to a partially full array that has become full, we just need to make a new array that is bigger than the existing array. The usual choice is to make a new array twice as big as the old. We need to meet one more requirement: At the end, the variable that referred to the old array must now point to the new array. That variable is what gives us access to the data, and in the end, the data is in the new array. Fortunately, a simple assignment statement will make the variable point to the correct array. Let's suppose that we are using playerList and playerCt to store the players in a game, as in the example above, and we want to add newPlayer to the game. Here is how we can do that even if the playerList array is full:

```
if ( playerCt == playerList.length ) {
            // The number of players is already equal to the size of the array.
            // The array is full.       Make a new array that has more space.
    Player[] temp;    // A variable to point to the new array.
    temp = new Player[ 2*playerList.length ];  // Twice as big as the old array.
    for ( int i = 0; i < playerList.length; i++ ) {
            temp[i] = playerList[i];    // Copy item from old array into new array.
    }
    playerList = temp;           // playerList now points to the new, bigger array.
}
// At this point, we know that there is room in the array for newPlayer. playerList[playerCt]
= newPlayer;
playerCt++;
```

After the new array has been created, there is no longer any variable that points to the old array, so it will be garbage collected.

3.2.2 Some Standard Array Methods

Copying an array seems like such a common method that you might expect Java to have a built- in method already defined to do it. In fact, Java comes with several standard array-processing methods. The methods are defined as static methods in a class named *Arrays*, which is in the package java.util. For example, for any array, list,

```
Arrays.copyOf( list, lengthOfCopy )
```

is a function that returns a new array whose length is given by lengthOfCopy, containing items copied from list. If lengthOfCopy is greater than list.length, then extra spaces in the new array will have their default value (zero for numeric arrays, null for object arrays, and so on). If lengthOfCopy is less than or equal to list.length, then only as many items are copied from list as will fit in the new array. So if A is any array, then

```
B = Arrays.copyOf( A, A.length );
```

sets B to refer to an exact copy of A, and

```
playerList = Arrays.copyOf( playerList, 2*playerList.length );
```

could be used to double the amount of space available in a partially full array with just one line of code. We can also use Arrays.copyOf to decrease the size of a partially full array. We might want to do that to avoid having a lot of excess, unused spaces. To implement this idea, the code for deleting player number k from the list of players might become

```
playerList[k] = playerList[playerCt-1]; playerCt--;
if ( playerCt < playerList.length/4 ) {
// More than 3/4 of the spaces are empty. Cut the array size in half. playerList = Arrays.
copyOf( playerList, playerList.length/2 );
}
```

I should mention that class *Arrays* actually contains a bunch of copyOf methods, one for each of the primitive types and one for objects. I should also note that when an array of objects is copied, it is only pointers to objects that are copied into the new array. The contents of the objects are not copied. This is the usual rule for assignment of pointers.

If what you want is a simple copy of an array, with the same size as the original, there is an even easier way to do it. Every array has an instance method named clone() that makes a copy of the array. To get a copy of an int array, A, for example, you can simply say

```
int[] B        =        A.clone();
```

The *Arrays* class contains other useful methods. I'll mention a few of them. As with Arrays.copyOf, there are actually multiple versions of all of these methods, for different array types.

- Arrays.fill(array, value) — Fill an entire array with a specified value. The type of value must be compatible with the base type of the array. For example, assuming that numlist is an array of type double[ ], then Arrays. fill(numlist,17) will set every element of numlist to have the value 17.
- Arrays.fill(array, fromIndex, toIndex, value) — Fills part of the array with value, starting at index number fromIndex and ending with index number toIndex-1. Note that toIndex itself is not included.
- Arrays.toString(array) — A function that returns a *String* containing all the values from array, separated by commas and enclosed between square brackets. The values in the array are converted into strings in the same way they would be if they were printed out.
- Arrays.sort(array) — Sorts the entire array. To sort an array means to rearrange the values in the array so that they are in increasing order. This method works for arrays of *String* and arrays of primitive type values

(except for boolean, which would be kind of silly). But it does not work for all arrays, since it must be meaningful to compare any two values in the array, to see which is "smaller." We will discuss array-sorting algorithms in Section 3.5.

- Arrays.sort(array, fromIndex, toIndex) — Sorts just the elements from array[fromIndex] up to array[toIndex-1]
- Arrays.binarySearch(array, value) — Searches for value in the array. The array must already be sorted into increasing order. This is a function that returns an int. If the value is found in the array, the return value is the index of an element that contains that value. If the value does not occur in the array, the return value is -1. We will discuss the binary search algorithm in Section 3.5.

3.2.3 RandomStrings Revisited

One of the examples in Subsection 2.2.4 was a GUI program, RandomStrings.java, that shows multiple copies of a message in random positions, colors, and fonts. When the user clicks a button, the positions, colors, and fonts are changed to new random values. But suppose that we want the message strings to move. That is, we want to run an animation where the strings drift around in the window. In that case, we need to store the properties of each string, since they will be needed to redraw the strings in each frame of the animation. A new version of the program that does that is RandomStringsWithArray.java.

There are 25 strings. We need to store the (x,y) coordinates where each string is drawn, the color of each string, and the font that is used for each string. To make the strings move, I also store a velocity for each string, represented as two numbers dx and dy. In each frame, the dx for each string, multiplied by the elapsed time since the previous frame, is added to the x coordinate of the string, similarly for dy. Now, the data for the string could be stored in six arrays

```
double[] x = new double[25];
double[] y = new double[25];
double[] dx = new double[25];
double[] dy = new double[25];
Color[] color = new Color[25];
Font[] font = new Font[25];
```

These arrays would be filled with random values. In the method that draws the strings, the i-th string would be drawn at the point (x[i],y[i]). Its color would be given by color[i]. And it would be drawn in the font font[i]. (The dx and dy would not be used for the drawing; they are used when updating the data for the next frame.) This would be accomplished by code such as:

```
g.setFill(Color.WHITE); // (Fill with white background.)
g.fillRect(0,0,canvas.getWidth(),canvas.getHeight());
for (int i = 0; i < 25; i++) {
    g.setFill( color[i] );
    g.setFont( font[i] );
    g.fillText( MESSAGE, x[i], y[i] );
    g.setStroke(Color.BLACK);
    g.strokeText( MESSAGE, x[i], y[i] );
}
```

This approach is said to use *parallel arrays*. The data for a given copy of the message is spread out across several arrays. If you think of the arrays as laid out in parallel columns— array x in the first column, array y in the second, array color in the third, and array font in the fourth—then the data for the i-th string can be found along the i-th row. There is nothing wrong with using parallel arrays in this simple example, but it does go against the object-oriented philosophy of keeping related data in one object. If we follow this rule, then we don't have to imagine the relationship among the data, because all the data for one copy of the message is physically in one place. So, when I wrote the program, I made a simple class to represent all the data that is needed for one copy of the message:

```
private static class StringData {        // Info needed to draw one string.
    double x,y;        // location of the string;
    double dx,dy;      // velocity of the string;
    Color color;       // color of the string;
    Font font;         // the font that is used to draw the string
}
```

To store the data for multiple copies of the message, I use an array of type StringData[ ]. The array is declared as an instance variable, with the name stringData:

```
StringData[] stringData;
```

Of course, the value of stringData is null until an actual array is created and assigned to it. The array has to be created and filled with data. Furthermore, each element of the array is an object of type *StringData* which has to be created before it can be used. The following subroutine creates the array and fills it with random data:

```
private void createStringData() {
    stringData = new StringData[25]; for (int i = 0; i < 25; i++) {
    stringData[i] = new StringData();
    stringData[i].x = canvas.getWidth() * Math.random();
    stringData[i].y = canvas.getHeight() * Math.random();
    stringData[i].dx = 1 + 3*Math.random();
    if (Math.random() < 0.5) // 50% chance that dx is negative
            stringData[i].dx = -stringData[i].dx;
    stringData[i].dy = 1 + 3*Math.random();
    if (Math.random() < 0.5) // 50% chance that dy is negative
            stringData[i].dy = -stringData[i].dy;
    stringData[i].color = Color.hsb( 360*Math.random(), 1.0, 1.0 );
    stringData[i].font = fonts[ (int)(5*Math.random()) ];
    }
}
```

This method is called in the start() method. It is also called to make new random data when the user clicks a button. The strings can now be drawn using a for loop such as:

```
for (int i = 0; i < 25; i++) {
    g.setFill( stringData[i].color );
    g.setFont( stringData[i].font );
    g.fillText( MESSAGE, stringData[i].x, stringData[i]. y );
    g.setStroke(Color.BLACK);
    g.strokeText( MESSAGE, stringData[i].x, stringData[i]. y );
}
```

But in fact, in my program, I used an equivalent for-each loop, which might be easier to understand:

```
for ( StringData data : stringData ) {
    g.setFill( data.color ); g.setFont( data.font);
    g.fillText( MESSAGE, data.x, data.y );
    g.setStroke( Color.BLACK );
    g.strokeText( MESSAGE, data.x, data.y );
}
```

In this loop, the loop control variable, data, holds a copy of one of the values from the array. That value is a reference to an object of type *StringData*, which has instance variables named color, font, x, and y. Once again, the use of a for-each loop has eliminated the need to work with array indices.

As for how the animation is done, you can check out the full source code. Animation was discussed in Subsection 2.3.5.

RandomStringsWithArray uses one other array of objects. The font for a given copy of the message is chosen at random from a set of five possible fonts. In the original version, there were five variables of type *Font* to represent the fonts. The variables were named font1, font2, font3, font4, and font5. To select one of these fonts at random, a switch statement could be used:

```
Font randomFont;    // One of the 5 fonts, chosen at random.
int rand;    // A random integer in the range 0 to 4.
fontNum = (int)(Math.random() * 5);
switch (fontNum) {
    case 0 -> randomFont = font1;
    case 1 -> randomFont = font2;
    case 2 -> randomFont = font3;
    case 3 -> randomFont = font4;
    case 4 -> randomFont = font5;
}
```

In the new version of the program, the five fonts are stored in an array, which is named fonts. This array is declared as a static final member variable of type Font[ ]:

```
private static final fonts= new Font[] {
    Font.font("Times New Roman", FontWeight.BOLD, 20),
    Font.font("Arial", FontWeight.BOLD, FontPosture .ITALIC, 28),
    Font.font("Verdana", 32),
    Font.font(40),
    Font.font("Times New Roman", FontWeight.BOLD, FontPosture .ITALIC, 60)
};
```

This makes it much easier to select one of the fonts at random. It can be done with the statements

```
Font randomFont;    // One of the 5 fonts, chosen at random.
int fontIndex;      // A random number in the range 0 to 4.
```

*fontIndex = (int)(Math.random() * 5);*

randomFont = fonts[fontIndex];

In fact, the preceding four lines can be replaced by the single line

*Font randomFont = fonts[(int)(Math.random() * 5)];*

The switch statement has been replaced by a single line of code. This is a very typical application of arrays. Note that this example uses the random access property: We can pick an array index at random and go directly to the array element at that index.

Here is another example of the same sort of thing. Months are often stored as numbers 1, 2, 3, . . . , 12. Sometimes, however, these numbers have to be translated into the names January, February, . . . , December. The translation can be done very easily with an array. The array can be declared and initialized as

```
static String[] monthName = { "January", "February", "March",
                              "April", "May", "June",
                              "July", "August",     "September",
                              "October", "November", "December" };
```

If mnth is a variable that holds one of the integers 1 through 12, then monthName[mnth-1] is the name of the corresponding month. We need the "-1" because months are numbered starting from 1, while array elements are numbered starting from 0. Simple array indexing does the translation for us!

3.2.4 Dynamic Arrays

Earlier, we discussed how a partially full array can be used to store a list of players in a game, allowing the list to grow and shrink over the course of the game. The list is "dynamic" in the sense that its size changes while the program is running. Dynamic lists are very common, and we might think about trying to write a class to represent the concept. By writing a class, we can avoid having to repeat the same code every time we want to use a similar data structure. We want something that is like an array, except that its size can change. Think about operations that we might want to perform on a dynamic array. Some essential and useful operations would include

- add an item to the end of the array
- remove the item at a specified position in the array
- get the value of one of the elements in the array
- set the value of one of the elements in the array
- get the number of items currently in the array

When we design our class, these operations will become instance methods in that class. The items in the dynamic array will actually be stored in a normal array, using the partially full array pattern. Using what we know, the class is not difficult to write. We do have to decide what to do when an attempt is made to access an array element that doesn't exist. It seems natural to throw an index-out-of-bounds exception in that case. Let's suppose that the items in the array will be of type int.

```
import java.util.Arrays;
/**
* Represents a list of int values that can grow and shrink.
*/
public class DynamicArrayOfInt {
    private int[] items = new int[8];   // partially full array holding the ints
    private int itemCt;
    /**
    Return the item at a given index in the array.
    Throws ArrayIndexOutOfBoundsException if the index is not valid.
    */
    public int get( int index ) {
            if ( index < 0 || index >= itemCt )
                    throw new ArrayIndexOutOfBoundsException("Illegal index, " + index);
            return items[index];
    }
    /**
    Set the value of the array element at a given index.
    Throws ArrayIndexOutOfBoundsException if the index is not valid.
    */
public void set( int index, int item ) {
    if ( index < 0 || index >= itemCt )
            throw new ArrayIndexOutOfBoundsException("Illegal index, " + index);
    items[index] = item;
}
/**
Returns the number of items currently in the array.
```

```
*/
public int size() {
    return itemCt;
}
/**
Adds a new item to the end of the array.        The size increases by one.
*/
public void add(int item) {
    if (itemCt == items.length)
            items = Arrays.copyOf( items, 2*items.length );
            items[itemCt] = item;
            itemCt++;
/**
Removes the item at a given index in the array.          The size of the array
decreases by one.     Items following the removed item are moved up one
space in the array.
Throws ArrayIndexOutOfBoundsException if the index is not valid.
*/
public void remove(int index) {
    if ( index < 0 || index >= itemCt )
            throw new ArrayIndexOutOfBoundsException("Illegal index, " + index)
for (int j = index+1; j < itemCt; j++)
            items[j-1] = items[j]; itemCt--;
    }
} // end class DynamicArrayOfInt
```

Everything here should be clear, except possibly why the original size of the items array is 8. In fact, the number 8 is arbitrary and has no effect on the functionality of the class. Any positive integer would work, but it doesn't make sense for the array to start off very big. The array will grow as needed if the number of items turns out to be large.

The example ReverseInputNumbers.java used a partially full array of int to print a list of input numbers in the reverse of the order in which they are input. In that program, an ordinary array of length 100 was used to hold the numbers. In any given run of the program, the size of the array could be much too large, or it could be too small, resulting in an exception. The program can now be written using a DynamicArrayOfInt, which will adapt itself to any reasonable number of inputs. For the program, see ReverseWithDynamicArray.java. It's a silly program, but the principle holds in any application where the amount of data cannot be predicted in advance: The size of a dynamic data structure can adapt itself to any amount of data, limited only by the amount of memory available to the program.

This is a nice example, but there is a real problem with it. Suppose that we want to have a dynamic array of *String*. We can't use a *DynamicArrayOfInt* object to hold strings, so it looks like we need to write a whole new class, *DynamicArrayOfString*. If we want a dynamic array to store players in a game, we would need a class *DynamicArrayOfPlayer*. And so on. It looks like we have to write a dynamic array class for every possible type of data! That can't be right! In fact, Java has a solution to this problem, a standard class that implements dynamic arrays and can work with any type of data. The class is called *ArrayList*, and we'll see how it works in the next section.

3.3 ARRAYLIST

As we have just seen in Subsection 3.2.4, we can easily encode the dynamic array pattern into a class, but it looks like we need a different class for each data type. In fact, Java has a feature called "parameterized types" that makes it possible to avoid the multitude of classes, and Java has a single class named *ArrayList* that implements the dynamic array pattern for all data types that are defined as classes (but not, directly, for primitive types).

3.3.1 ArrayList and Parameterized Types

Java has a standard type with the rather odd name ArrayList<String> that represents dynamic arrays of *Strings*. Similarly, there is a type ArrayList<Color> that can be used to represent dynamic arrays of *Colors*. And if *Player* is a class representing players in a game, then the type ArrayList<Player> can be used to represent a dynamic array of *Players*.

It might look like we still have a multitude of classes here, but in fact there is only one class, the *ArrayList* class, defined in the package java.util. But *ArrayList* is a *parameterized type*. A parameterized type can take a type parameter, so that from the single class *ArrayList*, we get a multitude of types including ArrayList<String>, ArrayList<Color>, and in fact ArrayList<T> for any object type *T*. The type parameter *T* must be an object type such as a class name or an interface name. It cannot be a primitive type. This means that, unfortunately, you can not have an ArrayList of int or an ArrayList of char.

Consider the type ArrayList<String>. As a type, it can be used to declare variables, such as

ArrayList<String> namelist;

It can also be used as the type of a formal parameter in a subroutine definition, or as the return type of a subroutine. It can be used with the new operator to create objects:

namelist = new ArrayList<String>();

The object created in this way is of type ArrayList<String> and represents a dynamic list of strings. It has instance methods such as namelist.add(str) for adding a *String* to the list, namelist.get(i) for getting the string at index i, and namelist.size() for getting the number of items currently in the list.

But we can also use *ArrayList* with other types. If *Player* is a class representing players in a game, we can create a list of players with

ArrayList<Player> playerList = new ArrayList<Player>();

Then to add a player, plr, to the game, we just have to say playerList.add(plr). And we can remove player number k with playerList.remove(k).

Furthermore if playerList is a local variable, then its declaration can be abbreviated to

var playlerList = new ArrayList<Player>();

using the alternative declaration syntax. The Java compiler uses the initial value that is assigned to playerList to deduce that its type is ArrayList<Player>. When you use a type such as ArrayList<T>, the compiler will ensure that only objects of type *T* can be added to the list. An attempt to add an object that is not of type *T* will be a syntax error, and the program will not compile. However, note that objects belonging to a subclass of *T* can be added to the list, since objects belonging to a subclass of *T* are still considered to be of type *T*. Thus, if class *Shape* has subclasses *Rectangle*, *Oval* and *RounRect*, then a variable of type ArrayList<Shape> can be used to hold objects of type *Rectangle*, *Oval*, and *RoundRect*. (Of course, this is the same way arrays work: An array of type T[ ] can hold objects belonging to any subclass of *T*.) Similarly, if *T* is an interface, then any object that implements interface *T* can be added to the list.

An object of type ArrayList<T> has all of the instance methods that you would expect in a dynamic array implementation. Here are some of the most useful. Suppose that list is a variable of type ArrayList<T>. Then we have:

- list.size() — This function returns the current size of the list, that is, the number of items currently in the list. The only valid positions in the list are numbers in the range 0 to list.size()-1. Note that the size can be zero. A call to the default constructor new ArrayList<T>() creates a list of size zero.

- list.add(obj) – Adds an object onto the end of the list, increasing the size by 1. The parameter, obj, can refer to an object of type *T*, or it can be null.
- list.get(N) – This function returns the value stored at position N in the list. The return type of this function is *T*. N must be an integer in the range 0 to list.size()-1. If N is outside this range, an error of type *IndexOutOfBoundsException* occurs. Calling this function is similar to referring to A[N] for an array, A, except that you can't use list.get(N) on the left side of an assignment statement.
- list.set(N, obj) – Assigns the object, obj, to position N in the *ArrayList*, replacing the item previously stored at position N. The parameter obj must be of type *T*. The integer N must be in the range from 0 to list.size()-1. A call to this function is equivalent to the command A[N] = obj for an array A.
- list.clear() – Removes all items from the list, setting its size to zero.
- list.remove(N) – For an integer, N, this removes the N-th item in the *ArrayList*. N must be in the range 0 to list.size()-1. Any items in the list that come after the removed item are moved up one position. The size of the list decreases by 1. This method returns the removed item.
- list.remove(obj) – If the specified object occurs somewhere in the list, it is removed from the list. Any items in the list that come after the removed item are moved up one position. The size of the *ArrayList* decreases by 1. If obj occurs more than once in the list, only the first copy is removed. If obj does not occur in the list, nothing happens; this is not an error. This method returns a boolean value that says whether or not an item was actually removed.
- list.indexOf(obj) – A function that searches for the object, obj, in the list. If the object is found in the list, then the first position number where it is found is returned. If the object is not found, then -1 is returned.

For the last two methods listed here, obj is compared to an item in the list by calling obj.equals(item), unless obj is null. This means, for example, that strings are tested for equality by checking the contents of the strings, not their location in memory.

Java comes with several parameterized classes representing different data structures. Those classes make up the *Java Collection Framework* . Here we consider only *ArrayList*, but we will return to this important topic in much more detail in Chapter 10.

By the way, *ArrayList* can also be used as a non-parametrized type. This means that you can declare variables and create objects of type *ArrayList* such as

ArrayList list = new ArrayList();

The effect of this is similar to declaring list to be of type ArrayList<Object>. That is, list can hold any object that belongs to a subclass of *Object*. Since every class is a subclass of *Object*, this means that any object can be stored in list.

3.3.2 Wrapper Classes

As I have already noted, parameterized types don't work with the primitive types. There is no such thing as "ArrayList<int>". However, this limitation turns out not to be very limiting after all, because of the so-called *wrapper classes* such as *Integer* and *Character*.

These classes contain the static methods Double.parseDouble() and Integer.parseInteger() that are used to convert strings to numerical values, and they contain constants such as Integer.MAX VALUE and Double.NaN. We have also encountered the *Character* class in some examples, with the static method Character.isLetter(), that can be used to test whether a given value of type char is a letter. There is a similar class for each of the other primitive types, *Long*, *Short*, *Byte*, *Float*, and *Boolean*. These classes are wrapper classes. Although they contain useful static members, they have another use as well: They are used for representing primitive type values as objects.

Remember that the primitive types are not classes, and values of primitive type are not objects. However, sometimes it's useful to treat a primitive value as if it were an object. This is true, for example, when you would like to store primitive type values in an *ArrayList*. You can't do that literally, but you can "wrap" the primitive type value in an object belonging to one of the wrapper classes.

For example, an object of type *Integer* contains a single instance variable, of type int. The object is a "wrapper" for the int value. You can get an object that wraps the int value 42 with

Integer n = Integer.valueOf(42);

The value of n has the same information as the value of type int, but it is an object. If you want to retrieve the int value that is wrapped in the object, you can call the function n.intValue(). Similarly, you can wrap a double in an object of type *Double*, a boolean value in an object of type *Boolean*, and so on. Each wrapper class has a static valueOf() method for wrapping a primitive type value in an object.

The method Integer.valueOf() is a static factory method that returns an object of type *Integer*. The *Integer* class also has a constructor for creating objects, but it has been *deprecated* , meaning that it should not be used in new code and might be removed from the language in the future. The static factory method has the advantage that if Integer.valueOf() is called more than once with the same parameter value, it has the option of returning the same object each time. This is OK because objects of type *Integer* are *immutable*, that is, the content of the object cannot be modified after the object has been created. Someone who gets their hands on an *Integer* will not be able to change the primitive int value that it represents. We saw something similar for the *Color* class in Subsection 2.2.1, which also has static factory methods for creating immutable objects.

To make the wrapper classes even easier to use, there is automatic conversion between a primitive type and the corresponding wrapper class. For example, if you use a value of type int in a context that requires an object of type *Integer*, the int will automatically be wrapped in an *Integer* object. If you say

Integer answer = 42;

the computer will silently read this as if it were

Integer answer = Integer.valueOf(42);

This is called *autoboxing* . It works in the other direction, too. For example, if d refers to an object of type Double, you can use d in a numerical expression such as 2*d. The double value inside d is automatically *unboxed* and multiplied by 2. Autoboxing and unboxing also apply to subroutine calls. For example, you can pass an actual parameter of type int to a subroutine that has a formal parameter of type *Integer*, and vice versa. In fact, autoboxing and unboxing make it possible in many circumstances to ignore the difference between primitive types and objects.

This is true in particular for parameterized types. Although there is no such thing as "ArrayList<int>", there is ArrayList<Integer>. An ArrayList<Integer> holds objects of type *Integer*, but any object of type *Integer* really just represents an int value in a rather thin wrapper. Suppose that we have an object of type ArrayList<Integer>:

ArrayList<Integer> integerList; integerList = new ArrayList<Integer>();

Then we can, for example, add an object to integerList that represents the number 42:

integerList.add(Integer.valueOf(42));

but because of autoboxing, we can actually say

integerList.add(42);

and the compiler will automatically wrap 42 in an object of type *Integer* before adding it to the list. Similarly, we can say

int num = integerList.get(3);

The value returned by integerList.get(3) is of type *Integer* but because of unboxing, the compiler will automatically convert the return value into an int, as if we had said

```
int num = integerList.get(3).intValue();
```

So, in effect, we can pretty much use integerList as if it were a dynamic array of int rather than a dynamic array of *Integer*. Of course, a similar statement holds for lists of other wrapper classes such as ArrayList<Double> and ArrayList<Character>.

There is one issue that sometimes causes problems: A list can hold null values, and a null does not correspond to any primitive type value. This means, for example, that the statement "int num = integerList.get(3);" can produce a null pointer exception in the case where integerList.get(3) returns null. Unless you are sure that all the values in your list are non-null, you need to take this possibility into account.

3.3.3 Programming With ArrayList

As a simple first example, we can redo ReverseWithDynamicArray.java, from the previous section, using an ArrayList instead of a custom dynamic array class. In this case, we want to store integers in the list, so we should use ArrayList<Integer>. Here is the complete program:

```
import textio.TextIO; import java.util.ArrayList;
/**
Reads a list of non-zero numbers from the user, then prints
out the input numbers in the reverse of the order in which
the were entered.     There is no limit on the number of inputs.
*/
public class ReverseWithArrayList {
    public static void main(String[] args) {
            ArrayList<Integer> list;
            list = new ArrayList<Integer>();
            System.out.println("Enter some non-zero integers. Enter 0 to end.");
            while (true) {
                    System.out.print("? ");
                    int number = TextIO.getlnInt();
                    if (number == 0)
                            break;
```

```
                list.add(number);
            }
            System.out.println();
            System.out.println("Your numbers in reverse are:");
            for (int i = list.size() - 1; i >= 0; i--) {
                System.out.printf("%10d%n", list.get(i));
            }
        }
    }
```

As illustrated in this example, ArrayLists are commonly processed using for loops, in much the same way that arrays are processed. for example, the following loop prints out all the items for a variable namelist of type ArrayList<String>:

```
for ( int i = 0; i < namelist.size(); i++ ) {
    String item = namelist.get(i);
    System.out.println(item);
}
```

You can also use for-each loops with ArrayLists, so this example could also be written

```
for ( String item : namelist ) { System.out.println(item);
}
```

When working with wrapper classes, the loop control variable in the for-each loop can be a primitive type variable. This works because of unboxing. For example, if numbers is of type ArrayList<Double>, then the following loop can be used to add up all the values in the list:

```
double sum = 0;
    for ( double num : numbers ) { sum = sum + num;
}
```

This will work as long as none of the items in the list are null. If there is a possibility of null values, then you will want to use a loop control variable of type *Double* and test for nulls. For example, to add up all the non-null values in the list:

```
double sum;
for ( Double num : numbers ) {
    if ( num != null ) {
```

```
            sum = sum + num;          // Here, num is SAFELY unboxed to get a double.
    }
}
```

For a more complete and useful example, we will look at the program SimplePaint2.java. This is a much improved version of SimplePaint.java from Subsection 2.3.3. In the new program, the user can sketch curves in a drawing area by clicking and dragging with the mouse. The user can select the drawing color using a menu. The background color of the drawing area can also be selected using a menu. And there is a "Control" menu that contains several commands: An "Undo" command, which removes the most recently drawn curve from the screen, a "Clear" command that removes all the curves, and a "Use Symmetry" checkbox that turns a symmetry feature on and off. Curves that are drawn by the user when the symmetry option is on are reflected horizontally and vertically to produce a symmetric pattern. (Symmetry is there just to look pretty.)

Unlike the original SimplePaint program, this new version uses a data structure to store information about the picture that has been drawn by the user. When the user selects a new background color, the canvas is filled with the new background color, and all of the curves that were there previously are redrawn on the new background. To do that, we need to store enough data to redraw all of the curves. Similarly, the Undo command is implemented by deleting the data for most recently drawn curve, and then redrawing the entire picture using the remaining data.

The data structure that we need is implemented using *ArrayLists*. The main data for an individual curve consists of a list of the points on the curve. This data is stored in an object of type ArrayList<Point2D>. (*Point2D* is standard class in package javafx.geometry: A *Point2D* can be constructed from two double values, giving the (x,y) coordinates of the point. And a *Point2D* object, pt, has getter methods pt.getX() and pt.getY() that return the x and y coordinates.) But in addition to a list of points on a curve, to redraw the curve, we also need

to know its color, and we need to know whether the symmetry option should be applied to the curve. All the data that is needed to redraw the curve is grouped into an object of type *CurveData* that is defined as a nested class in the program:

```
    private static class CurveData {
        Color color;       // The color of the curve.
        boolean symmetric;      // Are horizontal and vertical reflections also drawn?
        ArrayList<Point2D> points;      // The points on the curve.
    }
```

However, a picture can contain many curves, not just one, so to store all the data necessary to redraw the entire picture, we need a list of objects of type *CurveData*. For this list, the program uses an *ArrayList*, curves, declared as

```
ArrayList<CurveData> curves = new ArrayList<CurveData>();
```

Here we have a list of objects, where each object contains a list of points as part of its data! Let's look at a few examples of processing this data structure. When the user clicks the mouse on the drawing surface, it's the start of a new curve, and a new *CurveData* object must be created to represent that curve. The instance variables in the new *CurveData* object must also be initialized. Here is the code from the mousePressed() routine that does this, where currentCurve is a global variable of type CurveData:

```
currentCurve = new CurveData();              // Create a new CurveData object.
currentCurve.color = currentColor;           // The color of a curve is taken from an
                                             // instance variable that represents the
                                             // currently selected drawing color.
currentCurve.symmetric = useSymmetry;        // The "symmetric" property of the curve
                                             // is also copied from the current value
                                             // of an instance variable, useSymmetry.
currentCurve.points = new ArrayList<Point2D>();     // A new point list object.
```

As the user drags the mouse, new points are added to currentCurve, and line segments of the curve are drawn between points as they are added. When the user releases the mouse, the curve is complete, and it is added to the list of curves by calling

```
curves.add( currentCurve );
```

When the user changes the background color or selects the "Undo" command, the picture has to be redrawn. The program has a redraw() method that completely redraws the picture. That method uses the data in the list of *CurveData* to draw all the curves. The basic structure is a for-each loop that processes the data for each individual curve in turn. This has the form:

```
for ( CurveData curve : curves ) {
    .
    .        // Draw the curve represented by the object, curve, of type CurveData.
    .
}
```

In the body of this loop, curve.points is a variable of type ArrayList<Point2D> that holds the list of points on the curve. The i-th point on the curve can be obtained by calling the get() method of this list: curve.points.get(i). This returns a value of type *Point2D* which has getter methods named getX() and getY(). We can refer directly to the x-coordinate of the i-th point as:

```
curve.points.get(i).getX()
```

This might seem rather complicated, but it's a nice example of a complex name that specifies a path to a desired piece of data: Go to the object, curve. Inside curve, go to points. Inside points, get the i-th item. And from that item, get the x coordinate by calling its getX() method. Here is the complete definition of the method that redraws the picture:

```
private void redraw()
    g.setFill(backgroundColor);
    g.fillRect(0,0,canvas.getWidth(),canvas.getHeight());
    for ( CurveData curve : curves ) {
        g.setStroke(curve.color);
        for (int i = 1; i < curve.points.size(); i++) {
            // Draw a line segment from point number i-1 to point number i.
        double x1 = curve.points.get(i-1).getX();
        double y1 = curve.points.get(i-1).getY();
        double x2 = curve.points.get(i).getX();
        double y2 = curve.points.get(i).getY();
        drawSegment(curve.symmetric,x1,y1,x2,y2);
        }
    }
}
```

drawSegment() is a method that strokes the line segment from (x1,y1) to (x2,y2). If the first parameter is true, it also draws the horizontal and vertical reflections of that segment.

I have mostly been interested here in discussing how the program uses *ArrayList*, but I encourage you to read the full source code, SimplePaint2.java, and to try out the program. In addition to serving as an example of using parameterized types, it also serves as another example of creating and using menus. You should be able to understand the entire program.

3.4 RECORDS

Some programming languages have two basic kinds of built-in data structures: arrays and records. An array consists of a sequence of items, where individual items are referred to by their numerical position in the sequence. In a record, on the other hand, the positions in the data structure have names instead of numbers. The items in a record are called its "fields," and the names for the items are "field names." A field is accessed using its field name. We recognize records as similar to objects, with the fields in a record playing the same role as instance variables in an object, but records existed before object-oriented programming. The actual word "record" is used in programming languages such as Pascal and Cobol. The C programming language uses the term "struct" for the same idea. The "record" terminology might have originated with databases, which are just large, organized collections of data, where a record is a (typically small) set of related data items, and a database is a collection of records. In Java, classes can be used to represent records, but the term "record" has not traditionally been used. However, in Java 17, records have become an official part of the language in the form of a special kind of class. Java records are not really equivalent to records in other languages, since a record in Java is immutable, that is, its content cannot be modified after the record is created. However, they are similar to other records is that they are fairly simple containers for named fields.

3.4.1 Basic Java Records

A Java record is an object that belongs to a special kind of class, which I will call a record class. In the simplest case, a record class specifies nothing but the set of instance variables that represent the fields of the record. Here is an example:

public record FullName(String firstName, String lastName) { }

This is a class definition for a record class named *FullName* that has two instance variables of type *String* named firstName and lastName. These instance variables are the fields of the record. The "{ }" at the end of the definition is an empty class body. Note that the instance variables in a record class are listed in parentheses after the class name. The syntax is the same as the syntax for a list of formal parameters in a method definition, but the meaning is very different. A record of type *FullName*—that is, an instance of the record class—is created in the usual way, with the new operator. For example,

FullName fname = new FullName("Jane", "Doe");

This statement calls a constructor that has one parameter for each field of the record, whose effect is simply to provide a value for each field. Note that this constructor was not explicitly defined in the class. It is called the *canonical constructor* for the record class, and it is provided automatically by the compiler. In fact, many things are added implicitly to a record class definition by the compiler. The simple record definition of *FullName*, given above, is essentially equivalent to the following regular class definition:

```
public final class FullName {
    private final String firstName;
    private final String lastName;
    public FullName( String firstName, String lastName ) {
            this.firstName = firstName;
            this.lastName  =  lastName;
    }
    public firstName() {
            return firstName;
    }
    public lastName() {
            return lastName;
}
public String toString() {
            return "FullName[firstName=" + firstName
                    + ", lastName=" + lastName + "]";
}
public boolean equals(Object obj) {
            // (definition omitted)
}
public int hashCode() {
            // (definition omitted)
    }
}
```

We see that a record class is automatically final, that is, it cannot be extended by subclasses. Furthermore, a record class cannot extend another class (but it is a subclass of *Object*, as is true for any class).

The instance variables in a record are private and final. Accessor, or "getter", methods for the instance variables are automatically defined, but instead of using the typical getXXX() naming convention for getter methods, their names are the same as the names of the instance variables. For example, if fname is a variable of type *FullName*, then the instance variables would be accessed as fname. firstName() and fname.lastName(). Because its instance variables are final, a record is immutable, so no "setter" methods can be defined.

Furthermore, reasonable definitions are automatically provided for three methods inherited from class *Object*: toString(), equals(), and hashCode(). The toString() method returns a string that includes the name of the class and the names and values of its fields. The equals() method returns true if its parameter is an object of the same type that has the same values for its fields. (We will not encounter the hashCode() method until Section 6.3.)

We will see that record class definitions can be more complex, but you should expect basic record classes, with empty class bodies, to be very common, since they provide a simple way to group together a set of related data items. For example, the *CurveData* class from the SimplePaint2.java example in the previous section was created to group together all the data relevant to a single curve:

```
private static class CurveData {
    Color color;
    boolean symmetric;
    ArrayList<Point2D> points;
}
```

This nested class could be replaced by a nested record class:

```
private record CurveData(
    Color color,
    boolean symmetric,
    ArrayList<Point2D> points
) {}
```

Note that the nested *CurveData* record class does not have to be declared static, because nested record classes are automatically static.

After this change, when a *CurveData* object is created, values must be provided for its fields.

For example,

```
currentCurve = new CurveData(currentColor, useSymmetry, new ArrayList<Point2D>());
```

Another change is that *CurveData* objects are now immutable. That happens to be OK in SimplePaint2.java, but it's not something that will work in all cases. For example, class *Point2D* is a simple container for xy coordinates, but it could not be a record class because points are not immutable.

3.4.2 More Record Syntax

It is not possible to add additional instance variables to a record class, beyond those that are defined in the list after the class name. But almost anything else can be added in the class body. For example, a record class can contain static items of any kind. It can define instance methods, including replacements for the default toString(), equals(), and hashCode() methods. And it can define constructors, with just a few restrictions. First of all, it is possible to extend the definition for the canonical constructor that is defined automatically, using a syntax in which the parameter list for the constructor is omitted. For example, the canonical constructor for the *FullName* class might throw an exception if firstName is null:

```
public FullName { // canonical constructor for the FullName class
    if ( firstName == null) {
            throw new IllegalArgumentException("First name can't be null.");
    }
}
```

This extends the canonical constructor. Although the parameter list is omitted in the definition, a call to this constructor still requires two parameters, and it still uses those parameters to initialize firstName and lastName, before the code in the constructor definition is executed.

Additional constructors can be defined, but any non-canonical constructor must begin with a call to a constructor in the same class, using the special variable this as discussed in Subsection 1.6.3. This means that the canonical constructor will be called, directly or indirectly, by any other constructor.

As an example, noting that there are people who use only a single name, we might want to provide a *FullName* constructor that takes just one parameter representing that name:

```
public FullName(String onlyName) {
    this( onlyName, null ); // call the canonical constructor
}
```

This constructor calls the default constructor to set the firstName field equal to onlyName and the lastName field equal to null.

We might also want to define a more natural version of toString() for the *FullName* record class. For a full class definition that implements all of these ideas, see the sample file FullName.java.

A final syntax note: Although a record class cannot extend another class, it can implement one or more interfaces.

3.4.3 A Complex Example

A *complex number* consists of two real numbers, which are called the real part and the imaginary part of the complex number. Without knowing anything about the mathematics of complex numbers, you should see that this is a natural application for records. To represent a complex number in Java, we need a simple container for two values of type double. That could be done with a basic record class

```
record Complex( double re, double im ) { }
```

But there are many things that can be done with complex numbers, and we would want to include some of those things in a class that could truly be said to represent them. Here is a record class that includes a few of those things:

```
/**

A record type for representing complex numbers, where

a complex number consists of two real numbers called its

real and imaginary parts.     The class includes methods for

doing arithmetic with complex numbers.

*/

public record Complex(double re, double im)  {

    // Some named constants for common complex numbers.

    public final static Complex ONE = new Complex(1,0);

    public final static Complex ZERO = new Complex(0,0);

    public final static Complex I = new Complex(0,1);

    /**

    This constructor creates a complex number with a given

    real part and with imaginary part zero.

    */

    public Complex(double re) {

            this(re,0);

    }

    /**

    Creates string representations of complex number such

    * as:      3.0 + I*5.0,          -I*3.14,  2.7 - I*8.6,          3.14

    */

    public String toString() {
```

```
            if (im == 0)
                    return String.valueOf(re); else if (re == 0) {
            if (im < 0)
                    return "-I*" + (-im);
        else
    }
        else if (im < 0)
            return re + " - " + "I*" + (-im); else
            return re + " + " + "I*" + im;
        }
        // Some methods for doing arithmetic on two complex numbers
        public Complex plus(Complex c) {
            return new Complex(re + c.re, im + c.im);
        }
        public Complex minus(Complex c) {
            return new Complex(re - c.re, im - c.im);
        }
        public Complex times(Complex c) {
            return new Complex(re*c.re - im*c.im, re*c.im + im*c.re);
        }
        public Complex dividedBy(Complex c) {
            double denom = c.re*c.re + c.im*c.im;
            double real = (re*c.re + im*c.im)/denom;
            double imaginary = (im*c.re - re*c.im)/denom;
            return new Complex(real,imaginary);
        }
    } // end record Complex
```

This class adds some static member variables, a constructor that creates a complex number from a single real number, a toString() method that prints a complex number in a reasonable format, and some instance variables that implement arithmetic operations on complex numbers. Of course, it also has the canonical constructor that creates a complex number from two real numbers. The sample program RecordDemo.java tests both Complex.java and FullName.java.

It might be worth thinking about why record classes should be final and why records should be immutable. One reason for them to be final is that it can make it possible for a complier to apply certain kinds of optimization to the code that it generates. This applies not just to record classes but to final classes in general.

Here is an example. It is common to compute complicated arithmetic expressions involving complex numbers. Consider the quadratic formula Ax^2+Bx+C. If A, B, C, and x are objects of type *Complex*, then the value of this expression can be computed as

(A.times(x).times(x)).plus(B.times(x)).plus(C)

If you check the definitions of the times() and plus() methods, you can see that every time a method is called, it creates a new *Complex* object. In the quadratic formula example, five new objects are generated, but we are only interested in the one that represents the final answer. The other four objects are just scratch work: They are created, used very briefly and then immediately become eligible for garbage collection. Creating and garbage collecting large numbers of objects can be inefficient. However, in this case, the compiler might be able to avoid creating those extra objects by replacing the calls to plus() and times() with code that performs the same operations directly using temporary local variables of type double instead of objects. It can do this because it knows exactly what each method call does—but that is only the case because the *Complex* class is final. If that were not the case, then A, B, C, or x might actually refer to objects belonging to subclasses of *Complex* that have redefined plus() and times(). That is something that can only be checked at run time, not at compile time, so if the class were not final, a compiler would have no way of knowing what the calls to plus() and times() will do when the program is run.

As for immutability, it might also help with optimization, since a compiler can be sure that calling a method on an object will not modify the instance variables in that object. However, it is probably more important that immutability makes it easier to reason about a program. If you can prove that some property of an immutable object is true at some point in time, you can be sure that it won't become false later because the object has been modified.

3.5 SEARCHING AND SORTING

Two array processing techniques that are particularly common are *searching* and *sorting* . Searching here refers to finding an item in the array that meets some specified criterion. Sorting refers to rearranging all the items in the array into increasing or decreasing order (where the meaning of increasing and decreasing can depend on the context). We have seen in Subsection 3.2.2 that Java has some built-in methods for searching and sorting arrays. However, a computer science student should be familiar with the algorithms that are used in those methods. In this section, you will learn some algorithms for searching and sorting.

Sorting and searching are often discussed, in a theoretical sort of way, using an array of numbers as an example. In practical situations, though, more interesting types of data are usually involved. For example, the array might be a mailing list, and each element of the array might be an object containing a name and address. Given the name of a person, you might want to look up that person's address. This is an example of searching, since you want to find the object in the array that contains the given name. It would also be useful to be able to sort the array according to various criteria. One example of sorting would be ordering the elements of the array so that the names are in alphabetical order. Another example would be to order the elements of the array according to zip code before printing a set of mailing labels.

This example can be generalized to a more abstract situation in which we have an array that contains objects, and we want to search or sort the array based on the value of one of the instance variables in the objects. In that case, we might use the terminology of "records" and "fields" that originated in work with databases, as discussed in the previous section. In the mailing list example, we might have an array of records where each record contains a first name, last name, street address, state, city, and zip code as fields. For the purpose of searching or sorting, one of the fields is designated to be the *key* field. Searching then means finding a record in the array that has a specified value in its key field. Sorting means moving the records around in the array so that the key fields of the record are in increasing (or decreasing) order. In this section, most of my examples follow the tradition of using arrays of numbers. But I'll also give a few examples using objects, to remind you of the more practical applications.

3.5.1 Searching

There is an obvious algorithm for searching for a particular item in an array: Look at each item in the array in turn, and check whether that item is the one you are looking for. If so, the search is finished. If you look at every item without finding the one you want, then you can be sure that the item is not in the array. It's easy to write a subroutine to implement this algorithm. Let's say the array that you want to search is an array of ints. Here is a method that will search the array for a specified integer. If the integer is found, the method returns the index of the location in the array where it is found. If the integer is not in the array, the method returns the value -1 as a signal that the integer could not be found:

```
/**
Searches the array A for the integer N.      If N is not in the array,
```

```
then -1 is returned.   If N is in the array, then the return value is
the first integer i that satisfies A[i] == N.
*/
static int find(int[] A, int N) {
    for (int index = 0; index < A.length; index++) {
            if ( A[index] == N )
                    return index;     // N has been found at this index!
    }
    // If we get this far, then N has not been found
    // anywhere in the array.        Return a value of -1.
    return -1;
}
```

This method of searching an array by looking at each item in turn is called *linear search* . If nothing is known about the order of the items in the array, then there is really no better alternative algorithm. But if the elements in the array are known to be in increasing or decreasing order, then a much faster search algorithm can be used. An array in which the elements are in order is said to be *sorted* . Of course, it takes some work to sort an array, but if the array is to be searched many times, then the work done in sorting it can really pay off.

Binary search is a method for searching for a given item in a sorted array. Although the implementation is not trivial, the basic idea is simple: If you are searching for an item in a sorted list, then it is possible to eliminate half of the items in the list by inspecting a single item. For example, suppose that you are looking for the number 42 in a sorted array of 1000 integers. Let's assume that the array is sorted into increasing order. Suppose you check item number 500 in the array, and find that the item is 93. Since 42 is less than 93, and since the elements in the array are in increasing order, we can conclude that if 42 occurs in the array at all, then it must occur somewhere before location 500. All the locations numbered 500 or above contain values that are greater than or equal to 93. These locations can be eliminated as possible locations of the number 42.

Once we know that 42 can only be in the first half of the array, the obvious next step is to check location 250. If the number at that location is, say, -21, then you can eliminate locations before 250 and limit further search to locations between 251 and 499. The next test will limit the search to about 125 locations, and the one after that to about 62. After just 10 steps, there is only one location left. This is a whole lot better than looking through every element in the array. If there were a million items, it would still take only 20 steps for binary search to search the array! (Mathematically, the number of steps is approximately equal to the logarithm, in the base 2, of the number of items in the array.)

In order to make binary search into a Java subroutine that searches an array, A, for an item, N, we just have to keep track of the range of locations that could possibly contain N. At each step, as we eliminate possibilities, we reduce the size of this range. The basic operation is to look at the item in the middle of the range. If this item is greater than N, then the second half of the range can be eliminated. If it is less than N, then the first half of the range can be eliminated. If the number in the middle just happens to be N exactly, then the search is finished. If the size of the range decreases to zero, then the number N does not occur in the array. Here is a subroutine that implements this idea:

```
/**
Searches the array A for the integer N.
Precondition:        A must be sorted into increasing order.
Postcondition: If N is in the array, then the return value, i,
satisfies A[i] == N.    If N is not in the array, then the
return value is -1.
*/
static int binarySearch(int[] A, int N) {
    int lowestPossibleLoc = 0;
    int highestPossibleLoc = A.length - 1;
    while (highestPossibleLoc >= lowestPossibleLoc) {
            int middle = (lowestPossibleLoc + highestPossibleLoc) / 2;
            if (A[middle] == N) {
                    // N has been found at this index!
            return middle;
            }
            else if (A[middle] > N) {
                            // eliminate locations >= middle
                    highestPossibleLoc = middle - 1;
            }
            else {
                            // eliminate locations <= middle
```

```
                lowestPossibleLoc = middle + 1;
            }
        }
        // At this point, highestPossibleLoc < lowestPossibleLoc,
        // which means that N is known to be not in the array.    Return
        // a -1 to indicate that N could not be found in the array.
        return -1;
    }
```

3.5.2 Association Lists

One particularly common application of searching is with *association lists.* The standard example of an association list is a dictionary. A dictionary associates definitions with words. Given a word, you can use the dictionary to look up its definition. We can think of the dictionary as being a list of *pairs* of the form (w,d), where w is a word and d is its definition. A general association list is a list of pairs (k,v), where k is some "key" value, and v is a value associated to that key. In general, we want to assume that no two pairs in the list have the same key. There are two basic operations on association lists: Given a key, k, find the value v associated with k, if any. And given a key, k, and a value v, add the pair (k,v) to the association list (replacing the pair, if any, that had the same key value). The two operations are usually called *get* and *put* .

Association lists are very widely used in computer science. For example, a compiler has to keep track of the location in memory associated with each variable. It can do this with an association list in which each key is a variable name and the associated value is the address of that variable in memory. Another example would be a mailing list, if we think of it as associating an address to each name on the list. As a related example, consider a phone directory that associates a phone number to each name. We'll look at a highly simplified version of this example. (This is not meant to be a realistic way to implement a phone directory!)

The items in the phone directory's association list could be objects belonging to the class:

```
class PhoneEntry {
    String name;
    String phoneNum;
}
```

The data for a phone directory consists of an array of type PhoneEntry[ ] and an integer variable to keep track of how many entries are actually stored in the directory. The technique of dynamic arrays can be used in order to avoid putting an arbitrary limit on the number of entries that the phone directory can hold. A *PhoneDirectory* class should include instance methods that implement the "get" and "put" operations. Here is one possible simple definition of the class:

```
import java.util.Arrays;
/**
A PhoneDirectory holds a list of names with a phone number for
each name.  It is possible to find the number associated with
a given name, and to specify the phone number for a given name.
*/
public class PhoneDirectory {
    /**
    * An object of type PhoneEntry holds one name/number pair.
    */
    private static class PhoneEntry {
            String name;     // The name.
            String number;  // The associated phone number.
    }
    private PhoneEntry[] data;         // Array that holds the name/number pairs.
    private int dataCount;    // The number of pairs stored in the array.
    /**
    * Constructor creates an initially empty directory.
    */
    public PhoneDirectory() {
            data = new PhoneEntry[1];
            dataCount = 0;
    }
    /**
    Looks for a name/number pair with a given name. If found, the index of the pair in
    the data array is returned. If no pair contains the given name, then the return
    value is -1. This private method is used internally in getNumber() and putNumber().
    */
```

```
private int find( String name ) {
        for (int i = 0; i < dataCount; i++) {
                if (data[i].name.equals(name))
                        return i;// The name has been found in position i.
        }
        return -1;          // The name does not exist in the array.
}
/**
Finds the phone number, if any, for a given name.
@return The phone number associated with the name; if the name does
not occur in the phone directory, then the return value is null.
*/
public String getNumber( String name ) {
        int position = find(name);
        if (position == -1)
                return null;        // There is no phone entry for the given name
        else
                return data[position].number;
}
/**
Associates a given name with a given phone number. If the name already exists in the
phone directory, then the new number replaces the old one. Otherwise, a new name
number pair is added. The name and number should both be non-null. An
IllegalArgumentException is thrown if this is not the case.
*/
public void putNumber( String name, String number ) {
        if (name == null || number == null)
                throw new IllegalArgumentException("name and number cannot be null")
        int i = find(name);
        if (i >= 0) {
                // The name already exists, in position i in the array.
                // Just replace the old number at that position with the new
```

```
            data[i].number = number;
        }
        else {
                    // Add a new name/number pair to the array.   If the array is
                    // already full, first create a new, larger array.
            if (dataCount == data.length) {
                    data = Arrays.copyOf( data, 2*data.length );
            }
            PhoneEntry newEntry = new PhoneEntry();        // Create a new pair.
            newEntry.name = name;
            newEntry.number = number;
            data[dataCount] = newEntry;    // Add the new pair to the array.
            dataCount++;
            }
        }
    } // end class PhoneDirectory
```

The class defines a private instance method, find(), that uses linear search to find the position of a given name in the array of name/number pairs. The find() method is used both in the getNumber() method and in the putNumber() method. Note in particular that putNumber(name,number) has to check whether the name is in the phone directory. If so, it just changes the number in the existing entry; if not, it has to create a new phone entry and add it to the array.

This class could also have be written using an ArrayList instead of a dynamic array. And the nested *PhoneEntry* class is a natural candidate to be a record class. For a version that uses these ideas, see PhoneDirectory2.java.

This phone directory implementation could be improved by using binary search instead of simple linear search in the find() method. However, we could only do that if the list of *PhoneEntries* were sorted into alphabetical order according to name. In fact, it's really not all that hard to keep the list of entries in sorted order, as you'll see in the next subsection.

I will mention that association lists are also called "maps," and Java has a standard parameterized type named *Map* that implements association lists for keys and values of any type. The implementation is more efficient than anything you can do with basic arrays. You will encounter this class in Section 6.3.

3.5.3 Insertion Sort

We've seen that there are good reasons for sorting arrays. There are many algorithms available for doing so. One of the easiest to understand is the *insertion sort* algorithm. This technique is also applicable to the problem of keeping a list in sorted order as you add new items to the list. Let's consider that case first:

Suppose you have a sorted list and you want to add an item to that list. If you want to make sure that the modified list is still sorted, then the item must be inserted into the right location, with all the smaller items coming before it and all the bigger items after it. This will mean moving each of the bigger items up one space to make room for the new item.

```
/*
Precondition:       itemsInArray is the number of items that are
stored in A.  These items must be in increasing order
*    (A[0] <= A[1] <= ... <= A[itemsInArray-1]).
The array size is at least one greater than itemsInArray.
Postcondition:      The number of items has increased by one,
newItem has been added to the array, and all the items
in the array are still in increasing order.
Note:          To complete the process of inserting an item in the
array, the variable that counts the number of items
in the array must be incremented, after calling this
subroutine.
*/
static void insert(int[] A, int itemsInArray, int newItem) {
    int loc = itemsInArray - 1;          // Start at the end of the array.
    /* Move items bigger than newItem up one space; Stop when a smaller item is
    encountered or when the beginning of the array (loc == 0) is reached. */
    while (loc >= 0 && A[loc] > newItem) {
            A[loc + 1] = A[loc];         // Bump item from A[loc] up to loc+1.
            loc = loc - 1;       // Go on to next location.
    }
    A[loc + 1] = newItem;   // Put newItem in last vacated space.
}
```

Conceptually, this could be extended to a sorting method if we were to take all the items out of an unsorted array, and then insert them back into the array one-by-one, keeping the list in sorted order as we do so. Each insertion can be done using the insert routine given above. In the actual algorithm, we don't really take all the items from the array; we just remember what part of the array has been sorted:

```
static void insertionSort(int[] A) {
            // Sort the array A into increasing order.
    int itemsSorted; // Number of items that have been sorted so far.
    for (itemsSorted = 1; itemsSorted < A.length; itemsSorted++) {
            // Assume that items A[0], A[1], ... A[itemsSorted-1]
            // have already been sorted.      Insert A[itemsSorted]
            // into the sorted part of the list.
    int temp = A[itemsSorted];          // The item to be inserted.
    int loc = itemsSorted - 1;  // Start at end of list.
    while (loc >= 0 && A[loc] > temp) {
            A[loc + 1] = A[loc]; // Bump item from A[loc] up to loc+1.
            loc = loc - 1;       // Go on to next location.
            }
            A[loc + 1] = temp; // Put temp in last vacated space.
    }
}
```

Here is an illustration of one stage in insertion sort. It shows what happens during one execution of the for loop in the above method, when itemsSorted is 5:

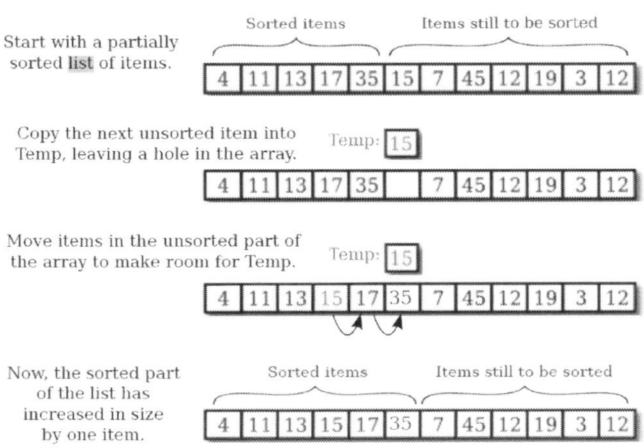

3.5.4 Selection Sort

Another typical sorting method uses the idea of finding the biggest item in the list and moving it to the end—which is where it belongs if the list is to be in increasing order. Once the biggest item is in its correct location, you can then apply the same idea to the remaining items. That is, find the next-biggest item, and move it into the next-to-last space, and so forth. This algorithm is called *selection sort*. It's easy to write:

```
static void selectionSort(int[] A) {
        // Sort A into increasing order, using selection sort
    for (int lastPlace = A.length-1; lastPlace > 0; lastPlace--) {
            // Find the largest item among A[0], A[1], ...,
            // A[lastPlace], and move it into position lastPlace
            // by swapping it with the number that is currently
            // in position lastPlace.
        int maxLoc = 0;  // Location of largest item seen so far.
        for (int j = 1; j <= lastPlace; j++) {
            if (A[j] > A[maxLoc]) {
                // Since A[j] is bigger than the maximum we've seen
                // so far, j is the new location of the maximum value
                // we've seen so far. maxLoc = j;
            }
        }
        int temp = A[maxLoc]; // Swap largest item with A[lastPlace].
        A[maxLoc] = A[lastPlace];
        A[lastPlace] = temp;
        }       // end of for loop
}
```

A variation of selection sort is used in the *Hand* class that was introduced in Subsection 1.4.1. (By the way, you are finally in a position to fully understand the source code for the *Hand* class from that section; note that it uses an *ArrayList*. The source file is Hand.java.)

In the *Hand* class, a hand of playing cards is represented by an ArrayList<Card>. The objects stored in the list are of type *Card*. A *Card* object contains instance methods getSuit() and getValue() that can be used to determine the suit and value of thc card. In my sorting method,

I actually create a new list and move the cards one-by-one from the old list to the new list. The cards are selected from the old list in increasing order. In the end, the new list becomes the hand and the old list is discarded. This is not the most efficient procedure, but hands of cards are so small that the inefficiency is negligible. Here is the code for sorting cards by suit:

```
/**
Sorts the cards in the hand so that cards of the same suit are
grouped together, and within a suit the cards are sorted by value.
Note that aces are considered to have the lowest value, 1.
*/
public void sortBySuit() {
    ArrayList<Card> newHand = new ArrayList<Card>();
    while (hand.size() > 0) {
            int pos = 0;        // Position of minimal card.
            Card c = hand.get(0);       // Minimal card.
            for (int i = 1; i < hand.size(); i++) {
                    Card c1 = hand.get(i);
                    if ( c1.getSuit() < c.getSuit() ||
                            (c1.getSuit() == c.getSuit() && c1.getValue() < c.getValue()) ) {
                    pos = i; // Update the minimal card and location.
                    c = c1;
            }
    }
    hand.remove(pos);       // Remove card from original hand.
    newHand.add(c);         // Add card to the new hand.
    }
    hand = newHand;
}
```

This example illustrates the fact that comparing items in a list is not usually as simple as using the operator "<". In this case, we consider one card to be less than another if the suit of the first card is less than the suit of the second, and also if the suits are the same and the value of the second card is less than the value of the first. The second part of this test ensures that cards with the same suit will end up sorted by value.

Sorting a list of *Strings* raises a similar problem: the “<” operator is not defined for strings. However, the *String* class does define a compareTo method. If str1 and str2 are of type *String*, then

```
str1.compareTo(str2)
```

returns an int that is 0 when str1 is equal to str2, is less than 0 when str1 precedes str2, and is greater than 0 when str1 follows str2. For example, you can test whether str1 precedes or is equal to str2 by testing

```
if ( str1.compareTo(str2) <= 0 )
```

The definition of “precedes” and “follows” for strings uses what is called *lexicographic ordering* , which is based on the Unicode values of the characters in the strings. Lexicographic ordering is not the same as alphabetical ordering, even for strings that consist entirely of letters (because in lexicographic ordering, all the upper case letters come before all the lower case letters). However, for words consisting strictly of the 26 lower case letters in the English alphabet, lexicographic and alphabetic ordering are the same. (The same holds true if the strings consist entirely of uppercase letters.) The method str1.compareToIgnoreCase(str2) compares the two strings after converting any characters that they contain to lower case.

Insertion sort and selection sort are suitable for sorting fairly small arrays (up to a few hundred elements, say). There are more complicated sorting algorithms that are much faster than insertion sort and selection sort for large arrays, to the same degree that binary search is faster than linear search. The standard method Arrays.sort uses these fast sorting algorithms.

3.5.5 Unsorting

I can’t resist ending this section on sorting with a related problem that is much less common, but is a bit more fun. That is the problem of putting the elements of an array into a random order. The typical case of this problem is shuffling a deck of cards. A good algorithm for shuffling is similar to selection sort, except that instead of moving the biggest item to the end of the list, an item is selected at random and moved to the end of the list. Here is a subroutine to shuffle an array of ints:

```
/**
* Postcondition:      The items in A have been rearranged into a random order.
*/
static void shuffle(int[] A) {
```

```
    for (int lastPlace = A.length-1; lastPlace > 0; lastPlace--) {
                // Choose a random location from among 0,1,...,lastPlace.
        int randLoc = (int)(Math.random()*(lastPlace+1));
                // Swap items in locations randLoc and lastPlace.
        int temp = A[randLoc];
        A[randLoc] = A[lastPlace];
        A[lastPlace] = temp;
    }
}
```

3.6 TWO-DIMENSIONAL ARRAYS

A 2D array has a type such as int[ ][ ] or String[ ][ ], with two pairs of square brackets. The elements of a 2D array are arranged in rows and columns, and the new operator for 2D arrays specifies both the number of rows and the number of columns. For example,

```
int[][] A;
A = new int[3][4];
```

This creates a 2D array of int that has 12 elements arranged in 3 rows and 4 columns. Although I haven't mentioned it, there are initializers for 2D arrays. For example, this statement creates the 3-by-4 array that is shown in the picture below:

```
int[][] A =   { { 1, 0, 12, -1 },
                { 7, -3, 2, 5 },
                { -5, -2, 2, -9 }
              };
```

An array initializer for a 2D array contains the rows of A, separated by commas and enclosed between braces. Each row, in turn, is a list of values separated by commas and enclosed between braces. There are also 2D array literals with a similar syntax that can be used anywhere, not just in declarations. For example,

```
A = new int[][]      { { 1, 0, 12, -1 },
                       { 7, -3, 2, 5 },
                       { -5, -2, 2, -9 }
                     };
```

All of this extends naturally to three-dimensional, four-dimensional, and even higher- dimensional arrays, but they are not used very often in practice.

3.6.1 The Truth About 2D Arrays

But before we go any farther, there is a little surprise. Java does not actually have two- dimensional arrays. In a true 2D array, all the elements of the array occupy a continuous block of memory, but that's not true in Java. The syntax for array types is a clue: For any type *BaseType*, we should be able to form the type BaseType[ ], meaning "array of *BaseType*." If we use int[ ] as the base type, the type that we get is "int[ ][ ] meaning "array of int[ ]" or "array of array of int." And in fact, that's what happens. The elements in a 2D array of type int[ ][ ] are variables of type int[ ]. And remember that a variable of type int[ ] can only hold a pointer to an array of int. So, a 2D array is really an array of pointers, where each pointer can refer to a one-dimensional array. Those one-dimensional arrays are the rows of the 2D array. A picture will help to explain this. Consider the 3-by-4 array A defined above.

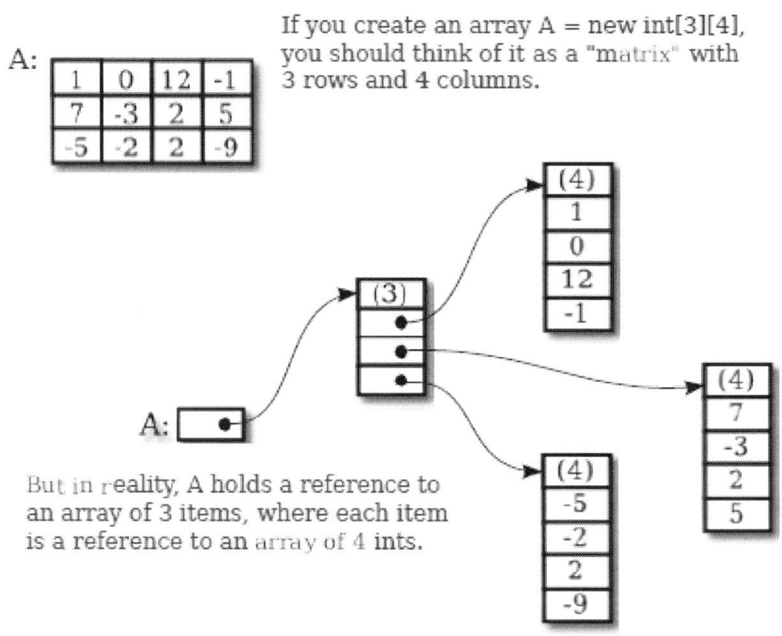

For the most part, you can ignore the reality and keep the picture of a grid in mind. Sometimes, though, you will need to remember that each row in the grid is really an array in itself. These arrays can be referred to as A[0], A[1], and A[2]. Each row is in fact a value of type int[ ]. It could, for example, be passed to a subroutine that asks for a parameter of type int[ ].

Some of the consequences of this structure are a little subtle. For example, thinking of a 2D array, A, as an array of arrays, we see that A.length makes sense and is equal to the number of rows of A. If A has the usual shape for a 2D array, then the number of columns in A would be the same as the number of elements in the first row, that is, A[0].length. But there is no rule that says that all of the rows of A must have the same length (although an array created with new BaseType[rows][columns] will always have that form). Each row in a 2D array is a separate one-dimensional array, and each of those arrays can have a different length. In fact, it's even possible for a row to be null. For example, the statement

```
A = new int[3][];
```

with no number in the second set of brackets, creates an array of 3 elements where all the elements are null. There are places for three rows, but no actual rows have been created. You can then create the rows A[0], A[1], and A[2] individually.

As an example, consider a *symmetric matrix* . A symmetric matrix, M, is a two Ñ dimensional array in which the number of rows is equal to the number of columns and satisfying M[i][j] equals M[j][i] for all i and j. Because of this equality, we only really need to store M[i][j] for i >= j. We can store the data in a "triangular matrix":

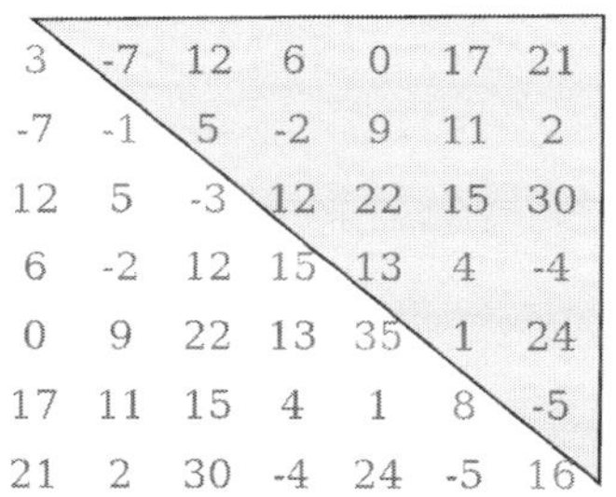

In a symmetric matrix, the elements above the diagonal (shown in red) duplicate elements below the diagonal (blue). So a symmetric matrix can be stored as a "triangular matrix" with rows of different lengths.

3						
-7	-1					
12	5	-3				
6	-2	12	15			
0	9	22	13	35		
17	11	15	4	1	8	
21	2	30	-4	24	-5	16

It's easy enough to make a triangular array, if we create each row separately. To create a 7-by-7 triangular array of double, we can use the code segment

```
double[][] matrix = new double[7][]; // rows have not yet been created!
for (int i = 0; i < 7; i++) {
    matrix[i] = new double[i+1];        // Create row i with i + 1 elements.
}
```

We just have to remember that if we want to know the value of the matrix at (i,j), and if i < j, then we actually have to get the value of matrix[j][i] in the triangular matrix. And similarly for setting values. It's easy to write a class to represent symmetric matrices:

```
/**
* Represents symmetric n-by-n matrices of real numbers.
*/
public class SymmetricMatrix {
    private double[][] matrix;          // A triangular matrix to hold the data.
    /**
```

```
* Creates an n-by-n symmetric matrix in which all entries are 0.
*/
public SymmetricMatrix(int n) {
        matrix = new double[n][];
        for (int i = 0; i < n; i++)
                matrix[i] = new double[i+1];
}
/**
Returns the matrix entry at position (row,col).     (If row < col,
the value is actually stored at position (col,row).)
*/
public double get( int row, int col ) {
        if (row >= col)
                return matrix[row][col];
        else
                return matrix[col][row];
}
/**
Sets the value of the matrix entry at (row,col).     (If row < col,
the value is actually stored at position (col,row).)
*/
public void set( int row, int col, double value ) {
        if (row >= col)
                matrix[row][col] = value;
        else
                matrix[col][row] = value;
}
/**
Returns the number of rows and columns in the matrix.
*/
public int size() {
```

```
            return matrix.length;     // The size is the number of rows.
        }
    } // end class SymmetricMatrix
```

This class is in the file SymmetricMatrix.java, and a small program to test it can be found in TestSymmetricMatrix.java.

By the way, the standard function Arrays.copyOf() can't make a full copy of a 2D array in a single step. To do that, you need to copy each row separately. To make a copy of a two-dimensional array of int, for example:

```
int[][] B = new int[A.length][];          // B has as many rows as A.
for (int i = 0; i < A.length; i++) {
    B[i] = Arrays.copyOf(A[i], A[i].length)); // Copy row i.
}
```

3.6.2 Conway's Game Of Life

As an example of more typical 2D array processing, let's look at a very well-known example: Conway's Game of Life, invented by mathematician John Horton Conway in 1970. This Game of Life is not really a game (although sometimes it's referred to as a "zero-person game" that plays itself). It's a "two-dimensional cellular automaton." This just means that it's a grid of cells whose content changes over time according to definite, deterministic rules. In Life, a cell can only have two possible contents: It can be "alive" or "dead." We will use a 2D array to represent the grid, with each element of the array representing the content of one cell in the grid. In the game, an initial grid is set up in which each cell is marked as either alive or dead. After that, the game "plays itself." The grid evolves through a series of time steps. The contents of the grid at each time step are completely determined by the contents at the previous time step, according to simple rules: Each cell in the grid looks at its eight neighbors (horizontal, vertical, and diagonal) and counts how many of its neighbors are alive. Then the state of the cell in the next step is determined by the rules:

- For a cell that is alive in the current time step: If the cell has 2 or 3 living neighbors, then the cell remains alive in the next time step; otherwise, it dies. (A living cell dies of loneliness if it has 0 or 1 living neighbor, and of overcrowding if it has more than 3 living neighbors.)
- For a cell that is dead in the current time step: If the cell has 3 living neighbors, then the cell becomes alive in the next time step; otherwise, it remains dead. (Three living cells give birth to a new living cell.)

Here's a picture of part of a Life board, showing the same board before and after the rules have been applied. The rules are applied to every cell in the grid. The picture shows how they apply to four of the cells:

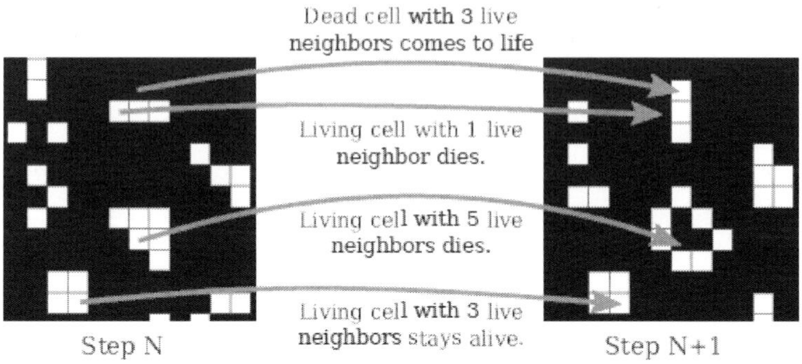

The Game of Life is interesting because it gives rise to many interesting and surprising patterns. (Look it up on Wikipedia.) Here, we are just interested in writing a program to simulate the game. The complete program can be found in the file Life.java. In the program, the life grid is shown as a grid of squares in which dead squares are black and living squares are white. (The program uses MosaicCanvas.java from Section 4.7 to represent the grid, so you will also need that file to compile and run the program.) In the program, you can fill the life board randomly with dead and alive cells, or you can use the mouse to set up the game board. There is a "Step" button that will compute one time-step of the game, and a "Start" button that will run time steps as an animation.

We'll look at some of the array processing involved in implementing the Game of Life for this program. Since a cell can only be alive or dead, it is natural to use a two-dimensional array of boolean[ ][ ] to represent the states of all the cells. The array is named alive, and alive[r][c] is true when the cell in row r, column c is alive. The number of rows and the number of columns are equal and are given by a constant, GRID SIZE. So, for example, to fill the Life grid with random values, the program uses simple nested for loops:

```
for (int r = 0; r < GRID SIZE; r++) {
    for (int c = 0; c < GRID SIZE; c++) {
                        // Use a 25% probability that the cell is alive.
        alive[r][c] = (Math.random() < 0.25);
    }
}
```

Note that the expression (Math.random() < 0.25) is a true/false value that can be assigned to a boolean array element. The array is also used to set the color of the cells on the screen. Since the grid of cells is displayed on screen as a *MosaicCanvas*, setting the colors is done using the MosaicCanvas API. Note that the actual drawing is done in the *MosaicCanvas* class (which has its own 2D array of type Color[ ][ ] to keep track of the colors of each cell). The Life program just has to set the colors in the mosaic, using the MosaicCanvas API. This is done in the program in a method named showBoard() that is called each time the board changes. Again, simple nested for loops are used to set the color of each square in the grid:

```
for (int r = 0; r < GRID SIZE; r++) {
    for (int c = 0; c < GRID SIZE; c++) {
        if (alive[r][c])
            display.setColor(r,c,Color.WHITE);
        else
            display.setColor(r,c,null);// Shows the background color, black.
    }
}
```

Of course, the most interesting part of the program is computing the new state of the board by applying the rules to the current state. The rules apply to each individual cell, so again we can use nested for loops to work through all the cells on the board, but this time the processing is more complicated. Note first that we can't make changes to the values in the array as we work through it, since we will need to know the old state of a cell when processing its neighboring cells. In fact, the program uses a second array to hold the new board as it is being created. When the new board is finished, it can be substituted for the old board. The algorithm goes like this in pseudocode:

let newboard be a new boolean[][] array for each row r:

for each column c:

Let N be the number of neighbors of cell (r,c) in the alive array if ((N is 3) or (N is 2 and alive[r][c]))

newboard[r][c] = true; else

newboard[r][c] = false; alive = newboard

Note that at the end of the process, alive is pointing to a new array. This doesn't matter as long as the contents of the array represent the new state of the game. The old array will be garbage collected. The test for whether newboard[r][c] should be true or false might not be obvious, but it implements the rules correctly. We still need to work on counting the neighbors. Consider the cell in row r and column c. If it's not at an edge of the board, then it's clear where its neighbors are:

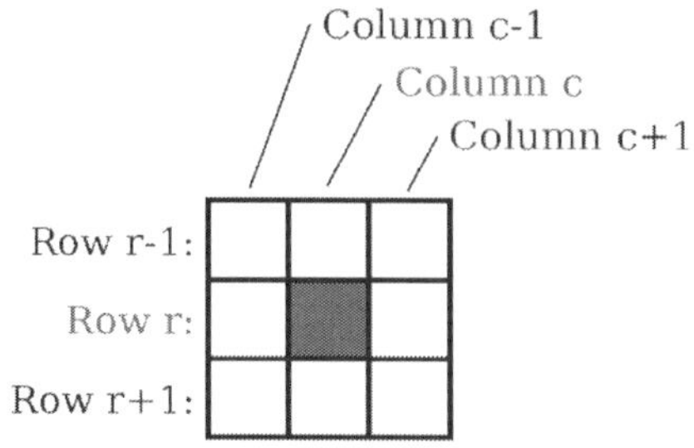

The row above row number r is row number r-1, and the row below is r+1. Similarly for the columns. We just have to look at the values of alive[r-1][c-1], alive[r-1][c], alive[r-1][c+1], alive[r][c-1], alive[r][c+1], alive[r+1][c-1], alive[r+1][c], and alive[r+1][c+1], and count the number that are true. (You should make sure that you understand how the array indexing works here.)

But there is a problem when the cell is along one of the edges of the grid. In that case, some of the array elements in the list don't exist, and an attempt to use them will cause an exception. To avoid the exception, we have to give special consideration to cells along the edges. One idea is that before referencing any array element, check that the array element actually exists. In that case, the code for neighbor counting becomes

```
if (r-1 >= 0 && c-1 >= 0 && alive[r-1][c-1])
    N++; // A cell at position (r-1,c-1) exists and is alive.
if (r-1 >= 0 && alive[r-1][c])
    N++; // A cell at position (r-1,c) exists and is alive.
if (r-1 >= 0 && c+1 <= GRID SIZE && alive[r-1][c+1])
    N++; // A cell at position (r-1,c+1) exists and is alive.
// and so on...
```

All the possible exceptions are avoided. But in my program, I actually do something that is common in 2D computer games—I pretend that the left edge of the board is attached to the right edge and the top edge to the bottom edge. For example, for a cell in row 0, we say that the row "above" is actually the bottom row, row number GRID SIZE-1. I use variables to represent the positions above, below, left, and right of a given cell. The code turns out to be simpler than the code shown above. Here is the complete method for computing the new board:

```
private void doFrame() { // Compute the new state of the Life board.
    boolean[][] newboard = new boolean[GRID SIZE][GRID SIZE];
    for ( int r = 0; r < GRID SIZE; r++ ) {
            int above, below; // rows considered above and below row number r
```

```
            int left, right;     // columns considered left and right of column c
            above = r > 0 ? r-1 : GRID SIZE-1;   //
            below = r < GRID SIZE-1 ? r+1 : 0;
            for ( int c = 0; c < GRID SIZE; c++ ) {
                left =     c > 0 ? c-1 : GRID SIZE-1;
                right = c < GRID SIZE-1 ? c+1 : 0;
                int n = 0; // number of alive cells in the 8 neighboring cells
                if (alive[above][left])
                    n++;
                if (alive[above][c])
                    n++;
                if (alive[above][right])
                    n++;
                if (alive[r][left])
                    n++;
                if (alive[r][right])
                    n++;
                if (alive[below][left])
                    n++;
                if (alive[below][c])
                    n++;
                if (alive[below][right])
                    n++;
                if (n == 3 || (alive[r][c] && n == 2))
                    newboard[r][c] = true;
                else
                    newboard[r][c] = false;
            }
        }
        alive = newboard;
    }
```

Again, I urge you to check out the source code, Life.java, and try the program. Don't forget that you will also need MosaicCanvas.java.

3.6.3 Checkers

As a final example for this chapter, we'll look at a more substantial example of using a 2D array. This is the longest program that we have encountered so far, with 741 lines of code. The program lets two users play checkers against each other. The checkers game is played on an eight-by-eight board, which is based on an example from Subsection 2.5.1. The players are called "red" and "black," after the color of their checkers. I'm not going to explain the rules of checkers here; possibly you can learn them by trying out the program.

In the program, a player moves by clicking on the piece that they want to move, and then clicking on the empty square to which it is to be moved. As an aid to the players, any square that the current player can legally click at a given time is highlighted with a brightly colored border. The square containing a piece that has been selected to be moved, if any, is surrounded by a yellow border. Other pieces that can legally be moved are surrounded by a cyan-colored border. If a piece has already been selected to be moved, each empty square that it can legally move to is highlighted with a green border. The game enforces the rule that if the current player can jump one of the opponent's pieces, then the player must jump. When a player's piece becomes a king, by reaching the opposite end of the board, a big white "K" is drawn on the piece. Here is a picture of the program early in a game. It is black's turn to move. Black has selected the piece in the yellow-outlined square to be moved. Black can click one of the squares outlined in green to complete the move, or can click one of the squares outlined in cyan to select a different piece to be moved.

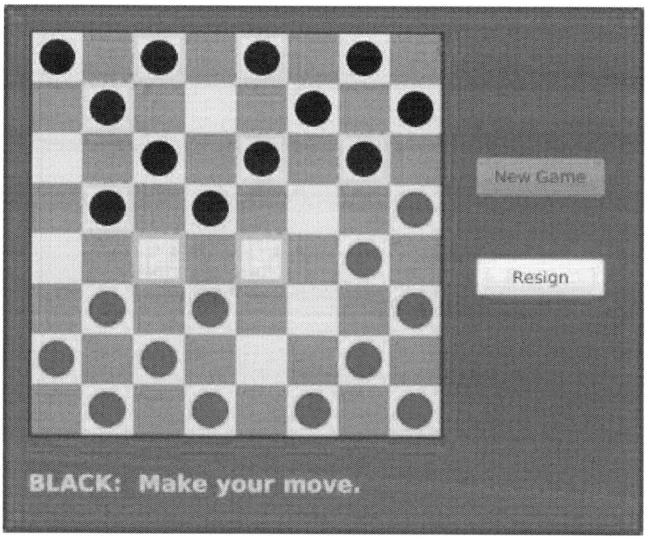

I will only cover a part of the programming for this example. I encourage you to read the complete source code, Checkers.java. It's long and complex, but with some study, you should understand all the techniques that it uses. The program is a good example of state-based, event-driven, object-oriented programming.

The data about the pieces on the board are stored in a two-dimensional array. Because of the complexity of the program, I wanted to divide it into several classes. In addition to the main class, there are several nested classes. One of these classes is *CheckersData*, which handles the data for the board. It is not directly responsible for any part of the graphics or event-handling, but it provides methods that can be called by other classes that handle graphics and events. It is mainly this class that I want to talk about.

The *CheckersData* class has an instance variable named board of type int[][]. The value of board is set to "new int[8][8]", an 8-by-8 grid of integers. The values stored in the grid are defined as constants representing the possible contents of a square on a checkerboard:

static final int

EMPTY = 0, *// Value representing an empty square.*

RED = 1, *// A regular red piece.*

RED KING = 2, *// A red king.*

BLACK = 3, *// A regular black piece. BLACK KING = 4; // A black king.*

The constants RED and BLACK are also used in my program (or, perhaps, misused) to represent the two players in the game. When a game is started, the values in the array are set to represent the initial state of the board. The grid of values looks like

	0	1	2	3	4	5	6	7
0	BLACK	EMPTY	BLACK	EMPTY	BLACK	EMPTY	BLACK	EMPTY
1	EMPTY	BLACK	EMPTY	BLACK	EMPTY	BLACK	EMPTY	BLACK
2	BLACK	EMPTY	BLACK	EMPTY	BLACK	EMPTY	BLACK	EMPTY
3	EMPTY	EMPTY	EMPTY	EMPTY	EMPTY	EMPTY	EMPTY	EMPTY
4	EMPTY	EMPTY	EMPTY	EMPTY	EMPTY	EMPTY	EMPTY	EMPTY
5	EMPTY	RED	EMPTY	RED	EMPTY	RED	EMPTY	RED
6	RED	EMPTY	RED	EMPTY	RED	EMPTY	RED	EMPTY
7	EMPTY	RED	EMPTY	RED	EMPTY	RED	EMPTY	RED

A regular black piece can only move "down" the grid. That is, the row number of the square it moves to must be greater than the row number of the square it comes from. A regular red piece can only move up the grid. Kings of either color can move in both directions.

One function of the *CheckersData* class is to take care of changes to the data structures that need to be made when one of the users moves a checker. An instance method named makeMove() is provided to do this. When a player moves a piece from one square to another, the values of two elements in the array are changed. But that's not all. If the move is a jump, then the piece that was jumped is removed from the board. (The method checks whether the move is a jump by checking if the square to which the piece is moving is two rows away from the square where it starts.) Furthermore, a RED piece that moves to row 0 or a BLACK piece that moves to row 7 becomes a king. Putting all that into a subroutine is good programming: the rest of the program doesn't have to worry about any of these details. It just calls this makeMove() method:

```
/**
Make the move from (fromRow,fromCol) to (toRow,toCol).       It is
ASSUMED that this move is legal!      If the move is a jump, the
jumped piece is removed from the board.       If a piece moves
to the last row on the opponent's side of the board, the
piece becomes a king.
*/
void makeMove(int fromRow, int fromCol, int toRow, int toCol) {
    board[toRow][toCol] = board[fromRow][fromCol]; // Move the piece.
    board[fromRow][fromCol] = EMPTY; // The square it moved from is now empty.
    if (fromRow - toRow == 2 || fromRow - toRow == -2) {
                // The move is a jump.    Remove the jumped piece from the board.
            int jumpRow = (fromRow + toRow) / 2; // Row of the jumped piece.
            int jumpCol = (fromCol + toCol) / 2; // Column of the jumped piece
            board[jumpRow][jumpCol] = EMPTY;
    }
    if (toRow == 0 && board[toRow][toCol] == RED)
            board[toRow][toCol] = RED KING; // Red piece becomes a king.
    if (toRow == 7 && board[toRow][toCol] == BLACK)
```

```
            board[toRow][toCol] = BLACK KING;        // Black piece becomes a king.
   }   // end makeMove()
```

An even more important function of the *CheckersData* class is to find legal moves on the board. In my program, a move in a Checkers game is represented by an object belonging to the following class:

```
   /**
   A CheckersMove object represents a move in the game of
   Checkers.   It holds the row and column of the piece that is
   to be moved and the row and column of the square to which
   it is to be moved.    (This class makes no guarantee that
   the move is legal.)
   */
   private static class CheckersMove {
      int fromRow, fromCol;    // Position of piece to be moved.
      int toRow, toCol; // Square it is to move to.
      CheckersMove(int r1, int c1, int r2, int c2) {
                  // Constructor.  Set the values of the instance variables.
         fromRow = r1;
         fromCol = c1; toRow = r2; toCol = c2;
      }
      boolean isJump() {
         // Test whether this move is a jump.      It is assumed that
         // the move is legal.      In a jump, the piece moves two
         // rows. (In a regular move, it only moves one row.)
      return (fromRow - toRow == 2 || fromRow - toRow == -2);
      }
   }   // end class CheckersMove.
```

The *CheckersData* class has an instance method which finds all the legal moves that are currently available for a specified player. This method is a function that returns an array of type CheckersMove[ ]. The array contains all the legal moves, represented as *CheckersMove* objects. The specification for this method reads

```
   /**
```

Return an array containing all the legal CheckersMoves

for the specified player on the current board. If the player

has no legal moves, null is returned. The value of player

should be one of the constants RED or BLACK; if not, null

is returned. If the returned value is non-null, it consists

entirely of jump moves or entirely of regular moves, since

if the player can jump, only jumps are legal moves.

**/*

CheckersMove[] getLegalMoves(int player)

A brief pseudocode algorithm for the method is

```
Start with an empty list of moves
Find any legal jumps and add them to the list
if there are no jumps:
    Find any other legal moves and add them to the list
if the list is empty:
    return null
else:
    return the list
```

Now, what is this "list"? We have to return the legal moves in an array. But since an array has a fixed size, we can't create the array until we know how many moves there are, and we don't know that until near the end of the method, after we've already made the list! A neat solution is to use an *ArrayList* instead of an array to hold the moves as we find them. In fact, I use an object defined by the parameterized type ArrayList<CheckersMove> so that the list is restricted to holding objects of type *CheckersMove*. As we add moves to the list, it will grow just as large as necessary. At the end of the method, we can create the array that we really want and copy the data into it:

```
Let "moves" be an empty ArrayList<CheckersMove>
Find any legal jumps and add them to moves
if moves.size() is 0:    // There are no legal jumps!
    Find any other legal moves and add them to moves
if moves.size() is 0:    // There are no legal moves at all!
    return null
```

else:

Let moveArray be an array of CheckersMoves of length moves.size()

Copy the contents of moves into moveArray

return moveArray

Now, how do we find the legal jumps or the legal moves? The information we need is in the board array, but it takes some work to extract it. We have to look through all the positions in the array and find the pieces that belong to the current player. For each piece, we have to check each square that it could conceivably move to, and check whether that would be a legal move. If we are looking for legal jumps, we want to look at squares that are two rows and two columns away from the piece. There are four squares to consider. Thus, the line in the algorithm that says "Find any legal jumps and add them to moves" expands to:

For each row of the board:

For each column of the board:

if one of the player's pieces is at this location:

if it is legal to jump to row + 2, column + 2

add this move to moves

if it is legal to jump to row - 2, column + 2

add this move to moves

if it is legal to jump to row + 2, column - 2

add this move to moves

if it is legal to jump to row - 2, column - 2

add this move to moves

The line that says "Find any other legal moves and add them to moves" expands to something similar, except that we have to look at the four squares that are one column and one row away from the piece. Testing whether a player can legally move from one given square to another given square is itself non-trivial. The square the player is moving to must actually be on the board, and it must be empty. Furthermore, regular red and black pieces can only move in one direction. I wrote the following utility method to check whether a player can make a given non-jump move:

*/***

This is called by the getLegalMoves() method to determine

whether the player can legally move from (r1,c1) to (r2,c2).

```
It is ASSUMED that (r1,c1) contains one of the player's
pieces and that (r2,c2) is a neighboring square.

*/
private boolean canMove(int player, int r1, int c1, int r2, int c2) {
    if (r2 < 0 || r2 >= 8 || c2 < 0 || c2 >= 8)
            return false;     // (r2,c2) is off the board.
    if (board[r2][c2] != EMPTY)
            return false;     // (r2,c2) already contains a piece.
    if (player == RED) {
            if (board[r1][c1] == RED && r2 > r1)
                    return false;     // Regular red piece can only move down.
            return true;      // The move is legal.
    }
    else {
            if (board[r1][c1] == BLACK && r2 < r1)
                    return false;     // Regular black piece can only move up.
            return true;      // The move is legal.
    }
}   // end canMove()
```

This method is called by my getLegalMoves() method to check whether one of the possible moves that it has found is actually legal. I have a similar method that is called to check whether a jump is legal. In this case, I pass to the method the square containing the player's piece, the square that the player might move to, and the square between those two, which the player would be jumping over. The square that is being jumped must contain one of the opponent's pieces. This method has the specification:

```
/**
This is called by other methods to check whether
the player can legally jump from (r1,c1) to (r3,c3).
It is assumed that the player has a piece at (r1,c1), that
(r3,c3) is a position that is 2 rows and 2 columns distant
```

```
from (r1,c1) and that (r2,c2) is the square between (r1,c1)
* and (r3,c3).
*/
private boolean canJump(int player, int r1, int c1,
                        int r2, int c2, int r3, int c3) {...
```

Given all this, you should be in a position to understand the complete getLegalMoves() method. It's a nice way to finish off this chapter, since it combines several topics that we've looked at: one-dimensional arrays, *ArrayLists*, and two-dimensional arrays:

```
CheckersMove[] getLegalMoves(int player) {
    if (player != RED && player != BLACK)
            return null;      // (This will not happen in a correct program.)
            int playerKing;  // The constant for a King belonging to the player
            if (player == RED)
                    playerKing = RED KING;
            else
                    playerKing = BLACK KING;
            ArrayList<CheckersMove> moves = new ArrayList<CheckersMove>();
                            // Moves will be stored in this list.
/*  First, check for any possible jumps.        Look at each square on the board.If  that square contains one of the player's pieces,
look at a possible jump in each of the four directions from that square.  If there is a legal jump in that direction, put it in the moves ArrayList.
*/
for (int row = 0; row < 8; row++) {
            for (int col = 0; col < 8; col++) {
                    if (board[row][col] == player || board[row][col] == playerKing) {
                            if (canJump(player, row, col, row+1, col+1, row+2, col+2))
                                    moves.add(new CheckersMove(row, col, row+2, col+2));
                            if (canJump(player, row, col, row-1, col+1, row-2, col+2))
                                    moves.add(new CheckersMove(row, col, row-2, col+2));
                            if (canJump(player, row, col, row+1, col-1, row+2, col-2))
```

```
                        moves.add(new CheckersMove(row, col, row+2, col-2));
                    if (canJump(player, row, col, row-1, col-1, row-2, col-2))
                        moves.add(new CheckersMove(row, col, row-2, col-2));
                }
            }
        }
        /*      If any jump moves were found, then the user must jump, so we don't add any
        regular moves. However, if no jumps were found, check for any legal regular
        moves. Look at each square on the board.If that square contains one of the player's
        pieces, look at a possible move in each of the four directions from that square.
        If there is a legal move in that direction, put it in the moves ArrayList.
    */
    if (moves.size() == 0) {
        for (int row = 0; row < 8; row++) {
                for (int col = 0; col < 8; col++) {
                if (board[row][col] == player || board[row][col] == playerKing) {
                    if (canMove(player,row,col,row+1,col+1))
                        moves.add(new CheckersMove(row,col,row+1,col+1));
                    if (canMove(player,row,col,row-1,col+1))
                        moves.add(new CheckersMove(row,col,row-1,col+1));
                    if (canMove(player,row,col,row+1,col-1))
                        moves.add(new CheckersMove(row,col,row+1,col-1));
                    if (canMove(player,row,col,row-1,col-1))
                        moves.add(new CheckersMove(row,col,row-1,col-1));
                }
            }
        }
    }
    /* If no legal moves have been found, return null.    Otherwise, create an array just
    big enough to hold all the legal moves, copy the
    legal moves from the ArrayList into the array, and return the array.
    */
```

```
if (moves.size() == 0) return null;
else {
        CheckersMove[] moveArray = new CheckersMove[moves.size()];
        for (int i = 0; i < moves.size(); i++)
            moveArray[i] = moves.get(i);
        return moveArray;
    }
}   // end getLegalMoves
```

The checkers program is complex, and you can be sure that it didn't just fall together. It took a good deal of design work to decide what classes and objects would be used, what methods should be written, and what algorithms the methods should use. The complete source code is in the file Checkers.java. Take a look!

Chapter 4 CORRECTNESS, ROBUSTNESS AND EFFICIENCY

In preceding chapters, we have addressed the principles of programming. The subsequent chapters will address more sophisticated facets of programming. The proposed concepts will typically be more intricate, and the systems employing them will be somewhat more elaborate. This concise chapter serves as a pivotal moment in which we examine the challenge of ensuring the accuracy of intricate programs. Malfunctioning computer programs are exceedingly prevalent. Software systems are delicate. A minor error might lead to a program malfunction or failure. Many of us recognize this from our personal experiences with computers. We have all seen narratives regarding software malfunctions that result in spacecraft collisions, website outages, telecommunication failures, and, in certain instances, fatalities. Programs need not be as deficient as they now are. While it may be infeasible to ensure that programs are devoid of issues, meticulous programming and well crafted programming tools can significantly mitigate problems. This chapter will examine the challenges of accuracy and robustness in programs. Examines methodologies for conceptualizing and evaluating programs to enhance the likelihood of their correctness, potentially achieving provable correctness. Examines exceptions and the try..catch statement in greater detail, while Section 4.4 presents assertions, an additional tool that Java offers to assist in the development of proper applications. Addresses another critical concern for real-world programs: efficiency. A program, regardless of its correctness, is rendered impractical if it requires an excessive duration to execute. The final section of this chapter presents methods for evaluating the runtime efficiency of algorithms. This chapter addresses subjects typically covered in advanced computer science courses, warranting just a succinct review here. However, the knowledge acquired here will be beneficial throughout the remainder of the book.

4.1 CORRECTNESS AND ROBUSTNESS: AN INTRODUCTION

A program is *correct* if it accomplishes the task that it was designed to perform. It is *robust* if it can handle illegal inputs and other unexpected situations in a reasonable way. For example, consider a program that is designed to read some numbers from the user and then print the same numbers in sorted order. The program is correct if it works for any set of input numbers. It is robust if it can also deal with non-numeric input by, for example, printing an error message and ignoring the bad input. A non-robust program might crash or give nonsensical output in the same circumstance.

Every program should be correct. (A sorting program that doesn't sort correctly is pretty useless.) It's not the case that every program needs to be completely robust. It depends on who will use it and how it will be used. For example, a small utility program that you write for your own use doesn't have to be particularly robust.

The question of correctness is actually more subtle than it might appear. A programmer works from a specification of what the program is supposed to do. The programmer's work is correct if the program meets its specification. But does that mean that the program itself is correct? What if the specification is incorrect or incomplete? A correct program should be a correct implementation of a complete and correct specification. The question is whether the specification correctly expresses the intention and desires of the people for whom the program is being written. This is a question that lies largely outside the domain of computer science.

4.1.1 Horror Stories

Most computer users have personal experience with programs that don't work or that crash. In many cases, such problems are just annoyances, but even on a personal computer there can be more serious consequences, such as lost work or lost money. When computers are given more important tasks, the consequences of failure can be proportionately more serious.

About twenty-three years ago, the failure of two multi-million dollar space missions to Mars was prominent in the news. Both failures were probably due to software problems, but in both cases the problem was not with an incorrect program as such. In September 1999, the Mars Climate Orbiter burned up in the Martian atmosphere because data that was expressed in English units of measurement (such as feet and pounds) was entered into a computer program that was designed to use metric units (such as centimeters and grams). A few months later, the Mars Polar Lander probably crashed because its software turned off its landing engines too soon. The program was supposed to detect the bump when the spacecraft landed and turn off the engines then. It has been determined that deployment of the landing gear might have jarred the spacecraft enough to activate the program, causing it to turn off the engines when the spacecraft was still high above the ground. The unpowered spacecraft would then have fallen to the Martian surface. A more robust system would have checked the altitude before turning off the engines!

There are many equally dramatic stories of problems caused by incorrect or poorly written software. Let's look at a few incidents recounted in the book *Computer Ethics* by Tom Forester and Perry Morrison. (This book covers various ethical issues in computing. It, or something like it, is essential reading for any student of computer science.)

- In 1985 and 1986, one person was killed and several were injured by excess radiation, while undergoing radiation treatments by a mis-programmed computerized radiation machine. In another case, over a ten-year period ending in 1992, almost 1,000 cancer patients received radiation dosages that were 30% less than prescribed because of a programming error.
- In 1985, a computer at the Bank of New York started destroying records of on-going security transactions because of an error in a program. It took less than 24 hours to fix the program, but by that time, the bank was out 5,000,000 in overnight interest payments on funds that it had to borrow to cover the problem.
- The programming of the inertial guidance system of the F-16 fighter plane would have turned the plane upside-down when it crossed the equator, if the problem had not been discovered in simulation. The Mariner 18 space probe was lost because of an error in one line of a program. The Gemini V space capsule missed its scheduled landing target by a hundred miles, because a programmer forgot to take into account the rotation of the Earth.
- In 1990, AT&T's long-distance telephone service was disrupted throughout the United States when a newly loaded computer program proved to contain a bug.

Of course, there have been more recent problems. For example, computer software error contributed to the Northeast Blackout of 2003, one of the largest power outages in history. In 2006, the Airbus A380 was delayed by software incompatibility problems, at a cost of perhaps billions of dollars. In 2007, a software problem grounded thousands of planes at the Los Angeles International Airport. On May 6, 2010, a flaw in an automatic trading program apparently resulted in a 1000-point drop in the Dow Jones Industrial Average.

These are just a few examples. Software problems are all too common. As programmers, we need to understand why that is true and what can be done about it.

4.1.2 Java to the Rescue

Part of the problem, according to the inventors of Java, can be traced to programming languages themselves. Java was designed to provide some protection against certain types of errors. How can a language feature help prevent errors? Let's look at a few examples.

Some programming languages do not require variables to be declared. In such languages, when a variable name is used in a program, the variable is created automatically. You might consider this more convenient than having to declare every variable explicitly, but there is an unfortunate consequence: An inadvertent spelling error might introduce an extra variable that you had no intention of creating. This type of error was responsible, according to one famous story, for yet another lost spacecraft. In the FORTRAN programming language, the command "DO 20 I = 1,5" is the first statement of a counting loop. Now, spaces are insignificant in FORTRAN, so this is equivalent to "DO20I=1,5". On the other hand, the command "DO20I=1.5", with a period instead of a comma, is an assignment statement that assigns the value 1.5 to the variable DO20I. Supposedly, the inadvertent substitution of a period for a comma in a statement of this type caused a rocket to blow up on take-off. Because FORTRAN doesn't require variables to be declared, the compiler would be happy to accept the statement "DO20I=1.5." It would just create a new variable named DO20I. If FORTRAN required variables to be declared, the compiler would have complained that the variable DO20I was undeclared.

While most programming languages today do require variables to be declared, there are other features in common programming languages that can cause problems. Java has eliminated some of these features. Some people complain that this makes Java less efficient and less powerful. While there is some justice in this criticism, the increase in security and robustness is probably worth the cost in most circumstances. The best defense against some types of errors is to design a programming language in which the errors are impossible. In other cases, where the error can't be completely eliminated, the language can be designed so that when the error does occur, it will automatically be detected. This will at least prevent the error from causing further harm, and it will alert the programmer that there is a bug that needs fixing. Let's look at a few cases where the designers of Java have taken these approaches.

An array is created with a certain number of locations, numbered from zero up to some specified maximum index. It is an error to try to use an array location that is outside of the specified range. In Java, any attempt to do so is detected automatically by the system. In some other languages, such as C and C++, it's up to the programmer to make sure that the index is within the legal range. Suppose that an array, A, has three locations, A[0], A[1], and A[2]. Then A[3], A[4], and so on refer to memory locations beyond the end of the array. In Java, an attempt to store data in A[3] will be detected. The program will be terminated (unless the error is "caught"). In C or C++, the computer will just go ahead and store the data in memory that is not part of the array. Since there is no telling what that memory location is being used for, the result will be unpredictable. The consequences could be much more serious than a terminated program. (See, for example, the discussion of buffer overflow errors later in this section.)

Pointers are a notorious source of programming errors. In Java, a variable of object type holds either a pointer to an object or the special value null. Any attempt to use a null value as if it were a pointer to an actual object will be detected by the system. In some other languages, again, it's up to the programmer to avoid such null pointer errors. In my first Macintosh computer, a long time ago, a null pointer was actually implemented as if it were a pointer to memory location zero. A program could use a null pointer to change values stored in memory near location zero. Unfortunately, the Macintosh stored important system data in those locations. Changing that data could cause the whole system to crash, a consequence more severe than a single failed program.

Another type of pointer error occurs when a pointer value is pointing to an object of the wrong type or to a segment of memory that does not even hold a valid object at all. These types of errors are impossible in Java, which does not allow programmers to manipulate pointers directly. In other languages, it is possible to set a pointer to point, essentially, to any location in memory. If this is done incorrectly, then using the pointer can have unpredictable results.

Another type of error that cannot occur in Java is a memory leak. In Java, once there are no longer any pointers that refer to an object, that object is "garbage collected" so that the memory that it occupied can be reused. In other languages, it is the programmer's responsibility to return unused memory to the system. If the programmer fails to do this, unused memory can build up, leaving less memory for programs and data. There is a story that many common programs for older Windows computers had so many memory leaks that the computer would run out of memory after a few days of use and would have to be restarted.

Many programs have been found to suffer from *buffer overflow errors*. Buffer overflow errors often make the news because they are responsible for many network security problems. When one computer receives data from another computer over a network, that data is stored in a buffer. The buffer is just a segment of memory that has been allocated by a program to hold data that it expects to receive. A buffer overflow occurs when more data is received than will fit in the buffer. The question is, what happens then? If the error is detected by the program or by the networking software, then the only thing that has happened is a failed network data transmission. The real problem occurs when the software does not properly detect buffer overflows. In that case, the software continues to store data in memory even after the buffer is filled, and the extra data goes into some part of memory that was not allocated by the program as part of the buffer. That memory might be in use for some other purpose. It might contain important data. It might even contain part of the program itself. This is where the real security issues come in. Suppose that a buffer overflow causes part of a program to be replaced with extra data received over a network. When the computer goes to execute the part of the program that was replaced, it's actually executing data that was received from another computer. That data could be anything. It could be a program that crashes the computer or takes it over. A malicious programmer who finds a convenient buffer overflow error in networking software can try to exploit that error to trick other computers into executing his programs.

For software written completely in Java, buffer overflow errors are impossible. The language simply does not provide any way to store data into memory that has not been properly allocated. To do that, you would need a pointer that points to unallocated memory or you would have to refer to an array location that lies outside the range allocated for the array. As explained above, neither of these is possible in Java. (However, there could conceivably still be errors in Java's standard classes, since some of the methods in these classes are actually written in the C programming language rather than in Java. In fact, Java's internal security errors have at times been a problem for the language.)

It's clear that language design can help prevent errors or detect them when they occur. Doing so involves restricting what a programmer is allowed to do. Or it requires tests, such as checking whether a pointer is null, that take some extra processing time. Some programmers feel that the sacrifice of power and efficiency is too high a price to pay for the extra security. In some applications, this is true. However, there are many situations where safety and security are primary considerations. Java is designed for such situations.

4.1.3 Problems Remain in Java

There is one area where the designers of Java chose not to detect errors automatically: numerical computations. In Java, a value of type int is represented as a 32-bit binary number. With 32 bits, it's possible to represent a little over four billion different values. The values of type int range from -2147483648 to 2147483647. What happens when the result of a computation lies outside this range? For example, what is 2147483647 + 1? And what is 2000000000 * 2? The mathematically correct result in each case cannot be represented as a value of type int. These are examples of *integer overflow* . In most cases, integer overflow should be considered an error. However, Java does not automatically detect such errors. For example, it will compute the value of 2147483647 + 1 to be the negative number, -2147483648. (What happens is that any extra bits beyond the 32-nd bit in the correct answer are discarded. Values greater than 2147483647 will "wrap around" to negative values. Mathematically speaking, the result is always "correct modulo 2^{32}.")

For example, consider the 3N+1 program starting from a positive integer N, the program computes a certain sequence of integers:

```
while ( N != 1 ) {
    if ( N % 2 == 0 )  // If N is even...
```

```
            N = N / 2;
      else
            N = 3 * N + 1;
      System.out.println(N);
   }
```

But there is a problem here: If N is too large, then the value of 3*N+1 will not be mathematically correct because of integer overflow. The problem arises whenever 3*N+1 > 2147483647, that is when N > 2147483646/3. For a completely correct program, we should check for this possibility before computing 3*N+1:

```
   while ( N != 1 ) {
      if ( N % 2 == 0 )   // If N is even...
            N = N / 2;
      else {
            if (N > 2147483646/3) {
                  System.out.println("Sorry, but the value of N has become");
                  System.out.println("too large for your computer!");
                  break;
            }
            N = 3 * N + 1;
      }
      System.out.println(N);
   }
```

(Be sure you understand why we can't just test "if (3*N+1 > 2147483647)".) The problem here is not that the original algorithm for computing 3N+1 sequences was wrong. The problem is that it just can't be correctly implemented using 32-bit integers. Many programs ignore this type of problem. But integer overflow errors have been responsible for their share of serious computer failures, and a completely robust program should take the possibility of integer overflow into account. (The infamous "Y2K" bug at the start of the year 2000 was, in fact, just this sort of error.)

For numbers of type double, there are even more problems. There are still overflow errors, which occur when the result of a computation is outside the range of values that can be represented as a value of type double. This range extends up to about 1.7 times 10 to the power 308. Numbers beyond this range do not "wrap around" to negative values. Instead, they are represented by special values that have no real numerical equivalent. The special values Double.POSITIVE INFINITY and Double. NEGATIVE INFINITY represent numbers outside the range of legal values. For example, 20 * 1e308 is computed to be Double.POSITIVE INFINITY. Another special value of type double, Double.NaN, represents an illegal or undefined result. ("NaN" stands for "Not a Number".) For example, the result of dividing zero by zero or taking the square root of a negative number is Double.NaN. You can test whether a number x is this special not-a-number value by calling the boolean-valued function Double.isNaN(x).

For real numbers, there is the added complication that most real numbers can only be represented approximately on a computer. A real number can have an infinite number of digits after the decimal point. A value of type double is only accurate to about 15 digits. The real number 1/3, for example, is the repeating decimal 0.333333333333..., and there is no way to represent it exactly using a finite number of digits. Computations with real numbers generally involve a loss of accuracy. In fact, if care is not exercised, the result of a large number of such computations might be completely wrong! There is a whole field of computer science, known as *numerical analysis*, which is devoted to studying algorithms that manipulate real numbers. So you see that not all possible errors are avoided or detected automatically in Java.

Furthermore, even when an error is detected automatically, the system's default response is to report the error and terminate the program. This is hardly robust behavior! So, a Java programmer still needs to learn techniques for avoiding and dealing with errors. These are the main topics of the next three sections.

4.2 WRITING CORRECT PROGRAMS

Correct programs don't just happen. It takes planning and attention to detail to avoid errors in programs. There are some techniques that programmers can use to increase the likelihood that their programs are correct.

4.2.1 Provably Correct Programs

In some cases, it is possible to prove that a program is correct. That is, it is possible to demonstrate mathematically that the sequence of computations represented by the program will always produce the correct result. Rigorous proof is difficult enough that in practice it can only be applied to fairly small programs. Furthermore, it depends on the fact that the "correct result" has been specified correctly and completely. As I've already pointed out, a program that correctly meets its specification is not useful if its specification was wrong. Nevertheless, even in everyday programming, we can apply some of the ideas and techniques that are used in proving that programs are correct.

The fundamental ideas are *process* and *state*. A state consists of all the information relevant to the execution of a program at a given moment during its execution. The state includes, for example, the values of all the variables in the program, the output that has been produced, any input that is waiting to be read, and a record of the position in the program where the computer is working. A process is the sequence of states that the computer goes through as it executes the program. From this point of view, the meaning of a statement in a program can be expressed in terms of the effect that the execution of that statement has on the computer's state. As a simple example, the meaning of the assignment statement "x = 7;" is that after this statement is executed, the value of the variable x will be 7. We can be absolutely sure of this fact, so it is something upon which we can build part of a mathematical proof.

In fact, it is often possible to look at a program and deduce that some fact must be true at a given point during the execution of a program. For example, consider the do loop:

```
do {
    System.out.print("Enter a positive integer: ");
    N = TextIO.getlnInt();
} while (N <= 0);
```

After this loop ends, we can be absolutely sure that the value of the variable N is greater than zero. The loop cannot end until this condition is satisfied. This fact is part of the meaning of the while loop. More generally, if a while loop uses the test "while ((*condition*))", and if there are no break statements in the loop, then after the loop ends, we can be sure that the (*condition*) is false. We can then use this fact to draw further deductions about what happens as the execution of the program continues. (With a loop, by the way, we also have to worry about the question of whether the loop will ever end. This is something that has to be verified separately.)

4.2.2 Preconditions and Postconditions

A fact that can be proven to be true after a given program segment has been executed is called a *postcondition* of that program segment. Postconditions are known facts upon which we can build further deductions about the behavior of the program. A postcondition of a program as a whole is simply a fact that can be proven to be true after the program has finished executing. A program can be proven to be correct by showing that the postconditions of the program meet the program's specification.

Consider the following program segment, where all the variables are of type double:

```
disc = B*B - 4*A*C;
x = (-B + Math.sqrt(disc)) / (2*A);
```

The quadratic formula (from high-school mathematics) assures us that the value assigned to x is a solution of the equation $A*x^2 + B*x + C = 0$, provided that the value of disc is greater than or equal to zero and the value of A is not zero. If we can guarantee that B*B-4*A*C >= 0 and that A != 0, then the fact that x is a solution of the equation becomes a postcondition of the program segment. We say that the condition, B*B-4*A*C >= 0 is a *precondition* of the program segment. The condition that A != 0 is another precondition. A precondition is defined to be a condition that must be true at a given point in the execution of a program in order for the program to continue correctly. A precondition is something that you want to be true. It's something that you have to check or force to be true, if you want your program to be correct.

That section introduced preconditions and postconditions as a way of specifying the contract of a subroutine. As the terms are being used here, a precondition of a subroutine is just a precondition of the code that makes up the definition of the subroutine, and the postcondition of a subroutine is a postcondition of the same code. In this section, we have generalized these terms to make them more useful in talking about program correctness in general.

Let's see how this works by considering a longer program segment:

```
do {
    System.out.println("Enter A, B, and C.");
    System.out.println("A must be non-zero and B*B-4*A*C must be >= 0.");
    System.out.print("A = ");
    A = TextIO.getlnDouble();
    System.out.print("B = ");
    B = TextIO.getlnDouble();
    System.out.print("C = ");
    C = TextIO.getlnDouble();
    if (A == 0 || B*B - 4*A*C < 0)
            System.out.println("Your input is illegal. Try again.");
} while (A == 0 || B*B - 4*A*C < 0);
disc = B*B - 4*A*C;
```

```
x = (-B + Math.sqrt(disc)) / (2*A);
```

After the loop ends, we can be sure that B*B-4*A*C >= 0 and that A != 0. The preconditions for the last two lines are fulfilled, so the postcondition that x is a solution of the equation $A*x^2 + B*x + C = 0$ is also valid. This program segment correctly and provably computes a solution to the equation. (Actually, because of problems with representing real numbers on computers, this is not 100% true. The algorithm is correct, but the program is not a perfect implementation of the algorithm. See the discussion in Subsection 4.1.3.)

Here is another variation, in which the precondition is checked by an if statement. In the first part of the if statement, where a solution is computed and printed, we know that the preconditions are fulfilled. In the other parts, we know that one of the preconditions fails to hold. In any case, the program is correct.

```
System.out.println("Enter your values for A, B, and C.");
System.out.print("A = ");
A = TextIO.getlnDouble();
System.out.print("B = ");
B = TextIO.getlnDouble();
System.out.print("C = ");
C = TextIO.getlnDouble();
    if (A != 0 && B*B - 4*A*C >= 0) {
            disc = B*B - 4*A*C;
            x = (-B + Math.sqrt(disc)) / (2*A);
            System.out.println("A solution of A*X*X + B*X + C = 0 is " + x);
    }
    else if (A == 0) {
            System.out.println("The value of A cannot be zero.");
    }
    else {
            System.out.println("Since B*B - 4*A*C is less than zero, the");
            System.out.println("equation A*X*X + B*X + C = 0 has no solution.");
    }
```

Whenever you write a program, it's a good idea to watch out for preconditions and think about how your program handles them. Often, a precondition can offer a clue about how to write the program.

For example, every array reference, such as A[i], has a precondition: The index must be within the range of legal indices for the array. For A[i], the precondition is that 0 <= i < A.length. The computer will check this condition when it evaluates A[i], and if the condition is not satisfied, the program will be terminated. In order to avoid this, you need to make sure that the index has a legal value. (There is actually another precondition, namely that A is not null, but let's leave that aside for the moment.) Consider the following code, which searches for the number x in the array A and sets the value of i to be the index of the array element that contains x:

```
i = 0;
while (A[i] != x) {
    i++;
}
```

As this program segment stands, it has a precondition, namely that x is actually in the array. If this precondition is satisfied, then the loop will end when A[i] == x. That is, the value of i when the loop ends will be the position of x in the array. However, if x is not in the array, then the value of i will just keep increasing until it is equal to A.length. At that time, the reference to A[i] is illegal and the program will be terminated. To avoid this, we can add a test to make sure that the precondition for referring to A[i] is satisfied:

```
i = 0;
while (i < A.length && A[i] != x) {
    i++;
}
```

Now, the loop will definitely end. After it ends, i will satisfy either i == A.length or A[i] == x. An if statement can be used after the loop to test which of these conditions caused the loop to end:

```
i = 0;
while (i < A.length && A[i] != x) {
    i++;
}
if (i == A.length)
    System.out.println("x is not in the array");
else
    System.out.println("x is in position " + i);
```

4.2.3 Invariants

Let's look at how loops work in more detail. Consider a subroutine for finding the sum of the elements in an array of int:

```
static int arraySum( int[] A ) {
    int total = 0;
    int i = 0;
    while ( i < A.length ) {
            total = total + A[i];
            i = i + 1;
    }
    return total;
}
```

(Note, by the way, that the requirements that A is not null is a precondition of the subroutine. If it is violated, the code in the subroutine will throw a NullPointerException.)

How can we be sure that this subroutine works? We need to prove that when the return statement is executed, the value of total is the sum of all the elements in A. One way to think about this problem is in terms of *loop invariants.*

A loop invariant is, roughly, a statement that remains true as the loop is executed. More precisely, we can show that a statement is an invariant for a loop if the following holds: As long as the statement is true before the code inside the loop is executed, then it will also be true after the code inside the loop has been executed. That is, a loop invariant is both a precondition and a postcondition of the body of the loop.

A loop invariant for the loop in the above subroutine is, "total is equal to the sum of the first i elements of A." Suppose this is true at the beginning of the while loop. That is, before the statement "total = total + A[i]" is executed, total is the sum of the first i elements of the array (namely A[0] through A[i-1]). After A[i] is added to total, total is now the sum of the first i+1 elements of the array. At this point, the loop invariant is not true. However, as soon as the next statement, "i = i + 1" is executed, replacing i with i+1, the loop invariant becomes true again. We have checked that if the loop invariant is true at the start of the body of the loop, then is also true at the end.

Note that a loop invariant is not necessarily true at every point during the execution of a loop. Executing one of the statements in the loop can make it false temporarily, as long as later statements in the loop make it true again.

So, have we proved that the subroutine arraySum() is correct? Not quite. There are still a few things to check. First of all, we need to make sure that the loop invariant is true before the very first time the loop is executed. At that point, i is zero, and total is also equal to zero, which is the correct sum of zero elements. So the loop invariant is true before the loop. Once we know that, we know that it remains true after each execution of the loop (because it's an invariant), and in particular, we know that it will still be true after the loop ends.

But for that to do us any good, we need to check that the loop actually does end! In each execution of the loop, the value of i goes up by one. That means that eventually it has to reach A.length. At that point, the condition in the while loop is false, and the loop ends.

After the loop ends, we know that i equals A.length, and we know that the loop invariant is true. At that point, since i is A.length, the loop invariant says, "total is the sum of the first A.length" elements of A." But that includes all of the elements of A. So, the loop invariant gives us exactly what we wanted to show: When total is returned by the subroutine, it is equal to the sum of all the elements of the array!

This might seem to you to be a lot of work to prove something that's obvious. But if you try to explain *why* it's obvious that arraySum() works, you'll probably find yourself using the logic behind loop invariants, even if you don't use the term.

Let's look more quickly at a similar example. Consider a subroutine that finds the maximum value in an array of int, where we assume that the array has length at least one:

```
static int maxInArray( int[] A ) {
    int max = A[0];
    int i = 1;
    while ( i < A.length ) {
            if ( A[i] > max )
                    max = A[i];
            i = i + 1;
    }
    return max;
}
```

In this case, we have a loop invariant that says, "max is the largest value among the first i elements of A." This statement is true before the loop starts, when i is 1 and max is A[0]. Suppose it is true at the start of the loop, before the if statement. After the if statement, max is greater than or equal to A[i], because that is a postcondition

In future chapters, I will occasionally point out how it can be useful to think in terms of preconditions, postconditions, and invariants.

I should note that reasoning about invariants becomes much more complicated in parallel programs, when several threads that are running at the same time and are accessing the same data.

4.2.4 Robust Handling of Input

One place where correctness and robustness are important—and especially difficult—is in the processing of input data, whether that data is typed in by the user, read from a file, or received over a network. Files and networking will be covered in Chapter 11, which will make essential use of material that will be covered in the next section of this chapter. For now, let's look at an example of processing user input.

Examples in this textbook use my *TextIO* class for reading input from the user. This class has built-in error handling. For example, the function TextIO.getDouble() is guaranteed to return a legal value of type double. If the user types an illegal value, then *TextIO* will ask the user to re-enter their response; your program never sees the illegal value. However, this approach can be clumsy and unsatisfactory, especially when the user is entering complex data. In the following example, I'll do my own error-checking.

Sometimes, it's useful to be able to look ahead at what's coming up in the input without actually reading it. For example, a program might need to know whether the next item in the input is a number or a word. For this purpose, the *TextIO* class includes the function TextIO.peek(). This function returns a char which is the next character in the user's input, but it does not actually read that character. If the next thing in the input is an end-of-line, then TextIO.peek() returns the new-line character, '\n'.

Often, what we really need to know is the next non-blank character in the user's input. Before we can test this, we need to skip past any spaces (and tabs). Here is a function that does this. It uses TextIO.peek() to look ahead, and it reads characters until the next character in the input is either an end-of-line or some non-blank character. (The function TextIO.getAnyChar() reads and returns the next character in the user's input, even if that character is a space. By contrast, the more common TextIO.getChar() would skip any blanks and then read and return the next non-blank character. We can't use TextIO.getChar() here since the object is to skip the blanks without reading the next non-blank character.)

/**

Reads past any blanks and tabs in the input.

```
Postcondition:      The next character in the input is an
end-of-line or a non-blank character.
*/
static void skipBlanks() {
    char ch;
    ch = TextIO.peek();
    while (ch == ' ' || ch == '\t') {
                    // Next character is a space or tab; read it
                    // and look at the character that follows it.
            ch = TextIO.getAnyChar();
            ch = TextIO.peek();
    }
} // end skipBlanks()
```

(In fact, this operation is so common that it is built into TextIO. The method TextIO. skipBlanks() does essentially the same thing as the skipBlanks() method presented here.)

It would then convert the measurement into inches, feet, yards, and miles. But people commonly use combined measurements such as "3 feet 7 inches". Let's improve the program so that it allows inputs of this form.

More specifically, the user will input lines containing one or more measurements such as "1 foot" or "3 miles 20 yards 2 feet". The legal units of measure are inch, foot, yard, and mile. The program will also recognize plurals (inches, feet, yards, miles) and abbreviations (in, ft, yd, mi). Let's write a subroutine that will read one line of input of this form and compute the equivalent number of inches. The main program uses the number of inches to compute the equivalent number of feet, yards, and miles. If there is any error in the input, the subroutine will print an error message and return the value -1. The subroutine assumes that the input line is not empty. The main program tests for this before calling the subroutine and uses an empty line as a signal for ending the program.

Ignoring the possibility of illegal inputs, a pseudocode algorithm for the subroutine is

```
inches = 0    // This will be the total number of inches
while there is more input on the line:
    read the numerical measurement
    read the units of measure
```

add the measurement to inches

return inches

We can test whether there is more input on the line by checking whether the next non-blank character is the end-of-line character. But this test has a precondition: We have to make sure that the next character in the input is in fact either an end-of-line or is a non-blank. To ensure that, we need to skip over any blank characters. So, the algorithm becomes

inches = 0

skipBlanks()

while TextIO.peek() is not '\n':

read the numerical measurement

read the unit of measure

add the measurement to inches skipBlanks()

return inches

Note the call to skipBlanks() at the end of the while loop. The call to skipBlanks() ensures that the precondition for the test is again true. More generally, if the test in a while loop has a precondition, then you have to make sure that this precondition holds at the end of the while loop, before the computer jumps back to re-evaluate the test, as well as before the start of the loop.

What about error checking? Before reading the numerical measurement, we have to make sure that there is really a number there to read. Before reading the unit of measure, we have to test that there is something there to read. (The number might have been the last thing on the line. An input such as "3", without a unit of measure, is not acceptable.) Also, we have to check that the unit of measure is one of the valid units: inches, feet, yards, or miles. Here is an algorithm that includes error-checking:

inches = 0

skipBlanks()

while TextIO.peek() is not '\n':

if the next character is not a digit:

report an error and return -1

Let measurement = TextIO.getDouble();

skipBlanks()   // Precondition for the next test!!

if the next character is end-of-line:

report an error and return -1

Let units = TextIO.getWord()

if the units are inches:

add measurement to inches

else if the units are feet:

*add 12*measurement to inches*

else if the units are yards:

*add 36*measurement to inches*

else if the units are miles:

*add 12*5280*measurement to inches*

else

report an error and return -1

skipBlanks()

return inches

As you can see, error-testing adds significantly to the complexity of the algorithm. Yet this is still a fairly simple example, and it doesn't even handle all the possible errors. For example, if the user enters a numerical measurement such as 1e400 that is outside the legal range of values of type double, then the program will fall back on the default error-handling in *TextIO*. Something even more interesting happens if the measurement is "1e308 miles". The number 1e308 is legal, but the corresponding number of inches is outside the legal range of values for type double. As mentioned in the previous section, the computer will get the value Double. POSITIVE INFINITY when it does the computation. You might want to run the program and try this out.

Here is the subroutine written out in Java:

```
/**
Reads the user's input measurement from one line of input.
Precondition:       The input line is not empty.
Postcondition:      If the user's input is legal, the measurement
is converted to inches and returned.   If the
input is not legal, the value -1 is returned.
The end-of-line is NOT read by this routine.
*/
```

```
static double readMeasurement() {
    double inches;          // Total number of inches in user's measurement.
    double measurement;     // One measurement,
                            //      such as the 12 in "12 miles"
    String units;           // The units specified for the measurement,
                            //      such as "miles"
    char ch;// Used to peek at next character in the user's input.
    inches = 0;      // No inches have yet been read.
    skipBlanks();
    ch = TextIO.peek();
    /* As long as there is more input on the line, read a measurement and add the
    equivalent number of inches to the variable, inches.      If an error is detected
    during the loop, end the subroutine immediately by returning -1. */
    while (ch != '\n') {
            /* Get the next measurement and the units. Before reading anything, make
            sure that a legal value is there to read. */
    if ( ! Character.isDigit(ch) ) {
            System.out.println(
                    "Error:  Expected to find a number, but found " + ch);
            return -1;
    }
    measurement = TextIO.getDouble();
    skipBlanks();
    if (TextIO.peek() == '\n') {
            System.out.println(
                    "Error:  Missing unit of measure at end of line.");
            return -1;
    }
    units = TextIO.getWord();
    units = units.toLowerCase();
    /* Convert the measurement to inches and add it to the total. */
    if (units.equals("inch")
```

```
                || units.equals("inches") || units.equals("in")) { inches += measurement;
        }
        else if (units.equals("foot")
                || units.equals("feet") || units.equals("ft")) {
        inches += measurement * 12;
        }
        else if (units.equals("yard")
                || units.equals("yards") || units.equals("yd")) {
        inches += measurement * 36;
        }
        else if (units.equals("mile")
                || units.equals("miles") || units.equals("mi")) {
        inches += measurement * 12 * 5280;
        }
        else {
                System.out.println("Error: \"" + units
                        + "\" is not a legal unit of measure.");
                return -1;
        }
        /* Look ahead to see whether the next thing on the line is the end-of-line. */
        skipBlanks();
        ch = TextIO.peek();
        }       // end while
        return inches;
    } // end readMeasurement()
```

The source code for the complete program can be found in the file LengthConverter2.java.

4.3 EXCEPTIONS AND TRY..CATCH

Getting a program to work under ideal circumstances is usually a lot easier than making the program *robust*. A robust program can survive unusual or "exceptional" circumstances without crashing. One approach to writing robust programs is to anticipate the problems that might arise and to include tests in the program for each possible problem. For example, a program will crash if it tries to use an array element A[i], when i is not within the declared range of indices for the array A. A robust program must anticipate the possibility of a bad index and guard against it. One way to do this is to write the program in a way that ensures (as a postcondition of the code that precedes the array reference) that the index is in the legal range. Another way is to test whether the index value is legal before using it in the array. This could be done with an if statement:

```
if (i < 0 || i >= A.length) {
    ...        // Do something to handle the out-of-range index, i
}
else {
    ...        // Process the array element, A[i]
}
```

There are some problems with this approach. It is difficult and sometimes impossible to anticipate all the possible things that might go wrong. It's not always clear what to do when an error is detected. Furthermore, trying to anticipate all the possible problems can turn what would otherwise be a straightforward algorithm into a messy tangle of if statements.

4.3.1 Exceptions and Exception Classes

Java provides a neater, more structured alternative technique for dealing with errors that can occur while a program is running. The technique is referred to as *exception handling* . The word "exception" is meant to be more general than "error." It includes any circumstance that arises as the program is executed which is meant to be treated as an exception to the normal flow of control of the program. An exception might be an error, or it might just be a special case that you would rather not have clutter up your elegant algorithm.

When an exception occurs during the execution of a program, we say that the exception is *thrown* . When this happens, the normal flow of the program is thrown off-track, and the program is in danger of crashing. However, the crash can be avoided if the exception is *caught* and handled in some way. An exception can be thrown in one part of a program and caught in a different part. An exception that is not caught will generally cause the program to crash. (More exactly, the thread that throws the exception will crash. In a multithreaded program, it is possible for other threads to continue even after one crashes. In particular, GUI programs are multithreaded, and parts of the program might continue to function even while other parts are non-functional because of exceptions.)

By the way, since Java programs are executed by a Java interpreter, having a program crash simply means that it terminates abnormally and prematurely. It doesn't mean that the Java interpreter will crash. In effect, the interpreter catches any exceptions that are not caught by the program. The interpreter responds by terminating the program. In many other programming languages, a crashed program will sometimes crash the entire system and freeze the computer until it is restarted. With Java, such system crashes should be impossible—which means that when they happen, you have the satisfaction of blaming the system rather than your own program.

When an exception occurs, the thing that is actually "thrown" is an object. This object can carry information (in its instance variables) from the point where the exception occurs to the point where it is caught and handled. This information always includes the *subroutine call stack* , which is a list of the subroutines that were being executed when the exception was thrown. (Since one subroutine can call another, several subroutines can be active at the same time.) Typically, an exception object also includes an error message describing what happened to cause the exception, and it can contain other data as well. All exception objects must belong to a subclass of the standard class java.lang.Throwable. In general, each different type of exception is represented by its own subclass of *Throwable*, and these subclasses are arranged in a fairly complex class hierarchy that shows the relationship among various types of exception. *Throwable* has two direct subclasses, *Error* and *Exception*. These two subclasses in turn have many other predefined subclasses. In addition, a programmer can create new exception classes to represent new types of exception.

Most of the subclasses of the class *Error* represent serious errors within the Java virtual machine that should ordinarily cause program termination because there is no reasonable way to handle them. In general, you should not try to catch and handle such errors. An example is a *ClassFormatError*, which occurs when the Java virtual machine finds some kind of illegal data in a file that is supposed to contain a compiled Java class. If that class was being loaded as part of the program, then there is really no way for the program to proceed.

On the other hand, subclasses of the class *Exception* represent exceptions that are meant to be caught. In many cases, these are exceptions that might naturally be called "errors," but they are errors in the program or in input data that a programmer can anticipate and possibly respond to in some reasonable way. (However, you should avoid the temptation of saying, "Well, I'll just put a thing here to catch all the errors that might occur, so my program won't crash." If you don't have a reasonable way to respond to the error, it's best just to let the program crash, because trying to go on will probably only lead to worse things down the road—in the worst case, a program that gives an incorrect answer without giving you any indication that the answer might be wrong!)

The class *Exception* has its own subclass, *RuntimeException*. This class groups together many common exceptions, including all those that have been covered in previous sections. For example, *IllegalArgumentException* and *NullPointerException* are subclasses of *RuntimeException*. A *RuntimeException* generally indicates a bug in the program, which the programmer should fix. *RuntimeExceptions* and *Errors* share the property that a program can simply ignore the possibility that they might occur. ("Ignoring" here means that you are content to let your program crash if the exception occurs.) For example, a program does this every time it uses an array reference like A[i] without making arrangements to catch a possible *ArrayIndexOutOfBoundsException*. For all other exception classes besides *Error*, *RuntimeException*, and their subclasses, exception-handling is "mandatory" in a sense that I'll discuss below.

The following diagram is a class hierarchy showing the class Throwable and just a few of its subclasses. Classes that require mandatory exception-handling are shown in red:

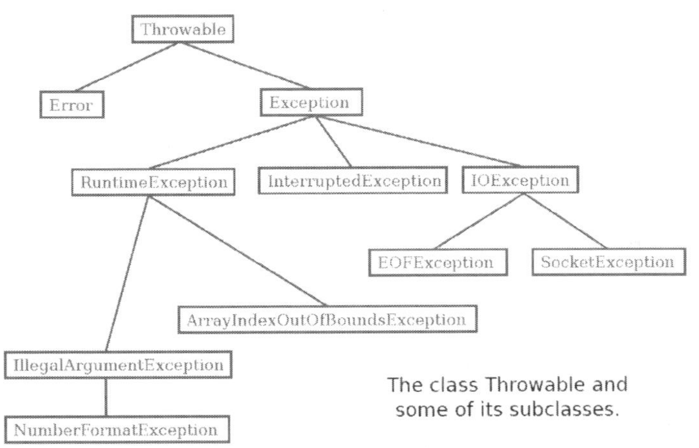

The class Throwable and some of its subclasses.

The class *Throwable* includes several instance methods that can be used with any exception object. If e is of type *Throwable* (or one of its subclasses), then e.getMessage() is a function that returns a *String* that describes the exception. The function e.toString(), which is used by the system whenever it needs a string representation of the object, returns a *String* that contains the name of the class to which the exception belongs as well as the same string that would be returned by e.getMessage(). And the method e.printStackTrace() writes a stack trace to standard output that tells which subroutines were active when the exception occurred. A stack trace can be very useful when you are trying to determine the cause of the problem. Information in the stack trace can tell you exactly where in the program the exception occurred. (Note that if an exception is not caught by the program, then the default response to the exception prints the stack trace to standard output.)

4.3.2 The try Statement

To catch exceptions in a Java program, you need a try statement. We have been using such statements, but the full syntax of the try statement is more complicated than what was presented there. The try statements that we have used so far had a syntax similar to the following example:

```
try {
    double determinant = M[0][0]*M[1][1] - M[0][1]*M[1][0];
    System.out.println("The determinant of M is " + determinant);
}
catch ( ArrayIndexOutOfBoundsException e ) {
    System.out.println("M is the wrong size to have a determinant.");
    e.printStackTrace();
}
```

Here, the computer tries to execute the block of statements following the word "try". If no exception occurs during the execution of this block, then the "catch" part of the statement is simply ignored. However, if an exception of type *ArrayIndexOutOfBoundsException* occurs, then the computer jumps immediately to the catch clause of the try statement. This block of statements is said to be an *exception handler* for *ArrayIndexOutOfBoundsException*. By handling the exception in this way, you prevent it from crashing the program. Before the body of the catch clause is executed, the object that represents the exception is assigned to the variable e, which is used in this example to print a stack trace.

However, the full syntax of the try statement has many options. It will take a while to go through them. For one thing, a try..catch statement can have more than one catch clause. This makes it possible to catch several different types of exception with one try statement. In the above example, in addition to the possible *ArrayIndexOutOfBoundsException*, there is a possible *NullPointerException* which will occur if the value of M is null. We can handle both possible exceptions by adding a second catch clause to the try statement:

```
try {
    double determinant = M[0][0]*M[1][1] - M[0][1]*M[1][0];
```

```
        System.out.println("The determinant of M is " + determinant);
    }
    catch ( ArrayIndexOutOfBoundsException e ) {
        System.out.println("M is the wrong size to have a determinant.");
    }
    catch ( NullPointerException e ) {
        System.out.print("Programming error!    M doesn't exist." + );
    }
```

Here, the computer tries to execute the statements in the try clause. If no error occurs, both of the catch clauses are skipped. If an *ArrayIndexOutOfBoundsException* occurs, the computer executes the body of the first catch clause and skips the second one. If a *NullPointerException* occurs, it jumps to the second catch clause and executes that.

Note that both *ArrayIndexOutOfBoundsException* and *NullPointerException* are subclasses of *RuntimeException*. It's possible to catch all *RuntimeExceptions* with a single catch clause. For example:

```
    try {
        double determinant = M[0][0]*M[1][1] - M[0][1]*M[1][0];
        System.out.println("The determinant of M is " + determinant);
    }
    catch ( RuntimeException err ) {
        System.out.println("Sorry, an error has occurred.");
        System.out.println("The error was: " + err);
    }
```

The catch clause in this try statement will catch any exception belonging to class *RuntimeEx- ception* or to any of its subclasses. This shows why exception classes are organized into a class hierarchy. It allows you the option of casting your net narrowly to catch only a specific type of exception. Or you can cast your net widely to catch a wide class of exceptions. Because of subclassing, when there are multiple catch clauses in a try statement, it is possible that a given exception might match several of those catch clauses. For example, an exception of type *NullPointerException* would match catch clauses for *NullPointerException*, *RuntimeException*, *Exception*, or *Throwable*. In this case, only the first catch clause that matches the exception is executed.

Of course, catching *RuntimeException* would catch many more types of exception than the two that we are interested in. It is possible to combine several specific exception types in a single catch clause. For example,

```
try {
    double determinant = M[0][0]*M[1][1] - M[0][1]*M[1][0];
    System.out.println("The determinant of M is " + determinant);
}
catch ( NullPointerException | ArrayIndexOutOfBoundsException err ) {
    System.out.println("Sorry, an error has occurred.");
    System.out.println("The error was: " + err);
}
```

Here, the two exception types are combined with a "|", the vertical line character that is also used in the boolean or operator. This example will catch errors of type *NullPointerException* or *ArrayIndexOutOfBoundsException*, and no other types.

The example I've been using here is not realistic, because you are not very likely to use exception-handling to guard against null pointers and bad array indices. This is a case where careful programming is better than exception handling: Just be sure that your program assigns a reasonable, non-null value to the array M. You would certainly resent it if the designers of Java forced you to set up a try..catch statement every time you wanted to use an array!

This is why handling of potential *RuntimeExceptions* is not mandatory. There are just too many things that might go wrong! (This also shows that exception-handling does not solve the problem of program robustness. It just gives you a tool that will in many cases let you approach the problem in a more organized way.)

I have still not completely specified the syntax of the try statement. The next variation is the possibility of a *finally clause* at the end of a try statement. With this addition, the syntax of the try statement can be described as:

```
try {
    (statements )
}
(optional-catch-clauses )
(optional-finally-clause )
```

Note that the catch clauses are also listed as optional. The try statement can include zero or more catch clauses and, optionally, a finally clause. The try statement must include one or the other. That is, a try statement can have either a finally clause, or one or more catch clauses, or both. The syntax for a catch clause is

```
catch ( (exception-class-names ) (variable-name ) ) {
    (statements )
}
```

where (*exception-class-names*) can be a single exception class or several classes separated by "|".

The syntax for a finally clause is

```
finally {
    (statements )
}
```

The semantics of the finally clause is that the block of statements in the finally clause is guaranteed to be executed as the last step in the execution of the try statement, whether or not any exception occurs and whether or not any exception that does occur is caught and handled. The finally clause is meant for doing essential cleanup that under no circumstances should be omitted. One example of this type of cleanup is closing a network connection. Although you don't yet know enough about networking to look at the actual programming in this case, we can consider some pseudocode:

```
try {
    open a network connection
    communicate over the connection
}
catch ( IOException e ) {
    report the error
}
finally {
    if the connection was successfully opened
            close the connection
}
```

The finally clause ensures that the network connection will definitely be closed, whether or not an error occurs during the communication. The pseudocode in this example follows a general pattern that can be used to robustly obtain a resource, use the resource, and then release the resource.

The pattern of obtaining a resource, then using the resource, and then releasing the resource is very common. Note that the resource can only be released if no error occurred while obtaining it. And, if it was successfully obtained, then it should be closed whether or not an error occurs while using it. This pattern is so common that it leads to one last option in the try statement syntax. With this option, you only need code to obtain the resource, and you don't need to worry about releasing it. That will happen automatically at the end of the try statement.

In order for this to work, the resource must be represented by an object that implements an interface named *AutoCloseable*, which defines a single method named close(), with no parameters. Standard Java classes that represent things like files and network connections already implement *AutoClosable*. So does the *Scanner* class. In that section, I showed how to use a Scanner to read from System.in. Although I didn't do it in that section, it's considered good form to close a Scanner after using it. Here is an example that uses the pattern in a try statement to make sure that the Scanner is closed automatically:

```
try( Scanner in = new Scanner(System.in) ) {
    // Use the Scanner to read from standard input
}
catch (Exception e) {
    // ... some error occurred while using the Scanner
}
```

The statement that allocates the *Scanner* goes in parentheses after the word "try". The statement must have the form of a variable declaration that includes an initialization of the variable. The variable is local to the try statement. (You can actually declare several variables in the parentheses, separated by semicolons.) In this example, we can be sure that in.close() will definitely be called by the system at the end of the try statement, as long as the Scanner was successfully initialized.

This is all getting quite complicated, and I won't continue the discussion here. The sample program TryStatementDemo.java demonstrates a try statement with all its options, and it includes a lot of comments to help you understand what can happen when you run the program.

4.3.3 Throwing Exceptions

There are times when it makes sense for a program to deliberately throw an exception. This is the case when the program discovers some sort of exceptional or error condition, but there is no reasonable way to handle the error at the point where the problem is discovered. The program can throw an exception in the hope that some other part of the program will catch and handle the exception. This can be done with a *throw statement*. In this section, we cover the throw statement more fully. The syntax of the throw statement is:

throw (exception-object) ;

The (*exception-object*) must be an object belonging to one of the subclasses of Throwable. Usually, it will in fact belong to one of the subclasses of Exception. In most cases, it will be a newly constructed object created with the new operator. For example:

throw new ArithmeticException("Division by zero");

The parameter in the constructor becomes the error message in the exception object; if e refers to the object, the error message can be retrieved by calling e.getMessage(). (You might find this example a bit odd, because you might expect the system itself to throw an *ArithmeticException* when an attempt is made to divide by zero. So why should a programmer bother to throw the exception? Recall that if the numbers that are being divided are of type int, then division by zero will indeed throw an *ArithmeticException*. However, no arithmetic operations with floating-point numbers will ever produce an exception. Instead, the special value Double. NaN is used to represent the result of an illegal operation. In some situations, you might prefer to throw an *ArithmeticException* when a real number is divided by zero.)

An exception can be thrown either by the system or by a throw statement. The exception is processed in exactly the same way in either case. Suppose that the exception is thrown inside a try statement. If that try statement has a catch clause that handles that type of exception, then the computer jumps to the catch clause and executes it. The exception has been *handled* . After handling the exception, the computer executes the finally clause of the try statement, if there is one. It then continues normally with the rest of the program, which follows the try statement. If the exception is not immediately caught and handled, the processing of the exception will continue.

When an exception is thrown during the execution of a subroutine and the exception is not handled in the same subroutine, then that subroutine is terminated (after the execution of any pending finally clauses). Then the routine that called that subroutine gets a chance to handle the exception. That is, if the subroutine was called inside a try statement that has an appropriate catch clause, then that catch clause will be executed and the program will continue on normally from there. Again, if the second routine does not handle the exception, then it also is terminated and the routine that called it (if any) gets the next shot at the exception. The exception will crash the program only if it passes up through the entire chain of subroutine calls without being handled. This is called "unwinding the call stack."

A subroutine that might generate an exception can announce this fact by adding a clause "throws (*exception-class-name*)" to the header of the routine. For example:

```
/**
Returns the larger of the two roots of the quadratic equation
A*x*x + B*x + C = 0, provided it has any roots.   If A == 0 or
if the discriminant, B*B - 4*A*C, is negative, then an exception
of type IllegalArgumentException is thrown.
*/
static public double root( double A, double B, double C )
                    throws IllegalArgumentException {
    if (A == 0) {
            throw new IllegalArgumentException("A can't be zero.");
    }
    else {
            double disc = B*B - 4*A*C;
            if (disc < 0)
                    throw new IllegalArgumentException("Discriminant < zero.");
            return  (-B + Math.sqrt(disc)) / (2*A);
    }
}
```

As discussed in the previous section, the computation in this subroutine has the precon- ditions that A != 0 and B*B-4*A*C >= 0. The subroutine throws an exception of type *Ille- galArgumentException* when either of these preconditions is violated. When an illegal condition is found in a subroutine, throwing an exception is often a reasonable response. If the program that called the subroutine knows some good way to handle the error, it can catch the exception. If not, the program will crash—and the programmer will know that the program needs to be fixed.

A throws clause in a subroutine heading can declare several different types of exception, separated by commas. For example:

```
void processArray(int[] A) throws NullPointerException,
                    ArrayIndexOutOfBoundsException { ...
```

4.3.4 Mandatory Exception Handling

In the preceding example, declaring that the subroutine root() can throw an *IllegalArgumentEx- ception* is just a courtesy to potential readers of this routine. This is because handling of *Il- legalArgumentExceptions* is not "mandatory." A routine can throw an *IllegalArgumentException* without announcing the possibility. And a program that calls that routine is free either to catch or to ignore the exception, just as a programmer can choose either to catch or to ignore an exception of type *NullPointerException*.

For those exception classes that require mandatory handling, the situation is different. If a subroutine can throw such an exception, that fact must be announced in a throws clause in the routine definition. Failing to do so is a syntax error that will be reported by the compiler. Exceptions that require mandatory handling are called *checked exceptions*. The compiler will check that such exceptions are handled by the program.

Suppose that some statement in the body of a subroutine can generate a checked exception, one that requires mandatory handling. The statement could be a throw statement, which throws the exception directly, or it could be a call to a subroutine that can throw the exception. In either case, the exception must be handled. This can be done in one of two ways: The first way is to place the statement in a try statement that has a catch clause that handles the exception; in this case, the exception is handled within the subroutine, so that no caller of the subroutine can ever see the exception. The second way is to declare that the subroutine can throw the exception. This is done by adding a "throws" clause to the subroutine heading, which alerts any callers to the possibility that the exception might be generated when the subroutine is executed. The caller will, in turn, be forced either to handle the exception in a try statement or to declare the exception in a throws clause in its own header.

Exception-handling is mandatory for any exception class that is not a subclass of either *Error* or *RuntimeException*. These checked exceptions generally represent conditions that are outside the control of the programmer. For example, they might represent bad input or an illegal action taken by the user. There is no way to avoid such errors, so a robust program has to be prepared to handle them. The design of Java makes it impossible for programmers to ignore the possibility of such errors.

Among the checked exceptions are several that can occur when using Java's input/ output routines. This means that you can't even use these routines unless you understand something about exception-handling. Chapter 11 deals with input/ output and uses checked exceptions extensively.

4.3.5 Programming with Exceptions

Exceptions can be used to help write robust programs. They provide an organized and structured approach to robustness. Without exceptions, a program can become cluttered with if statements that test for various possible error conditions. With exceptions, it becomes possible to write a clean implementation of an algorithm that will handle all the normal cases. The exceptional cases can be handled elsewhere, in a catch clause of a try statement.

When a program encounters an exceptional condition and has no way of handling it immediately, the program can throw an exception. In some cases, it makes sense to throw an exception belonging to one of Java's predefined classes, such as *IllegalArgumentException* or *IOException*. However, if there is no standard class that adequately represents the exceptional condition, the programmer can define a new exception class. The new class must extend the standard class *Throwable* or one of its subclasses. In general, if the programmer does not want to require mandatory exception handling, the new class will extend *RuntimeException* (or one of its subclasses). To create a new checked exception class, which does require mandatory handling, the programmer can extend one of the other subclasses of *Exception* or can extend *Exception* itself.

Here, for example, is a class that extends *Exception*, and therefore requires mandatory exception handling when it is used:

```
public class ParseError extends Exception {
    public ParseError(String message) {
            // Create a ParseError object containing
            // the given message as its error message. super(message);
    }
}
```

The class contains only a constructor that makes it possible to create a *ParseError* object containing a given error message. (The statement "super(message)" calls a constructor in the superclass, *Exception*.) Of course the class inherits the getMessage() and printStackTrace() routines from its superclass. If e refers to an object of type *ParseError*, then the function call e.getMessage() will retrieve the error message that was specified in the constructor. But the main point of the *ParseError* class is simply to exist. When an object of type *ParseError* is thrown, it indicates that a certain type of error has occurred. (*Parsing* , by the way, refers to figuring out the syntax of a string. A *ParseError* would indicate, presumably, that some string that is being processed by the program does not have the expected form.)

A throw statement can be used in a program to throw an error of type *ParseError*. The constructor for the *ParseError* object must specify an error message. For example:

```
throw new ParseError("Encountered an illegal negative number.");
```

or

```
throw new ParseError("The word '" + word
            + "' is not a valid file name.");
```

Since *ParseError* is defined as a subclass of *Exception*, it is a checked exception. If the throw statement does not occur in a try statement that catches the error, then the subroutine that contains the throw must declare that it can throw a *ParseError* by adding the clause "throws ParseError" to the subroutine heading. For example,

```
void getUserData() throws ParseError {
    . . .
}
```

This would not be required if *ParseError* were defined as a subclass of *RuntimeException* instead of *Exception*, since in that case *ParseErrors* would not be checked exceptions.

A routine that wants to handle *ParseErrors* can use a try statement with a catch clause that catches *ParseErrors*. For example:

```
try {
    getUserData();
    processUserData();
}
catch (ParseError pe) {
    . . .       // Handle the error
}
```

Note that since *ParseError* is a subclass of *Exception*, a catch clause of the form "catch (Exception e)" would also catch *ParseErrors*, along with any other object of type *Exception*.

Sometimes, it's useful to store extra data in an exception object. For example,

```
class ShipDestroyed extends RuntimeException {
    Ship ship;          // Which ship was destroyed.
    int where x, where y;       // Location where ship was destroyed.
    ShipDestroyed(String message, Ship s, int x, int y) {
                    // Constructor creates a ShipDestroyed object
```

```
            // carrying an error message plus the information
            // that the ship s was destroyed at location (x,y)
            // on the screen.
        super(message);
        ship = s;
        where x = x; where y = y;
    }
}
```

Here, a *ShipDestroyed* object contains an error message and some information about a ship that was destroyed. This could be used, for example, in a statement:

```
if ( userShip.isHit() )
    throw new ShipDestroyed("You've been hit!", userShip, xPos, yPos);
```

Note that the condition represented by a *ShipDestroyed* object might not even be considered an error. It could be just an expected interruption to the normal flow of a game. Exceptions can sometimes be used to handle such interruptions neatly.

The ability to throw exceptions is particularly useful in writing general-purpose methods and classes that are meant to be used in more than one program. In this case, the person writing the method or class often has no reasonable way of handling the error, since that person has no way of knowing exactly how the method or class will be used. In such circumstances, a novice programmer is often tempted to print an error message and forge ahead, but this is almost never satisfactory since it can lead to unpredictable results down the line. Printing an error message and terminating the program is almost as bad, since it gives the program no chance to handle the error.

The program that calls the method or uses the class needs to know that the error has occurred. In languages that do not support exceptions, the only alternative is to return some special value or to set the value of some global variable to indicate that an error has occurred. For example, the readMeasurement() function in Subsection 4.2.2 returns the value -1 if the user's input is illegal. However, this only does any good if the main program bothers to test the return value. It is very easy to be lazy about checking for special return values every time a subroutine is called. And in this case, using -1 as a signal that an error has occurred makes it impossible to allow negative measurements. Exceptions are a cleaner way for a subroutine to react when it encounters an error.

It is easy to modify the readMeasurement() function to use exceptions instead of a special return value to signal an error. My modified subroutine throws a *ParseError* when the user's input is illegal, where *ParseError* is the subclass of *Exception* that was defined above. (Arguably, it might be reasonable to avoid defining a new class by using the standard exception class *IllegalArgumentException* instead.) The changes from the original version are shown in italic:

```
/**
Reads the user's input measurement from one line of input.
Precondition:      The input line is not empty.
Postcondition:     If the user's input is legal, the measurement
is converted to inches and returned.
* @throws ParseError if the user's input is not legal.
*/
static double readMeasurement() throws ParseError {
    double inches;          // Total number of inches in user's measurement.
    double measurement;     // One measurement,
                            //      such as the 12 in "12 miles."
    String units;           // The units specified for the measurement,
                            //      such as "miles."
    char ch;// Used to peek at next character in the user's input.
    inches = 0;      // No inches have yet been read.
    skipBlanks();
    ch = TextIO.peek();
    /* As long as there is more input on the line, read a measurement and add the
    equivalent number of inches to the variable, inches.      If an error is detected
    during the loop, end the subroutine immediately by throwing a ParseError. */
    while (ch != '\n') {
        /* Get the next measurement and the units. Before reading anything, make
        sure that a legal value is there to read. */
    if ( ! Character.isDigit(ch) ) {
        throw new ParseError("Expected to find a number, but found " + ch);
    }
    measurement = TextIO.getDouble();
    skipBlanks();
    if (TextIO.peek() == '\n') {
```

```
            throw new ParseError("Missing unit of measure at end of line.");
    }
    units = TextIO.getWord();
    units = units.toLowerCase();
    /* Convert the measurement to inches and add it to the total. */
    if (units.equals("inch")
                    || units.equals("inches") || units.equals("in")) {
            inches += measurement;
    }
    else if (units.equals("foot")
                    || units.equals("feet") || units.equals("ft")) {
    inches += measurement * 12;
    }
    else if (units.equals("yard")
                    || units.equals("yards") || units.equals("yd")) {
    inches += measurement * 36;
    }
    else if (units.equals("mile")
                    || units.equals("miles") || units.equals("mi")) {
    inches += measurement * 12 * 5280;
    }
    else {
            throw new ParseError("\"" + units
                    + "\" is not a legal unit of measure.");
    }
    /* Look ahead to see whether the next thing on the line is the end-of-line. */
            skipBlanks();
            ch = TextIO.peek();
    }       // end while
    return inches;
} // end readMeasurement()
```

In the main program, this subroutine is called in a try statement of the form

```
try {
inches = readMeasurement();
}
catch (ParseError e) {
. . . // Handle the error.
}
```

The complete program can be found in the file LengthConverter3.java. From the user's point of view, this program has exactly the same behavior as the program LengthConverter2 from the previous section. Internally, however, the programs are significantly different, since LengthConverter3 uses exception handling.

4.4 ASSERTIONS AND ANNOTATIONS

In this short section, we look briefly at two features of Java that are not covered or used elsewhere in this textbook, assertions and annotations. They are included here for completeness, but they are mostly meant for more advanced programming. (Annotations, in particular, don't really belong in this chapter, but I could not find a better place to put my short introduction to the topic.)

4.4.1 Assertions

Recall that a precondition is a condition that must be true at a certain point in a program, for the execution of the program to continue correctly from that point. In the case where there is a chance that the precondition might not be satisfied—for example, if it depends on input from the user—then it's a good idea to insert an if statement to test it. But then the question arises, What should be done if the precondition does not hold? One option is to throw an exception. This will terminate the program, unless the exception is caught and handled elsewhere in the program.

In many cases, of course, instead of using an if statement to *test* whether a precondition holds, a programmer tries to write the program in a way that will *guarantee* that the precondition holds. In that case, the test should not be necessary, and the if statement can be avoided. The problem is that programmers are not perfect. In spite of the programmer's intention, the program might contain a bug that screws up the precondition. So maybe it's a good idea to check the precondition after all—at least during the debugging phase of program development.

Similarly, a postcondition is a condition that is true at a certain point in the program as a consequence of the code that has been executed before that point. Assuming that the code is correctly written, a postcondition is guaranteed to be true, but here again testing whether a desired postcondition is actually true is a way of checking for a bug that might have screwed up the postcondition. This is something that might be desirable during debugging.

And the same thing applies to loop invariants and class invariants. These are things that should be true at certain points in a program. If they are not true at those points, it means that the program contains a bug.

The programming languages C and C++ have always had a facility for adding what are called *assertions* to a program. These assertions take the form "assert((*condition*))", where (*condition*) is a boolean-valued expression. This condition expresses a precondition or postcondition that should hold at that point in the program. When the computer encounters an assertion during the execution of the program, it evaluates the condition. If the condition is false, the program is terminated. Otherwise, the program continues normally. This allows the programmer's belief that the condition is true to be tested; if it is not true, that indicates that the part of the program that preceded the assertion contained a bug. One nice thing about assertions in C and C++ is that they can be "turned off" at compile time. That is, if the program is compiled in one way, then the assertions are included in the compiled code. If the program is compiled in another way, the assertions are not included. During debugging, the first type of compilation is used, with assertions turned on. The release version of the program is compiled with assertions turned off. The release version will be more efficient, because the computer won't have to evaluate all the assertions.

Although early versions of Java did not have assertions, an assertion facility similar to the one in C/C++ has been available in Java since version 1.4. As with the C/C++ version, Java assertions can be turned on during debugging and turned off during normal execution. In Java, however, assertions are turned on and off at run time rather than at compile time. An assertion in the Java source code is always included in the compiled class file. When the program is run in the normal way, these assertions are ignored; since the condition in the assertion is not evaluated in this case, there is little or no performance penalty for having the assertions in the program. When the program is being debugged, it can be run with assertions enabled, as discussed below, and then the assertions can be a great help in locating and identifying bugs.

An assertion statement in Java takes one of the following two forms:

assert (condition) ;

or

assert (condition) : (error-message) ;

where (*condition*) is a boolean-valued expression and (*error-message*) is a string or an expression of type *String*. The word "assert" is a reserved word in Java, which cannot be used as an identifier. An assertion statement can be used anyplace in Java where a statement is legal.

If a program is run with assertions disabled, an assertion statement is equivalent to an empty statement and has no effect. When assertions are enabled and an assertion statement is encountered in the program, the (*condition*) in the assertion is evaluated. If the value is true, the program proceeds normally. If the value of the condition is false, then an exception of type java.lang.AssertionError is thrown, and the program will crash (unless the error is caught by a try statement). If the assert statement includes an (*error-message*), then the error message string becomes the message in the *AssertionError*.

So, the statement "assert (condition) : (error-message);" is similar to

```
if ( (condition ) == false )
        throw new AssertionError( (error-message ) );
```

except that the if statement is executed whenever the program is run, and the assert statement is executed only when the program is run with assertions enabled.

The question is, when to use assertions instead of exceptions? The general rule is to use assertions to test conditions that should definitely be true, if the program is written correctly. Assertions are useful for testing a program to see whether or not it is correct and for finding the errors in an incorrect program. After testing and debugging, when the program is used inc the normal way, the assertions in the program will be ignored. However, if a problem turns up later, the assertions are still there in the program to be used to help locate the error. If someone writes to you to say that your program doesn't work when he does such-and-such, you can run the program with assertions enabled, do such-and-such, and hope that the assertions in the program will help you locate the point in the program where it goes wrong.

Consider, for example, the root() method from Subsection 4.3.3 that calculates a root of a quadratic equation. If you believe that your program will always call this method with legal arguments, then it would make sense to write the method using assertions instead of exceptions:

```
/**
Returns the larger of the two roots of the quadratic equation
*    A*x*x + B*x + C = 0.
Precondition: A != 0 and B*B - 4*A*C >= 0.
*/
static public double root( double A, double B, double C )        {
```

```
        assert A != 0 : "Leading coefficient of quadratic equation cannot be zero.";
        double disc = B*B - 4*A*C;
        assert disc >= 0 : "Discriminant of quadratic equation cannot be negative.";
        return   (-B + Math.sqrt(disc)) / (2*A);
    }
```

The assertions are not checked when the program is run in the normal way. If you are correct in your belief that the method is never called with illegal arguments, then checking the conditions in the assertions would be unnecessary. If your belief is not correct, the problem should turn up during testing or debugging, when the program is run with the assertions enabled.

If the root() method is part of a software library that you expect other people to use, then the situation is less clear. Oracle's Java documentation advises that assertions should not be used for checking the contract of public methods: If the caller of a method violates the contract by passing illegal parameters, then an exception should be thrown. This will enforce the contract whether or not assertions are enabled. (However, while it's true that Java programmers *expect* the contract of a method to be enforced with exceptions, there are reasonable arguments for using assertions instead, in some cases.) One might say that assertions are for you, to help you in debugging your code, while exceptions are for people who use your code, to alert them that they are misusing it.

On the other hand, it never hurts to use an assertion to check a postcondition or an invariant. These are conditions that are definitely expected to be true in any bug-free program, so an assertion is the natural way to check the condition while debugging, without imposing an efficiency penalty when the program is executed normally. If the postcondition or invariant is false, there is a bug, and that is something that needs to be found during the testing and debugging phase of programming.

To have any effect, assertions must be enabled when the program is run. How to do this depends on what programming environment you are using. In the usual command line environment, assertions are enabled by adding the option -enableassertions to the java command that is used to run the program.

For example, if the class that contains the main program is *RootFinder*, then the command

```
java    -enableassertions    RootFinder
```

will run the program with assertions enabled. The -enableassertions option can be abbreviated to -ea, so the command can alternatively be written as

```
java    -ea    RootFinder
```

In fact, it is possible to enable assertions in just part of a program. An option of the form "-ea:(*class-name*)" enables only the assertions in the specified class. Note that there are no spaces between the -ea, the ":", and the name of the class. To enable all the assertions in a package and in its subpackages, you can use an option of the form "-ea:(*package-name*)...". To enable assertions in the "default package" (that is, classes that are not specified to belong to a package, like almost all the classes in this book), use "-ea:...". For example, to run a Java program named "MegaPaint" with assertions enabled for every class in the packages named "paintutils" and "drawing", you would use the command:

java -ea:paintutils... -ea:drawing... MegaPaint

If you are using the Eclipse integrated development environment, you can specify the -ea option by creating a *run configuration* . Right-click the name of the main program class in the Package Explorer pane, and select "Run As" from the pop-up menu and then "Run. . . " from the submenu. This will open a dialog box where you can manage run configurations. The name of the project and of the main class will be already be filled in. Click the "Arguments" tab, and enter -ea in the box under "VM Arguments". The contents of this box are added to the java command that is used to run the program. You can enter other options in this box, including more complicated enableassertions options such as -ea:paintutils When you click the "Run" button, the options will be applied. Furthermore, they will be applied whenever you run the program, unless you change the run configuration or add a new configuration. Note that it is possible to make two run configurations for the same class, one with assertions enabled and one with assertions disabled.

4.4.2 Annotations

The term "annotation" commonly refers to notes added to or written alongside a main text, to help you understand or appreciate the text. An annotation might be a note that you make to yourself in the margin of a book. It might be a footnote added to an old novel by an editor to explain the historical context of some event. The annotation is metadata or "metatext," that is, text written *about* the main text rather than as *part of* the main text itself.

Comments on a program are actually a kind of annotation. Since they are ignored by the compiler, they have no effect on the meaning of the program. They are there to explain that meaning to a human reader. It is possible, of course, for another computer program (not the compiler) to process comments. That's what is done in the case of Javadoc comments, which are processed by a program that uses them to create API documentation. But comments are only one type of metadata that might be added to programs.

In Java 5.0, a new feature called *annotations* was added to the Java language to make it easier to create new kinds of metadata for Java programs. This has made it possible for programmers to devise new ways of annotating programs, and to write programs that can read and use their annotations.

Java annotations have no direct effect on the program that they annotate. But they do have many potential uses. Some annotations are used to make the programmer's intent more explicit. Such annotations might be checked by a compiler to make sure that the code is consistent with the programmer's intention. For example, @ Override is a standard annotation that can be used to annotate method definitions. It means that the method is intended to override (that is replace) a method with the same signature that was defined in some superclass. A compiler can check that the superclass method actually exists; if not, it can inform the programmer. An annotation used in this way is an aid to writing correct programs, since the programmer can be warned about a potential error in advance, instead of having to hunt it down later as a bug. To annotate a method definition with the @Override annotation, simply place it in front of the definition. Syntactically, annotations are modifiers that are used in much the same way as built-in modifiers like "public" and "final." For example,

@Override public void WindowClosed(WindowEvent evt) { ... }

If there is no "WindowClosed(WindowEvent)" method in any superclass, then the compiler can issue an error. In fact, this example is based on a hard-to-find bug that I once introduced when trying to override a method named "windowClosed" with a method that I called "WindowClosed" (with an upper case "W"). If the @ Override annotation had existed at that time—and if I had used it—the compiler could have rejected my code and saved me the trouble of tracking down the bug.

(Annotations are a fairly advanced feature, and I might not have mentioned them in this textbook, except that some notations, such as @Override, can show up in code generated by Eclipse and other integrated development environments.)

There are two other standard annotations. One is @Deprecated, which can be used to mark deprecated classes, methods, and variables. (A deprecated item is one that is considered to be obsolete, but is still part of the Java language for backwards compatibility for old code.) Use of this annotation would allow a compiler to generate warnings when the deprecated item is used.

The other standard annotation is @SurpressWarnings, which can be used by a compiler to turn off warning messages that would ordinarily be generated when a class or method is compiled. @SuppressWarnings is an example of an annotation that has a parameter. The parameter tells what class of warnings are to be suppressed. For example, when a class or method is annotated with

@SuppressWarnings("deprecation")

then no warnings about the use of deprecated items will be emitted when the class or method is compiled. There are other types of warning that can be suppressed; unfortunately the list of warnings and their names is not standardized and will vary from one compiler to another.

Note, by the way, that the syntax for annotation parameters—especially for an annotation that accepts multiple parameters—is not the same as the syntax for method parameters. I won't cover the annotation syntax here.

Programmers can define new annotations for use in their code. Such annotations are ignored by standard compilers and programming tools, but it's possible to write programs that can understand the annotations and check for their presence in source code. It is even possible to create annotations that will be retained at run-time and become part of the running program. In that case, a program can check for annotations in the actual compiled code that is being executed, and take actions that depend on the presence of the annotation or the values of its parameters.

Annotations can help programmers to write correct programs. To use an example from the Java documentation, they can help with the creation of "boilerplate" code—that is, code that has a very standardized format and that can be generated mechanically. Often, boilerplate code is generated based on other code. Doing that by hand is a tedious and error-prone process. A simple example might be code to save certain aspects of a program's state to a file and to restore it later. The code for reading and writing the values of all the relevant state variables is highly repetitious. Instead of writing that code by hand, a programmer could use an annotation to mark the variables that are part of the state that is to be saved. A program could then be used to check for the annotations and generate the save-and-restore code. In fact, it would even be possible to do without that code altogether, if the program checks for the presence of the annotation at run time to decide which variables to save and restore.

4.5 ANALYSIS OF ALGORITHMS

This chapter has concentrated mostly on correctness of programs. In practice, another issue is also important: *efficiency* . When analyzing a program in terms of efficiency, we want to look at questions such as, "How long does it take for the program to run?" and "Is there another approach that will get the answer more quickly?" Efficiency will always be less important than correctness; if you don't care whether a program works correctly, you can make it run very quickly indeed, but no one will think it's much of an achievement! On the other hand, a program that gives a correct answer after ten thousand years isn't very useful either, so efficiency is often an important issue.

The term "efficiency" can refer to efficient use of almost any resource, including time, computer memory, disk space, or network bandwidth. In this section, however, we will deal exclusively with time efficiency, and the major question that we want to ask about a program is, how long does it take to perform its task?

It really makes little sense to classify an individual program as being "efficient" or "inefficient." It makes more sense to compare two (correct) programs that perform the same task and ask which one of the two is "more efficient," that is, which one performs the task more quickly. However, even here there are difficulties. The running time of a program is not well-defined. The run time can be different depending on the number and speed of the processors in the computer on which it is run and, in the case of Java, on the design of the Java Virtual Machine which is used to interpret the program. It can depend on details of the compiler which is used to translate the program from high-level language to machine language. Furthermore, the run time of a program depends on the size of the problem which the program has to solve. It takes a sorting program longer to sort 10000 items than it takes it to sort 100 items. When the run times of two programs are compared, it often happens that Program A solves small problems faster than Program B, while Program B solves large problems faster than Program A, so that it is simply not the case that one program is faster than the other in all cases.

In spite of these difficulties, there is a field of computer science dedicated to analyzing the efficiency of programs. The field is known as *Analysis of Algorithms.* The focus is on algorithms, rather than on programs as such, to avoid having to deal with multiple implementations of the same algorithm written in different languages, compiled with different compilers, and running on different computers. Analysis of Algorithms is a mathematical field that abstracts away from these down-and-dirty details. Still, even though it is a theoretical field, every working programmer should be aware of some of its techniques and results. This section is a very brief introduction to some of those techniques and results. Because this is not a mathematics book, the treatment will be rather informal.

One of the main techniques of analysis of algorithms is *asymptotic analysis.* The term "asymptotic" here means basically "the tendency in the long run, as the size of the input is increased." An asymptotic analysis of an algorithm's run time looks at the question of how the run time depends on the size of the problem. The analysis is asymptotic because it only considers what happens to the run time as the size of the problem increases without limit; it is not concerned with what happens for problems of small size or, in fact, for problems of any fixed finite size. Only what happens in the long run, as the problem size increases without limit, is important. Showing that Algorithm A is asymptotically faster than Algorithm B doesn't necessarily mean that Algorithm A will run faster than Algorithm B for problems of size 10 or size 1000 or even size 1000000—it only means that if you keep increasing the problem size, you will eventually come to a point where Algorithm A is faster than Algorithm B. An asymptotic analysis is only a first approximation, but in practice it often gives important and useful information.

Central to asymptotic analysis is *Big-Oh notation* . Using this notation, we might say, for example, that an algorithm has a running time that is $O(n^2)$ or $O(n)$ or $O(\log(n))$. These notations are read "Big-Oh of n squared," "Big-Oh of n," and "Big-Oh of log n" (where log is a logarithm function). More generally, we can refer to $O(f(n))$ ("Big-Oh of f of n"), where f(n) is some function that assigns a positive real number to every positive integer n. The "n" in this notation refers to the size of the problem. Before you can even begin an asymptotic analysis, you need some way to measure problem size. Usually, this is not a big issue. For example, if the problem is to sort a list of items, then the problem size can be taken to be the number of items in the list. When the input to an algorithm is an integer, as in the case of an algorithm that checks whether a given positive integer is prime, the usual measure of the size of a problem is the number of bits in the input integer rather than the integer itself. More generally, the number of bits in the input to a problem is often a good measure of the size of the problem.

To say that the running time of an algorithm is $O(f(n))$ means that for large values of the problem size, n, the running time of the algorithm is no bigger than some constant times f(n). (More rigorously, there is a number C and a positive integer M such that whenever n is greater than M, the run time is less than or equal to $C*f(n)$.) The constant takes into account details such as the speed of the computer on which the algorithm is run; if you use a slower computer, you might have to use a bigger constant in the formula, but changing the constant won't change the basic fact that the run time is $O(f(n))$. The constant also makes it unnecessary to say whether we are measuring time in seconds, years, CPU cycles, or any other unit of measure; a change from one unit of measure to another is just multiplication by a constant. Note also that $O(f(n))$ doesn't depend at all on what happens for small problem sizes, only on what happens in the long run as the problem size increases without limit.

To look at a simple example, consider the problem of adding up all the numbers in an array. The problem size, n, is the length of the array. Using A as the name of the array, the algorithm can be expressed in Java as:

```
total = 0;
for (int i = 0; i < n; i++)
    total = total + A[i];
```

This algorithm performs the same operation, total = total + A[i], n times. The total time spent on this operation is a*n, where a is the time it takes to perform the operation once. Now, this is not the only thing that is done in the algorithm. The value of i is incremented and is compared to n each time through the loop. This adds an additional time of b*n to the run time, for some constant b. Furthermore, i and total both have to be initialized to zero; this adds some constant amount c to the running time. The exact running time would then be (a+b)*n+c, where the constants a, b, and c depend on factors such as how the code is compiled and what computer it is run on. Using the fact that c is less than or equal to c*n for any positive integer n, we can say that the run time is less than or equal to (a+b+c)*n. That is, the run time is less than or equal to a constant times n. By definition, this means that the run time for this algorithm is O(n).

If this explanation is too mathematical for you, we can just note that for large values of n, the c in the formula (a+b)*n+c is insignificant compared to the other term, (a+b)*n. We say that c is a "lower order term." When doing asymptotic analysis, lower order terms can be discarded. A rough, but correct, asymptotic analysis of the algorithm would go something like this: Each iteration of the for loop takes a certain constant amount of time. There are n iterations of the loop, so the total run time is a constant times n, plus lower order terms (to account for the initialization). Disregarding lower order terms, we see that the run time is O(n).

Note that to say that an algorithm has run time O(f(n)) is to say that its run time is no bigger than some constant times f(n) (for large values of n). O(f(n)) puts an upper limit on the run time. However, the run time could be smaller, even much smaller. For example, if the run time is O(n), it would also be correct to say that the run time is $O(n^2)$ or even $O(n^{10})$. If the run time is less than a constant times n, then it is certainly less than the same constant times n^2 or n^{10}.

Of course, sometimes it's useful to have a lower limit on the run time. That is, we want to be able to say that the run time is greater than or equal to some constant times f(n) (for large values of n). The notation for this is Ω(f(n)), read "Omega of f of n" or "Big Omega of f of n." "Omega" is the name of a letter in the Greek alphabet, and Ω is the upper case version of that letter. (To be technical, saying that the run time of an algorithm is Ω(f(n)) means that there is a positive number C and a positive integer M such that whenever n is greater than M, the run time is greater than or equal to C*f(n).) O(f(n)) tells you something about the maximum amount of time that you might have to wait for an algorithm to finish; Ω(f(n)) tells you something about the minimum time.

The algorithm for adding up the numbers in an array has a run time that is Ω(n) as well as O(n). When an algorithm has a run time that is both Ω(f(n)) and O(f(n)), its run time is said to be Θ(f(n)), read "Theta of f of n" or "Big Theta of f of n." (Theta is another letter from the Greek alphabet.) To say that the run time of an algorithm is $\Theta(f(n))$ means that for large values of n, the run time is between a*f(n) and b*f(n), where a and b are constants (with b greater than a, and both greater than 0).

Let's look at another example. Consider the algorithm that can be expressed in Java in the following method:

```
/**
 * Sorts the n array elements A[0], A[1], ..., A[n-1] into increasing order.
 */
public static void simpleBubbleSort( int[] A, int n ) {
    for (int i = 0; i < n; i++) {
                // Do n passes through the array...
        for (int j = 0; j < n-1; j++) {
                if ( A[j] > A[j+1] ) {
                            // A[j] and A[j+1] are out of order, so swap them
                    int temp = A[j];
                    A[j] = A[j+1];
                    A[j+1] = temp;
                }
        }
    }
}
```

Here, the parameter n represents the problem size. The outer for loop in the method is executed n times. Each time the outer for loop is executed, the inner for loop is executed n-1 times, so the if statement is executed n*(n-1) times. This is n^2-n, but since lower order terms are not significant in an asymptotic analysis, it's good enough to say that the if statement is executed about n^2 times. In particular, the test A[j] > A[j+1] is executed about n^2 times, and this fact by itself is enough to say that the run time of the algorithm is $\Omega(n^2)$, that is, the run time is at least some constant times n^2. Furthermore, if we look at other operations—the assignment statements, incrementing i and j, etc.—none of them are executed more than n^2 times, so the run time is also $O(n^2)$, that is, the run time is no more than some constant times n^2. Since it is both $\Omega(n^2)$ and $O(n^2)$, the run time of the simpleBubbleSort algorithm is $\Theta(n^2)$.

You should be aware that some people use the notation $O(f(n))$ as if it meant $\Theta(f(n))$. That is, when they say that the run time of an algorithm is $O(f(n))$, they mean to say that the run time is about equal to a constant times f(n). For that, they should use Θ(f(n)). Properly speaking, O(f(n)) means that the run time is less than a constant times f(n), possibly much less.

So far, my analysis has ignored an important detail. We have looked at how run time depends on the problem size, but in fact the run time usually depends not just on the size of the problem but on the specific data that has to be processed. For example, the run time of a sorting algorithm can depend on the initial order of the items that are to be sorted, and not just on the number of items.

To account for this dependency, we can consider either the *worst case* run time analysis or the *average case* run time analysis of an algorithm. For a worst case run time analysis, we consider all possible problems of size n and look at the longest possible run time for all such problems. For an average case analysis, we consider all possible problems of size n and look at the average of the run times for all such problems. Usually, the average case analysis assumes that all problems of size n are equally likely to be encountered, although this is not always realistic—or even possible in the case where there is an infinite number of different problems of a given size.

In many cases, the average and the worst case run times are the same to within a constant multiple. This means that as far as asymptotic analysis is concerned, they are the same. That is, if the average case run time is O(f(n)) or Θ(f(n)), then so is the worst case. However, later in the book, we will encounter a few cases where the average and worst case asymptotic analyses differ.

It is also possible to talk about *best case* run time analysis, which looks at the shortest possible run time for all inputs of a given size. However, a best case analysis is only occasionally useful.

So, what do you really have to know about analysis of algorithms to read the rest of this book? We will not do any rigorous mathematical analysis, but you should be able to follow informal discussion of simple cases such as the examples that we have looked at in this section. Most important, though, you should have a feeling for exactly what it means to say that the running time of an algorithm is O(f(n)) or Θ(f(n)) for some common functions f(n). The main point is that these notations do not tell you anything about the actual numerical value of the running time of the algorithm for any particular case. They do not tell you anything at all about the running time for small values of n. What they do tell you is something about the *rate of growth* of the running time as the size of the problem increases.

Suppose you compare two algorithms that solve the same problem. The run time of one algorithm is $\Theta(n^2)$, while the run time of the second algorithm is $\Theta(n^3)$. What does this tell you? If you want to know which algorithm will be faster for some particular problem of size, say, 100, nothing is certain. As far as you can tell just from the asymptotic analysis, either algorithm could be faster for that particular case—or in any particular case. But what you can say for sure is that if you look at larger and larger problems, you will come to a point where the $\Theta(n^2)$ algorithm is faster than the $\Theta(n^3)$ algorithm. Furthermore, as you continue to increase the problem size, the relative advantage of the $\Theta(n^2)$ algorithm will continue to grow. There will be values of n for which the $\Theta(n^2)$ algorithm is a thousand times faster, a million times faster, a billion times faster, and so on. This is because for any positive constants a and b, the function $a*n^3$ grows faster than the function $b*n^2$ as n gets larger. (Mathematically, the limit of the ratio of $a*n^3$ to $b*n^2$ is infinite as n approaches infinity.)

This means that for "large" problems, a $\Theta(n^2)$ algorithm will definitely be faster than a $\Theta(n^3)$ algorithm. You just don't know—based on the asymptotic analysis alone—exactly how large "large" has to be. In practice, in fact, it is likely that the $\Theta(n^2)$ algorithm will be faster even for fairly small values of n, and absent other information you would generally prefer a $\Theta(n^2)$ algorithm to a $\Theta(n^3)$ algorithm.

So, to understand and apply asymptotic analysis, it is essential to have some idea of the rates of growth of some common functions. For the power functions n, n^2, n^3, n^4, . . . , the larger the exponent, the greater the rate of growth of the function. Exponential functions such as 2^n and 10^n, where the n is in the exponent, have a growth rate that is faster than that of any power function. In fact, exponential functions grow so quickly that an algorithm whose run time grows exponentially is almost certainly impractical even for relatively modest values of n, because the running time is just too long. Another function that often turns up in asymptotic analysis is the logarithm function, log(n). There are actually many different logarithm functions, but the one that is usually used in computer science is the so-called logarithm to the base two, which is defined by the fact that $\log(2^x) = x$ for any number x. (Usually, this function is written $\log_2(n)$, but I will leave out the subscript 2, since I will only use the base-two logarithm in this book.) The logarithm function grows very slowly. The growth rate of log(n) is much smaller than the growth rate of n. The growth rate of n*log(n) is a little larger than the growth rate of n, but much smaller than the growth rate of n^2. The following table should help you understand the differences among the rates of growth of various functions:

n	log(n)	n*log(n)	n2	n / log(n)
16	4	64	256	4.0
64	6	384	4096	10.7
256	8	2048	65536	32.0
1024	10	10240	1048576	102.4
1000000	20	19931568	1000000000000	50173.1
1000000000	30	29897352854	1000000000000000000	33447777.3

The reason that log(n) shows up so often is because of its association with multiplying and dividing by two: Suppose you start with the number n and divide it by 2, then divide by 2 again, and so on, until you get a number that is less than or equal to 1. Then the number of divisions is equal (to the nearest integer) to log(n).

For instance, examine the binary search technique presented in Subsection 3.5.1. This approach locates an item within a sorted array. The issue size, n, may be defined as the length of the array. The binary search algorithm reduces the number of objects under consideration by half at each stage, terminating when this number is less than or equal to one (or earlier). The maximum number of steps for an array of length n is log(n). The worst-case runtime for binary search is $\Theta(\log(n))$. The average case runtime is $\Theta(\log(n))$. In contrast, the linear search technique, discussed in Subsection 3.5.1, has a runtime of $\Theta(n)$. The Θ notation provides a mathematical method to articulate and comprehend why binary search is significantly more efficient than linear search.

In binary search, each iteration of the method reduces the problem size by half. It frequently occurs that a certain action within an algorithm (not exclusively a singular step) reduces the issue size by half. In such instances, the logarithmic function is likely to appear in the asymptotic analysis of the algorithm's runtime.

The analysis of algorithms constitutes a vast and intriguing domain. We will utilize simply a select number of fundamental concepts from this domain, nevertheless even these can significantly aid in comprehending the distinctions between algorithms.

5 Chapter LINKED DATA STRUCTURES AND RECURSION

This chapter examines two sophisticated programming techniques: recursion and linked data structures, along with their applications. Both strategies pertain to the ostensibly paradoxical concept of defining an entity in terms of itself. This proves to be an exceptionally potent concept.

A subroutine is classified as recursive if it invokes itself, either directly or indirectly. This indicates that the subroutine is utilized within its own definition. Recursion frequently facilitates the resolution of intricate problems by deconstructing them into more manageable instances of the same nature.

An instance variable of one object can store a reference to another object. The objects are then described as "linked." Intricate data structures can be constructed by interconnecting things. A particularly intriguing scenario arises when an object possesses a reference to another object of the same class. In this instance, the class is utilized within its own definition. Numerous significant data structure types are constructed utilizing such classes.

5.1 RECURSION

At one time or another, you've probably been told that you can't define something in terms of itself. Nevertheless, if it's done right, defining something at least partially in terms of itself can be a very powerful technique. A *recursive* definition is one that uses the concept or thing that is being defined as part of the definition. For example: An "ancestor" is either a parent or an *ancestor* of a parent. A "sentence" can be, among other things, two *sentences* joined by a conjunction such as "and." A "directory" is a part of a disk drive that can hold files and *directories*. In mathematics, a "set" is a collection of elements, which can themselves be *sets*. A "statement" in Java can be a while statement, which is made up of the word "while", a boolean-valued condition, and a *statement*.

Recursive definitions can describe very complex situations with just a few words. A definition of the term "ancestor" without using recursion might go something like "a parent, or a grandparent, or a great-grandparent, or a great-great-grandparent, and so on." But saying "and so on" is not very rigorous. (I've often thought that recursion is really just a rigorous way of saying "and so on.") You run into the same problem if you try to define a "directory" as "a file that is a list of files, where some of the files can be lists of files, where some of those files can be lists of files, and so on." Trying to describe what a Java statement can look like, without using recursion in the definition, would be difficult and probably pretty comical.

Recursion can be used as a programming technique. A *recursive subroutine* (or *recursive method*) is one that calls itself, either directly or indirectly. To say that a subroutine calls itself directly means that its definition contains a subroutine call statement that calls the subroutine that is being defined. To say that a subroutine calls itself indirectly means that it calls a second subroutine which in turn calls the first subroutine (either directly or indirectly). A recursive subroutine can define a complex task in just a few lines of code. In the rest of this section, we'll look at a variety of examples, and we'll see other examples in the rest of the book.

5.1.1 Recursive Binary Search

Let's start with an example that you've seen before: the binary search algorithm from Subsection 3.5.1. Binary search is used to find a specified value in a sorted list of items (or, if it does not occur in the list, to determine that fact). The idea is to test the element in the middle of the list. If that element is equal to the specified value, you are done. If the specified value is less than the middle element of the list, then you should search for the value in the first half of the list. Otherwise, you should search for the value in the second half of the list. The method used to search for the value in the first or second half of the list is binary search. That is, you look at the middle element in the half of the list that is still under consideration, and either you've found the value you are looking for, or you have to apply binary search to one half of the remaining elements. And so on! This is a recursive description, and we can write a recursive subroutine to implement it.

Before we can do that, though, there are two considerations that we need to take into account. Each of these illustrates an important general fact about recursive subroutines. First of all, the binary search algorithm begins by looking at the "middle element of the list." But what if the list is empty? If there are no elements in the list, then it is impossible to look at the middle element. In the terminology of Subsection 4.2.2, having a non-empty list is a "precondition" for looking at the middle element, and this is a clue that we have to modify the algorithm to take this precondition into account. What should we do if we find ourselves searching for a specified value in an empty list? The answer is easy: If the list is empty, we can be sure that the value does not occur in the list, so we can give the answer without any further work. An empty list is a *base case* for the binary search algorithm. A base case for a recursive algorithm is a case that is handled directly, rather than by applying the algorithm recursively. The binary search algorithm actually has another type of base case: If we find the element we are looking for in the middle of the list, we are done. There is no need for further recursion.

The second consideration has to do with the parameters to the subroutine. The problem is phrased in terms of searching for a value in a list. In the original, non-recursive binary search subroutine, the list was given as an array. However, in the recursive approach, we have to be able to apply the subroutine recursively to just a part of the original list. Where the original subroutine was designed to search an entire array, the recursive subroutine must be able to search part of an array. The parameters to the subroutine must tell it what part of the array to search. This illustrates a general fact that in order to solve a problem recursively, it is often necessary to generalize the problem slightly.

Here is a recursive binary search algorithm that searches for a given value in part of an array of integers:

```
/**
Search in the array A in positions numbered loIndex to hiIndex,
inclusive, for the specified value.     If the value is found, return
the index in the array where it occurs.         If the value is not found,


return -1.    Precondition:    The array must be sorted into increasing
order.
*/
static int binarySearch(int[] A, int loIndex, int hiIndex, int value) {
    if (loIndex > hiIndex) {
                // The starting position comes after the final index,
                // so there are actually no elements in the specified
                // range.         The value does not occur in this empty list!
        return -1;
        }
        else {
                // Look at the middle position in the list.   If the
                // value occurs at that position, return that position.
                // Otherwise, search recursively in either the first
                // half or the second half of the list.
        int middle = (loIndex + hiIndex) / 2;
        if (value == A[middle])
```

```
            return middle;
        else if (value < A[middle])
            return binarySearch(A, loIndex, middle - 1, value);
        else    // value must be > A[middle]
            return binarySearch(A, middle + 1, hiIndex, value);
    }
} // end binarySearch()
```

In this routine, the parameters loIndex and hiIndex specify the part of the array that is to be searched. To search an entire array, it is only necessary to call binarySearch(A, 0, A.length - 1, value). In the two base cases—when there are no elements in the specified range of indices and when the value is found in the middle of the range—the subroutine can return an answer immediately, without using recursion. In the other cases, it uses a recursive call to compute the answer and returns that answer.

Most people find it difficult at first to convince themselves that recursion actually works. The key is to note two things that must be true for recursion to work properly: There must be one or more base cases, which can be handled without using recursion. And when recursion is applied during the solution of a problem, it must be applied to a problem that is in some sense smaller—that is, closer to the base cases—than the original problem. The idea is that if you can solve small problems and if you can reduce big problems to smaller problems, then you can solve problems of any size. Ultimately, of course, the big problems have to be reduced, possibly in many, many steps, to the very smallest problems (the base cases). Doing so might involve an immense amount of detailed bookkeeping. But the computer does that bookkeeping, not you! As a programmer, you lay out the big picture: the base cases and the reduction of big problems to smaller problems. The computer takes care of the details involved in reducing a big problem, in many steps, all the way down to base cases. Trying to think through this reduction in detail is likely to drive you crazy, and will probably make you think that recursion is hard. Whereas in fact, recursion is an elegant and powerful method that is often the simplest approach to solving a complex problem.

A common error in writing recursive subroutines is to violate one of the two rules: There must be one or more base cases, and when the subroutine is applied recursively, it must be applied to a problem that is smaller than the original problem. If these rules are violated, the result can be an *infinite recursion* , where the subroutine keeps calling itself over and over, without ever reaching a base case. Infinite recursion is similar to an infinite loop. However, since each recursive call to the subroutine uses up some of the computer's memory, a program that is stuck in an infinite recursion will run out of memory and crash before long. In Java, the program will crash with an exception of type StackOverflowError.

5.1.2 Towers of Hanoi

We have been studying an algorithm, binary search, that can easily be implemented with a while loop, instead of with recursion. Next, we turn to a problem that is easy to solve with recursion but difficult to solve without it. This is a standard example known as "The Towers of Hanoi." The problem involves a stack of various-sized disks, piled up on a base in order of decreasing size. The object is to move the stack from one base to another, subject to two rules: Only one disk can be moved at a time, and no disk can ever be placed on top of a smaller disk. There is a third base that can be used as a "spare." The starting situation for a stack of ten disks is shown in the top half of the following picture. The situation after a number of moves have been made is shown in the bottom half of the picture. (These illustrations are from a sample program from Chapter 12, TowersOfHanoiGUI.java, which displays an animation of the step-by-step solution of the problem; however, that program uses some techniques that you haven't learned yet.)

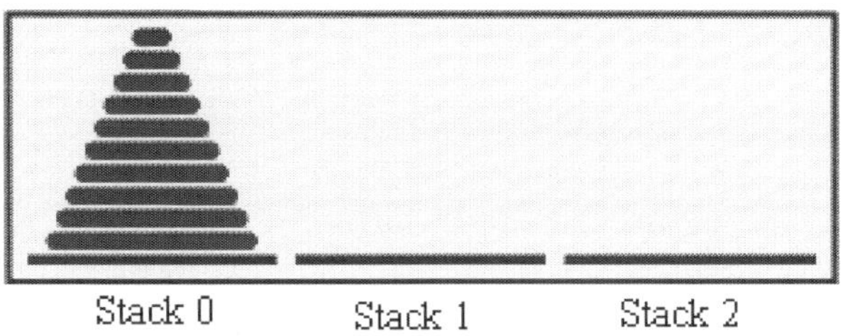

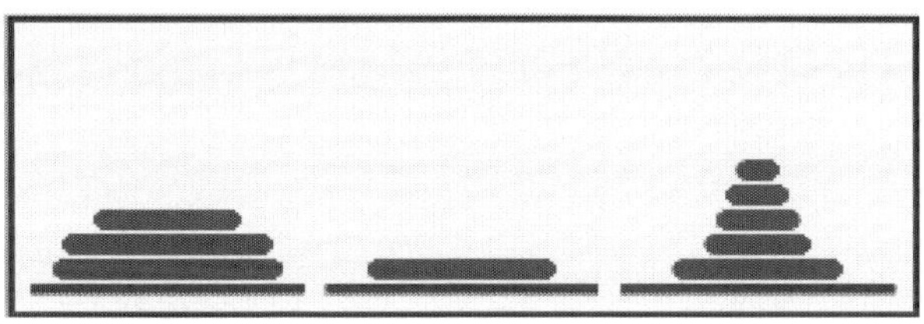

The stacks after a number of moves.

The problem is to move ten disks from Stack 0 to Stack 1, subject to the rules given above. Stack 2 can be used as a spare location. Can we reduce this to smaller problems of the same type, possibly generalizing the problem a bit to make this possible? It seems natural to consider the size of the problem to be the number of disks to be moved. If there are N disks in Stack 0, we know that we will eventually have to move the bottom disk from Stack 0 to Stack 1. But before we can do that, according to the rules, the first N-1 disks must be on Stack 2. Once we've moved the N-th disk to Stack 1, we must move the other N-1 disks from Stack 2 to Stack 1 to complete the solution. But moving N-1 disks is the same type of problem as moving N disks, except that it's a smaller version of the problem. This is exactly what we need to do recursion! The problem has to be generalized a bit, because the smaller problems involve moving disks from Stack 0 to Stack 2 or from Stack 2 to Stack 1, instead of from Stack 0 to Stack 1. In the recursive subroutine that solves the problem, the stacks that serve as the source and destination of the disks have to be specified. It's also convenient to specify the stack that is to be used as a spare, even though we could figure that out from the other two parameters. The base case is when there is only one disk to be moved. The solution in this case is trivial: Just move the disk in one step. Here is a version of the subroutine that will print out step-by-step instructions for solving the problem:

```
/**
Solve the problem of moving the number of disks specified
by the first parameter from the stack specified by the
second parameter to the stack specified by the third
parameter.  The stack specified by the fourth parameter
is available for use as a spare.          Stacks are specified by
number: 0, 1, or 2.
*/
static void towersOfHanoi(int disks, int from, int to, int spare) {
    if (disks == 1) {
                    // There is only one disk to be moved.      Just move it.
            System.out.printf("Move disk 1 from stack %d to stack %d%n",
                    from, to);
    }
    else {
                    // Move all but one disk to the spare stack, then
                    // move the bottom disk, then put all the other
                    // disks on top of it.
            towersOfHanoi(disks-1, from, spare, to);
            System.out.printf("Move disk %d from stack %d to stack %d%n",
                            disks, from, to);
            towersOfHanoi(disks-1, spare, to, from);
    }
}
```

This subroutine just expresses the natural recursive solution. The recursion works because each recursive call involves a smaller number of disks, and the problem is trivial to solve in the base case, when there is only one disk. To solve the "top level" problem of moving N disks from Stack 0 to Stack 1, the subroutine should be called with the command TowersOfHanoi(N,0,1,2). The subroutine is used in the sample program TowersOfHanoi.java. Here, for example, is the output from the program when it is run with the number of disks set equal to 4:

```
Move disk 1 from stack 0 to stack 2
Move disk 2 from stack 0 to stack 1
Move disk 1 from stack 2 to stack 1
Move disk 3 from stack 0 to stack 2
Move disk 1 from stack 1 to stack 0
Move disk 2 from stack 1 to stack 2
Move disk 1 from stack 0 to stack 2
Move disk 4 from stack 0 to stack 1
Move disk 1 from stack 2 to stack 1
Move disk 2 from stack 2 to stack 0
Move disk 1 from stack 1 to stack 0
Move disk 3 from stack 2 to stack 1
Move disk 1 from stack 0 to stack 2
Move disk 2 from stack 0 to stack 1
Move disk 1 from stack 2 to stack 1
```

The output of this program shows you a mass of detail that you don't really want to think about! The difficulty of following the details contrasts sharply with the simplicity and elegance of the recursive solution. Of course, you really want to leave the details to the computer. (You might think about what happens when the precondition that the number of disks is positive is violated. The result is an example of infinite recursion.)

There is, by the way, a story that explains the name of this problem. According to this story, on the first day of creation, a group of monks in an isolated tower near Hanoi were given a stack of 64 disks and were assigned the task of moving one disk every day, according to the rules of the Towers of Hanoi problem. On the day that they complete their task of moving all the disks from one stack to another, the universe will come to an end. But don't worry. The number of steps required to solve the problem for N disks is $2^N - 1$, and $2^{64} - 1$ days is over 50,000,000,000,000 years. We have a long way to go.

(In the terminology of Section 4.5, the Towers of Hanoi algorithm has a run time that is $\Theta(2^n)$, where n is the number of disks that have to be moved. Since the exponential function 2^n grows so quickly, the Towers of Hanoi problem can be solved in practice only for a small number of disks.)

By the way, in addition to the graphical Towers of Hanoi program, mentioned above, there are two more demo programs that you might want to look at. Each program provides a visual demonstration of a recursive algorithm. In Maze.java, recursion is used to solve a maze. In LittlePentominos.java, it is used to solve a well-known kind of puzzle. (LittlePentominos.java also requires the file MosaicCanvas.java.)

The Maze program first creates a random maze. It then tries to solve the maze by finding a path through the maze from the upper left corner to the lower right corner. This problem is actually very similar to a "blob-counting" problem that is considered later in this section. The recursive maze-solving routine starts from a given square, and it visits each neighboring square and calls itself recursively from there. The recursion ends if the routine finds itself at the lower right corner of the maze. When it can't find a solution from a square, it "backs up" out of that square and tries somewhere else. This common technique is referred to as *recursive backtracking* .

The LittlePentominos program is an implementation of a classic puzzle. A pentomino is a connected figure made up of five equal-sized squares. There are exactly twelve figures that can be made in this way, not counting all the possible rotations and reflections of the basic figures. The problem is to place the twelve pentominos on an 8-by-8 board in which four of the squares have already been marked as filled. The recursive solution looks at a board that has already been partially filled with pentominos. The subroutine looks at each remaining piece in turn. It tries to place that piece in the next available place on the board. If the piece fits, it calls itself recursively to try to fill in the rest of the solution. If that fails, then the subroutine goes on to the next piece—another example of recursive backtracking. A generalized version of the pentominos program with many more features can be found at https://math.hws.edu/eck/js/pentominos/pentominos.html.

5.1.3 A Recursive Sorting Algorithm

Turning next to an application that is perhaps more practical, we'll look at a recursive algorithm for sorting an array. The selection sort and insertion sort algorithms, which were covered in Section .5, are fairly simple, but they are rather slow when applied to large arrays. Faster sorting algorithms are available. One of these is *Quicksort*, a recursive algorithm which turns out to be the fastest sorting algorithm in most situations.

The Quicksort algorithm is based on a simple but clever idea: Given a list of items, select any item from the list. This item is called the *pivot* . (In practice, I'll just use the first item in the list.) Move all the items that are smaller than the pivot to the beginning of the list, and move all the items that are larger than the pivot to the end of the list. Now, put the pivot between the two groups of items. This puts the pivot in the position that it will occupy in the final, completely sorted array. It will not have to be moved again. We'll refer to this procedure as QuicksortStep.

To apply QuicksortStep to a list of numbers, select one of the numbers, 23 in this case. Arrange the numbers so that numbers less than 23 lie to its left and numbers greater than 23 lie to its right.

23 10 7 45 16 86 56 2 31 18

18 10 7 2 16 23 86 56 31 45

To finish sorting the list, sort the numbers to the left of 23, and sort the numbers to the right of 23. The nuber 23 itself is already in its final position and doesn't have to be moved again

QuicksortStep is not recursive. It is used as a subroutine by Quicksort. The speed of Quicksort depends on having a fast implementation of QuicksortStep. Since it's not the main point of this discussion, I present one without much comment.

```
/**
Apply QuicksortStep to the list of items in locations lo through hi
in the array A.        The value returned by this routine is the final
position of the pivot item in the array.
*/
static int quicksortStep(int[] A, int lo, int hi) {
    int pivot = A[lo]; // Get the pivot value.
    // The numbers hi and lo mark the endpoints of a range
    // of numbers that have not yet been tested.        Decrease hi
    // and increase lo until they become equal, moving numbers
    // bigger than pivot so that they lie above hi and moving
    // numbers less than the pivot so that they lie below lo.
    // When we begin, A[lo] is an available space, since its
    // value has been moved into the local variable, pivot.
    while (hi > lo) {
            // Loop invariant (See Subsection Subsection 4.2.3):        A[i] <= pivot
            // for i < lo, and A[i] >= pivot for i > hi.
```

```
            while (hi > lo && A[hi] >= pivot) {
                        // Move hi down past numbers greater than pivot.
                        // These numbers do not have to be moved.
            hi--;
      }
      if (hi == lo)
            break;
      // The number A[hi] is less than pivot.    Move it into
      // the available space at A[lo], leaving an available
      // space at A[hi].
      A[lo] = A[hi];
      lo++;
      while (hi > lo && A[lo] <= pivot) {
            // Move lo up past numbers less than pivot.
            // These numbers do not have to be moved.
      lo++;
      }
      if (hi == lo)
            break;
      // The number A[lo] is greater than pivot.Move it into
      // the available space at A[hi], leaving an available
      // space at A[lo].
      A[hi] = A[lo];
      hi--;
   } // end while
      // At this point, lo has become equal to hi, and there is
      // an available space at that position.    This position lies
      // between numbers less than pivot and numbers greater than
      // pivot.Put pivot in this space and return its location.
      A[lo] = pivot;
      return lo;
   }  // end QuicksortStep
```

With this subroutine in hand, Quicksort is easy. The Quicksort algorithm for sorting a list consists of applying QuicksortStep to the list, then applying Quicksort recursively to the items that lie to the left of the new position of the pivot and to the items that lie to the right of that position. Of course, we need base cases. If the list has only one item, or no items, then the list is already as sorted as it can ever be, so Quicksort doesn't have to do anything in these cases.

```
/**
Apply quicksort to put the array elements between
position lo and position hi into increasing order.
*/
static void quicksort(int[] A, int lo, int hi) {
    if (hi <= lo) {
                // The list has length one or zero. Nothing needs
                // to be done, so just return from the subroutine.
        return;
    }
    else {
                // Apply quicksortStep and get the new pivot position.
                // Then apply quicksort to sort the items that
                // precede the pivot and the items that follow it.
        int pivotPosition = quicksortStep(A, lo, hi);
        quicksort(A, lo, pivotPosition - 1);
        quicksort(A, pivotPosition + 1, hi);
    }
}
```

As usual, we had to generalize the problem. The original problem was to sort an array, but the recursive algorithm is set up to sort a specified part of an array. To sort an entire array, A, using the quickSort() subroutine, you would call quicksort(A, 0, A.length - 1).

Quicksort is an interesting example from the point of view of the analysis of algorithms (Section 4.5), because its average case run time differs greatly from its worst case run time. Here is a very informal analysis, starting with the average case: Note that an application of quicksortStep divides a problem into two subproblems. On the average, the subproblems will be of approximately the same size.

A problem of size n is divided into two problems that are roughly of size n/2; these are then divided into four problems that are roughly of size n/4; and so on. Since the problem size is divided by 2 on each level, there will be approximately log(n) levels of subdivision. The amount of processing on each level is proportional to n. (On the top level, each element in the array is looked at and possibly moved. On the second level, where there are two subproblems, every element but one in the array is part of one of those two subproblems and must be looked at and possibly moved, so there is a total of about n steps in both subproblems combined. Similarly, on the third level, there are four subproblems and a total of about n steps in the four subproblems on that level. . . .) With a total of n steps on each level and approximately log(n) levels in the average case, the average case run time for Quicksort is $\Theta(n*\log(n))$. This analysis assumes that quicksortStep divides a problem into two approximately equal parts. However, in the worst case, each application of quicksortStep divides a problem of size n into a problem of size 0 and a problem of size n-1. This happens when the pivot element ends up at the beginning or end of the array. In this worst case, there are n levels of subproblems, and the worst-case run time is $\Theta(n^2)$. The worst case is very rare—it depends on the items in the array being arranged in a very special way, so the average performance of Quicksort can be very good even though it is not so good in certain rare cases. (One of these "rare" cases is when the original array is already sorted or almost sorted, which is really not all that rare in practice. Applying the Quicksort algorithm as given above to a large sorted array will take a long time. One way to avoid that—with high probablility—is to pick the pivot for QuickSort step at random, rather than always using the first item.)

There are sorting algorithms that have both an average case and a worst case run time of $\Theta(n*\log(n))$. One example that is fairly easy to understand is MergeSort, which you can look up if you are interested.

5.1.4 Blob Counting

Next, we will look at counting the number of squares in a group of connected squares. I call a group of connected squares a "blob," and the sample program that we will consider is Blobs.java. The program displays a grid of small white, gray, and red squares. Here is a screenshot from the program, showing the grid of squares along with some controls:

The gray or red squares are considered to be "filled" and the white squares are "empty." For the purposes of this example, we define a "blob" to consist of a filled square and all the filled squares that can be reached from it by moving up, down, left, and right through other filled squares. If the user clicks on any filled square in the program, the computer will count the squares in the blob that contains the clicked square, and it will change the color of those squares to red. In the picture, one of the blobs is shown in red. The program has several controls. There is a "New Blobs" button; clicking this button will create a new random pattern in the grid. A pop-up menu specifies the approximate percentage of squares that will be filled in the new pattern. The more filled squares, the larger the blobs. And a button labeled "Count the Blobs" will tell you how many different blobs there are in the pattern.

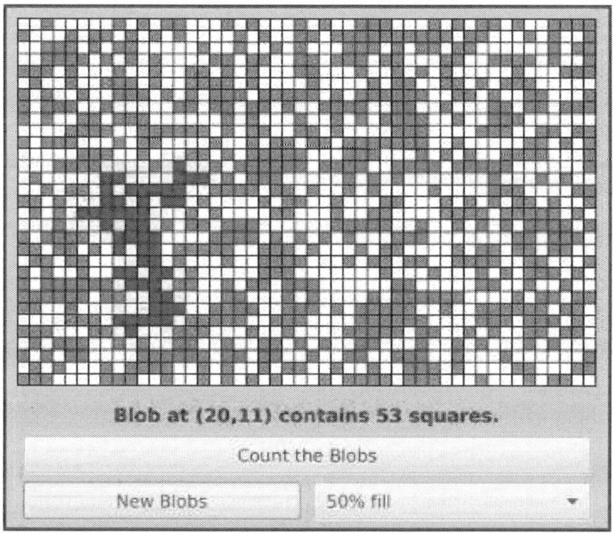

Recursion is used in this program to count the number of squares in a blob. Without recursion, this would be a very difficult thing to implement. Recursion makes it relatively easy, but it still requires a new technique, which is also useful in a number of other applications.

The data for the grid of squares is stored in a two dimensional array of boolean values,

boolean[][] filled;

The value of filled[r][c] is true if the square in row r and in column c of the grid is filled. The number of rows in the grid is stored in an instance variable named rows, and the number of columns is stored in columns. The program uses a recursive instance method named getBlobSize(r,c) to count the number of squares in a blob. The parameters r and c tell which blob to count, namely the blob that includes the square in a row r and column c. If there is no filled square at position (r,c), then the answer is zero. Otherwise, getBlobSize() has to count all the filled squares that can be reached from the square at position (r,c). The idea is to use getBlobSize() recursively to get the number of filled squares that can be reached from each of the neighboring positions: (r+1,c), (r-1,c), (r,c+1), and (r,c-1). Add up these numbers, and add one to count the square at (r,c) itself, and you get the total number of filled squares that can be reached from (r,c). Here is an implementation of this algorithm, as stated. Unfortunately, it has a serious flaw: It leads to an infinite recursion!

```
int getBlobSize(int r, int c) {  // BUGGY, INCORRECT VERSION!!
                          // This INCORRECT method tries to count all the filled
                          // squares that can be reached from position (r,c) in the grid.
   if (r < 0 || r >= rows || c < 0 || c >= columns) {
                          // This position is not in the grid, so there is
                          // no blob at this position.     Return a blob size of zero.
         return 0;
   }
   if (filled[r][c] == false) {
   // This square is not part of a blob, so return zero.
   return 0;
   }
   int size = 1;          // Count the square at this position, then count the
                          //      the blobs that are connected to this square
                          //      horizontally or vertically.
   size += getBlobSize(r-1,c);
   size += getBlobSize(r+1,c);
   size += getBlobSize(r,c-1);
   size += getBlobSize(r,c+1);
   return size;
}  // end INCORRECT getBlobSize()
```

Unfortunately, this routine will count the same square more than once. In fact, if there are at least two squares in the blob, then it will try to count each square infinitely often! Think of yourself standing at position (r,c) and trying to follow these instructions. The first instruction tells you to move up one row. You do that, and then you apply the same procedure. As one of the steps in that procedure, you have to move down one row and apply the same procedure yet again. But that puts you back at position (r,c)! From there, you move up one row, and from there you move down one row. . . . Back and forth forever! We have to make sure that a square is only counted and processed once, so we don't end up going around in circles. The solution is to leave a trail of breadcrumbs—or on the computer a trail of boolean values—to mark the squares that you've already visited. Once a square is marked as visited, it won't be processed again. The remaining, unvisited squares are reduced in number, so definite progress has been made in reducing the size of the problem. Infinite recursion is avoided!

A second boolean array, visited[r][c], is used to keep track of which squares have already been visited and processed. It is assumed that all the values in this array are set to false before getBlobSize() is called. As getBlobSize() encounters unvisited squares, it marks them as visited by setting the corresponding entry in the visited array to true. When getBlobSize() encounters a square that it has already visited, it doesn't count it or process it further. The technique of "marking" items as they are encountered is one that is used over and over in the programming of recursive algorithms. Here is the corrected version of getBlobSize(), with changes shown in italic:

```
/**
Counts the squares in the blob at position (r,c) in the
grid.        Squares are only counted if they are filled and
unvisited.   If this routine is called for a position that
has been visited, the return value will be zero.
*/
int getBlobSize(int r, int c) {
    if (r < 0 || r >= rows || c < 0 || c >= columns) {
                // This position is not in the grid, so there is
                // no blob at this position.       Return a blob size of zero.
          return 0;
    }
    if (filled[r][c] == false || visited[r][c] == true) {
                // This square is not part of a blob, or else it has
                // already been counted, so return zero.
          return 0;
    }
    visited[r][c] = true;      // Mark the square as visited so that
                               //      we won't count it again during the
                               //      following recursive calls.
    int size = 1;              // Count the square at this position, then count the
                               //      the blobs that are connected to this square
                               //      horizontally or vertically.
    size += getBlobSize(r-1,c);
```

```
        size += getBlobSize(r+1,c);
        size += getBlobSize(r,c-1);
        size += getBlobSize(r,c+1);
        return size;
    } // end getBlobSize()
```

In the program, this method is used to determine the size of a blob when the user clicks on a square. After getBlobSize() has performed its task, all the squares in the blob are still marked as visited. The method that draws the grid of squares shows visited squares in red, which makes the blob visible.

The getBlobSize() method is also used for the other task that can be done by the program: counting all the blobs. This is done by the following method, which includes comments to explain how it works:

```
    /**
    When the user clicks the "Count the Blobs" button, find the
    number of blobs in the grid and report the number in the
    message label.
    */
    void countBlobs() {
        int count = 0; // Number of blobs.
            /*Firstclearoutthevisitedarray.ThegetBlobSize()methodwillmarkeveryfilled
            square that it finds by setting the corresponding element of the array to true.
            Onceasquarehasbeenmarkedasvisited,itwillstaymarkeduntilalltheblobshave
            been counted. This will prevent the same blob from being counted more than
            once. */
        for (int r = 0; r < rows; r++)
            for (int c = 0; c < columns; c++)
                visited[r][c] = false;
            /* For each position in the grid, call getBlobSize() to get the size of the blob at
            that position.    If the size is not zero, count a blob.    Note that if we
            come to a position that was part of a previously counted blob, getBlobSize()
            will return 0 and the blob will not be counted again. */
        for (int r = 0; r < rows; r++)
            for (int c = 0; c < columns; c++) {
                if (getBlobSize(r,c) > 0)
```

```
                count++;
            }
        draw();             // Redraw the entire grid of squares.
                            // Note that all the filled squares will be red,
                            //        since they have all now been visited.
        message.setText("The number of blobs is " + count);
    } // end countBlobs()
```

5.2 LINKED DATA STRUCTURES

Every useful object contains instance variables. When the type of an instance variable is given by a class or interface name, the variable can hold a reference to another object. Such a reference is also called a pointer, and we say that the variable *points to* the object. (Of course, any variable that can contain a reference to an object can also contain the special value null, which points to nowhere.) When one object contains an instance variable that points to another object, we think of the objects as being "linked" by the pointer. Data structures of great complexity can be constructed by linking objects together.

5.2.1 Recursive Linking

Something interesting happens when an object contains an instance variable that can refer to another object of the same type. In that case, the definition of the object's class is recursive. Such recursion arises naturally in many cases. For example, consider a class designed to represent employees at a company. Suppose that every employee except the boss has a supervisor, who is another employee of the company. Then the *Employee* class would naturally contain an instance variable of type *Employee* that points to the employee's supervisor:

```
    /**
    * An object of type Employee holds data about one employee.
    */
    public class Employee {
        String name;      // Name of the employee.
        Employee supervisor;      // The employee's supervisor.
                .
                .         // (Other instance variables and methods.)
                .
    } // end class Employee
```

If emp is a variable of type *Employee*, then emp.supervisor is another variable of type *Employee*. If emp refers to the boss, then the value of emp.supervisor should be null to indicate the fact that the boss has no supervisor. If we wanted to print out the name of the employee's supervisor, for example, we could use the following Java statement:

```
if ( emp.supervisor == null) {
    System.out.println( emp.name + " is the boss and has no supervisor!" );
}
else {
    System.out.print( "The supervisor of " + emp.name + " is " );
    System.out.println( emp.supervisor.name );
}
```

Now, suppose that we want to know how many levels of supervisors there are between a given employee and the boss. We just have to follow the chain of command through a series of supervisor links, and count how many steps it takes to get to the boss:

```
if ( emp.supervisor == null ) {
    System.out.println( emp.name + " is the boss!" );
}
else {
    Employee runner;          // For "running" up the chain of command.
    runner = emp.supervisor;
    if ( runner.supervisor == null) {
        System.out.println(  emp.name     + " reports directly to the boss." );
    }
    else {
        int count = 0;
        while ( runner.supervisor != null ) {
            count++;// Count the supervisor on this level.
            runner = runner.supervisor; // Move up to the next level.
        }
        System.out.println( "There are " + count
                + " supervisors between " + emp.name
```

```
                        + " and the boss." );
    }
}
```

As the while loop is executed, runner points in turn to the original employee (emp), then to emp's supervisor, then to the supervisor of emp's supervisor, and so on. The count variable is incremented each time runner "visits" a new employee. The loop ends when runner.supervisor is null, which indicates that runner has reached the boss. At that point, count has counted the number of steps between emp and the boss.

In this example, the supervisor variable is quite natural and useful. In fact, data structures that are built by linking objects together are so useful that they are a major topic of study in computer science. We'll be looking at a few typical examples. In this section and the next, we'll be looking at *linked lists*. A linked list consists of a chain of objects of the same type, linked together by pointers from one object to the next. This is much like the chain of supervisors between emp and the boss in the above example. It's also possible to have more complex situations, in which one object can contain links to several other objects. We'll look at an example of this in Section 5.4.

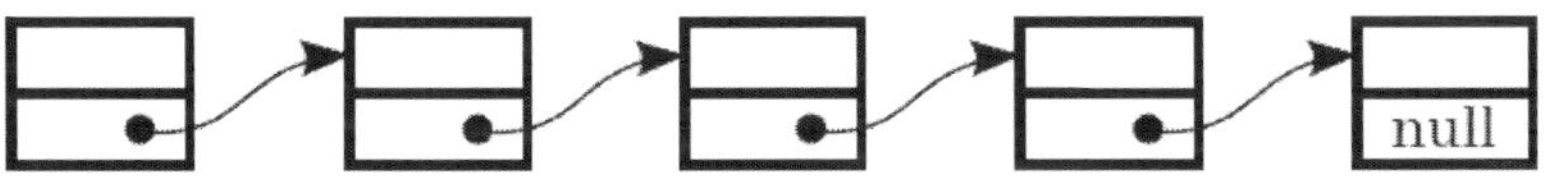

When an object contains a reference to an object of the same type, then several objects can be linked together into a list. Each object refers to the next object.

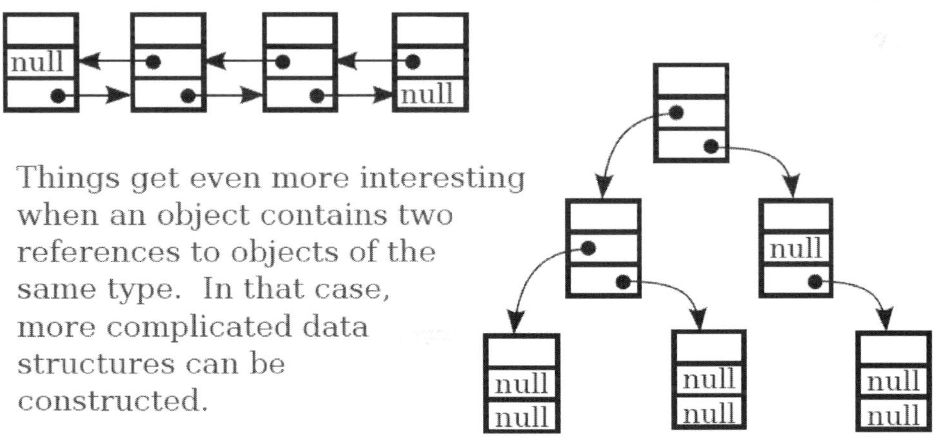

Things get even more interesting when an object contains two references to objects of the same type. In that case, more complicated data structures can be constructed.

5.2.2 Linked Lists

For most of the examples in the rest of this section, linked lists will be constructed out of objects belonging to the class *Node* which is defined as follows:

class Node {

String item;

Node next;

}

The term *node* is often used to refer to one of the objects in a linked data structure. Objects of type *Node* can be chained together as shown in the top part of the above illustration. Each node holds a *String* and a pointer to the next node in the list (if any). The last node in such a list can always be identified by the fact that the instance variable next in the last node holds the value null instead of a pointer to another node. The purpose of the chain of nodes is to represent a list of strings. The first string in the list is stored in the first node, the second string is stored in the second node, and so on. The pointers and the node objects are used to build the structure, but the data that we want to represent is the list of strings. Of course, we could just as easily represent a list of integers or a list of *Colors* or a list of any other type of data by changing the type of the item that is stored in each node.

Although the *Nodes* in this example are very simple, we can use them to illustrate the common operations on linked lists. Typical operations include deleting nodes from the list, inserting new nodes into the list, and searching for a specified *String* among the items in the list. We will look at subroutines to perform all of these operations, among others.

For a linked list to be used in a program, that program needs a variable that refers to the first node in the list. It only needs a pointer to the first node since all the other nodes in the list can be accessed by starting at the first node and following links along the list from one node to the next. In my examples, I will always use a variable named head, of type *Node*, that points to the first node in the linked list. When the list is empty, the value of head is null.

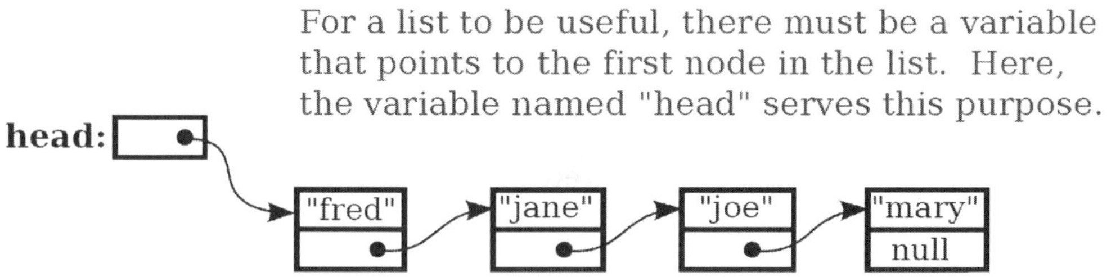

5.2.3 Basic Linked List Processing

It is very common to want to process all the items in a linked list in some way. The common pattern is to start at the head of the list, then move from each node to the next by following the pointer in the node, stopping when the null that marks the end of the list is reached. If head is a variable of type *Node* that points to the first node in the list, then the general form of the code for processing all the items in a linked list is:

```
Node runner;          // A pointer that will be used to traverse the list. runner = head;
// Start with runner pointing to the head of the list. while ( runner != null ) {    /       /
Continue until null is encountered.

    process( runner.item );    // Do something with the item in the current node.

    runner = runner.next;      // Move on to the next node in the list.

}
```

Our only access to the list is through the variable head, so we start by getting a copy of the value in head with the assignment statement runner = head. We need a copy of head because we are going to change the value of runner. We can't change the value of head, or we would lose our only access to the list! The variable runner will point to each node of the list in turn. When runner points to one of the nodes in the list, runner.next is a pointer to the next node in the list, so the assignment statement runner = runner.next moves the pointer along the list from each node to the next. We know that we've reached the end of the list when runner becomes equal to null. Note that our list-processing code works even for an empty list, since for an empty list the value of head is null and the body of the while loop is not executed at all. As an example, we can print all the strings in a list of *Strings* by saying:

```
Node runner = head;

while ( runner != null ) {

    System.out.println( runner.item );

    runner = runner.next;

}
```

The while loop can, by the way, be rewritten as a for loop. Remember that even though the loop control variable in a for loop is often numerical, that is not a requirement. Here is a for loop that is equivalent to the above while loop:

```
for ( Node runner = head; runner != null; runner = runner.next ) {

    System.out.println( runner.item );

}
```

Similarly, we can traverse a list of integers to add up all the numbers in the list. A linked list of integers can be constructed using the class

```
public class IntNode {
    int item;          // One of the integers in the list.
    IntNode next;      // Pointer to the next node in the list.
}
```

If head is a variable of type *IntNode* that points to a linked list of integers, we can find the sum of the integers in the list using:

```
int sum = 0;
IntNode runner = head;
while ( runner != null ) {
    sum = sum + runner.item;          // Add current item to the sum.
    runner = runner.next;
}
System.out.println("The sum of the list of items is " + sum);
```

It is also possible to use recursion to process a linked list. Recursion is rarely the natural way to process a list, since it's so easy to use a loop to traverse the list. However, understanding how to apply recursion to lists can help with understanding the recursive processing of more complex data structures. A non-empty linked list can be thought of as consisting of two parts: the *head* of the list, which is just the first node in the list, and the *tail* of the list, which consists of the remainder of the list after the head. Note that the tail is itself a linked list and that it is shorter than the original list (by one node). This is a natural setup for recursion, where the problem of processing a list can be divided into processing the head and recursively processing the tail. The base case occurs in the case of an empty list (or sometimes in the case of a list of length one). For example, here is a recursive algorithm for adding up the numbers in a linked list of integers:

```
if the list is empty then
    return 0 (since there are no numbers to be added up)
otherwise
    let listsum = the number in the head node
    let tailsum be the sum of the numbers in the tail list (recursively)
    add tailsum to listsum
    return listsum
```

One remaining question is, how do we get the tail of a non-empty linked list? If head is a variable that points to the head node of the list, then head.next is a variable that points to the second node of the list—and that node is in fact the first node of the tail. So, we can view head.next as a pointer to the tail of the list. One special case is when the original list consists of a single node. In that case, the tail of the list is empty, and head.next is null. Since an empty list is represented by a null pointer, head.next represents the tail of the list even in this special case. This allows us to write a recursive list-summing function in Java as

```
/**
Compute the sum of all the integers in a linked list of integers.
@param head a pointer to the first node in the linked list
*/
public static int addItemsInList( IntNode head ) {
    if ( head == null ) {
                // Base case:   The list is empty,      so the sum is zero.
        return 0;
    }
    else {
                // Recursive case:     The list is non-empty.    Find the sum of
                // the tail list, and add that to the item in the head node.
                // (Note that this case could be written simply as
                //      return head.item + addItemsInList( head.next );)
        int listsum = head.item;
        int tailsum = addItemsInList( head.next );
        listsum = listsum + tailsum;
        return listsum;
    }
}
```

I will finish by presenting a list-processing problem that is easy to solve with recursion, but quite tricky to solve without it. The problem is to print out all the strings in a linked list of strings in the reverse of the order in which they occur in the list. Note that when we do this, the item in the head of a list is printed out after all the items in the tail of the list. This leads to the following recursive routine. You should convince yourself that it works, and you should think about trying to do the same thing without using recursion:

```
public static void printReversed( Node head ) {
    if ( head == null ) {
            // Base case:    The list is empty, and there is nothing to print.
    return;
    }
    else {
            // Recursive case:      The list is non-empty.
    printReversed( head.next );     // Print strings from tail, in reverse order.
    System.out.println( head.item );        // Then print string from head node.
    }
}
```

In the rest of this section, we'll look at a few more advanced operations on a linked list of strings. The subroutines that we consider are instance methods in a class that I wrote named *StringList*. An object of type *StringList* represents a linked list of strings. The class has a private instance variable named head of type *Node* that points to the first node in the list, or is null if the list is empty. Instance methods in class *StringList* access head as a global variable. The source code for *StringList* is in the file StringList.java, and it is used in a sample program named ListDemo.java, so you can take a look at the code in context if you want.

One of the methods in the *StringList* class searches the list, looking for a specified string. If the string that we are looking for is searchItem, then we have to compare searchItem to each item in the list. This is an example of basic list traversal and processing. However, in this case, we can stop processing if we find the item that we are looking for.

```
/**
Searches the list for a specified item.
@param searchItem the item that is to be searched for
@return true if searchItem is one of the items in the list or false if
searchItem does not occur in the list.
*/
public boolean find(String searchItem) {
    Node runner;            // A pointer for traversing the list.
    runner = head;          // Start by looking at the head of the list.
                            //      (head is an instance variable! )
```

```
      while ( runner != null ) {
                              // Go through the list looking at the string in each
                              // node. If the string is the one we are looking for,
                              // return true, since the string has been found in the list.
            if ( runner.item.equals(searchItem) )
                  return true;
            runner = runner.next;     // Move on to the next node.
      }
      // At this point, we have looked at all the items in the list
      // without finding searchItem.    Return false to indicate that
      // the item does not exist in the list.
      return false;
   } // end find()
```

It is possible that the list is empty, that is, that the value of head is null. We should be careful that this case is handled properly. In the above code, if head is null, then the body of the while loop is never executed at all, so no nodes are processed and the return value is false. This is exactly what we want when the list is empty, since the searchItem can't occur in an empty list.

5.2.4 Inserting into a Linked List

The problem of inserting a new item into a linked list is more difficult, at least in the case where the item is inserted into the middle of the list. (In fact, it's probably the most difficult operation on linked data structures that you'll encounter in this chapter.)

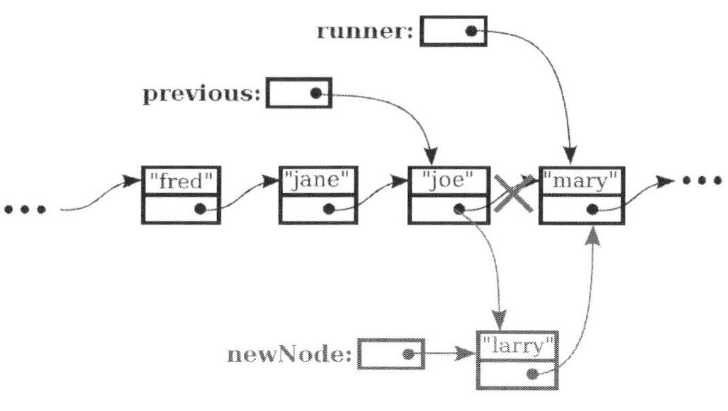

Inserting a new node
into the middle of a list.

In the *StringList* class, the items in the nodes of the linked list are kept in increasing order. When a new item is inserted into the list, it must be inserted at the correct position according to this ordering. This means that, usually, we will have to insert the new item somewhere in the middle of the list, between two existing nodes. To do this, it's convenient to have two variables of type *Node*, which refer to the existing nodes that will lie on either side of the new node. In the following illustration, these variables are previous and runner. Another variable, newNode, refers to the new node. In order to do the insertion, the link from previous to runner must be "broken," and new links from previous to newNode and from newNode to runner must be added:

Once we have previous and runner pointing to the right nodes, the command "previous.next = newNode;" can be used to make previous.next point to the new node.

And the command "newNode.next = runner" will set newNode.next to point to the correct place. However, before we can use these commands, we need to set up runner and previous as shown in the illustration. The idea is to start at the first node of the list, and then move along the list past all the items that are less than the new item. While doing this, we have to be aware of the danger of "falling off the end of the list." That is, we can't continue if runner reaches the end of the list and becomes null. If insertItem is the item that is to be inserted, and if we assume that it does, in fact, belong somewhere in the middle of the list, then the following code would correctly position previous and runner:

```
Node runner, previous;
previous = head;       // Start at the beginning of the list. runner = head.next;
while ( runner != null && runner.item.compareTo(insertItem) < 0 ) {
    previous = runner;         // "previous = previous.next" would also work
    runner = runner.next;
}
```

(This uses the compareTo() instance method from the *String* class to test whether the item in the node is less than the item that is being inserted.

This is fine, except that the assumption that the new node is inserted into the middle of the list is not always valid. It might be that insertItem is less than the first item of the list. In that case, the new node must be inserted at the head of the list. This can be done with the instructions

```
newNode.next = head;         // Make newNode.next point to the old head.
head = newNode;      // Make newNode the new head of the list.
```

It is also possible that the list is empty. In that case, newNode will become the first and only node in the list. This can be accomplished simply by setting head = newNode. The following insert() method from the *StringList* class covers all of these possibilities:

```
/**
Insert a specified item into the list, keeping the list in order.
@param insertItem the item that is to be inserted.
*/
public void insert(String insertItem) {
    Node newNode; // A Node to contain the new item.
    newNode = new Node();
    newNode.item = insertItem;        // (N.B. newNode.next is null.)
    if ( head == null ) {
                // The new item is the first (and only) one in the list.
                // Set head to point to it.
        head = newNode;
    }
    else if ( head.item.compareTo(insertItem) >= 0 ) {
                // The new item is less than the first item in the list,
                // so it has to be inserted at the head of the list.
        newNode.next = head;
        head = newNode;
    }
    else {
                // The new item belongs somewhere after the first item
                // in the list.    Search for its proper position and insert it.
        Node runner;    // A node for traversing the list.
        Node previous;  // Always points to the node preceding
        runner. runner = head.next;      // Start by looking at the SECOND position.
        previous = head;
        while ( runner != null && runner.item.compareTo(insertItem) < 0 ) {
                // Move previous and runner along the list until runner
```

```
                    // falls off the end or hits a list element that is
                    // greater than or equal to insertItem.     When this
                    // loop ends, previous indicates the position where
                    // insertItem must be inserted.
                previous = runner;
                runner = runner.next;
                }
                newNode.next = runner;  // Insert newNode after previous.
                previous.next = newNode;
            }
        }  // end insert()
```

If you were paying close attention to the above discussion, you might have noticed that there is one special case which is not mentioned. What happens if the new node has to be inserted at the end of the list? This will happen if all the items in the list are less than the new item. In fact, this case is already handled correctly by the subroutine, in the last part of the if statement. If insertItem is greater than all the items in the list, then the while loop will end when runner has traversed the entire list and become null. However, when that happens, previous will be left pointing to the last node in the list. Setting previous.next = newNode adds newNode onto the end of the list. Since runner is null, the command newNode.next = runner sets newNode.next to null, which is exactly what is needed to mark the end of the list.

5.2.5 Deleting from a Linked List

The delete operation is similar to insert, although a little simpler. There are still special cases to consider. When the first node in the list is to be deleted, then the value of head has to be changed to point to what was previously the second node in the list. Since head.next refers to the second node in the list, this can be done by setting head = head.next. (Once again, you should check that this works when head.next is null, that is, when there is no second node in the list. In that case, the list becomes empty.)

If the node that is being deleted is in the middle of the list, then we can set up previous and runner with runner pointing to the node that is to be deleted and with previous pointing to the node that precedes that node in the list. Once that is done, the command "previous.next = runner.next;" will delete the node. The deleted node will be garbage collected. I encourage you to draw a picture for yourself to illustrate this operation. Here is the complete code for the delete() method:

```
/**
Delete a specified item from the list, if that item is present.
If multiple copies of the item are present in the list, only
the one that comes first in the list is deleted.
@param deleteItem the item to be deleted
@return true if the item was found and deleted, or false if the item
was not in the list.
*/

public boolean delete(String deleteItem) {
    if ( head == null ) {
            // The list is empty, so it certainly doesn't contain deleteString.
        return false;
    }
    else if ( head.item.equals(deleteItem) ) {
            // The string is the first item of the list.    Remove it.
        head = head.next;
        return true;
    }
    else {
            // The string, if it occurs at all, is somewhere beyond the
            // first element of the list.          Search the list.
        Node runner;      // A node for traversing the list.
        Node previous;  // Always points to the node preceding runner.
        runner = head.next;        // Start by looking at the SECOND list node.
        previous = head;
        while ( runner != null && runner.item.compareTo(deleteItem) < 0 ) {
            // Move previous and runner along the list until runner
            // falls off the end or hits a list element that is
            // greater than or equal to deleteItem.      When this
            // loop ends, runner indicates the position where
```

```
                    // deleteItem must be, if it is in the list.
                previous = runner;
                runner = runner.next;
        }
        if ( runner != null && runner.item.equals(deleteItem) ) {
                    // Runner points to the node that is to be deleted.
                    // Remove it by changing the pointer in the previous node.
                previous.next = runner.next;
                return true;
        }
        else {
                    // The item does not exist in the list.
                return false;
                }
        }
    } // end delete()
```

5.3 STACKS, QUEUES, AND ADTS

A linked list is a particular type of data structure, made up of objects linked together by pointers. In the previous section, we used a linked list to store an ordered list of *Strings*, and we implemented insert, delete, and find operations on that list. However, we could easily have stored the list of *Strings* in an array or *ArrayList*, instead of in a linked list. We could still have implemented the same operations on the list. The implementations of these operations would be different, but their interfaces and logical behavior would still be the same.

The term *abstract data type*, or *ADT* , refers to a set of possible values and a set of operations on those values, without any specification of how the values are to be represented or how the operations are to be implemented. An "ordered list of strings" can be defined as an abstract data type. Any sequence of *Strings* that is arranged in increasing order is a possible value of this data type. The operations on the data type include inserting a new string, deleting a string, and finding a string in the list. There are often several different ways to implement the same abstract data type. For example, the "ordered list of strings" ADT can be implemented as a linked list or as an array. A program that only depends on the abstract definition of the ADT can use either implementation, interchangeably. In particular, the implementation of the ADT can be changed without affecting the program as a whole. This can make the program easier to debug and maintain, so ADTs are an important tool in software engineering. Abstraction is an important general concept in computer science.

In this section, we'll look at two common abstract data types, *stacks* and *queues.* Both stacks and queues are often implemented as linked lists, but that is not the only possible implementation. You should think of the rest of this section partly as a discussion of stacks and queues and partly as a case study in ADTs.

5.3.1 Stacks

A stack consists of a sequence of items, which should be thought of as piled one on top of the other like a physical stack of boxes or cafeteria trays. Only the top item on the stack is accessible at any given time. It can be removed from the stack with an operation called *pop.* An item lower down on the stack can only be removed after all the items on top of it have been popped off the stack. A new item can be added to the top of the stack with an operation called *push* . We can make a stack of any type of items. If, for example, the items are values of type int, then the push and pop operations can be implemented as instance methods

- void push(int newItem) — Add newItem to top of stack.
- int pop() — Remove the top int from the stack and return it.

It is an error to try to pop an item from an empty stack, so it is important to be able to tell whether a stack is empty. We need another stack operation to do the test, implemented as an instance method

- boolean isEmpty() — Returns true if the stack is empty.

This defines "stack of ints" as an abstract data type. This ADT can be implemented in several ways, but however it is implemented, its behavior must correspond to the abstract mental image of a stack.

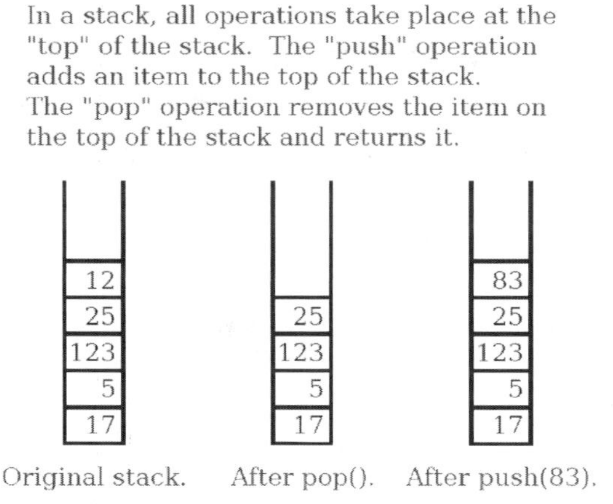

In the linked list implementation of a stack, the top of the stack is actually the node at the head of the list. It is easy to add and remove nodes at the front of a linked list—much easier than inserting and deleting nodes in the middle of the list. Here is a class that implements the "stack of ints" ADT using a linked list. (It uses a static nested class to represent the nodes of the linked list, but that is part of the private implementation of the ADT.)

```
public class StackOfInts {
    /**
    An object of type Node holds one of the items in the linked list
    that represents the stack.
    */
    private static class Node {
            int item;
            Node next;
    }
    private Node top;          // Pointer to the Node that is at the top of
                               //      of the stack.    If top == null, then the
                               //      stack is empty.
    /**
    Add N to the top of the stack.
    */
    public void push( int N ) {
            Node newTop;   // A Node to hold the new item.
            newTop = new Node();
            newTop.item = N;          // Store N in the new Node.
            newTop.next = top;        // The new Node points to the old top.
            top = newTop;   // The new item is now on top.
    }
    /**
    Remove the top item from the stack, and return it.
    Throws an IllegalStateException if the stack is empty when
    this method is called.
    */
```

```
public int pop() {
        if ( top == null )
                throw new IllegalStateException("Can't pop from an empty stack.");
        int topItem = top.item;    // The item that is being popped.
        top = top.next;    // The previous second item is now on top.
        return topItem;
}
/**
Returns true if the stack is empty.          Returns false
if there are one or more items on the stack.
*/
public boolean isEmpty() {
return (top == null);
}
} // end class StackOfInts
```

You should make sure that you understand how the push and pop operations operate on the linked list. Drawing some pictures might help. Note that the linked list is part of the private implementation of the *StackOfInts* class. A program that uses this class doesn't even need to know that a linked list is being used.

(As an aside, the nested *Node* class in *StackOfInts* could have been record class (Section 3.4), since nodes don't need to be modified after they are created. The implementation of push() would have to be changed to use the record class constructor. See StackOfInt.java, which uses this approach.)

Now, it's pretty easy to implement a stack as an array instead of as a linked list. Since the number of items on the stack varies with time, a counter is needed to keep track of how many spaces in the array are actually in use. If this counter is called top, then the items on the stack are stored in positions 0, 1, . . . , top-1 in the array. The item in position 0 is on the bottom of the stack, and the item in position top-1 is on the top of the stack. Pushing an item onto the stack is easy: Put the item in position top and add 1 to the value of top. If we don't want to put a limit on the number of items that the stack can hold, we can use the dynamic array techniques from Subsection 3.2.4. Note that the typical picture of the array would show the stack "upside down," with the bottom of the stack at the top of the array. This doesn't matter. The array is just an implementation of the abstract idea of a stack, and as long as the stack operations work the way they are supposed to, we are OK. Here is a second implementation of the *StackOfInts* class, using a dynamic array:

```
import java.util.Arrays;        // For the Arrays.copyOf() method. public class StackOfInts
{   // (alternate version, using an array)
    private int[] items = new int[10];  // Holds the items on the stack.
    private int top = 0;          // The number of items currently on the stack.
    /**
    Add N to the top of the stack.
    */
    public void push( int N ) {
            if (top == items.length) {
                            // The array is full, so make a new, larger array and
                            // copy the current stack items into it.
                    items = Arrays.copyOf( items, 2*items.length );
    }
    items[top] = N;   // Put N in next available spot.
            top++;    // Number of items goes up by one.
    }
    /**
    Remove the top item from the stack, and return it.
    Throws an IllegalStateException if the stack is empty when
    this method is called.
    */
    public int pop() {
            if ( top == 0 )
                    throw new IllegalStateException("Can't pop from an empty stack.");
            int topItem = items[top - 1];        // Top item in the stack.
            top--;   // Number of items on the stack goes down by one.
            return topItem;
    }
    /**
    Returns true if the stack is empty.          Returns false
    if there are one or more items on the stack.
```

```
    */
    public boolean isEmpty() {
        return (top == 0);
    }
} // end class StackOfInts
```

Once again, the implementation of the stack (as an array) is private to the class. The two versions of the *StackOfInts* class can be used interchangeably, since their public interfaces are identical—including the fact that an attempt to pop from an empty stack will result in an *IllegalStateException*.

It's interesting to look at the run time analysis of stack operations. We can measure the size of the problem by the number of items that are on the stack. For the linked list implementation of a stack, the worst case run time both for the push and for the pop operation is $\Theta(1)$. This just means that the run time is less than some constant, independent of the number of items on the stack. This is easy to see if you look at the code. The operations are implemented with a few simple assignment statements, and the number of items on the stack has no effect.

For the array implementation, on the other hand, a special case occurs in the push operation when the array is full. In that case, a new array is created and all the stack items are copied into the new array. This takes an amount of time that is proportional to the number of items on the stack. So, although the run time for push is usually $\Theta(1)$, the worst case run time is $\Theta(n)$, where n is the number of items on the stack. (However, the worst case occurs only rarely, and there is a natural sense in which the *average* case run time for the array implementation is still $\Theta(1)$.)

5.3.2 Queues

Queues are similar to stacks in that a queue consists of a sequence of items, and there are restrictions about how items can be added to and removed from the list. However, a queue has two ends, called the front and the back of the queue. Items are always added to the queue at the back and removed from the queue at the front. The operations of adding and removing items are called *enqueue* and *dequeue* in this book. (These names are not completely standardized, in the way that "push" and "pop" are. For example, the operations are sometimes called "put" and "take.") An item that is added to the back of the queue will remain on the queue until all the items in front of it have been removed. This should sound familiar. A queue is like a "line" or "queue" of customers waiting for service. Customers are serviced in the order in which they arrive on the queue.

A queue can hold items of any type. For a queue of ints, the enqueue and dequeue operations can be implemented as instance methods in a "*QueueOfInts*" class. We also need an instance method for checking whether the queue is empty:

- void enqueue(int N) — Add N to the back of the queue.
- int dequeue() — Remove the item at the front and return it.
- boolean isEmpty() — Return true if the queue is empty.

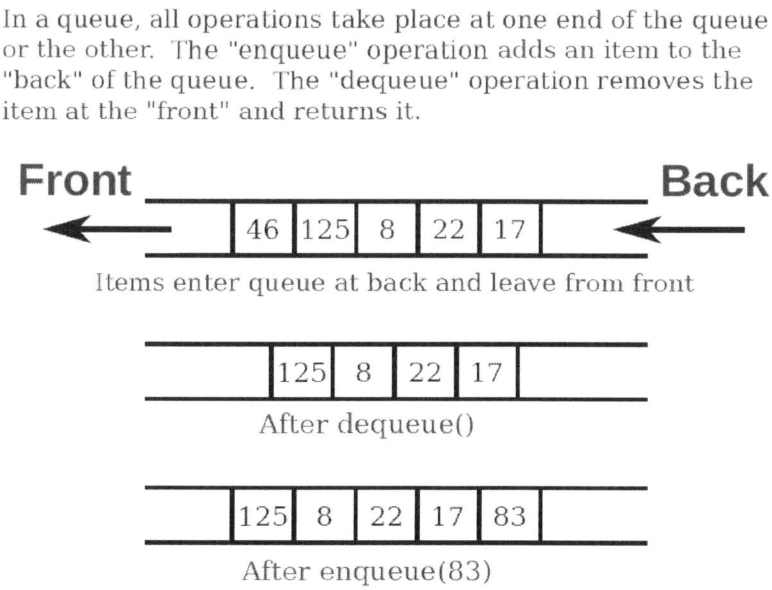

A queue can be implemented as a linked list or as an array. An efficient array implementation is trickier than the array implementation of a stack, so I won't give it here. In the linked list implementation, the first item of the list is at the front of the queue. Dequeueing an item from the front of the queue is just like popping an item off a stack. The back of the queue is at the end of the list. Enqueueing an item involves setting a pointer in the last node of the current list to point to a new node that contains the item. To do this, we'll need a command like "tail.next = newNode;", where tail is a pointer to the last node in the list. If head is a pointer to the first node of the list, it would always be possible to get a pointer to the last node of the list by saying:

```
Node tail;    // This will point to the last node in the list.
tail = head;  // Start at the first node.
while (tail.next != null) {
    tail = tail.next;   // Move to next node.
}
```

```
// At this point, tail.next is null, so tail points to
// the last node in the list.
```

However, it would be very inefficient to do this over and over every time an item is enqueued. For the sake of efficiency, we'll use another instance variable to store a pointer to the last node. This complicates the class somewhat; we have to be careful to update the value of this variable

whenever a new node is added to the end of the list. Given all this, writing the *QueueOfInts* class is not all that difficult:

```
public class QueueOfInts {
    /**
    An object of type Node holds one of the items
    in the linked list that represents the queue.
    */
    private static class Node {
            int item;
            Node next;
    }
    private Node head = null;        // Points to first Node in the queue.
                                     // The queue is empty when head is null.
    private Node tail = null;        // Points to last Node in the queue
                                     // when the queue is not empty.
    /**
    Add N to the back of the queue.
    */
    public void enqueue( int N ) {
            Node newTail = new Node();       // A Node to hold the new item.
            newTail.item = N;
            if (head == null) {
                    // The queue was empty. The new Node becomes
                    // the only node in the list.       Since it is both
                    // the first and last node, both head and tail
                    // point to it.
```

```
            head = newTail;
            tail = newTail;
        }
        else {
            // The new node becomes the new tail of the list.
            // (The head of the list is unaffected.
        tail.next = newTail;
        tail = newTail;
        }
    }
    /**
    Remove and return the front item in the queue.
    Throws an IllegalStateException if the queue is empty.
    */
    public int dequeue() {
        if ( head == null)
            throw new IllegalStateException("Can't dequeue from an empty queue.");
        int firstItem = head.item;
        head = head.next;          // The previous second item is now first.
                                   // If we have just removed the last item,
                                   // then head is null.
        if (head == null) {
                                   // The queue has become empty.  The Node that was
                                   // deleted was the tail as well as the head of the
                                   // list, so now there is no tail.      (Actually, the
                                   // class would work fine without this step.)
                tail = null;
            }
            return firstItem;
        }
        /**
```

```
        Return true if the queue is empty.
        */
        boolean isEmpty() {
                return (head == null);
        }
} // end class QueueOfInts
```

To help you follow what is being done here with the tail pointer, it might help to think in terms of a class invariant. "If the queue is non-empty, then tail points to the last node in the queue." This invariant must be true at the beginning and at the end of each method call. For example, applying this to the enqueue() method, in the case of a non-empty list, the invariant tells us that a new node can be added to the back of the list simply by saying "tail.next = newNode. It also tells us how the value of tail must be set before returning from the method: it must be set to point to the node that was just added to the queue.

Queues are typically used in a computer (as in real life) when only one item can be processed at a time, but several items can be waiting for processing. For example:

- In a Java program that has multiple threads, the threads that want processing time on the CPU are kept in a queue. When a new thread is started, it is added to the back of the queue. A thread is removed from the front of the queue, it is given some processing time, and then—if it has not terminated—is sent to the back of the queue to wait for another turn.
- Events such as keystrokes and mouse clicks are stored in a queue called the "event queue." A program removes events from the event queue and processes them. It's possible for several more events to occur while one event is being processed, but since the events are stored in a queue, they will always be processed in the order in which they occurred.
- A web server is a program that receives requests from web browsers for "pages." It is easy for new requests to arrive while the web server is still fulfilling a previous request. Requests that arrive while the web server is busy are placed into a queue to await processing. Using a queue ensures that requests will be processed in the order in which they were received.

Queues are said to implement a *FIFO* policy: First In, First Out. Or, as it is more commonly expressed, first come, first served. Stacks, on the other hand implement a *LIFO* policy: Last In, First Out. The item that comes out of the stack is the last one that was put in. Just like queues, stacks can be used to hold items that are waiting for processing (although in applications where queues are typically used, a stack would be considered "unfair").

To get a better handle on the difference between stacks and queues, consider the sample program DepthBreadth.java. I suggest that you try out the program. The program shows a grid of squares. Initially, all the squares are white. When you click on a white square, that square is "marked" by turning it red. The program than starts marking squares that are connected, horizontally or vertically, to squares that have already been marked. This process will eventually process every square in the grid. To understand how the program works, think of yourself in the place of the program. When the user clicks a square, you are handed an index card. The location of the square—its row and column—is written on the card. You put the card in a pile, which then contains just that one card. Then, you repeat the following: If the pile is empty, you are done. Otherwise, remove an index card from the pile. The index card specifies a square. Look at each horizontal and vertical neighbor of that square. If the neighbor has not already been encountered, write its location on a new index card and put the card in the pile. You are done when there are no more index cards waiting in the pile to be processed. In the program, while a square is in the pile, waiting to be processed, it is colored red; that is, red squares have been *encountered* but not yet *processed*. When a square is taken from the pile and processed, its color changes to gray. Once a square has been colored gray, the program will never consider it again, since all of its neighbors have already been accounted for. Eventually, all the squares have been processed, all the squares are gray, and the procedure ends. In the index card analogy, the pile of cards has been emptied.

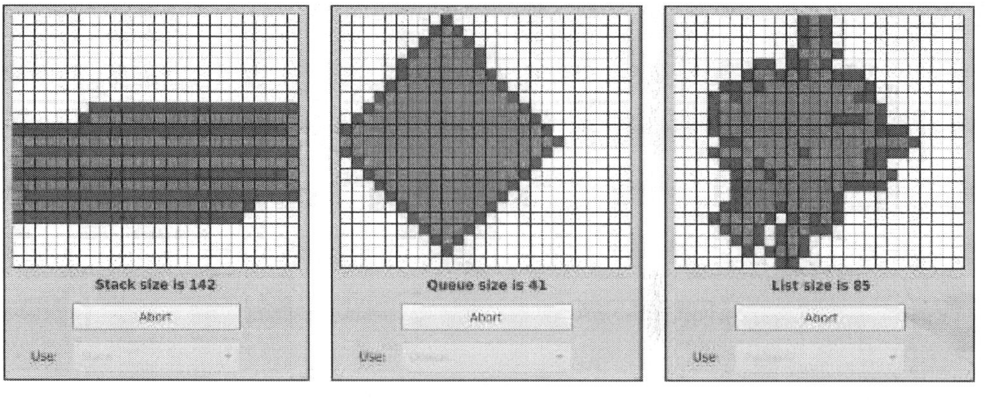

The program can use your choice of three methods: Stack, Queue, and Random. In each case, the same general procedure is used. The only difference is how the "pile of index cards" is managed. For a stack, cards are added and removed at the top of the pile. For a queue, cards are added to the bottom of the pile and removed from the top. In the random case, the card to be processed is picked at random from among all the cards in the pile. The order of processing is very different in these three cases. Here are three pictures from the program, using the three different processing methods. In each case, the process was started by selecting a square near the middle of the grid. A stack is used for the picture on the left, a queue for the picture in the middle, and random selection for the picture on the right:

The patterns that are produced are very different. When using a stack, the program explores out as far as possible before it starts backtracking to look at previously encountered squares. With a queue, squares are processed roughly in the order of their distance from the starting point. When random selection is used, the result is an irregular blob, but it is a connected blob since a square can only be encountered if it is next to a previously encountered square.

You should experiment with the program to see how it all works. Try to understand how stacks and queues are being used. Try starting from one of the corner squares. While the process is going on, you can click on other white squares, and they will be added to the list of encountered squares. When you do this with a stack, you should notice that the square you click is processed immediately, and all the red squares that were already waiting for processing have to wait. On the other hand, if you do this with a queue, the square that you click will wait its turn until all the squares that were already in the pile have been processed. Again, the source code for the program is DepthBreadth.java.

Queues seem very natural because they occur so often in real life, but there are times when stacks are appropriate and even essential. For example, consider what happens when a routine calls a subroutine. The first routine is suspended while the subroutine is executed, and it will continue only when the subroutine returns. Now, suppose that the subroutine calls a second subroutine, and the second subroutine calls a third, and so on. Each subroutine is suspended while the subsequent subroutines are executed. The computer has to keep track of all the subroutines that are suspended. It does this with a stack.

When a subroutine is called, an *activation record* is created for that subroutine. The activation record contains information relevant to the execution of the subroutine, such as its local variables, parameters, and return address (the the point in the program where the computer should return to when the subroutine ends). The activation record for the subroutine is placed on a stack. It will be removed from the stack and destroyed when the subroutine returns. If the subroutine calls another subroutine, the activation record of the second subroutine is pushed onto the stack, on top of the activation record of the first subroutine. The stack can continue to grow as more subroutines are called, and it shrinks as those subroutines return.

In the case of a recursive subroutine, which calls itself, there can be several activation records on the stack for the same subroutine. This is how the computer keeps track of many recursive calls at the same time: It has a different activation record for each call.

5.3.3 Postfix Expressions

As another example, stacks can be used to evaluate *postfix expressions.* An ordinary mathematical expression such as 2+(15-12)*17 is called an *infix expression* . In an infix expression, an operator comes in between its two operands, as in "2 + 2". In a postfix expression, an operator comes after its two operands, as in "2 2 +". The infix expression "2+(15-12)*17" would be written in postfix form as "2 15 12 - 17 * +". The "-" operator in this expression applies to the two operands that precede it, namely "15" and "12". The "*" operator applies to the two operands that precede it, namely "15 12 -" and "17". And the "+" operator applies to "2" and "15 12 - 17 *". These are the same computations that are done in the original infix expression.

Now, suppose that we want to process the expression "2 15 12 - 17 * +", from left to right and find its value. The first item we encounter is the 2, but what can we do with it? At this point, we don't know what operator, if any, will be applied to the 2 or what the other operand might be. We have to remember the 2 for later processing. We do this by pushing it onto a stack. Moving on to the next item, we see a 15, which is pushed onto the stack on top of the 2. Then the 12 is added to the stack. Now, we come to the operator, "-". This operation applies to the two operands that preceded it in the expression. We have saved those two operands on the stack. So, to process the "-" operator, we pop two numbers from the stack, 12 and 15, and compute 15 - 12 to get the answer 3. This 3 must be remembered to be used in later processing, so we push it onto the stack, on top of the 2 that is still waiting there. The next item in the expression is a 17, which is processed by pushing it onto the stack, on top of the 3. To process the next item, "*", we pop two numbers from the stack. The numbers are 17 and the 3 that represents the value of "15 12 -". These numbers are multiplied, and the result, 51, is pushed onto the stack. The next item in the expression is a "+" operator, which is processed by popping 51 and 2 from the stack, adding them, and pushing the result, 53, onto the stack. Finally, we've come to the end of the expression. The number on the stack is the value of the entire expression, so all we have to do is pop the answer from the stack, and we are done! The value of the expression is 53.

Although it's easier for people to work with infix expressions, postfix expressions have some advantages. For one thing, postfix expressions don't require parentheses or precedence rules. The order in which operators are applied is determined entirely by the order in which they occur in the expression. This allows the algorithm for evaluating postfix expressions to be fairly straightforward:

Start with an empty stack

for each item in the expression:

if the item is a number:

Push the number onto the stack

else if the item is an operator:

Pop the operands from the stack // Can generate an error

Apply the operator to the operands

Push the result onto the stack

else

There is an error in the expression

Pop a number from the stack // Can generate an error

if the stack is not empty:

There is an error in the expression

else:

The last number that was popped is the value of the expression

Errors in an expression can be detected easily. For example, in the expression "2 3 + *", there are not enough operands for the "*" operation. This will be detected in the algorithm when an attempt is made to pop the second operand for "*" from the stack, since the stack will be empty. The opposite problem occurs in "2 3 4 +". There are not enough operators for all the numbers. This will be detected when the 2 is left still sitting in the stack at the end of the algorithm.

This algorithm is demonstrated in the sample program PostfixEval.java. This program lets you type in postfix expressions made up of non-negative real numbers and the operators "+", "-", "*", "/", and "^". The "^" represents exponentiation. That is, "2 3 ^" is evaluated as 23. The program prints out a message as it processes each item in the expression. The stack class that is used in the program is defined in the file StackOfDouble.java. The *StackOfDouble* class is identical to the first *StackOfInts* class, given above, except that it has been modified to store values of type double instead of values of type int.

The only interesting aspect of this program is the method that implements the postfix evaluation algorithm. It is a direct implementation of the pseudocode algorithm given above:

*/***

Read one line of input and process it as a postfix expression.

If the input is not a legal postfix expression, then an error

message is displayed. Otherwise, the value of the expression

is displayed. It is assumed that the first character on

the input line is a non-blank.

```
*/
private static void readAndEvaluate() {
    StackOfDouble stack;      // For evaluating the expression.
    stack = new StackOfDouble();      // Make a new, empty stack.
    System.out.println();
    while (TextIO.peek() != '\n') {
            if ( Character.isDigit(TextIO.peek()) ) {
                    // The next item in input is a number.      Read it and
                    // save it on the stack.
            double num = TextIO.getDouble();
            stack.push(num);
            System.out.println("      Pushed constant " + num);
    }
    else {
                    // Since the next item is not a number, the only thing
                    // it can legally be is an operator. Get the operator
                    // and perform the operation.
            char op;// The operator, which must be +, -, *, /, or ^.
            double x,y;        // The operands, from the stack, for the operation.
            double answer;  // The result, to be pushed onto the stack.
            op = TextIO.getChar();
            if (op != '+' && op != '-' && op != '*' && op != '/' && op != '^') {
                            // The character is not one of the acceptable operations.
                    System.out.println("\nIllegal operator found in input: " + op);
            return;
    }
    if (stack.isEmpty()) {
                    System.out.println("        Stack is empty while trying to evaluate " + op);
                    System.out.println("\nNot enough numbers in expression!");
                    return;
            }
            y = stack.pop();
```

```
            if (stack.isEmpty()) {
                    System.out.println("        Stack is empty while trying to evaluate " + op);
                    System.out.println("\nNot enough numbers in expression!");
                    return;
    }
                    x = stack.pop();
                    switch (op) {
                    case '+' -> answer = x + y;
                    case '-' -> answer = x - y;
                    case '*' -> answer = x * y;
                    case '/' -> answer = x / y;
                    default  -> answer = Math.pow(x,y);        // (op must be '^'.)
                    }
                    stack.push(answer);
                    System.out.println("        Evaluated " + op + " and pushed " + answer);
            }
            TextIO.skipBlanks();
    }       // end while
    // If we get to this point, the input has been read successfully.
    // If the expression was legal, then the value of the expression is
    // on the stack, and it is the only thing on the stack.
    if  (stack.isEmpty())  {    // Impossible if the input is really non-empty.
            System.out.println("No expression provided.");
            return;
    }
    double value = stack.pop();          // Value of the expression.
    System.out.println("       Popped " + value + " at end of expression.");
    if (stack.isEmpty() == false) {
            System.out.println("       Stack is not empty.");
            System.out.println("\nNot enough operators for all the numbers!");
            return;
    }
```

```
        System.out.println("\nValue = " + value);
    } // end readAndEvaluate()
```

Postfix expressions are often used internally by computers. In fact, the Java virtual machine is a "stack machine" which uses the stack-based approach to expression evaluation that we have been discussing. The algorithm can easily be extended to handle variables, as well as constants. When a variable is encountered in the expression, the value of the variable is pushed onto the stack. It also works for operators with more or fewer than two operands. As many operands as are needed are popped from the stack and the result is pushed back onto the stack. For example, the *unary minus* operator, which is used in the expression "-x", has a single operand. We will continue to look at expressions and expression evaluation in the next two sections.

5.4 BINARY TREES

We have seen in the two previous sections how objects can be linked into lists. When an object contains two pointers to objects of the same type, structures can be created that are much more complicated than linked lists. In this section, we'll look at one of the most basic and useful structures of this type: *binary trees*. Each of the objects in a binary tree contains two pointers, typically called left and right. In addition to these pointers, of course, the nodes can contain other types of data. For example, a binary tree of integers would be made up of objects of the following type:

```
class TreeNode {
    int item;           // The data in this node.
    TreeNode left;      // Pointer to the left subtree.
    TreeNode right;     // Pointer to the right subtree.
}
```

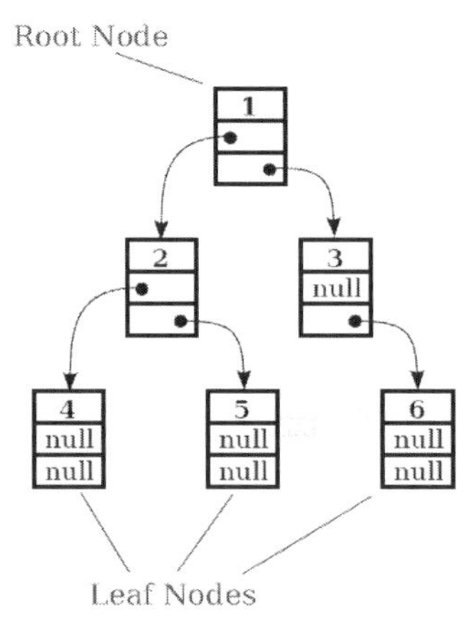

The left and right pointers in a TreeNode can be null or can point to other objects of type TreeNode. A node that points to another node is said to be the *parent* of that node, and the node it points to is called a *child* . In a binary tree, a child is either a "left child" or a "right child," and a node can have a right child even if it has no left child. In the picture below, for example, node 3 is the parent of node 6, and nodes 4 and 5 are children of node 2. Not every linked structure made up of tree nodes is a binary tree. A binary tree must have the following properties: There is exactly one node in the tree which has no parent; this node is called the *root* of the tree. Every other node in the tree has exactly one parent. Finally, there can be no loops in a binary tree. That is, it is not possible to follow a chain of pointers starting at some node and arriving back at the same node.

A node that has no children is called a *leaf*. A leaf node can be recognized by the fact that both the left and right pointers in the node are null. In the standard picture of a binary tree, the root node is shown at the top and the leaf nodes at the bottom—which doesn't show much respect for the analogy to real trees. But at least you can see the branching, tree-like structure that gives a binary tree its name.

5.4.1 Tree Traversal

Consider any node in a binary tree. Look at that node together with all its descendants (that is, its children, the children of its children, and so on). This set of nodes forms a binary tree, which is called a *subtree* of the original tree. For example, in the picture, nodes 2, 4, and 5 form a subtree. This subtree is called the *left subtree* of the root. Similarly, nodes 3 and 6 make up the *right subtree* of the root. We can consider any non-empty binary tree to be made up of a root node, a left subtree, and a right subtree. Either or both of the subtrees can be empty. This is a recursive definition, matching the recursive definition of the *TreeNode* class. So it should not be a surprise that recursive subroutines are often used to process trees.

Consider the problem of counting the nodes in a binary tree. As an exercise, you might try to come up with a non-recursive algorithm to do the counting, but you shouldn't expect to find one easily. The heart of the problem is keeping track of which nodes remain to be counted. It's not so easy to do this, and in fact it's not even possible without an auxiliary data structure such as a stack or queue. With recursion, however, the algorithm is almost trivial. Either the tree is empty or it consists of a root and two subtrees. If the tree is empty, the number of nodes is zero. (This is the base case of the recursion.) Otherwise, use recursion to count the nodes in each subtree. Add the results from the subtrees together, and add one to count the root. This gives the total number of nodes in the tree. Written out in Java:

```
/**
   Count the nodes in the binary tree to which root points, and
```

```
return the answer.    If root is null, the answer is zero.
*/
static int countNodes( TreeNode root ) {
    if ( root == null ) {          // Base case:      empty tree.
            return 0;              // An empty tree contains no nodes.
    }
    else {    // Recursive case:          root node plus two subtrees.
            int count = 1;     // Start by counting the root.
            count += countNodes(root.left);    // Add the number of nodes
                                               //       in the left subtree.
            count += countNodes(root.right); // Add the number of nodes
                                               //       in the right subtree.
            return count;     // Return the total.
    }
} // end countNodes()
```

Or, consider the problem of printing the items in a binary tree. If the tree is empty, there is nothing to do. If the tree is non-empty, then it consists of a root and two subtrees. Print the item in the root and use recursion to print the items in the subtrees. Here is a subroutine that prints all the items on one line of output:

```
/**
Print all the items in the tree to which root points.
The item in the root is printed first, followed by the
items in the left subtree and then the items in the
right subtree.
*/
static void preorderPrint( TreeNode root ) {
    if ( root != null ) { // (Otherwise, there's nothing to print.)
            System.out.print( root.item + " " ); // Print the root item.
            preorderPrint( root.left ); // Print items in left subtree.
            preorderPrint( root.right ); // Print items in right subtree.
    }
} // end preorderPrint()
```

This routine is called "preorderPrint" because it uses a *preorder traversal* of the tree. In a preorder traversal, the root node of the tree is processed first, then the left subtree is traversed, then the right subtree. In a *postorder traversal* , the left subtree is traversed, then the right subtree, and then the root node is processed. And in an *inorder traversal* , the left subtree is traversed first, then the root node is processed, then the right subtree is traversed. Subroutines that use postorder and inorder traversal to print the contents of a tree differ from preorderPrint() only in the placement of the statement that outputs the root item:

```
/**
Print all the items in the tree to which root points.
The items in the left subtree are printed first, followed
by the items in the right subtree and then the item
in the root node.
*/
static void postorderPrint( TreeNode root ) {
    if ( root != null ) {          // (Otherwise, there's nothing to print.)
            postorderPrint( root.left );        // Print items in left subtree.
            postorderPrint( root.right );       // Print items in right subtree.
            System.out.print( root.item + " " );          // Print the root item.
    }
    } // end postorderPrint()


    /**
    Print all the items in the tree to which root points.
    The items in the left subtree are printed first, followed
    by the item in the root node and then the items
    in the right subtree.
    */
    static void inorderPrint( TreeNode root ) {
            if ( root != null ) {          // (Otherwise, there's nothing to print.)
                    inorderPrint( root.left );  // Print items in left subtree.
                    System.out.print( root.item + " " );          // Print the root item.
                    inorderPrint( root.right );          // Print items in right subtree.
```

```
    }
} // end inorderPrint()
```

Each of these subroutines can be applied to the binary tree shown in the illustration at the beginning of this section. The order in which the items are printed differs in each case:

preorderPrint outputs:	1	2	4	5	3	6
postorderPrint outputs:	4	5	2	6	3	1
inorderPrint outputs:	4	2	5	1	3	6

In preorderPrint, for example, the item at the root of the tree, 1, is output before anything else. But the preorder printing also applies to each of the subtrees of the root. The root item of the left subtree, 2, is printed before the other items in that subtree, 4 and 5. As for the right subtree of the root, 3 is output before 6. A preorder traversal applies at all levels in the tree. The other two traversal orders can be analyzed similarly.

5.4.2 Binary Sort Trees

One of the examples in Section 5.2 was a linked list of strings, in which the strings were kept in increasing order. While a linked list works well for a small number of strings, it becomes inefficient for a large number of items. When inserting an item into the list, searching for that item's position requires looking at, on average, half the items in the list. Finding an item in the list requires a similar amount of time. If the strings are stored in a sorted array instead of in a linked list, then searching becomes more efficient because binary search can be used. However, inserting a new item into the array is still inefficient since it means moving, on average, half of the items in the array to make a space for the new item. A binary tree can be used to store an ordered list in a way that makes both searching and insertion efficient. A binary tree used in this way is called a *binary sort tree* or *BST* .

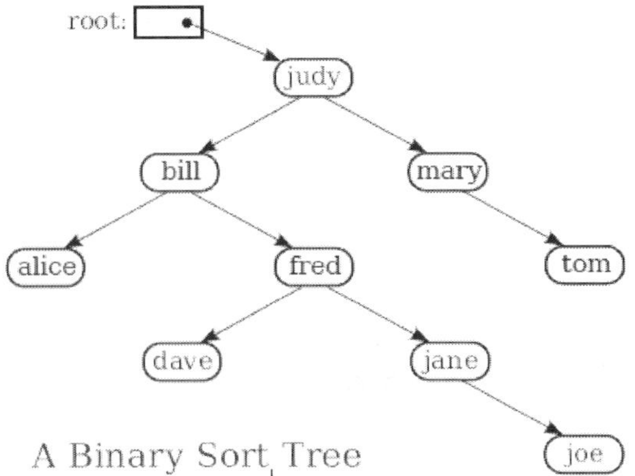

A Binary Sort Tree

A binary sort tree is a binary tree with the following property: For every node in the tree, the item in that node is greater than or equal to every item in the left subtree of that node, and it is less than or equal to all the items in the right subtree of that node. Here for example is a binary sort tree containing items of type *String*. (In this picture, I haven't bothered to draw all the pointer variables. Non-null pointers are shown as arrows.)

Binary sort trees have this useful property: An inorder traversal of the tree will process the items in increasing order. In fact, this is really just another way of expressing the definition. For example, if an inorder traversal is used to print the items in the tree shown above, then the items will be in alphabetical order. The definition of an inorder traversal guarantees that all the items in the left subtree of "judy" are printed before "judy", and all the items in the right subtree of "judy" are printed after "judy". But the binary sort tree property guarantees that the items in the left subtree of "judy" are precisely those that precede "judy" in alphabetical order, and all the items in the right subtree follow "judy" in alphabetical order. So, we know that "judy" is output in its proper alphabetical position. But the same argument applies to the subtrees. "Bill" will be output after "alice" and before "fred" and its descendants. "Fred" will be output after "dave" and before "jane" and "joe". And so on.

Suppose that we want to search for a given item in a binary search tree. Compare that item to the root item of the tree. If they are equal, we're done. If the item we are looking for is less than the root item, then we need to search the left subtree of the root—the right subtree can be eliminated because it only contains items that are greater than or equal to the root. Similarly, if the item we are looking for is greater than the item in the root, then we only need to look in the right subtree. In either case, the same procedure can then be applied to search the subtree. Inserting a new item is similar: Start by searching the tree for the position where the new item belongs. When that position is found, create a new node and attach it to the tree at that position.

Searching and inserting are efficient operations on a binary search tree, provided that the tree is close to being *balanced* . A binary tree is balanced if for each node, the left subtree of that node contains approximately the same number of nodes as the right subtree. In a perfectly balanced tree, the two numbers differ by at most one. Not all binary trees are balanced, but if the tree is created by inserting items in a random order, there is a high probability that the tree is approximately balanced. (If the order of insertion is not random, however, it's quite possible for the tree to be very unbalanced.) During a search of any binary sort tree, every comparison eliminates one of two subtrees from further consideration. If the tree is balanced, that means cutting the number of items still under consideration in half. This is exactly the same as the binary search algorithm, and the result is a similarly efficient algorithm.

In terms of asymptotic analysis, searching, inserting, and deleting in a binary search tree have average case run time Θ(log(n)). The problem size, n, is the number of items in the tree, and the average is taken over all the different orders in which the items could have been inserted into the tree. As long as the actual insertion order is random, the actual run time can be expected to be close to the average. However, the worst case run time for binary search tree operations is Θ(n), which is much worse than Θ(log(n)). The worst case occurs for particular insertion orders. For example, if the items are inserted into the tree in order of increasing size, then every item that is inserted moves always to the right as it moves down the tree. The result is a "tree" that looks more like a linked list, since it consists of a linear string of nodes strung together by their right child pointers. Operations on such a tree have the same performance as operations on a linked list. Now, there are data structures that are similar to simple binary sort trees, except that insertion and deletion of nodes are implemented in a way that will always keep the tree balanced, or almost balanced. For these data structures, searching, inserting, and deleting have both average case and worst case run times that are Θ(log(n)). Here, however, we will look at only the simple versions of inserting and searching.

The sample program SortTreeDemo.java is a demonstration of binary sort trees. The program includes subroutines that implement inorder traversal, searching, and insertion. We'll look at the latter two subroutines below. The main() routine tests the subroutines by letting you type in strings to be inserted into the tree.

In *SortTreeDemo*, nodes in the binary tree are represented using the following static nested class, which includes a simple constructor to make creating nodes easier:

```
/**
 * An object of type TreeNode represents one node in a binary tree of strings.
 */
private static class TreeNode {
    String item;       // The data in this node.
    TreeNode left;     // Pointer to left subtree.
    TreeNode right;    // Pointer to right subtree.
    TreeNode(String str) {
                       // Constructor.  Make a node containing str.
                       // Note that left and right pointers are null.
        item = str;
```

```
    }
} // end class TreeNode
```

A static member variable of type *TreeNode* points to the binary sort tree that is used by the program:

```
private static TreeNode root; // Pointer to the root node in the tree.
                              // When the tree is empty, root is null.
```

A recursive subroutine named treeContains is used to search for a given item in the tree. This routine implements the search algorithm for binary trees that was outlined above:

```
/**
Return true if item is one of the items in the binary
sort tree to which root points.        Return false if not.
*/
static boolean treeContains( TreeNode root, String item ) {
    if ( root == null ) {
                // Tree is empty, so it certainly doesn't contain item.
        return false;
    }
    else if ( item.equals(root.item) ) {
                // Yes, the item has been found in the root node. return true;
    }
    else if ( item.compareTo(root.item) < 0 ) {
                // If the item occurs, it must be in the left subtree.
        return treeContains( root.left, item );
    }
    else {
                // If the item occurs, it must be in the right subtree.
        return treeContains( root.right, item );
    }
} // end treeContains()
```

When this routine is called in the main() routine, the first parameter is the static member variable root, which points to the root of the entire binary sort tree.

It's worth noting that recursion is not really essential in this case. A simple, non-recursive algorithm for searching a binary sort tree follows the rule: Start at the root and move down the tree until you find the item or reach a null pointer. Since the search follows a single path down the tree, it can be implemented as a while loop. Here is a non-recursive version of the search routine:

```
private static boolean treeContainsNR( TreeNode root, String item ) {
    TreeNode runner;          // For "running" down the tree.
    runner = root;            // Start at the root node.
    while (true) {
        if (runner == null) {
                    // We've fallen off the tree without finding item.
            return false;
        }
        else if ( item.equals(runner.item) ) {
                    // We've found the item.
            return true;
        }
        else if ( item.compareTo(runner.item) < 0 ) {
                    // If the item occurs, it must be in the left subtree.
                    // So, advance the runner down one level to the left.
            runner = runner.left;
        }
        else {
                    // If the item occurs, it must be in the right subtree.
                    // So, advance the runner down one level to the right.
            runner = runner.right;
        }
    }       // end while
} // end treeContainsNR();
```

The subroutine for inserting a new item into the tree turns out to be more similar to the non-recursive search routine than to the recursive. The insertion routine has to handle the case where the tree is empty. In that case, the value of root must be changed to point to a node that contains the new item:

```
root = new TreeNode( newItem );
```

But this means, effectively, that the root can't be passed as a parameter to the subroutine, because it is impossible for a subroutine to change the value stored in an actual parameter. (I should note that this is something that is possible in other languages.) Recursion uses parameters in an essential way. There are ugly ways to work around the problem, but the easiest thing is just to use a non-recursive insertion routine that accesses the static member variable root directly. One difference between inserting an item and searching for an item is that we have to be careful not to fall off the tree. That is, we have to stop searching just before runner becomes null. When we get to an empty spot in the tree, that's where we have to insert the new node:

```
/**
Add the item to the binary sort tree to which the global variable
"root" refers.        (Note that root can't be passed as a parameter to
this routine because the value of root might change, and a change
in the value of a formal parameter does not change the actual parameter.)
*/
private static void treeInsert(String newItem) {
    if ( root == null ) {
                // The tree is empty.     Set root to point to a new node containing
                // the new item. This becomes the only node in the tree.
        root = new TreeNode( newItem );
        return;
    }
    TreeNode runner;                    // Runs down the tree to find a place for newItem.
    runner = root;    // Start at the root.
    while (true) {
        if ( newItem.compareTo(runner.item) < 0 ) {
                // Since the new item is less than the item in runner,
                // it belongs in the left subtree of runner.  If there
                // is an open space at runner.left, add a new node there.
                // Otherwise, advance runner down one level to the left.
        if ( runner.left == null ) {
                runner.left = new TreeNode( newItem );
```

```
                return;  // New item has been added to the tree.
            }
            else
                runner = runner.left;
        }
        else {
                // Since the new item is greater than or equal to the item in
                // runner, it belongs in the right subtree of runner.          If there
                // is an open space at runner.right, add a new node there.
                // Otherwise, advance runner down one level to the right.
            if ( runner.right == null ) {
                runner.right = new TreeNode( newItem );
                return;  // New item has been added to the tree.
            }
            else
                runner = runner.right;
        }
    } // end while
}   // end treeInsert()
```

5.4.3 Expression Trees

Another application of trees is to store mathematical expressions such as 15*(x+y) or sqrt(42)+7 in a convenient form. Let's stick for the moment to expressions made up of numbers and the operators +, -, *, and /. Consider the expression 3*((7+1)/4)+(17-5).

This expression is made up of two subexpressions, 3*((7+1)/4) and (17-5), combined with the operator "+". When the expression is represented as a binary tree, the root node holds the operator +, while the subtrees of the root node represent the subexpressions 3*((7+1)/4) and (17-5). Every node in the tree holds either a number or an operator. A node that holds a number is a leaf node of the tree. A node that holds an operator has two subtrees representing the operands to which the operator applies. The tree is shown in the illustration below. I will refer to a tree of this type as an *expression tree*.

Given an expression tree, it's easy to find the value of the expression that it represents. Each node in the tree has an associated value. If the node is a leaf node, then its value is simply the number that the node contains. If the node contains an operator, then the associated value is computed by first finding the values of its child nodes and then applying the operator to those values. The process is shown by the upward-directed arrows in the illustration. The value computed for the root node is the value of the expression as a whole. There are other uses for expression trees. For example, a postorder traversal of the tree will output the postfix form of the expression.

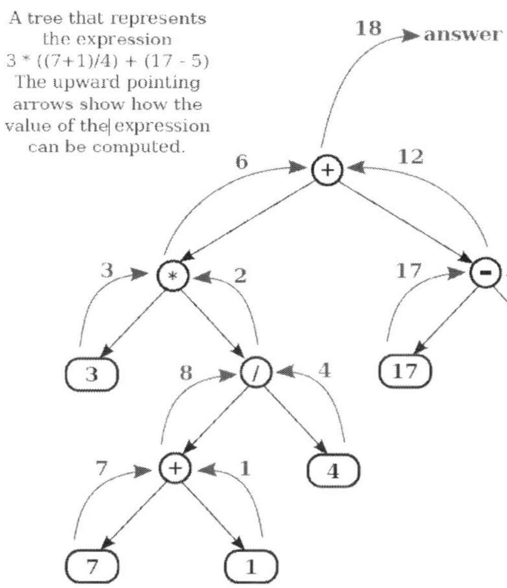

An expression tree contains two types of nodes: nodes that contain numbers and nodes that contain operators. Furthermore, we might want to add other types of nodes to make the trees more useful, such as nodes that contain variables. If we want to work with expression trees in Java, how can we deal with this variety of nodes? One way—which will be frowned upon by object-oriented purists—is to include an instance variable in each node object to record which type of node it is:

```
enum NodeType { NUMBER, OPERATOR }        // Possible kinds of node.
class ExpNode {        // A node in an expression tree.
    NodeType kind; // Which type of node is this?
    double number; // The value in a node of type NUMBER.
    char op;// The operator in a node of type OPERATOR.
    ExpNode left;      // Pointers to subtrees,
    ExpNode right;  //         in a node of type OPERATOR.
    ExpNode( double val ) {
                    // Constructor for making a node of type NUMBER.
```

```
        kind = NodeType.NUMBER;
        number = val;
    }
    ExpNode( char op, ExpNode left, ExpNode right ) {
                // Constructor for making a node of type OPERATOR.
        kind = NodeType.OPERATOR;
        this.op = op;
        this.left = left;
        this.right = right;
    }
} // end class ExpNode
```

Given this definition, the following recursive subroutine will find the value of an expression tree:

```
static double getValue( ExpNode node ) {
                // Return the value of the expression represented by
                // the tree to which node refers.   Node must be non-null.
        if ( node.kind == NodeType.NUMBER ) {
                // The value of a NUMBER node is the number it holds.
        return node.number;
    }
    else {      // The kind must be OPERATOR.
                // Get the values of the operands and combine them
                //      using the operator.
        double leftVal = getValue( node.left );
        double rightVal = getValue( node.right );
        switch ( node.op ) {
                case '+': return leftVal + rightVal;
                case '-': return leftVal - rightVal;
                case '*': return leftVal * rightVal;
                case '/': return leftVal / rightVal;
                default: return Double.NaN; // Bad operator.
```

```
            }
        }
    } // end getValue()
```

Although this approach works, a more object-oriented approach is to note that since there are two types of nodes, there should be two classes to represent them, perhaps named *ConstNode* and *BinOpNode*. To represent the general idea of a node in an expression tree, we need another class, *ExpNode*. Both *ConstNode* and *BinOpNode* will be subclasses of *ExpNode*. Since any actual node will be either a ConstNode or a *BinOpNode*, *ExpNode* should be an abstract class. Since one of the things we want to do with nodes is find their values, each class should have an instance method for finding the value:

```
    abstract class ExpNode {
                    // Represents a node of any type in an expression tree.
            abstract double value();  // Return the value of this node.
    } // end class ExpNode
    class ConstNode extends ExpNode {
                    // Represents a node that holds a number.
            double number; // The number in the node.
            ConstNode( double val ) {
                    // Constructor.   Create a node to hold val.
            number = val;
        }
        double value() {
                    // The value is just the number that the node holds.
            return number;
        }
    } // end class ConstNode
    class BinOpNode extends ExpNode {
                    // Represents a node that holds an operator.
            char op;// The operator.
            ExpNode left;      // The left operand.
            ExpNode right;   // The right operand.
    BinOpNode( char op, ExpNode left, ExpNode right ) {
```

```
            // Constructor.   Create a node to hold the given data.
        this.op = op;
        this.left = left;
        this.right = right;
    }
    double value() {
            // To get the value, compute the value of the left and
            // right operands, and combine them with the operator.
        double leftVal = left.value();
        double rightVal = right.value();
        switch ( op ) {
            case '+': return leftVal + rightVal;
            case '-': return leftVal - rightVal;
            case '*': return leftVal * rightVal;
            case '/': return leftVal / rightVal;
            default: return Double.NaN; // Bad operator.
        }
    }
} // end class BinOpNode
```

Note that the left and right operands of a *BinOpNode* are of type *ExpNode*, not *BinOpNode*. This allows the operand to be either a *ConstNode* or another *BinOpNode*—or any other type of *ExpNode* that we might eventually create. Since every *ExpNode* has a value() method, we can call left.value() to compute the value of the left operand. If left is in fact a *ConstNode*, this will call the value() method in the *ConstNode* class. If it is in fact a *BinOpNode*, then left.value() will call the value() method in the *BinOpNode* class. Each node knows how to compute its own value.

Although it might seem more complicated at first, the object-oriented approach has some real advantages. For one thing, it doesn't waste memory. In the original *ExpNode* class, only some of the instance variables in each node were actually used, and we needed an extra instance variable to keep track of the type of node. More important, though, is the fact that new types of nodes can be added more cleanly, since it can be done by creating a new subclass of *ExpNode* rather than by modifying an existing class.

We'll return to the topic of expression trees in the next section, where we'll see how to create an expression tree to represent a given expression.

5.5 A SIMPLE RECURSIVE DESCENT PARSER

I have always been fascinated by language—both natural languages like English and the artificial languages that are used by computers. There are many difficult questions about how languages can convey information, how they are structured, and how they can be processed. Natural and artificial languages are similar enough that the study of programming languages, which are pretty well understood, can give some insight into the much more complex and difficult natural languages. And programming languages raise more than enough interesting issues to make them worth studying in their own right. How can it be, after all, that computers can be made to "understand" even the relatively simple languages that are used to write programs? Computers can only directly use instructions expressed in very simple machine language. Higher level languages must be translated into machine language. But the translation is done by a compiler, which is just a program. How could such a translation program be written?

5.5.1 Backus-Naur Form

Natural and artificial languages are similar in that they have a structure known as grammar or syntax. Syntax can be expressed by a set of rules that describe what it means to be a legal sentence or program. For programming languages, syntax rules are often expressed in *BNF* (Backus-Naur Form), a system that was developed by computer scientists John Backus and Peter Naur in the late 1950s. Interestingly, an equivalent system was developed independently at about the same time by linguist Noam Chomsky to describe the grammar of natural language. BNF cannot express all possible syntax rules. For example, it can't express the fact that a variable must be defined before it is used. Furthermore, it says nothing about the meaning or semantics of the language. The problem of specifying the semantics of a language—even of an artificial programming language—is one that is still far from being completely solved. However, BNF does express the basic structure of the language, and it plays a central role in the design of compilers.

A variety of different notations are used for BNF. The one that I will use here is fairly common. Although other notations are used, they express the same concepts.

In English, terms such as "noun", "transitive verb," and "prepositional phrase" are *syntactic categories* that describe building blocks of sentences. Similarly, "statement", "number," and "while loop" are syntactic categories that describe building blocks of Java programs. In BNF, a syntactic category is written as a word enclosed between "<" and ">". For example: <noun>, <verb-phrase>, or <while-loop>. A *rule* in BNF specifies the structure of an item in a given syntactic category, in terms of other syntactic categories and/or basic symbols of the language. For example, one BNF rule for the English language might be

<sentence> ::=   <noun-phrase> <verb-phrase>

The symbol "::=" is read "can be", so this rule says that a <sentence> can be a <noun-phrase> followed by a <verb-phrase>. (The term is "can be" rather than "is" because there might be other rules that specify other possible forms for a sentence.) This rule can be thought of as a recipe for a sentence: If you want to make a sentence, make a noun-phrase and follow it by a verb-phrase. Noun-phrase and verb-phrase must, in turn, be defined by other BNF rules.

In BNF, a choice between alternatives is represented by the symbol "|", which is read "or". For example, the rule

<verb-phrase> ::= <intransitive-verb> |
(<transitive-verb> <noun-phrase>)

says that a <verb-phrase> can be an <intransitive-verb>, or a <transitive-verb> followed by a <noun-phrase>. Note also that parentheses can be used for grouping. To express the fact that an item is optional, it can be enclosed between "[" and "]". An optional item that can be repeated any number of times is enclosed between "[" and "]...". And a symbol that is an actual part of the language that is being described is enclosed in quotes. For example,

<noun-phrase> ::= <common-noun> ["that" <verb-phrase>] |
<common-noun> [<prepositional-phrase>]...

says that a <noun-phrase> can be a <common-noun>, optionally followed by the literal word "that" and a <verb-phrase>, or it can be a <common-noun> followed by zero or more <prepositional-phrase>'s. Obviously, we can describe very complex structures in this way. The real power comes from the fact that BNF rules can be recursive. In fact, the two preceding rules, taken together, are recursive. A <noun-phrase> is defined partly in terms of <verb-phrase>, while <verb-phrase> is defined partly in terms of <noun-phrase>. For example, a <noun-phrase> might be "the rat that ate the cheese", since "ate the cheese" is a <verb-phrase>. But then we can, recursively, make the more complex <noun-phrase> "the cat that caught the rat that ate the cheese" out of the <common-noun> "the cat", the word "that" and the <verb-phrase> "caught the rat that ate the cheese". Building from there, we can make the <noun-phrase> "the dog that chased the cat that caught the rat that ate the cheese". The recursive structure of language is one of the most fundamental properties of language, and the ability of BNF to express this recursive structure is what makes it so useful.

BNF can be used to describe the syntax of a programming language such as Java in a formal and precise way. For example, a <while-loop> can be defined as

<while-loop> ::= "while" "(" <condition> ")" <statement>

This says that a <while-loop> consists of the word "while", followed by a left parenthesis, followed by a <condition>, followed by a right parenthesis, followed by a <statement>. Of course, it still remains to define what is meant by a condition and by a statement. Since a statement can be, among other things, a while loop, we can already see the recursive structure of the Java language. The exact specification of an if statement, which is hard to express clearly in words, can be given as

<if-statement> ::=

"if" "(" <condition> ")" <statement>

["else" "if" "(" <condition> ")" <statement>]...

["else" <statement>]

This rule makes it clear that the "else" part is optional and that there can be, optionally, one or more "else if" parts.

5.5.2 Recursive Descent Parsing

In the rest of this section, I will show how a BNF grammar for a language can be used as a guide for constructing a parser. A parser is a program that determines the grammatical structure of a phrase in the language. This is the first step in determining the meaning of the phrase—which for a programming language means translating it into machine language. Although we will look at only a simple example, I hope it will be enough to convince you that compilers can in fact be written and understood by mortals and to give you some idea of how that can be done.

The parsing method that we will use is called *recursive descent parsing* . It is not the only possible parsing method, or the most efficient, but it is the one most suited for writing compilers by hand (rather than with the help of so called "parser generator" programs). In a recursive descent parser, every rule of the BNF grammar is the model for a subroutine. Not every BNF grammar is suitable for recursive descent parsing. The grammar must satisfy a certain property. Essentially, while parsing a phrase, it must be possible to tell what syntactic category is coming up next just by looking at the next item in the input. Many grammars are designed with this property in mind.

When we try to parse a phrase that contains a syntax error, we need some way to respond to the error. A convenient way of doing this is to throw an exception. I'll use an exception class called *ParseError*, defined as follows:

*/***

An object of type ParseError represents a syntax error found in

the user's input.

```
*/
private static class ParseError extends Exception {
    ParseError(String message) {
        super(message);
    }
} // end nested class ParseError
```

Another general point is that our BNF rules don't say anything about spaces between items, but in reality we want to be able to insert spaces between items at will. To allow for this, I'll always call the routine TextIO.skipBlanks() before trying to look ahead to see what's coming up next in input. TextIO.skipBlanks() skips past any whitespace, such as spaces and tabs, in the input, and stops when the next character in the input is either a non-blank character or the end-of-line character.

Let's start with a very simple example. A "fully parenthesized expression" can be specified in BNF by the rules

```
<expression>    ::=    <number>    |
                       "(" <expression> <operator> <expression> ")"
<operator>  ::=    "+" | "-" | "*" | "/"
```

where <number> refers to any non-negative real number. An example of a fully parenthesized expression is "(((34-17)*8)+(2*7))". Since every operator corresponds to a pair of parentheses, there is no ambiguity about the order in which the operators are to be applied. Suppose we want a program that will read and evaluate such expressions. We'll read the expressions from standard input, using *TextIO*. To apply recursive descent parsing, we need a subroutine for each rule in the grammar. Corresponding to the rule for <operator>, we get a subroutine that reads an operator. The operator can be a choice of any of four things. Any other input will be an error.

```
/**
If the next character in input is one of the legal operators,
read it and return it. Otherwise, throw a ParseError.
*/
static char getOperator() throws ParseError {
    TextIO.skipBlanks();
    char op = TextIO.peek(); // look ahead at the next char, without reading it
    if ( op == '+' || op == '-' || op == '*' || op == '/' ) {
        TextIO.getAnyChar();    // read the operator, to remove it from the input
```

```
            return op;
        }
        else if (op == '\n')
            throw new ParseError("Missing operator at end of line.");
        else
            throw new ParseError("Missing operator. Found \"" +
                    op + "\" instead of +, -, *, or /.");
    } // end getOperator()
```

I've tried to give a reasonable error message, depending on whether the next character is an end-of-line or something else. I use TextIO.peek() to look ahead at the next character before I read it, and I call TextIO.skipBlanks() before testing TextIO.peek() in order to ignore any blanks that separate items. I will follow this same pattern in every case.

When we come to the subroutine for <expression>, things are a little more interesting. The rule says that an expression can be either a number or an expression enclosed in parentheses. We can tell which it is by looking ahead at the next character. If the character is a digit, we have to read a number. If the character is a "(", we have to read the "(", followed by an expression, followed by an operator, followed by another expression, followed by a ")". If the next character is anything else, there is an error. Note that we need recursion to read the nested expressions. The routine doesn't just read the expression. It also computes and returns its value. This requires semantical information that is not specified in the BNF rule.

```
    /**
    Read an expression from the current line of input and return its value.
    @throws ParseError if the input contains a syntax error
    */
    private static double expressionValue() throws ParseError {
        TextIO.skipBlanks();
        if ( Character.isDigit(TextIO.peek()) ) {
                    // The next item in input is a number, so the expression
                    // must consist of just that number.      Read and return
                    // the number.
            return TextIO.getDouble();
        }
```

```
else if ( TextIO.peek() == '(' ) {
            // The expression must be of the form
            //         "(" <expression> <operator> <expression> ")"
            // Read all these items, perform the operation, and
            // return the result.
      TextIO.getAnyChar();      // Read the "("
      double leftVal = expressionValue(); // Read and evaluate first operand.
      char op = getOperator();  // Read the operator.
      double rightVal = expressionValue(); // Read and evaluate second operand.
      TextIO.skipBlanks();
      if ( TextIO.peek() != ')' ) {
                  // According to the rule, there must be a ")" here.
                  // Since it's missing, throw a ParseError.
            throw new ParseError("Missing right parenthesis.");
      }
      TextIO.getAnyChar(); // Read the ")"
      switch (op) { // Apply the operator and return the result.
            case '+': return leftVal + rightVal;
            case '-': return leftVal - rightVal;
            case '*': return leftVal * rightVal;
            case '/': return leftVal / rightVal;
            default: return 0; // Can't occur since op is one of the above.
                        // (But Java syntax requires a return value.)
      }
}
else {    // No other character can legally start an expression.
      throw new ParseError("Encountered unexpected character, \"" +
            TextIO.peek() + "\" in input.");
}
} // end expressionValue()
```

I hope that you can see how this routine corresponds to the BNF rule. Where the rule uses “|” to give a choice between alternatives, there is an if statement in the routine to determine which choice to take. Where the rule contains a sequence of items, “(“ <expression> <operator> <expression> “)”, there is a sequence of statements in the subroutine to read each item in turn.

When expressionValue() is called to evaluate the expression (((34-17)*8)+(2*7)), it sees the “(“ at the beginning of the input, so the else part of the if statement is executed. The “(“ is read. Then the first recursive call to expressionValue() reads and evaluates the subexpression ((34-17)*8), the call to getOperator() reads the “+” operator, and the second recursive call to expressionValue() reads and evaluates the second subexpression (2*7). Finally, the “)” at the end of the expression is read. Of course, reading the first subexpression, ((34-17)*8), involves further recursive calls to the expressionValue() routine, but it’s better not to think too deeply about that! Rely on the recursion to handle the details.

You’ll find a complete program that uses these routines in the file SimpleParser1.java.

Fully parenthesized expressions aren’t very natural for people to use. But with ordinary expressions, we have to worry about the question of operator precedence, which tells us, for example, that the “*” in the expression “5+3*7” is applied before the “+”. The complex expression “3*6+8*(7+1)/4-24” should be seen as made up of three “terms”, 3*6, 8*(7+1)/4, and 24, combined with “+” and “-” operators. A term, on the other hand, can be made up of several factors combined with “*” and “/” operators. For example, 8*(7+1)/4 contains the factors 8, (7+1) and 4. This example also shows that a factor can be either a number or an expression in parentheses. To complicate things a bit more, we allow for leading minus signs in expressions, as in “-(3+4)” or “-7”. (Since a <number> is a positive number, this is the only way we can get negative numbers. It’s done this way to avoid “3 * -7”, for example.) This structure can be expressed by the BNF rules

<expression> ::= [“-”] <term> [(“+” | “-”) <term>]...

<term> ::= <factor> [(“” | “/”) <factor>]...*

<factor> ::= <number> | “(“ <expression> “)”

The first rule uses the “[ ]...” notation, which says that the items that it encloses can occur zero, one, two, or more times. The rule means that an <expression> can begin, optionally, with a “-”. Then there must be a <term> which can optionally be followed by one of the operators “+” or “-” and another <term>, optionally followed by another operator and <term>, and so on. In a subroutine that reads and evaluates expressions, this repetition is handled by a while loop. An if statement is used at the beginning of the loop to test whether a leading minus sign is present:

```
/**
Read an expression from the current line of input and return its value.
@throws ParseError if the input contains a syntax error
*/
private static double expressionValue() throws ParseError {
    TextIO.skipBlanks();
    boolean negative;        // True if there is a leading minus sign.
    negative = false;
    if (TextIO.peek() == '-') {
            TextIO.getAnyChar();    // Read the minus sign.
            negative = true;
    }
    double val;      // Value of the expression.
    val = termValue();        // Read and evaluate the first term.
    if (negative)
            val = -val;       // Apply the leading minus sign to the first term.
    TextIO.skipBlanks();
    while ( TextIO.peek() == '+' || TextIO.peek() == '-' ) {
                        // Read the next term and add it to or subtract it from
                        // the value of previous terms in the expression.
                char op = TextIO.getAnyChar(); // Read the operator.
                double nextVal = termValue(); // Read and evaluate the next term.
                if (op == '+')
                        val += nextVal;
                else
                        val -= nextVal;
                TextIO.skipBlanks();
            }
    return val;
} // end expressionValue()
```

The subroutine for <term> is very similar to this, and the subroutine for <factor> is similar to the example given above for fully parenthesized expressions. A complete program that reads and evaluates expressions based on the above BNF rules can be found in the file SimpleParser2.java.

5.5.3 Building an Expression Tree

Now, so far, we've only evaluated expressions. What does that have to do with translating programs into machine language? Well, instead of actually evaluating the expression, it would be almost as easy to generate the machine language instructions that are needed to evaluate the expression. If we are working with a "stack machine," these instructions would be stack operations such as "push a number" or "apply a + operation". The program SimpleParser3.java can both evaluate the expression and print a list of stack machine operations for evaluating the expression.

It's quite a jump from this program to a recursive descent parser that can read a program written in Java and generate the equivalent machine language code—but the conceptual leap is not huge.

The SimpleParser3 program doesn't actually generate the stack operations directly as it parses an expression. Instead, it builds an expression tree, as discussed in Subsection 5.4.3, to represent the expression. The expression tree is then used to find the value and to generate the stack operations. The tree is made up of nodes belonging to classes *ConstNode* and *BinOpNode* that are similar to those given in Subsection 5.4.3. Another subclass of *ExpNote*, *UnaryMinusNode*, has been introduced to represent the unary minus operation. I've added a method, printStackCommands(), to each class. This method is responsible for printing out the stack operations that are necessary to evaluate an expression. Here for example is the new BinOpNode class from SimpleParser3.java:

```
private static class BinOpNode extends ExpNode {
    char op;// The operator.
    ExpNode left;     // The expression for its left operand.
    ExpNode right;  // The expression for its right operand.
    BinOpNode(char op, ExpNode left, ExpNode right) {
                // Construct a BinOpNode containing the specified data.
        assert op == '+' || op == '-' || op == '*' || op == '/';
        assert left != null && right != null;
                // (for assert statements, see Subsection 8.4.1)
        this.op = op;
```

```
        this.left = left;
        this.right = right;
}
double value() {
                // The value is obtained by evaluating the left and right
                // operands and combining the values with the operator.
        double x = left.value();
        double y = right.value();
        switch (op) {
        case '+':
                return x + y;
        case '-':
                return x - y;
        case '*':
                return x * y;
        case '/':
                return x / y;
        default:
                return Double.NaN;      // Bad operator! Should not be possible.
        }
}
void    printStackCommands() {
                // To evaluate the expression on a stack machine, first do
                // whatever is necessary to evaluate the left operand, leaving
                // the answer on the stack.  Then do the same thing for the
                // second operand. Then apply the operator (which means popping
                // the operands, applying the operator, and pushing the result).
        left.printStackCommands();
        right.printStackCommands();
        System.out.println("      Operator " + op);
}
```

```
}
```

It's also interesting to look at the new parsing subroutines. Instead of computing a value, each subroutine builds an expression tree. For example, the subroutine corresponding to the rule for <expression> becomes

```
static ExpNode expressionTree() throws ParseError {
            // Read an expression from the current line of input and
            // return an expression tree representing the expression.
            // (The return value is a pointer to the root of the tree.)
      TextIO.skipBlanks();
      boolean negative;         // True if there is a leading minus sign.
      negative = false;
      if (TextIO.peek() == '-') {
            TextIO.getAnyChar();
            negative = true;
      }
      ExpNode exp;    // The expression tree for the expression
      exp = termTree();         // Start with a tree for first term.
      if (negative) {
                  // Build the tree that corresponds to applying a
                  // unary minus operator to the term we've
                  // just read.
            exp = new UnaryMinusNode(exp);
      }
      TextIO.skipBlanks();
      while ( TextIO.peek() == '+' || TextIO.peek() == '-' ) {
                  // Read the next term and combine it with the
                  // previous terms into a bigger expression tree.
            char op = TextIO.getAnyChar();
            ExpNode nextTerm = termTree();
                  // Create a tree that applies the binary operator
                  // to the previous tree and the term we just read.
            exp = new BinOpNode(op, exp, nextTerm);
```

```
            TextIO.skipBlanks();
        }
        return exp;
    } // end expressionTree()
```

In some real compilers, the parser creates a tree to represent the program that is being parsed. This tree is called a *parse tree* or *abstract syntax tree*. Parse trees are somewhat different in form from expression trees, but the purpose is the same. Once you have the tree, there are a number of things you can do with it. For one thing, it can be used to generate machine language code. But there are also techniques for examining the tree and detecting certain types of programming errors, such as an attempt to reference a local variable before it has been assigned a value. (The Java compiler, of course, will reject the program if it contains such an error.) It's also possible to manipulate the tree to *optimize* the program.

In optimization, the tree is transformed to make the program more efficient before the code is generated.

And so we are back where we started in Chapter 1, looking at programming languages, compilers, and machine language. But looking at them, I hope, with a lot more understanding and a much wider perspective.

Chapter 6 GENERIC PROGRAMMING AND COLLECTION FRAMEWORKS

How can one prevent the duplication of existing solutions? Numerous data structures and algorithms, including those from Chapter 5, have been examined, implemented, and re-implemented by successive generations of computer science students. This constitutes a significant educational opportunity. Regrettably, they have been repeatedly programmed and reprogrammed by successive generations of computer specialists, consuming time that could be allocated to innovative and creative endeavors. A programmer requiring a list or a binary tree should not be compelled to implement these data structures from the ground up. They are comprehensively understood and have been coded numerous times previously. The challenge is in providing programmers access to pre-existing, resilient data structures. This chapter examines Java's efforts to resolve this issue.

A portion of the answer has previously been presented in Section 3.3. The section presented parameterized types and the ArrayList class. Parameterized types enable a single class to operate with various data types. The concept that identical code can be applied to multiple data types is referred to as generic programming.

6.1 GENERIC PROGRAMMING

Generic programming refers to writing code that will work for many types of data. We encountered the alternative to generic programming in Subsection 3.2.4, where we looked at dynamic arrays of integers. The source code presented there for working with dynamic arrays of integers works only for data of type int. But the source code for dynamic arrays of double, *String*, *Color*, or any other type would be almost identical, except for the substitution of one type name for another. It seems silly to write essentially the same code over and over. Java's approach to this problem is parameterized types. As we saw in Section 3.3, the parameterized class *ArrayList* implements dynamic arrays. Since it is parameterized, there are types such as ArrayList<String> to represent dynamic arrays of *String*, ArrayList<Color> for dynamic arrays of colors, and more generally ArrayList<T> for any object type *T*. *ArrayList* is just one class, but the source code works for many different types. This is generic programming.

The *ArrayList* class is just one of many standard classes that are used for generic programming in Java. We will spend the next three sections looking at some of these classes and how they are used, and we'll see that there are also generic methods and generic interfaces. The classes and interfaces discussed in these sections are defined in the package java.util, and you will need import statements at the beginning of your programs to get access to them.

In Section 6.5, we will see that it is possible to define new generic classes, interfaces, and methods. Until then, we will stick to using Java's predefined generics. And in Section 6.6, we will look at *streams*, a relatively new feature of Java that makes extensive use of generics.

It is no easy task to design a library for generic programming. Java's solution has many nice features but is certainly not the only possible approach. It is almost certainly not the best, and has a few features that in my opinion can only be called bizarre, but in the context of the overall design of Java, it might be close to optimal. To get some perspective on generic programming in general, it might be useful to look very briefly at some other approaches to generic programming.

6.1.1 Generic Programming in Smalltalk

Smalltalk was one of the very first object-oriented programming languages. It is still used today, although its use is not very common. It never achieved anything like the popularity of Java or C++, but it is the source of many ideas used in these languages. In Smalltalk, essentially all programming is generic, because of two basic properties of the language.

First of all, variables in Smalltalk are typeless. A data value has a type, such as integer or string, but variables do not have types. Any variable can hold data of any type. Parameters are also typeless, so a subroutine can be applied to parameter values of any type. Similarly, a data structure can hold data values of any type. For example, once you've defined a binary tree data structure in SmallTalk, you can use it for binary trees of integers or strings or dates or data of any other type. There is simply no need to write new code for each data type.

Secondly, all data values are objects, and all operations on objects are defined by methods in a class. This is true even for types that are "primitive" in Java, such as integers. When the "+" operator is used to add two integers, the operation is performed by calling a method in the integer class. When you define a new class, you can define a "+" operator, and you will then be able to add objects belonging to that class by saying "a + b" just as if you were adding numbers. Now, suppose that you write a subroutine that uses the "+" operator to add up the items in a list. The subroutine can be applied to a list of integers, but it can also be applied, automatically, to any other data type for which "+" is defined. Similarly, a subroutine that uses the "<" operator to sort a list can be applied to lists containing any type of data for which "<" is defined. There is no need to write a different sorting subroutine for each type of data.

Put these two features together and you have a language where data structures and algorithms will work for any type of data for which they make sense, that is, for which the appropriate operations are defined. This is real generic programming. This might sound pretty good, and you might be asking yourself why all programming languages don't work this way. This type of freedom makes it easier to write programs, but unfortunately it makes it harder to write programs that are correct and robust (see Chapter 8). Once you have a data structure that can contain data of any type, it becomes hard to ensure that it only holds the type of data that you want it to hold. If you have a subroutine that can sort any type of data, it's hard to ensure that it will only be applied to data for which the "<" operator is defined. More particularly, there is no way for a compiler to ensure these things. The problem will only show up at run time when an attempt is made to apply some operation to a data type for which it is not defined, and the program will crash.

6.1.2 Generic Programming in C++

Unlike Smalltalk, C++ is a very strongly typed language. Every variable has a type, and can only hold data values of that type. This means that the kind of generic programming that is used in Smalltalk is impossible in C++. Nevertheless, C++ has a powerful and flexible system of generic programming. It is made possible by a language feature known as *templates*. In C++, instead of writing a different sorting subroutine for each type of data, you can write a single subroutine template. The template is not a subroutine; it's more like a factory for making subroutines. We can look at an example, since the syntax of C++ is very similar to Java's:

```
template<class ItemType>
void sort( ItemType A[], int count ) {
            // Sort items in the array, A, into increasing order.
            // The items in positions 0, 1, 2, ..., (count-1) are sorted.
            // The algorithm that is used here is selection sort.
      for int i = count-1; i > 0; i--) {
            int position of max = 0;
            for (int j = 1; j <= i ; j++)
                  if ( A[j] > A[position of max] )
                        position of max = j;
            ItemType temp = A[i];
            A[i] = A[position of max];
            A[position of max] = temp;
}
}
```

This piece of code defines a subroutine template. If you remove the first line, "template<class ItemType>", and substitute the word "int" for the word "ItemType" in the rest of the template, you get a subroutine for sorting arrays of ints. (Even though it says "class ItemType", you can actually substitute any type for ItemType, including the primitive types.) If you substitute "string" for "ItemType", you get a subroutine for sorting arrays of strings. This is pretty much what the compiler does with the template. If your program says "sort(list,10)" where list is an array of ints, the compiler uses the template to generate a subroutine for sorting arrays of ints. If you say "sort(cards,10)" where cards is an array of objects of type *Card*, then the compiler generates a subroutine for sorting arrays of *Cards*. At least, it tries to. The template uses the ">" operator to compare values. If this operator is defined for values of type *Card*, then the compiler will successfully use the template to generate a subroutine for sorting cards. If ">" is not defined for *Cards*, then the compiler will fail—but this will happen at compile time, not, as in Smalltalk, at run time where it would make the program crash. (By the way, in C++, it is possible to write definitions of operators like > for any type, so that it is possible that > might work for values of type *Card*.)

In addition to subroutine templates, C++ also has templates for making classes. If you write a template for a binary tree class, you can use it to generate classes for binary trees of ints, binary trees of strings, binary trees of dates, and so on—all from one template. Modern C++ comes with a large number of pre-written templates called the *Standard Template Library* or STL. The STL is quite complex. Many people would say that it's much too complex. But it is also one of the most interesting features of C++.

6.1.3 Generic Programming in Java

Java's generic programming features have gone through several stages of development. Early versions of Java did not have parameterized types, but they did have classes to represent common data structures. Those classes were designed to work with *Objects*; that is, they could hold objects of any type, and there was no way to restrict the types of objects that could be stored in a given data structure. For example, *ArrayList* was not originally a parameterized type, so that any ArrayList could hold any type of object. This means that if list was an *ArrayList*, then list.get(i) would return a value of type *Object*. If the programmer was actually using the list to store *Strings*, the value returned by list.get(i) would have to be type-cast to treat it as a string:

```
String item = (String)list.get(i);
```

This is still a kind of generic programming, since one class can work for any kind of object, but it was closer in spirit to Smalltalk than it was to C++, since there is no way to do type checks at compile time. Unfortunately, as in Smalltalk, the result is a category of errors that show up only at run time, rather than at compile time. If a programmer assumes that all the items in a data structure are strings and tries to process those items as strings, a run-time error will occur if other types of data have inadvertently been added to the data structure. In Java, the error will most likely occur when the program retrieves an *Object* from the data structure and tries to type-cast it to type *String*. If the object is not actually of type *String*, the illegal type-cast will throw an error of type *ClassCastException*.

Java 5.0 introduced parameterized types, which made it possible to create generic data structures that can be type-checked at compile time rather than at run time. For example, if list is of type ArrayList<String>, then the compiler will only allow objects of type *String* to be added to list. Furthermore, the return type of list.get(i) is *String*, so type-casting is not necessary. Java's parameterized classes are similar to template classes in C++ (although the implementation is very different), and their introduction moves Java's generic programming model closer to C++ and farther from Smalltalk. In this chapter, I will use the parameterized types exclusively, but you should remember that their use is not mandatory. It is still legal to use a parameterized class as a non-parameterized type, such as a plain *ArrayList*. In that case, any type of object can be stored in the data structure. (But if that is what you really want to do, it would be preferable to use the type ArrayList<Object>.)

Note that there is a significant difference between parameterized classes in Java and template classes in C++. A template class in C++ is not really a class at all—it's a kind of factory for generating classes. Every time the template is used with a new type, a new compiled class is created. With a Java parameterized class, there is only one compiled class file. For example, there is only one compiled class file, ArrayList.class, for the parameterized class *ArrayList*. The parameterized types *ArrayList<String>* and *ArrayList<Integer>* both use the same compiled class file, as does the plain *ArrayList* type. The type parameter—*String* or *Integer* —just tells the compiler to limit the type of object that can be stored in the data structure. The type parameter has no effect at run time and is not even known at run time. The type information is said to be "erased" at run time. This *type erasure* introduces a certain amount of weirdness. For example, you can't test "if (list instanceof ArrayList<String>)" because the instanceof operator is evaluated at run time, and at run time only the plain *ArrayList* exists. Similarly, you can't type-cast to the type ArrayList<String>. Even worse, you can't create an array that has base type ArrayList<String> by using the new operator, as in "new ArrayList<String>[N]". This is because the new operator is evaluated at run time, and at run time there is no such thing as "ArrayList<String>"; only the non- parameterized type *ArrayList* exists at run time. (However, although you can't have an array of ArrayList<String>, you can have an ArrayList of ArrayList<String>—with the type written as ArrayList<ArrayList<String>>—which is just as good or better.)

Fortunately, most programmers don't have to deal with such problems, since they turn up only in fairly advanced programming. Most people who use parameterized types will not encounter the problems, and they will get the benefits of type-safe generic programming with little difficulty.

It's worth noting that if the type parameter in a parameterized type can be deduced by the compiler, then the name of the type parameter can be omitted. For example, the word "String" is optional in the constructor in the following statement, because the *ArrayList* that is created must be an ArrayList<String> to match the type of the variable:

ArrayList<String> words = new ArrayList<>();

6.1.4 The Java Collection Framework

As I've said, Java comes with a number of parameterized types that implement common data structures. This collection of data structure classes and interfaces is referred to as the *Java Collection Framework* , or *JCF* . We will spend the next few sections learning about the JCF.

The generic data structures in the Java Collection Framework can be divided into two categories: *collections* and *maps.* A collection is more or less what it sounds like: a collection of objects. A map associates objects in one set with objects in another set in the way that a dictionary associates definitions with words or a phone book associates phone numbers with names. A map is similar to what I called an "association list" in Subsection 3.5.2. In Java, collections and maps are represented by the parameterized interfaces *Collection<T>* and *Map<T,S>*. Here, "T" and "S" stand for any type except for the primitive types. *Map<T,S>* is an example of a parameterized type that has two type parameters, *T* and *S* ; we will not deal further with this possibility until we look at maps more closely in Section 6.3. In this section and the next, we look at collections only.

There are two types of collections: *lists* and *sets.* A list is a collection in which the objects are arranged in a linear sequence. A list has a first item, a second item, and so on. For any item in the list, except the last, there is an item that directly follows it. For collections that are "sets," the defining property is that no object can occur more than once in a set; the elements of a set are not necessarily thought of as being in any particular order. The ideas of lists and sets are represented as parameterized interfaces *List<T>* and *Set<T>*. These are sub- interfaces of *Collection<T>*. That is, any object that implements the interface *List<T>* or *Set<T>* automatically implements *Collection<T>* as well. The interface *Collection<T>* specifies general operations that can be applied to any collection at all. *List<T>* and *Set<T>* add additional operations that are appropriate for lists and sets respectively.

Of course, any actual object that is a collection, list, or set must belong to a concrete class that implements the corresponding interface. For example, the class *ArrayList<T>* implements the interface *List<T>* and therefore also implements *Collection<T>*. This means that all the methods that are defined in the list and collection interfaces can be used with an ArrayList. We will look at various classes that implement the list and set interfaces in the next section. But before we do that, we'll look briefly at some of the general operations that are available for all collections.

The interface *Collection<T>* specifies methods for performing some basic operations on any collection of objects. Since "collection" is a very general concept, operations that can be applied to all collections are also very general. They are generic operations in the sense that they can be applied to various types of collections containing various types of objects. Suppose that coll is an object that implements the interface *Collection<T>* (for some specific non-primitive type *T*). Then the following operations, which are specified in the interface *Collection<T>*, are defined for coll:

- coll.size() — returns an int that gives the number of objects in the collection.
- coll.isEmpty() — returns a boolean value which is true if the size of the collection is 0.
- coll.clear() — removes all objects from the collection.
- coll.add(tobject) — adds tobject to the collection. The parameter must be of type *T* ; if not, a syntax error occurs at compile time. (Remember that if *T* is a class, this includes objects belonging to a subclass of *T*, and if *T* is an interface, it includes any object that implements *T*.) The add() method returns a boolean value which tells you whether the operation actually modified the collection. For example, adding an object to a Set has no effect if that object was already in the set.
- coll.contains(object) — returns a boolean value that is true if object is in the collection. Note that object is not required to be of type *T*, since it makes sense to check whether object is in the collection, no matter what type object has. (For testing equality, null is considered to be equal to itself. The criterion for testing non-null objects for equality can differ from one kind of collection to another; see Subsection 6.1.6, below.)
- coll.remove(object) — removes object from the collection, if it occurs in the collection, and returns a boolean value that tells you whether the object was found. Again, object is not required to be of type *T*. The test for equality is the same test that is used by contains().

- coll.containsAll(coll2) — returns a boolean value that is true if every object in coll2 is also in coll. The parameter can be any collection.
- coll.addAll(coll2) — adds all the objects in coll2 to coll. The parameter, coll2, can be any collection of type *Collection<T>*. However, it can also be more general. For example, if *T* is a class and *S* is a sub-class of *T*, then coll2 can be of type *Collection<S>*. This makes sense because any object of type *S* is automatically of type *T* and so can legally be added to coll.
- coll.removeAll(coll2) — removes every object from coll that also occurs in the collection coll2. coll2 can be any collection.
- coll.retainAll(coll2) — removes every object from coll that does not occur in the collection coll2. It "retains" only the objects that do occur in coll2. coll2 can be any collection.
- coll.toArray() — returns an array of type Object[ ] that contains all the items in the collection. Note that the return type is Object[ ], not T[ ]! However, there is another version of this method that takes an array of type T[ ] as a parameter: the method coll.toArray(tarray) returns an array of type T[ ] containing all the items in the collection. If the array parameter tarray is large enough to hold the entire collection, then the items are stored in tarray and tarray is also the return value of the collection. If tarray is not large enough, then a new array is created to hold the items; in that case tarray serves only to specify the type of the array. For example, coll. toArray(new String[0]) can be used if coll is a collection of *Strings* and will return a new array of type String[ ].

Since these methods are part of the *Collection<T>* interface, they must be defined for every object that implements that interface. There is a problem with this, however. For example, the size of some collections cannot be changed after they are created. Methods that add or remove objects don't make sense for these collections. While it is still legal to call the methods, an exception will be thrown when the call is evaluated at run time. The type of the exception is *UnsupportedOperationException.* Furthermore, since *Collection<T>* is only an interface, not a concrete class, the actual implementation of the method is left to the classes that implement the interface. This means that the semantics of the methods, as described above, are not guaranteed to be valid for all collection objects; they are valid, however, for classes in the Java Collection Framework.

There is also the question of efficiency. Even when an operation is defined for several types of collections, it might not be equally efficient in all cases. Even a method as simple as size() can vary greatly in efficiency. For some collections, computing the size() might involve counting the items in the collection. The number of steps in this process is equal to the number of items. Other collections might have instance variables to keep track of the size, so evaluating size() just means returning the value of a variable. In this case, the computation takes only one step, no matter how many items there are. When working with collections, it's good to have some idea of how efficient operations are and to choose a collection for which the operations that you need can be implemented most efficiently. We'll see specific examples of this in the next two sections.

6.1.5 Iterators and for-each Loops

The interface *Collection<T>* defines a few basic generic algorithms, but suppose you want to write your own generic algorithms. Suppose, for example, you want to do something as simple as printing out every item in a collection. To do this in a generic way, you need some way of going through an arbitrary collection, accessing each item in turn. We have seen how to do this for specific data structures: For an array, you can use a for loop to iterate through all the array indices. For a linked list, you can use a while loop in which you advance a pointer along the list. For a binary tree, you can use a recursive subroutine to do an inorder traversal. Collections can be represented in any of these forms and many others besides. With such a variety of traversal mechanisms, how can we even hope to come up with a single generic method that will work for collections that are stored in wildly different forms? This problem is solved by *iterators*. An iterator is an object that can be used to traverse a collection. Different types of collections have iterators that are implemented in different ways, but all iterators are used in the same way. An algorithm that uses an iterator to traverse a collection is generic, because the same technique can be applied to any type of collection. Iterators can seem rather strange to someone who is encountering generic programming for the first time, but you should understand that they solve a difficult problem in an elegant way.

The interface *Collection<T>* defines a method that can be used to obtain an iterator for any collection. If coll is a collection, then coll.iterator() returns an iterator that can be used to traverse the collection. You should think of the iterator as a kind of generalized pointer that starts at the beginning of the collection and can move along the collection from one item to the next. Iterators are defined by a parameterized interface named *Iterator<T>*. If coll implements the interface *Collection<T>* for some specific type *T*, then coll.iterator() returns an iterator of type *Iterator<T>*, with the same type *T* as its type parameter. The interface *Iterator<T>* defines just three methods. If iter refers to an object that implements *Iterator<T>*, then we have:

- iter.next() — returns the next item, and advances the iterator. The return value is of type *T*. This method lets you look at one of the items in the collection. Note that there is no way to look at an item without advancing the iterator past that item. If this method is called when no items remain, it will throw a *NoSuchElementException*.

- iter.hasNext() – returns a boolean value telling you whether there are more items to be processed. In general, you should test this before calling iter.next().
- iter.remove() – if you call this after calling iter.next(), it will remove the item that you just saw from the collection. Note that this method has no parameter. It removes the item that was most recently returned by iter.next(). This might produce an *UnsupportedOperationException*, if the collection does not support removal of items.

Using iterators, we can write code for printing all the items in any collection. Suppose, for example, that coll is of type *Collection<String>*. In that case, the value returned by coll.iterator() is of type *Iterator<String>*, and we can say:

```
Iterator<String> iter;              // Declare the iterator variable.
iter = coll.iterator();             // Get an iterator for the collection.
while ( iter.hasNext() ) {
    String item = iter.next();      // Get the next item.
    System.out.println(item);
}
```

The same general form will work for other types of processing. For example, the following code will remove all null values from any collection of type *Collection<Color>* (as long as that collection supports removal of values):

```
Iterator<Color> iter = coll.iterator():
while ( iter.hasNext() ) {
    Color item = iter.next();
    if (item == null)
            iter.remove();
    }
```

(Note, by the way, that when *Collection<T>*, *Iterator<T>*, or any other parameterized type is used in actual code, they are always used with actual types such as *String* or *Color* in place of the "formal type parameter" *T*. An iterator of type *Iterator<String>* is used to iterate through a collection of *Strings*; an iterator of type *Iterator<Color>* is used to iterate through a collection of *Color* ; and so on.)

An iterator is often used to apply the same operation to all the elements in a collection. In many cases, it's possible to avoid the use of iterators for this purpose by using a for-each loop. The for-each loop was discussed in Subsection 3.1.1 for use with arrays and in Subsection 3.3.3 for use with ArrayLists. But in fact, a for-each loop can be used to iterate through any collection. For a collection coll of type *Collection<T>*, a for-each loop takes the form:

```
for ( T x : coll ) { // "for each object x, of type T, in coll"
    //      process x
}
```

Here, x is the loop control variable. Each object in coll will be assigned to x in turn, and the body of the loop will be executed for each object. Since objects in coll are of type *T*, x is declared to be of type *T*. For example, if namelist is of type *Collection<String>*, we can print out all the names in the collection with:

```
for ( String name : namelist ) {
    System.out.println( name );
}
```

This for-each loop could, of course, be written as a while loop using an iterator, but the for-each loop is much easier to follow.

6.1.6 Equality and Comparison

There are several methods in the *Collection* interface that test objects for equality. For example, the methods coll.contains(object) and coll.remove(object) look for an item in the collection that is equal to object. However, equality is not such a simple matter. The obvious technique for testing equality—using the == operator—does not usually give a reasonable answer when applied to objects. The == operator tests whether two objects are identical in the sense that they share the same location in memory. Usually, however, we want to consider two objects to be equal if they represent the same value, which is a very different thing. Two values of type *String* should be considered equal if they contain the same sequence of characters. The question of whether those characters are stored in the same location in memory is irrelevant. Two values of type *Date* should be considered equal if they represent the same time.

We have seen that the *Object* class defines the boolean-valued method equals(Object) for testing whether one object is equal to another. This method is used by many, but not by all, collection classes for deciding whether two objects are to be considered the same. In the *Object* class, obj1.equals(obj2) is defined to be the same as obj1 == obj2. However, for many sub-classes of Object, this definition is not reasonable, and it should be overridden. The *String* class, for example, overrides equals() so that for a *String* str, the value of str.equals(obj) is true when obj is also a *String* and obj contains the same sequence of characters as str.

If you write your own class, you might want to define an equals() method in that class to get the correct behavior when objects are tested for equality. For example, a *Card* class that will work correctly when used in collections could be defined as:

```
public class Card {   // Class to represent playing cards.
    private int suit; // Number from 0 to 3 that codes for the suit --
                      // spades, diamonds, clubs or hearts.
    private int value; // Number from 1 to 13 that represents the value.
    public boolean equals(Object obj) {
            try {
                    Card other = (Card)obj;    // Type-cast obj to a Card.
                    if (suit == other.suit && value == other.value) {
                            // The other card has the same suit and value as
                            // this card, so they should be considered equal.
                    return true;
            }
            else {
                    return false;
            }
    }
    catch (Exception e) {
                    // This will catch the NullPointerException that occurs if obj
                    // is null and the ClassCastException that occurs if obj is
                    // not of type Card.        In these cases, obj is not equal to
                    // this Card, so return false.
            return false;
            }
    }
    .
    . // other methods and constructors
    .
}
```

Without the equals() method in this class, methods such as contains() and remove() from the interface *Collection<Card>* will not work as expected.

A similar concern arises when items in a collection are sorted. Sorting refers to arranging a sequence of items in ascending order, according to some criterion. The problem is that there is no natural notion of ascending order for arbitrary objects. Before objects can be sorted, some method must be defined for comparing them. Objects that are meant to be compared should implement the interface java.lang.Comparable. In fact, *Comparable* is defined as a parameterized interface, *Comparable<T>*, which represents the ability to be compared to an object of type *T*. The interface *Comparable<T>* defines one method:

public int compareTo(T obj)

The value returned by obj1.compareTo(obj2) should be negative if and only if obj1 comes before obj2, when the objects are arranged in ascending order. It should be positive if and only if obj1 comes after obj2. A return value of zero means that the objects are considered to be the same for the purposes of this comparison. This does not necessarily mean that the objects are equal in the sense that obj1.equals(obj2) is true. But in general, classes that implement *Comparable* should try to define .equals() and compareTo() so that obj1.equals(obj2) and obj1.compareTo(obj2) == 0 always have the same value. (Some classes in the JCF use compareTo() rather than equals() to test objects for equality.)

The *String* class implements the interface *Comparable<String>* and defines compareTo in a reasonable way. In this case, the return value of compareTo is zero if and only if the two strings that are being compared are equal. If you define your own class and want to be able to sort objects belonging to that class, you should do the same. For example:

```
/**
* Represents a full name consisting of a first name and a last name.
*/
public class FullName implements Comparable<FullName> {
    private String firstName, lastName;        // Non-null first and last names.
    public FullName(String first, String last) {// Constructor.
            if (first == null || last == null)
                    throw new IllegalArgumentException("Names must be non-null.");
            firstName = first;
            lastName = last;
    }
```

```
public boolean equals(Object obj) {
        try {
        FullName other = (FullName)obj; // Type-cast obj to type FullName
        return firstName.equals(other.firstName)
                        && lastName.equals(other.lastName);
        }
        catch (Exception e) {
                return false;       // if obj is null or is not of type FullName
        }
}
public int compareTo( FullName other ) {
        int compareLast = lastName.compareTo(other.lastName);
        if ( compareLast < 0 ) {
                        // If lastName comes before the last name of
                        // the other object, then this FullName comes
                        // before the other FullName.     Return a negative
                        // value to indicate this.
                return -1;
}
else if ( compareLast > 0 ) {
                        // If lastName comes after the last name of
                        // the other object, then this FullName comes
                        // after the other FullName.      Return a positive
                        // value to indicate this.
                return 1;
}
else {
                        // Last names are the same, so base the comparison on
                        // the first names, using compareTo from class String.
                return firstName.compareTo(other.firstName);
        }
```

```
    }
    .
    . // other methods
    .
}
```

I find it a little odd that the class here is declared as "class FullName implements Comparable<FullName>", with "FullName" repeated as a type parameter in the name of the interface. However, it does make sense. It means that we are going to compare objects that belong to the class *FullName* to other objects of the same type. Even though this is the only reasonable thing to do, that fact is not obvious to the Java compiler—and the type parameter in *Comparable<FullName>* is there for the compiler.

There is another way to allow for comparison of objects in Java, and that is to provide a separate object that is capable of making the comparison. The object must implement the interface *Comparator<T>*, where *T* is the type of the objects that are to be compared. The interface *Comparator<T>* defines the method:

public int compare(T obj1, T obj2)

This method compares two objects of type *T* and returns a value that is negative, or positive, or zero, depending on whether obj1 comes before obj2, or comes after obj2, or is considered to be the same as obj2 for the purposes of this comparison. Comparators are useful for comparing objects that do not implement the *Comparable* interface and for defining several different orderings on the same collection of objects. Since *Comparator* is a functional interface, comparators are often defined by lambda expressions (see Section 4.5).

Note that it can often make sense to use a *Comparator* for which obj1.equals(obj2) does not always have the same value as compare(obj1,obj2) == 0. For example, when sorting addresses by zip code, you would use a *Comparator* that looks at the zip code field in the addresses that it compares.

In the next two sections, we'll see how *Comparable* and *Comparator* are used in the context of collections and maps.

6.1.7 Generics and Wrapper Classes

As noted in Section 3.3 about *ArrayLists*, Java's generic programming does not apply to the primitive types. This is because generic data structures can only hold objects, and values of primitive type are not objects. However, the "wrapper classes" that were introduced in Subsection 3.3.2 make it possible to get around this restriction to a great extent.

Recall that each primitive type has an associated wrapper class: class *Integer* for type int, class *Boolean* for type boolean, class *Character* for type char, and so on.

An object of type *Integer* contains a value of type int. The object serves as a "wrapper" for the primitive type value, which allows it to be used in contexts where objects are required, such as in generic data structures. For example, a list of *Integers* can be stored in a variable of type *ArrayList<Integer>*, and interfaces such as *Collection<Integer>* and *Set<Integer>* are defined. Furthermore, class *Integer* defines equals(), compareTo(), and toString() methods that do what you would expect (that is, that compare and write out the corresponding primitive type values in the usual way). Similar remarks apply for all the wrapper classes.

Recall also that Java does automatic conversions between a primitive type and the corresponding wrapper type. (These conversions, which are called autoboxing and unboxing, were also introduced in Subsection 3.3.3.) This means that once you have created a generic data structure to hold objects belonging to one of the wrapper classes, you can use the data structure pretty much as if it actually contained primitive type values. For example, if numbers is a variable of type *Collection<Integer>*, it is legal to call numbers.add(17) or numbers.remove(42). You can't literally add the primitive type value 17 to numbers, but Java will automatically convert the 17 to the corresponding wrapper object, Integer.valueOf(17), and the wrapper object will be added to the collection. (The creation of the object does add some time and memory overhead to the operation, and you should keep that in mind in situations where efficiency is important. An array of int is more efficient than an *ArrayList<Integer>*.)

6.2 LISTS AND SETS

In the previous section, we looked at the general properties of collection classes in Java. In this section, we look at some specific collection classes and how to use them. These classes can be divided into two main categories: lists and sets. A list consists of a sequence of items arranged in a linear order. A list has a definite order, but is not necessarily sorted. A set is a collection that has no duplicate entries. The elements of a set might or might not be arranged into some definite order. I will also briefly discuss a third category of collection known as a "priority queue."

6.2.1 ArrayList and LinkedList

There are two obvious ways to represent a list: as a dynamic array and as a linked list. We've encountered these already in Section 3.3 and Section 5.2. Both of these options are available in generic form as the collection classes java.util.ArrayList and java.util.LinkedList. These classes are part of the Java Collection Framework. Each implements the interface *List<T>*, and therefore the interface *Collection<T>*. An object of type *ArrayList<T>* represents an ordered sequence of objects of type *T*, stored in an array that will grow in size whenever necessary as new items are added. An object of type *LinkedList<T>* also represents an ordered sequence of objects of type *T*, but the objects are stored in nodes that are linked together with pointers.

Both list classes support the basic list operations that are defined in the interface *List<T>*, and an abstract data type is defined by its operations, not by its representation. So why two classes? Why not a single List class with a single representation? The problem is that there is no single representation of lists for which all list operations are efficient. For some operations, linked lists are more efficient than arrays. For others, arrays are more efficient. In a particular application of lists, it's likely that only a few operations will be used frequently. You want to choose the representation for which the frequently used operations will be as efficient as possible.

Broadly speaking, the *LinkedList* class is more efficient in applications where items will often be added or removed at the beginning of the list or in the middle of the list. In an array, these operations require moving a large number of items up or down one position in the array, to make a space for a new item or to fill in the hole left by the removal of an item. In terms of asymptotic analysis (Section 4.5), adding an element at the beginning or in the middle of an array has run time Θ(n), where n is the number of items in the array. In a linked list, nodes can be added or removed at any position by changing a few pointer values, an operation that has run time Θ(1). That is, the operation takes only some constant amount of time, independent of how many items are in the list.

On the other hand, the *ArrayList* class is more efficient when *random access* to items is required. Random access means accessing the k-th item in the list, for any integer k. Random access is used when you get or change the value stored at a specified position in the list. This is trivial for an array, with run time Θ(1). But for a linked list it means starting at the beginning of the list and moving from node to node along the list for k steps, an operation that has run time Θ(k).

Operations that can be done efficiently for both types of lists include sorting and adding an item at the end of the list.

All lists implement the methods from interface *Collection<T>* that were discussed in Subsection 6.1.4. These methods include size(), isEmpty(), add(T), remove(Object), and clear(). The add(T) method adds the object at the end of the list. The remove(Object) method involves first finding the object, which uses linear search and is not very efficient for any list since it involves going through the items in the list from beginning to end until the object is found. The interface *List<T>* adds some methods for accessing list items according to their numerical positions in the list. Suppose that list is an object of type *List<T>*. Then we have the methods:

- list.get(index) — returns the object of type *T* that is at position index in the list, where index is an integer. Items are numbered 0, 1, 2, . . . , list.size()-1. The parameter must be in this range, or an *IndexOutOfBoundsException* is thrown.
- list.set(index,obj) — stores the object obj at position number index in the list, replacing the object that was there previously. The object obj must be of type *T*. This does not change the number of elements in the list or move any of the other elements.
- list.add(index,obj) — inserts an object obj into the list at position number index, where obj must be of type *T*. The number of items in the list increases by one, and items that come after position index move down one position to make room for the new item. The value of index must be in the range 0 to list.size(), inclusive. If index is equal to list.size(), then obj is added at the end of the list.
- list.remove(index) — removes the object at position number index, and returns that object as the return value of the method. Items after this position move up one space in the list to fill the hole, and the size of the list decreases by one. The value of index must be in the range 0 to list.size()-1.
- list.indexOf(obj) — returns an int that gives the position of obj in the list, if it occurs. If it does not occur, the return value is -1. The object obj can be of any type, not just of type *T*. If obj occurs more than once in the list, the index of the first occurrence is returned.

These methods are defined both in class *ArrayList<T>* and in class *LinkedList<T>*, although some of them—such as get and set—are only efficient for *ArrayLists*. The class *LinkedList<T>* adds a few additional methods, which are not defined for an *ArrayList*. If linkedlist is an object of type *LinkedList<T>*, then we have

- linkedlist.getFirst() — returns the object of type *T* that is the first item in the list. The list is not modified. If the list is empty when the method is called, an exception of type *NoSuchElementException* is thrown (the same is true for the next three methods as well).
- linkedlist.getLast() — returns the object of type *T* that is the last item in the list. The list is not modified.
- linkedlist.removeFirst() — removes the first item from the list, and returns that object of type *T* as its return value. The functions linkedlist.remove() and linkedlist.pop() are also defined, with the same meaning as removeFirst().
- linkedlist.removeLast() — removes the last item from the list, and returns that object of type *T* as its return value.

- linkedlist.addFirst(obj) – adds the obj, which must be of type *T*, to the beginning of the list. The function linkedlist.push(obj) has the same meaning.
- linkedlist.addLast(obj) – adds the object obj, which must be of type *T*, to the end of the list. This is exactly the same as linkedlist.add(obj) but is defined to keep the naming consistent.

There is some redundancy here, apparently to make it easy to use a *LinkedList* as if it were a stack or a queue. For example, we can use a *LinkedList* as a stack by using the methods named push() and pop(), or as a queue by using add() and remove() to implement the enqueue and dequeue operations.

If list is an object of type *List<T>*, then the method list.iterator(), defined in the interface *Collection<T>*, returns an *Iterator* that can be used to traverse the list from beginning to end. However, for *Lists*, there is a special type of *Iterator*, called a *ListIterator*, which offers additional capabilities. *ListIterator<T>* is an interface that extends the interface *Iterator<T>*. The method list.listIterator() returns an object of type *ListIterator<T>*.

A *ListIterator* has the usual *Iterator* methods, hasNext(), next(), and remove(), but it also has methods hasPrevious(), previous(), add(obj), and set(obj) that make it possible to move backwards in the list, to add an item at the current position of the iterator, and to replace one of the items in the list. To understand how these work, it's best to think of an iterator as pointing to a position between two list elements, or at the beginning or end of the list. In this diagram, the items in a list are represented by squares, and arrows indicate the possible positions of an iterator:

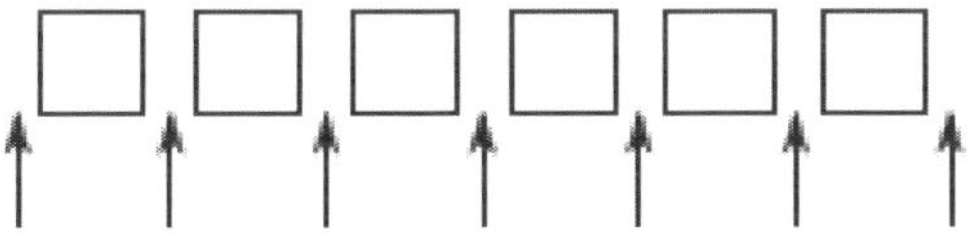

If iter is of type *ListIterator<T>*, then iter.next() moves the iterator one space to the right along the list and returns the item that the iterator passes as it moves. The method iter.previous() moves the iterator one space to the left along the list and returns the item that it passes. The method iter.remove() removes an item from the list; the item that is removed is the item that the iterator passed most recently in a call to either iter.next() or iter.previous(). The method iter.set(obj) works similarly; it replaces the item that would be removed by iter.remove(). There is also a method iter.add(obj) that adds the specified object to the list at the current position of the iterator (where obj must be of type *T*). This can be between two existing items or at the beginning of the list or at the end of the list.

(By the way, the lists that are used in class LinkedList<T> are *doubly linked lists*. That is, each node in the list contains two pointers—one to the next node in the list and one to the previous node. This makes it possible to efficiently implement both the next() and previous() methods of a ListIterator. Also, to make the addLast() and getLast() methods of a *LinkedList* efficient, the class *LinkedList<T>* includes a "tail pointer" that points to the last node in the list.)

As an example of using a *ListIterator*, suppose that we want to maintain a list of items that is always sorted into increasing order. When adding an item to the list, we can use a *ListIterator* to find the position in the list where the item should be added. Once the position has been found, we use the same list iterator to place the item in that position. The idea is to start at the beginning of the list and to move the iterator forward past all the items that are smaller than the item that is being inserted. At that point, the iterator's add() method can be used to insert the item. To be more definite, suppose that stringList is a variable of type *List<String>*. Assume that the strings that are already in the list are stored in ascending order and that newItem is a string that we would like to insert into the list. The following code will place newItem in the list in its correct position, so that the modified list is still in ascending order:

- ListIterator<String> iter = stringList.listIterator();
- // Move the iterator so that it points to the position where
- // newItem should be inserted into the list. If newItem is
- // bigger than all the items in the list, then the while loop
- // will end when iter.hasNext() becomes false, that is, when
- // the iterator has reached the end of the list.

```
while (iter.hasNext()) {
    String item = iter.next();
    if (newItem.compareTo(item) <= 0) {
                // newItem should come BEFORE item in the list.
                // Move the iterator back one space so that
                // it points to the correct insertion point,
                // and end the loop.
        iter.previous();
        break;
    }
}
iter.add(newItem);
```

Here, stringList might be of type *ArrayList<String>* or of type *LinkedList<String>*. The algorithm that is used to insert newItem into the list will be about equally efficient for both types of lists, and it will even work for other classes that implement the interface *List<String>*. You would probably find it easier to design an insertion algorithm that uses array-like indexing with the methods get(index) and add(index,obj). However, that algorithm would be horribly inefficient for *LinkedLists* because random access is so inefficient for linked lists. (By the way, the insertion algorithm works when the list is empty, and it works when the new item has to be inserted at the beginning or at the end of the list. It might be useful for you to think about why this is true.)

6.2.2 Sorting

Sorting a list is a fairly common operation, and there should really be a sorting method in the *List* interface. There is not, presumably because it only makes sense to sort lists of certain types of objects. However, methods for sorting lists are available as static methods in the class java.util.Collections. This class contains a variety of static utility methods for working with collections. The methods are generic; that is, they will work for collections of objects of various types. (You have already seen similar methods for arrays in the *Arrays* class.) Suppose that list is of type *List<T>*. The command

Collections.sort(list);

can be used to sort the list into ascending order. The items in the list should implement the interface *Comparable<T>* (see Subsection 6.1.6). The method Collections.sort() will work, for example, for lists of *String* and for lists of any of the wrapper classes such as *Integer* and *Double*. There is also a sorting method that takes a *Comparator* as its second argument:

Collections.sort(list,comparator);

In this method, the comparator will be used to compare the items in the list. As mentioned in the previous section, a *Comparator* is an object that defines a compare() method that can be used to compare two objects. We'll see an example of using a *Comparator* in Section 6.4.

The sorting method that is used by Collections.sort() is the so-called "merge sort" algorithm, which has both worst-case and average-case run times that are $\Theta(n*\log(n))$ for a list of size n. Although the average run time for MergeSort is a little slower than that of QuickSort, its worst-case performance is much better than QuickSort's. (QuickSort was covered in Subsection 5.1.3.) MergeSort also has a nice property called "stability" that we will encounter at the end of Subsection 6.4.3.

The *Collections* class has at least two other useful methods for modifying lists. Collections.shuffle(list) will rearrange the elements of the list into a random order. Collections.reverse(list) will reverse the order of the elements, so that the last element is moved to the beginning of the list, the next-to-last element to the second position, and so on. Since an efficient sorting method is provided for *Lists*, there is no need to write one yourself.

6.2.3 TreeSet and HashSet

A set is a collection of objects in which no object occurs more than once. Sets implement all the methods in the interface *Collection<T>*, but do so in a way that ensures that no element occurs twice in the set. For example, if set is an object of type *Set<T>*, then set.add(obj) will have no effect on the set if obj is already an element of the set. Java has two classes that implement the interface *Set<T>*: java.util.TreeSet and java.util.HashSet.

In addition to being a *Set*, a *TreeSet* has the property that the elements of the set are arranged into ascending sorted order. That is, an *Iterator* (or a for-each loop) for a TreeSet will always visit the elements of the set in ascending order.

A *TreeSet* cannot hold arbitrary objects, since there must be a way to determine the sorted order of the objects it contains. Ordinarily, this means that the objects in a set of type *TreeSet<T>* should implement the interface *Comparable<T>* and that obj1.compareTo(obj2) should be defined in a reasonable way for any two objects obj1 and obj2 in the set. Alternatively, an object of type *Comparator<T>* can be provided as a parameter to the constructor when the *TreeSet* is created. In that case, the compare() method of the *Comparator* will be used to compare objects that are added to the set.

A *TreeSet* does not use the equals() method to test whether two objects are the same. Instead, it uses the compareTo() or compare() method. This can be a problem. Recall from Subsection 6.1.6 that the compare() method of a *Comparator* might consider two objects to be the same for the purpose of the comparison even though the objects are not equal. (This is less likely, but still possible for a properly defined compareTo() method.) For a *TreeSet* that uses the *Comparator*, this means that only one of those objects can be in the set. For example, if the *TreeSet* contains mailing addresses and if the compare() method for addresses just compares their zip codes, then the set can contain only one address in each zip code. Clearly, this is not right! But that only means that you have to be aware of the semantics of *TreeSets*, and you need to make sure that the compare() or compareTo() is defined in a reasonable way for objects that you put into a *TreeSet*. This will be true, by the way, for *Strings*, *Integers*, and many other built-in types, since the compareTo() method for these types considers two objects to be the same only if they are actually equal.

In the implementation of a *TreeSet*, the elements are stored in something similar to a binary sort tree. However, the data structure that is used is balanced in the sense that the left and right subtrees of any node in the tree are at about the same size. This ensures that all the basic operations—inserting, deleting, and searching—are efficient, with worst-case run time Θ(log(n)), where n is the number of items in the set.

The fact that a *TreeSet* sorts its elements and removes duplicates makes it very useful in some applications. Exercise 7.6 asked you to write a program that would read a file and output an alphabetical list of all the words that occurred in the file, with duplicates removed. The words were to be stored in an *ArrayList*, so it was up to you to make sure that the list was sorted and contained no duplicates. The same task can be programmed much more easily using a *TreeSet* instead of a list. A *TreeSet* automatically eliminates duplicates, and an iterator for the set will automatically visit the items in the set in sorted order. An algorithm for the program, using a *TreeSet*, would be:

```
TreeSet<String> words = new TreeSet<String>();
while there is more data in the input file:
    Let word = the next word from the file
    Convert word to lower case
    words.add(word)          // Adds the word only if not already present.
for ( String w : words ) // for each String w in words
    Output w          // words are output in sorted order
```

If you would like to see a complete, working program, you can find it in the file WordListWith- TreeSet.java.

As another example, suppose that coll is any Collection of *Strings*. (This would also work for any other type for which compareTo() is properly defined.) We can use a *TreeSet* to sort the items of coll and remove the duplicates simply by saying:

```
TreeSet<String> set = new TreeSet<String>();
set.addAll(coll);
```

The second statement adds all the elements of the collection to the set. Since it's a *Set*, duplicates are ignored. Since it's a *TreeSet*, the elements of the set are sorted. If you would like to have the data in some other type of data structure, it's easy to copy the data from the set. For example, to place the answer in an *ArrayList*, you could say:

```
TreeSet<String> set = new TreeSet<String>();
set.addAll(coll);
```

```
ArrayList<String> list = new ArrayList<String>();
list.addAll(set);
```

Now, in fact, every one of Java's collection classes has a constructor that takes a *Collection* as an argument. All the items in that *Collection* are added to the new collection when it is created. So, if coll is of type *Collection<String>*, then "new TreeSet<String>(coll)" creates a *TreeSet* that contains the same elements as coll, but with duplicates removed and in sorted order. This means that we can abbreviate the four lines in the above example to the single command:

```
ArrayList<String> list = new ArrayList<>( new TreeSet<>(coll) );
```

This makes a sorted list of the elements of coll with no duplicates. This is a nice example of the power of generic programming. (Note that the type parameter, String, is optional in the two constructors in this example, since it can be deduced by the compiler.)

A *HashSet* stores its elements in a *hash table*, a type of data structure that I will discuss in the next section. The operations of finding, adding, and removing elements are implemented very efficiently in hash tables, even more so than for *TreeSets*. The elements of a *HashSet* are not stored in any particular order, and so do not need to implement the *Comparable* interface. (They do, however, need to define a proper "hash code," as we'll see in the next section.)

The equals() method is used to determine whether two objects in a *HashSet* are to be considered the same. An *Iterator* for a *HashSet* will visit its elements in what seems to be a completely arbitrary order, and it's even possible for the order to change when a new element is added. Use a *HashSet* instead of a *TreeSet* when the elements it contains are not comparable, or when the order is not important, or when the small advantage in efficiency is important.

A note about the mathematics of sets: In mathematical set theory, the items in a set are called *members* or *elements* of that set. Important operations include adding an element to a set, removing an element from a set, and testing whether a given entity is an element of a set. Operations that can be performed on two sets include *union* , *intersection* , and *set difference*. All these operations are defined in Java for objects of type *Set*, but with different names. Suppose that A and B are *Sets*. Then:

- A.add(x) adds the element x to the set A.
- A.remove(x) removes the element x from the set A.
- A.contains(x) tests whether x is an element of the set A.
- A.addAll(B) computes the union of A and B.
- A.retainAll(B) computes the intersection of A and B.
- A.removeAll(B) computes the set difference, A - B.

There are of course, differences between mathematical sets and sets in Java. Most important, perhaps, sets in Java must be finite, while in mathematics, most of the fun in set theory comes from working with infinity. In mathematics, a set can contain arbitrary elements, while in Java, a set of type *Set<T>* can only contain elements of type *T*. The operation A.addAll(B) acts by modifying the value of A, while in mathematics the operation A union B computes a new set, without changing the value of A or B. See Exercise 10.2 for an example of mathematical set operations in Java.

6.2.4 Priority Queues

A *priority queue* is an abstract data type that represents a collection of items, where each item has an assigned "priority" that allows any two items to be compared. Operations on a priority queue include *add*, which adds an item to the collection, and *remove*, which removes and returns an item from the collection that has the minimum priority among items currently in the collection. (Maximum priority would also be possible, but in Java's version, the *remove* operation removes a minimum priority item.)

A simple implementation of priority queue could be achieved by using a linked list to store the items in the queue in order of increasing priority. In that case, *remove* would simply remove and return the first item in the list. However, *add* would have to insert the new item into its correct position in the list, an operation with average run time $\Theta(n)$, where n is the number of items in the list. In fact, priority queues can be implemented so that both *add* and *remove* have run time $\Theta(\log(n))$, which is much more efficient. (The efficient implementation uses something called a "heap," which is not to be confused with the heap where objects are created. I will not discuss the implementation here.)

The parameterized class *PriorityQueue<T>* implements a priority queue of objects of type *T*. This class implements the interface *Collection<T>*. So, if pq is a *PriorityQueue*, then it has all the methods defined in that interface. But the essential priority queue operations are

- pq.add(obj) — adds obj to the priority queue, where obj must be an object of type *T*
- pq.remove() — removes and returns an item of minimal priority. The return value is an object of type *T*. Throws an exception if the queue is empty.
- pq.isEmpty() — tests whether the priority queue is empty.

You've probably noticed that I haven't yet mentioned how the priority of items in the priority queue are determined. The situation is much like sorting: We need to be able to compare any two items in the queue. As with sorting, there are two solutions. If the items implement the *Comparable* interface, then they can be compared using the compareTo() method from that interface. Alternatively, a *Comparator* object can be provided as a parameter to the *PriorityQueue* constructor. In that case, the Comparator's compare() method will be used to compare items.

Classes such as *String*, *Integer*, and *Date* that implement *Comparable* can be used in a priority queue. For example, a *PriorityQueue<String>* can be used to sort strings into lexicographic order: Just *add* all the strings to the priority queue, then *remove* them one-by-one. Since items are removed from the queue in order of priority, they will be removed in lexicographic order. Earlier,

I showed how to use a *TreeSet* to sort and remove duplicates from a collection. A *PriorityQueue* can be used in a similar way to sort a collection without removing duplicates. For example, if coll is of type *Collection<String>*, then the following code segment will print all the items from coll in order, including duplicates:

```
PriorityQueue<String> pq = new PriorityQueue<>();
pq.addAll( coll );
while ( ! pq.isEmpty() ) {
    System.out.println( pq.remove() );
}
```

Note, by the way, that we can't use an iterator or a for-each loop to print the items in this example, since iterators and for-each loops do not traverse a priority queue in ascending order.

The sample program WordListWithPriorityQueue.java makes a sorted list of words from a file without removing duplicates, using a priority queue to hold the words. It is a minor modification of WordListWithTreeSet.java.

Although priority queues can be used for sorting, they have other natural applications. For example, consider the problem of scheduling "jobs" to be executed on a computer, where each job is assigned a priority and jobs with lower priority should always be executed before jobs with higher priority. Jobs can be placed into a priority queue as they are created. When the computer removes jobs from the queue for execution, they will be removed in order of increasing priority.

6.3 MAPS

An array of N elements can be thought of as a way of associating some item with each of the integers 0, 1, . . . , N-1. If i is one of these integers, it's possible to *get* the item associated with i, and it's possible to *put* a new item in the i-th position. These "get" and "put" operations define what it means to be an array.

A *map* is a kind of generalized array. Like an array, a map is defined by "get" and "put" operations. But in a map, these operations are defined not for integers 0, 1, . .

. , N-1, but for arbitrary objects of some specified type *T*. Associated to these objects of type *T* are objects of some possibly different type *S*.

In fact, some programming languages use the term *associative array* instead of "map" and use the same notation for associative arrays as for regular arrays. In those languages, for example, you might see the notation A["fred"] used to indicate the item associated to the string "fred" in an associative array A. Java does not use array notation for maps, unfortunately, but the idea is the same: A map is like an array, but the indices for a map are objects, not integers. In a map, an object that serves as an "index" is called a *key* . The object that is associated with a key is called a *value*. Note that a key can have at most one associated value, but the same value can be associated to several different keys. A map can be considered to be a set of "associations," where each association is a key/value pair.

6.3.1 The Map Interface

In Java, maps are defined by the interface java.util.Map, which includes put and get methods as well as other general methods for working with maps. The map interface, *Map<K,V>*, is parameterized by two types. The first type parameter, *K*, specifies the type of objects that are possible keys in the map; the second type parameter, *V*, specifies the type of objects that are possible values in the map. For example, a map of type *Map<Date,Color>* would associate values of type *Color* to keys of type *Date*. For a map of type *Map<String,String>*, both the keys and the values are of type *String*.

Suppose that map is a variable of type *Map<K,V>* for some specific types *K* and *V*. Then the following are some of the methods that are defined for map:

map.get(key) — returns the object of type *V* that is associated by the map to the key. If the map does not associate any value with key, then the return value is null. Note that it's also possible for the return value to be null when the map explicitly associates the value null with the key. Referring to "map.get(key)" is similar to referring to "A[key]" for an array A. (But note that there is nothing like an *IndexOutOfBoundsException* for maps.)

- map.put(key,value) — Associates the specified value with the specified key, where key must be of type *K* and value must be of type *V*. If the map already associated some other value with the key, then the new value replaces the old one. This is similar to the command "A[key] = value" for an array.
- map.putAll(map2) — if map2 is another map of type *Map<K,V>*, this copies all the associations from map2 into map.
- map.remove(key) — if map associates a value to the specified key, that association is removed from the map.

- map.containsKey(key) — returns a boolean value that is true if the map associates some value to the specified key.
- map.containsValue(value) — returns a boolean value that is true if the map associates the specified value to some key.
- map.size() — returns an int that gives the number of key/value associations in the map.
- map.isEmpty() — returns a boolean value that is true if the map is empty, that is if it contains no associations.
- map.clear() — removes all associations from the map, leaving it empty.

The put and get methods are certainly the most commonly used of the methods in the *Map* interface. In many applications, these are the only methods that are needed, and in such cases a map is really no more difficult to use than a standard array.

Java includes two classes that implement the interface *Map<K,V>*: *TreeMap<K,V>* and *HashMap<K,V>*. In a *TreeMap*, the key/value associations are stored in a sorted tree, in which they are sorted according to their keys. For this to work, it must be possible to compare the keys to one another. This means either that the keys must implement the interface *Comparable<K>*, or that a *Comparator* must be provided for comparing keys. (The *Comparator* can be provided as a parameter to the *TreeMap* constructor.) Note that in a *TreeMap*, as in a *TreeSet*, the compareTo() (or compare()) method is used to decide whether two keys are to be considered the same. This can have undesirable consequences if the comparison method does not agree with the usual notion of equality, and you should keep this in mind when using *TreeMaps*.

A *HashMap* does not store associations in any particular order, so the keys that can be used in a *HashMap* do not have to be comparable. However, the key class should have reasonable definitions for the equals() method and for a hashCode() method that is discussed later in this section; most of Java's standard classes define these methods correctly. Most operations are a little faster on *HashMaps* than they are on *TreeMaps*. In general, you should use a *HashMap* unless you have some particular need for the ordering property of a *TreeMap*. In particular, if you are only using the put and get operations, you can safely use a *HashMap*.

Let's consider an example where maps would be useful. In Subsection 3.5.2, I presented a simple *PhoneDirectory* class that associated phone numbers with names. That class defined operations addEntry(name,number) and getNumber(name), where both name and number are given as *Strings*. In fact, the phone directory is acting just like a map, with the addEntry method playing the role of the put operation and getNumber playing the role of get. In a real programming application, there would be no need to define a new class; we could simply use a map of type *Map<String,String>*. A directory could be defined as

```
Map<String,String> directory = new TreeMap<>();
```

(using *TreeMap* so that the entries are kept in sorted order by name). Then directory.put(name,number) would record a phone number in the directory and directory.get(name) would retrieve the phone number associated with a given name.

6.3.2 Views, SubSets, and SubMaps

A *Map* is not a *Collection*, and maps do not implement all the operations defined on collections. In particular, there are no iterators for maps. Sometimes, though, it's useful to be able to iterate through all the associations in a map. Java makes this possible in a roundabout but clever way. If map is a variable of type *Map<K,V>*, then the method

```
map.keySet()
```

returns the set of all objects that occur as keys for associations in the map. The value returned by this method is an object that implements the interface *Set<K>*. The elements of this set are the map's keys. The obvious way to implement the keySet() method would be to create a new set object, add all the keys from the map, and return that set. But that's not how it's done. The value returned by map.keySet() is not an independent object. It is what is called a *view* of the actual objects that are stored in the map. This "view" of the map implements the *Set<K>* interface, but it does it in such a way that the methods defined in the interface refer directly to keys in the map. For example, if you remove a key from the view, that key—along with its associated value—is actually removed from the map. It's not legal to add an object to the view, since it doesn't make sense to add a key to a map without specifying the value that should be associated to the key. Since map.keySet() does not create a new set, it's very efficient, even for very large maps.

One of the things that you can do with a *Set* is get an *Iterator* for it and use the iterator to visit each of the elements of the set in turn. We can use an iterator for the key set of a map to traverse the map. For example, if map is of type *Map<String,Double>*, we could write:

```
Set<String> keys = map.keySet();       // The set of keys in the map.
Iterator<String> keyIter = keys.iterator();
System.out.println("The map contains the following associations:");
while (keyIter.hasNext()) {
    String key = keyIter.next();        // Get the next key.
    Double value = map.get(key);        // Get the value for that key.
```

```
        System.out.println( "     (" + key + "," + value + ")" );
    }
```

Or we could do the same thing more easily, avoiding the explicit use of an iterator, with a for-each loop:

```
    System.out.println("The map contains the following associations:");
    for ( String key : map.keySet() ) {      // "for each key in the map's key set"
        Double value = map.get(key);
        System.out.println( "     (" + key + "," + value + ")" );
    }
```

If the map is a *TreeMap*, then the key set of the map is a sorted set, and the iterator will visit the keys in ascending order. For a *HashMap*, the keys are visited in an arbitrary, unpredictable order.

The *Map* interface defines two other views. If map is a variable of type *Map<K,V>*, then the method:

```
    map.values()
```

returns an object of type *Collection<V>* that contains all the values from the associations that are stored in the map. The return value is a *Collection* rather than a *Set* because it can contain duplicate elements (since a map can associate the same value to any number of keys). The method:

```
    map.entrySet()
```

returns a set that contains all the associations from the map. The elements in the set are objects of type *Map.Entry<K,V>*. *Map.Entry<K,V>* is defined as a static nested interface inside the interface *Map<K,V>*, so its full name contains a period. However, the name can be used in the same way as any other type name. (The return type of the method map.entrySet() is written as *Set<Map.Entry<K,V>>*. The type parameter in this case is itself a parameterized type. Although this might look confusing, it's just Java's way of saying that the elements of the set are of type *Map.Entry<K,V>*.) The information in the set returned by map.entrySet() is actually no different from the information in the map itself, but the set provides a different view of this information, with different operations. Each Map.Entry object contains one key/value pair, and defines methods getKey() and getValue() for retrieving the key and the value. There is also a method, setValue(value), for setting the value; calling this method for a Map.Entry object will modify the map itself, just as if the map's put method were called. As an example, we can use the entry set of a map to print all the key/value pairs in the map. This is more efficient than using the key set to print the same information, as I did in the above example, since we don't have to use the get() method to look up the value associated with each key. Suppose again that map is of type *Map<String,Double>*. Then we can write:

```
Set<Map.Entry<String,Double>> entries = map.entrySet();
Iterator<Map.Entry<String,Double>> entryIter = entries.iterator();
System.out.println("The map contains the following associations:");
while (entryIter.hasNext()) {
Map.Entry<String,Double> entry = entryIter.next();
String key = entry.getKey();        // Get the key from the entry.
Double value = entry.getValue();  // Get the value.
System.out.println( "     (" + key + "," + value + ")" );
}
```

or, using a for-each loop to avoid some of the ugly type names:

```
System.out.println("The map contains the following associations:");
for ( Map.Entry<String,Double> entry : map.entrySet() ) {
    System.out.println( "     (" + entry.getKey() + "," + entry.getValue() + ")" );
}
```

This is certainly a place where it would be convenient to use var to declare the variables (See Subsection 4.8.2). With var, the example using an iterator becomes:

```
var entries = map.entrySet();
var entryIter = entries.iterator();
System.out.println("The map contains the following associations:");
while (entryIter.hasNext()) { . . .
```

Maps are not the only place in Java's generic programming framework where views are used. For example, the interface *List<T>* defines a *sublist* as a view of a part of a list. If list implements the interface *List<T>*, then the method

```
list.subList( fromIndex, toIndex )
```

where fromIndex and toIndex are integers, returns a view of the part of the list consisting of the list elements in positions between fromIndex and toIndex (including fromIndex but excluding toIndex). This view lets you operate on the sublist using any of the operations defined for lists, but the sublist is not an independent list. Changes made to the sublist are actually made to the original list.

Similarly, it is possible to obtain views that represent certain subsets of a sorted set. If set is of type *TreeSet<T>*, then set.subSet(fromElement,toElement) returns a *Set<T>* that contains all the elements of set that are between fromElement and toElement (including fromElement and excluding toElement). The parameters fromElement and toElement must be objects of type *T*. For example, if words is a set of type *TreeSet<String>* in which all the elements are strings of lower case letters, then words.subSet("m","n") contains all the elements of words that begin with the letter 'm'. This subset is a view of part of the original set. That is, creating the subset does not involve copying elements. And changes made to the subset, such as adding or removing elements, are actually made to the original set. The view set.headSet(toElement) consists of all elements from the set which are strictly less than toElement, and set.tailSet(fromElement) is a view that contains all elements from the set that are greater than or equal to fromElement.

The class *TreeMap<K,V>* defines three submap views. A submap is similar to a subset. A submap is a *Map* that contains a subset of the keys from the original *Map*, along with their associated values. If map is a variable of type *TreeMap<K,V>*, and if fromKey and toKey are of type *K*, then map.subMap(fromKey,toKey) returns a view that contains all key/value pairs from map whose keys are between fromKey and toKey (including fromKey and excluding toKey). There are also views map.headMap(toKey) and map.tailMap(fromKey) which are defined analogously to headSet and tailSet. Suppose, for example, that phoneBook is a map of type *TreeMap<String,String>* in which the keys are names and the values are phone numbers. We can print out all the entries from phoneBook where the name begins with "M" as follows:

```
Map<String,String> ems = phoneBook.subMap("M","N");
            // This submap contains entries for which the key is greater
            // than or equal to "M" and strictly less than "N".
    if (ems.isEmpty()) {
            System.out.println("No entries beginning with M.");
    }
    else {
            System.out.println("Entries beginning with M:");
            for ( var entry : ems.entrySet() ) {
                    // Note: type for entry is Map.Entry<String,String>
                    // but it's easier to user var to declare the variable!
            System.out.println( "     " + entry.getKey() + ": " + entry.getValue() );
    }
}
```

Subsets and submaps are probably best thought of as generalized search operations that make it possible to find all the items in a range of values, rather than just to find a single value. For example, suppose that a database of scheduled events is stored in a map of type *TreeMap<DateTime,Event>* in which the a key gives the date and time of an event, and suppose you want a listing of all events that are scheduled for some time on July 4, 2022. Just make a submap containing all keys in the range from 12:00 AM, July 4, 2022 to 12:00 AM, July 5, 2022, and output all the entries from that submap. This type of search, which is known as a *subrange query*, is quite common.

6.3.3 Hash Tables and Hash Codes

HashSets and *HashMaps* are implemented using a data structure known as a *hash table.* You don't need to understand hash tables to use *HashSets* or *HashMaps*, but any computer programmer should be familiar with hash tables and how they work.

Hash tables are an elegant solution to the search problem. A hash table, like a *HashMap*, stores key/value pairs. Given a key, you have to search the table for the corresponding key/value pair. When a hash table is used to implement a set, there are no values, and the only question is whether or not the key occurs in the set. You still have to search for the key to check whether it is there or not.

In most search algorithms, in order to find the item you are interested in, you have to look through a bunch of other items that don't interest you. To find something in an unsorted list, you have to go through the items one-by-one until you come to the one you are looking for. In a binary sort tree, you have to start at the root and move down the tree until you find the item you want. When you search for a key/value pair in a hash table, you can go directly to the location that contains the item you want. You don't have to look through any other items. (This is not quite true, but if the hash table is working properly, it's close.) The location of the key/value pair is computed from the key: You just look at the key, and then you go directly to the location where it is stored.

How can this work? If the keys were integers in the range 0 to 99, we could store the key/value pairs in an array, A, of 100 elements. The key/value pair with key K would be stored in A[K]. The key takes us directly to the location of the key/value pair. The problem is that there are usually far too many different possible keys for us to be able to use an array with one location for each possible key. For example, if the key can be any value of type int, then we would need an array with over four billion locations—quite a waste of space if we are only going to store, say, a few thousand items! If the key can be a string of any length, then the number of possible keys is infinite, and using an array with one location for each possible key is simply impossible.

Nevertheless, hash tables store their data in an array, and the array index where a key is stored is based on the key. The index is not equal to the key, but it is computed from the key. The array index for a key is called the *hash code* for that key. A function that computes a hash code, given a key, is called a *hash function* . To find a key in a hash table, you just have to compute the hash code of the key and go directly to the array location given by that hash code. If the hash code is 17, look in array location number 17.

Now, since there are fewer array locations than there are possible keys, it's possible that we might try to store two or more keys in the same array location. This is called a *collision* . A collision is not an error. We can't reject a key just because another key happened to have the same hash code. A hash table must be able to handle collisions in some reasonable way. In the type of hash table that is used in Java, each array location actually holds a linked list of key/value pairs (possibly an empty list). When two items have the same hash code, they are in the same linked list. The structure of the hash table looks something like this:

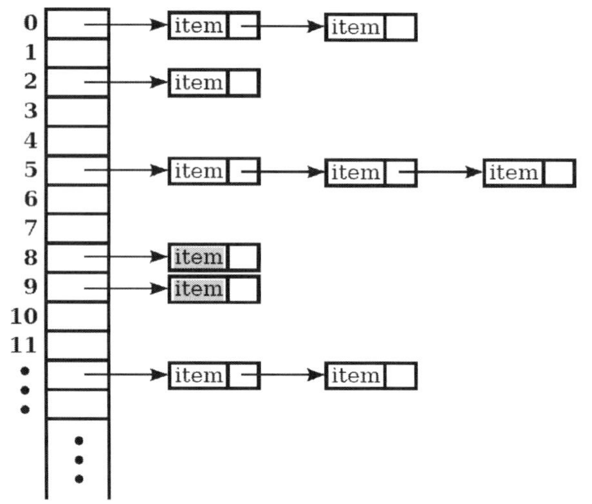

In this diagram, there are two items with hash code 0, no items with hash code 1, one item with hash code 2, and so on. In a properly designed hash table, most of the linked lists are of length zero or one, and the average length of the lists is less than one. Although the hash code of a key doesn't necessarily take you directly to that key, there are probably no more than one or two other items that you have to look through before finding the key you want. For this to work properly, the number of items in the hash table should be somewhat less than the number of locations in the array. In Java's implementation, whenever the number of items exceeds 75% of the array size, the array is replaced by a larger one and all the items in the old array are inserted into the new one. (This is why adding one new item will sometimes cause the ordering of all the items in the hash table to change completely.)

There is still the question of where hash codes come from. Every object in Java has a hash code. The *Object* class defines the method hashCode(), which returns a value of type int. When an object, obj, is stored in a hash table that has N locations, a hash code in the range 0 to N-1 is needed. This hash code is computed as Math.abs(obj.hashCode()) % N, the remainder when the absolute value of obj.hashCode() is divided by N. (The Math.abs is necessary because obj.hashCode() can be a negative integer, and we need a non-negative number to use as an array index.)

For hashing to work properly, two objects that are equal according to the equals() method must have the same hash code. In the *Object* class, this condition is satisfied because both equals() and hashCode() are based on the address of the memory location where the object is stored. However, as noted in Subsection 6.1.6, many classes redefine the equals() method. If a class redefines the equals() method, and if objects of that class will be used as keys in hash tables, then the class must also redefine the hashCode() method. For example, in the *String* class, the equals() method is redefined so that two objects of type *String* are considered to be equal if they contain the same sequence of characters. The hashCode() method is also redefined in the *String* class, so that the hash code of a string is computed from the characters in that string rather than from its location in memory. For Java's standard classes, you can expect equals() and hashCode() to be correctly defined. However, you might need to define these methods in classes that you write yourself.

Writing a good hash function is something of an art. In order to work well, the hash function must spread the possible keys fairly evenly over the hash table. Otherwise, the items in a table can be concentrated in a subset of the available locations, and the linked lists at those locations can grow to a large size; that would destroy the efficiency that is the major reason for hash tables to exist in the first place. However, I won't cover techniques for creating good hash functions in this book.

6.4 PROGRAMMING WITH THE JAVA COLLECTION FRAMEWORK

In this section, we'll look at some programming examples that use classes from the Java Collection Framework. The Collection Framework is easy to use, especially compared to the difficulty of programming new data structures from scratch.

6.4.1 Symbol Tables

We begin with a straightforward but important application of maps. When a compiler reads the source code of a program, it encounters definitions of variables, subroutines, and classes. The names of these things can be used later in the program. The compiler has to remember the definition of each name, so that it can recognize the name and apply the definition when the name is encountered later in the program. This is a natural application for a *Map*. The name can be used as a key in the map. The value associated to the key is the definition of the name, encoded somehow as an object. A map that is used in this way is called a *symbol table.*

In a compiler, the values in a symbol table can be quite complicated, since the compiler has to deal with names for various sorts of things, and it needs a different type of information for each different type of name. We will keep things simple by looking at a symbol table in another context. Suppose that we want a program that can evaluate expressions entered by the user, and suppose that the expressions can contain variables, in addition to operators, numbers, and parentheses. For this to make sense, we need some way of assigning values to variables. When a variable is used in an expression, we need to retrieve the variable's value. A symbol table can be used to store the data that we need. The keys for the symbol table are variable names. The value associated with a key is the value of that variable, which is of type double. The symbol table will be an object of type *Map<String,Double>*. (Remember that primitive types such as double can't be used as type parameters; a wrapper class such as *Double* must be used instead. See Subsection 6.1.7.)

To demonstrate the idea, we'll use a rather simple-minded program in which the user types commands such as:

let x = 3 + 12

print 2 + 2

*print 10*x +17 let rate = 0.06*

print 1000(1+rate)*

The program is an interpreter for a very simple language. The only two commands that the program understands are "print" and "let". When a "print" command is executed, the computer evaluates the expression and displays the value. If the expression contains a variable, the computer has to look up the value of that variable in the symbol table. A "let" command is used to give a value to a variable. The computer has to store the value of the variable in the symbol table. (Note: The "variables" I am talking about here are not variables in the Java program. The Java program is executing a sort of program typed in by the user. I am talking about variables in the user's program. The user gets to make up variable names, so there is no way for the Java program to know in advance what the variables will be.)

In Subsection 5.5.2, we saw how to write a program, SimpleParser2.java, that can evaluate expressions that do not contain variables. Here, I will discuss another example program, SimpleInterpreter.java, that is based on the older program. I will only talk about the parts that are relevant to the symbol table.

The program uses a *HashMap* as the symbol table. A *TreeMap* could also be used, but since the program does not need to access the variables in alphabetical order, we don't need to have the keys stored in sorted order. The symbol table in the program is represented by a variable named symbolTable of type *HashMap<String,Double>*. At the beginning of the program, the symbol table object is created with the command:

symbolTable = new HashMap<>();

This creates a map that initially contains no key/value associations. To execute a "let" command, the program uses the symbol table's put() method to associate a value with the variable name. Suppose that the name of the variable is given by a *String*, varName, and the value of the variable is stored in a variable, val, of type double. The following command would then set the value associated with the variable in the symbol table:

symbolTable.put(varName, val);

In the program SimpleInterpreter.java, you'll find this in the method named doLetCommand(). The actual value that is stored in the symbol table is an object of type *Double*. We can use the double value val in the call to put because Java does an automatic conversion of type double to *Double* when necessary.

Just for fun, I decided to pre-define two variables named "pi" and "e" whose values are the usual mathematical constants π and *e*. In Java, the values of these constants are given by Math.PI and Math.E. To make these variables available to the user of the program, they are added to the symbol table with the commands:

symbolTable.put("pi", Math.PI); symbolTable.put("e", Math.E);

When the program encounters a variable while evaluating an expression, the symbol table's get() method is used to retrieve its value. The function symbolTable.get(varName) returns a value of type *Double*. It is possible that the return value is null; this will happen if no value has ever been assigned to varName in the symbol table. It's important to check this possibility. It indicates that the user is trying to use a variable that the user has not defined. The program considers this to be an error, so the processing looks something like this:

```
Double val = symbolTable.get(varName);
if (val == null) {
    ... // Throw an exception:        Undefined variable.
}
// The value associated to varName is val.doubleValue()
```

You will find this code, more or less, in a method named primaryValue() in SimpleInter- preter.java.

As you can see from this example, *Maps* are very useful and are really quite easy to use.

6.4.2 Sets Inside a Map

The objects in a collection or map can be of any type. They can even be collections. Here's an example where it's natural to store sets as the value objects in a map.

Consider the problem of making an index for a book. An index consists of a list of terms that appear in the book. Next to each term is a list of the pages on which that term appears. To represent an index in a program, we need a data structure that can hold a list of terms, along with a list of pages for each term. Adding new data should be easy and efficient. When it's time to print the index, it should be easy to access the terms in alphabetical order. There are many ways this could be done, but I'd like to use Java's generic data structures and let them do as much of the work as possible.

We can think of an index as a *Map* that associates a list of page references to each term. The terms are keys, and the value associated with a given key is the list of page references for that term. A *Map* can be either a *TreeMap* or a *HashMap*, but only a *TreeMap* will make it easy to access the terms in sorted order. The value associated with a term is a list of page references. How can we represent such a value? If you think about it, you see that it's not really a list in the sense of Java's generic classes. If you look in any index, you'll see that a list of page references has no duplicates, so it's really a set rather than a list. Furthermore, the page references for a given term are always printed in increasing order, so we want a sorted set. This means that we should use a *TreeSet* to represent each list of page references. The values that we really want to put in this set are of type int, but once again we have to deal with the fact that generic data structures can only hold objects, so we must use the wrapper class, *Integer*, for the objects in the set.

To summarize, an index will be represented by a *TreeMap*. The keys for the map will be terms, which are of type *String*. The values in the map will be *TreeSets* that contain *Integers* representing page numbers. The parameterized type that we should use for the sets is *TreeSet<Integer>*. For the *TreeMap* that represents the index as a whole, the key type is *String* and the value type is *TreeSet<Integer>*. This means that the index has type

TreeMap< String, TreeSet<Integer> >

This is just the usual *TreeMap<K,V>* with K=String and V=TreeSet<Integer>. A type name as complicated as this one can look intimidating, but if you think about the data structure that we want to represent, it makes sense.

To make an index, we need to start with an empty *TreeMap*. We then work through the book, and we insert into the map every reference that we want to be in the index. We then need to print out the data from the map. Let's leave aside the question of how we find the references to put in the index, and just look at how the

TreeMap is used. It can be created with the commands:

```
TreeMap<String,TreeSet<Integer>>   index; // Declare the variable. index = new
TreeMap<>();          // Create the map object.
```

(Note that even for this complex type, the type parameters can be omitted from the constructor.)

Now, suppose that we find a reference to some term (of type *String*) on some pageNum (of type int). We need to insert this information into the index. To do this, we should look up the term in the index, using index.get(term). The return value is either null or is the set of page references that we have previously found for the term. If the return value is null, then this is the first page reference for the term, so we should add the term to the index, with a new set that contains the page reference we've just found. If the return value is non-null, we already have a set of page references, and we should just add the new page reference to the set. Here is a subroutine that does this:

```
/**
* Add a page reference to the index.
*/
void addReference(String term, int pageNum) {
    TreeSet<Integer> references; // The set of page references that we
                                 //      have so far for the term.
    references = index.get(term);
    if (references == null){
                    // This is the first reference that we have
                    // found for the term.    Make a new set containing
                    // the page number and add it to the index, with
                    // the term as the key.
        TreeSet<Integer> firstRef = new TreeSet<>();
        firstRef.add( pageNum ); // pageNum is "autoboxed" to give an Integer!
        index.put(term,firstRef);
    }
    else {
                    // references is the set of page references
                    // that we have found previously for the term.
```

```
                // Add the new page number to that set.   This
                // set is already associated to term in the index.
            references.add( pageNum );
        }
    }
```

The only other thing we need to do with the index is print it out. We want to iterate through the index and print out each term, together with the set of page references for that term. We could use an *Iterator* to iterate through the index, but it's much easier to do it with a for-each loop. The loop will iterate through the entry set of the map. Each "entry" is a key/value pair from the map; the key is a term and the value is the associated set of page references. Inside the for-each loop, we will have to print out a set of *Integers*, which can also be done with a for-each loop. So, here we have an example of nested for-each loops. (You might try to do the same thing entirely with iterators; doing so should give you some appreciation for the for-each loop!) Here is a subroutine that will print the index:

```
/**
 * Print each entry in the index.
 */
void printIndex() {
    for ( Map.Entry<String,TreeSet<Integer>> entry :   index.entrySet() ) {
        String term = entry.getKey();
        TreeSet<Integer> pageSet = entry.getValue();
        System.out.print( term + ": " );
        for ( int page : pageSet ) {
            System.out.print( page + " " );
        }
        System.out.println();
    }
}
```

The hardest thing here is the name of the type Map.Entry<String,TreeSet<Integer>>! Remember that the entries in a map of type *Map<K,V>* have type *Map.Entry<K,V>*, so the type parameters in Map.Entry<String,TreeSet<Integer>> are simply copied from the declaration of index. Another thing to note is that I used a loop control variable, page, of type *int* to iterate through the elements of pageSet, which is of type *TreeSet<Integer>*. You might have expected page to be of type *Integer*, not int, and in fact *Integer* would have worked just as well here. However, int does work, because of automatic type conversion: It's legal to assign a value of type *Integer* to a variable of type int. (To be honest, I was sort of surprised that this worked when I first tried it!)

This is not a lot of code, considering the complexity of the operations. I have not written a complete indexing program, but Exercise 10.6 presents a problem that is almost identical to the indexing problem.

(By the way, the printIndex() method could have used var to declare all of its local variables. This would have avoided the complex type names, but you would still need to be aware of the types, since you have to know what methods, such as entry. getKey(), can be used with the variables.)

By the way, in this example, I would prefer to print each list of page references with the integers separated by commas. In the printIndex() method given above, they are separated by spaces. There is an extra space after the last page reference in the list, but it does no harm since it's invisible in the printout. An extra comma at the end of the list would be annoying. The lists should be in a form such as "17,42,105" and not "17,42,105,". The problem is, how to leave that last comma out. Unfortunately, this is not so easy to do with a for-each loop. It might be fun to look at a few ways to solve this problem. One alternative is to use an iterator:

```
Iterator<Integer>    iter = pageSet.iterator();
int firstPage = iter.next();     // In this program, we know the set has
                                 // at least one element.
System.out.print(firstPage);
while ( iter.hasNext() ) {
    int nextPage = iter.next();
    System.out.print("," + nextPage);
}
```

Another possibility is to use the fact that the *TreeSet* class defines a method first() that returns the first item in the set, that is, the one that is smallest in terms of the ordering that is used to compare items in the set. (It also defines the method last().) We can solve our problem using this method and a for-each loop:

```
int firstPage = pageSet.first();// Find out the first page number in the set.
for ( int page : pageSet ) {
    if ( page != firstPage )
```

```
            System.out.print(","); // Output comma only if this is not the first page.
        System.out.print(page);
    }
```

Finally, here is an elegant solution using a subset view of the tree. Actually, this solution might be a bit extreme:

```
int firstPage = pageSet.first();// Get first item, which we know exists.
System.out.print(firstPage);   // Print first item, with no comma.
for ( int page : pageSet.tailSet( firstPage+1 ) ) // Process remaining items.
    System.out.print( "," + page );
```

6.4.3 Using a Comparator

There is a potential problem with our solution to the indexing problem. If the terms in the index can contain both upper case and lower case letters, then the terms will not be in alphabetical order! The ordering on *String* is not alphabetical. It is based on the Unicode codes of the characters in the string. The codes for all the upper case letters are less than the codes for the lower case letters. So, for example, terms beginning with "Z" come before terms beginning with "a". If the terms are restricted to use lower case letters only (or upper case only), then the ordering would be alphabetical. But suppose that we allow both upper and lower case, and that we insist on alphabetical order. In that case, our index can't use the usual ordering for Strings. Fortunately, it's possible to specify a different method to be used for comparing the keys of a map. This is a typical use for a *Comparator*.

Recall that an object that implements the interface *Comparator<T>* defines a method for comparing two objects of type *T* :

```
public int compare( T obj1, T obj2 )
```

This method should return an integer that is negative, zero, or positive, depending on whether obj1 is less than, equal to, or greater than obj2. We want to compare two *Strings* ignoring case. The *String* class already includes a method that does that, compareToIgnoreCase(). But to use a non-default comparison in a *TreeMap*, we need an object of type *Comparator<String>*. Since *Comparator* is a functional interface, an easy way to specify the comparator is to use a lambda expression:

```
(a,b) -> a.compareToIgnoreCase(b)
```

To solve our indexing problem, we just need to pass this comparator as a parameter to the *TreeMap* constructor:

```
index = new TreeMap<>( (a,b) -> a.compareToIgnoreCase(b) );
```

In fact, since the lambda expression is just calling a method that already exists in the *String* class, it could actually be given as a method reference:

index = new TreeMap<>(String::compareToIgnoreCase);

This does work. However, there one technicality. Suppose, for example, that the indexing program calls addReference("aardvark",56) and that it later calls addReference("Aardvark",102). The words "aardvark" and "Aardvark" differ only in that one of them begins with an upper case letter; when converted to lower case, they are the same. When we insert them into the index, do they count as two different terms or as one term? The answer depends on the way that a *TreeMap* tests objects for equality. In fact, *TreeMaps* and *TreeSets* always use a *Comparator* object or a compareTo method to test for equality. They do not use the equals() method for this purpose. The *Comparator* that is used for the *TreeMap* in this example returns the value zero when it is used to compare "aardvark" and "Aardvark", so the *TreeMap* considers them to be the same. Page references to "aardvark" and "Aardvark" are combined into a single list, and when the index is printed it will contain only the first version of the word that was encountered by the program. This is probably acceptable behavior in this example. If not, some other technique must be used to sort the terms into alphabetical order.

6.4.4 Word Counting

The final example in this section also deals with storing information about words. The problem here is to make a list of all the words that occur in a file, along with the number of times that each word occurs. The file will be selected by the user. The output of the program will consist of two lists. Each list contains all the words from the file, along with the number of times that the word occurred. One list is sorted alphabetically, and the other is sorted according to the number of occurrences, with the most common words at the top and the least common at the bottom. The problem here is a generalization of Exercise 7.6, which asked you to make an alphabetical list of all the words in a file, without counting the number of occurrences.

My word counting program can be found in the file WordCount.java. As the program reads an input file, it must keep track of how many times it encounters each word. We could simply throw all the words, with duplicates, into a list and count them later. But that would require a lot of extra storage space and would not be very efficient. A better method is to keep a counter for each word. The first time the word is encountered, the counter is initialized to 1. On subsequent encounters, the counter is incremented. To keep track of the data for one word, the program uses a simple class that holds a word and the counter for that word. The class is a static nested class:

*/***

Represents the data we need about a word: the word and

```
the number of times it has been encountered.
*/
private static class WordData {
     String word;
     int count;
     WordData(String w) {
                    // Constructor for creating a WordData object when
                    // we encounter a new word.
          word = w;
          count = 1;          // The initial value of count is 1.
     }
} // end class WordData
```

The program has to store all the *WordData* objects in some sort of data structure. We want to be able to add new words efficiently. Given a word, we need to check whether a *WordData* object already exists for that word, and if it does, we need to find that object so that we can increment its counter. A *Map* can be used to implement these operations. Given a word, we want to look up a *WordData* object in the *Map*. This means that the word is the key, and the *WordData* object is the value. (It might seem strange that the key is also one of the instance variables in the value object, but in fact this is a very common situation: The value object contains all the information about some entity, and the key is one of those pieces of information; the partial information in the key is used to retrieve the full information in the value object.) After reading the file, we want to output the words in alphabetical order, so we should use a *TreeMap* rather than a *HashMap*. This program converts all words to lower case so that the default ordering on Strings will put the words in alphabetical order. The data is stored in a variable named words of type *TreeMap<String,WordData>*. The variable is declared and the map object is created with the statement:

```
TreeMap<String,WordData> words = new TreeMap<>();
```

When the program reads a word from a file, it calls words.get(word) to find out if that word is already in the map. If the return value is null, then this is the first time the word has been encountered, so a new *WordData* object is created and inserted into the map with the command words.put(word, new WordData(word)). If words.get(word) is not null, then its value is the *WordData* object for this word, and the program only has to increment the counter in that object. The program uses a method readNextWord(), which was given in Exercise 7.6, to read one word from the file. This method returns null when the end of the file is encountered. Here is the complete code segment that reads the file and collects the data:

```
String word = readNextWord();
while (word != null) {
    word = word.toLowerCase();        // convert word to lower case
    WordData data = words.get(word);
    if (data == null)
            words.put( word, new WordData(word) );
    else
            data.count++;
    word = readNextWord();
}
```

After reading the words and printing them out in alphabetical order, the program has to sort the words by frequency and print them again. To do the sorting using a generic algorithm, we can copy the *WordData* objects into a list and then use the generic method Collections.sort(list,comparator), which specifies a comparator as its second parameter. Since we want to sort the data into decreasing order by count, we want a comparator for two *WordData* values a and b that puts a before b if a.count > b.count. You should check that the following lambda expression defines a comparator that will work here:

```
(a,b) -> b.count - a.count
```

The *WordData* objects that we need are the values in the map, words. Recall that words.values() returns a *Collection* that contains all the values from the map. The constructor for the *ArrayList* class lets you specify a collection to be copied into the list when it is created. So, we can use the following commands to create a list of type *ArrayList<WordData>* containing the word data and then sort that list according to frequency:

```
ArrayList<WordData> wordsByFrequency = new ArrayList<>( words.values() );
Collections.sort( wordsByFrequency, (a,b) -> b.count - a.count );
```

You should notice that these two lines replace a lot of code! It requires some practice to think in terms of generic data structures and algorithms, but the payoff is significant in terms of saved time and effort.

The only remaining problem is to print the data. We have to print the data from all the *WordData* objects twice, first in alphabetical order and then sorted according to frequency count. The data is in alphabetical order in the *TreeMap*, or more precisely, in the values of the *TreeMap*. We can use a for-each loop to print the data in the collection words.values(), and the words will appear in alphabetical order. Another for-each loop can be used to print the data in the list wordsByFrequency, and the words will be printed in order of decreasing frequency. Here is the code that does it:

```
TextIO.putln("List of words in alphabetical order"
    + " (with counts in parentheses):\n");
for ( WordData data : words.values() )
    TextIO.putln("   " + data.word + " (" + data.count + ")");
TextIO.putln("\n\nList of words by frequency of occurrence:\n");
for ( WordData data : wordsByFrequency )
    TextIO.putln("   " + data.word + " (" + data.count + ")");
```

You can find the complete word-counting program in the file WordCount.java. Note that for reading and writing files, it uses the file I/O capabilities of TextIO.java, which were discussed in Subsection 2.4.4.

By the way, if you run the WordCount program on a reasonably large file and take a look at the output, it will illustrate something about the Collections.sort() method. The second list of words in the output is ordered by frequency, but if you look at a group of words that all have the same frequency, you will see that the words in that group are in alphabetical order. The method Collections.sort() was applied to sort the words by frequency, but before it was applied, the words were already in alphabetical order. When Collections.sort() rearranged the words, it did not change the ordering of words that have the same frequency, so they were still in alphabetical order within the group of words with that frequency. This is because the algorithm used by Collections.sort() is a *stable* sorting algorithm. A sorting algorithm is said to be stable if it satisfies the following condition: When the algorithm is used to sort a list according to some property of the items in the list, then the sort does not change the relative order of items that have the same value of that property. That is, if item B comes after item A in the list before the sort, and if both items have the same value for the property that is being used as the basis for sorting, then item B will still come after item A after the sorting has been done. Neither SelectionSort nor QuickSort are stable sorting algorithms. Insertion sort is stable, but is not very fast. Merge sort, the sorting algorithm used by Collections.sort(), is both stable and fast.

I hope that the programming examples in this section have convinced you of the usefulness of the Java Collection Framework!

6.5 WRITING GENERIC CLASSES AND METHODS

So far in this chapter, you have learned about using the generic classes and methods that are part of the Java Collection Framework. Now, it's time to learn how to write new generic classes and methods from scratch. Generic programming produces highly general and reusable code—it's very useful for people who write reusable software libraries to know how to do generic programming, since it enables them to write code that can be used in many different situations.

Not every programmer needs to write reusable software libraries, but every programmer should know at least a little about how to do it. In fact, just to read the Javadoc documentation for Java's standard generic classes, you need to know some of the syntax that is introduced in this section.

I will not cover every detail of generic programming in Java in this section, but the material presented here should be sufficient to cover the most common cases.

6.5.1 Simple Generic Classes

Let's start with an example that illustrates the motivation for generic programming. In Subsection 6.2.1, I remarked that it would be easy to use a *LinkedList* to implement a queue. To ensure that the only operations that are performed on the list are the queue operations enqueue, dequeue, and isEmpty, we can create a new class that contains the linked list as a private instance variable. To implement queues of strings, for example, we can define the class:

```
class QueueOfStrings {
    private LinkedList<String> items = new LinkedList<>();
    public void enqueue(String item) {
            items.addLast(item);
    }
    public String dequeue() {
            return items.removeFirst();
    }
    public boolean isEmpty() {
            return (items.size() == 0);
    }
}
```

This is a fine and useful class. But, if this is how we write queue classes, and if we want queues of *Integers* or *Doubles* or *Colors* or any other type, then we will have to write a different class for each type. The code for all of these classes will be almost identical, which seems like a lot of redundant programming. To avoid the redundancy, we can write a generic *Queue* class that can be used to define queues of any type of object.

The syntax for writing the generic class is straightforward: We replace the specific type *String* with a type parameter such as *T*, and we add the type parameter to the name of the class:

```
class Queue<T> {
    private LinkedList<T> items = new LinkedList<>();
    public void enqueue(T item) {
        items.addLast(item);
    }
    public T dequeue() {
        return items.removeFirst();
    }
    public boolean isEmpty() {
        return (items.size() == 0);
    }
}
```

Note that within the class, the type parameter *T* is used just like any regular type name. It's used to declare the return type for dequeue, as the type of the formal parameter item in enqueue, and even as the actual type parameter in *LinkedList<T>*. Given this class definition, we can use parameterized types such as *Queue<String>* and *Queue<Integer>* and *Queue<Color>*. That is, the *Queue* class is used in exactly the same way as built-in generic classes like *LinkedList* and *HashSet*.

Note that you don't have to use "T" as the name of the type parameter in the definition of the generic class. Type parameters are like formal parameters in subroutines. You can make up any name you like in the definition of the class. The name in the definition will be replaced by an actual type name when the class is used to declare variables or create objects. If you prefer to use a more meaningful name for the type parameter, you might define the *Queue* class as:

```
class Queue<ItemType> {
    private LinkedList<ItemType> items = new LinkedList<>();
    public void enqueue(ItemType item) {
        items.addLast(item);
    }
```

```
        public ItemType dequeue() {
                return  items.removeFirst();
    }
        public boolean isEmpty() {
                return (items.size() == 0);
        }
    }
```

Changing the name from "T" to "ItemType" has absolutely no effect on the meaning of the class definition or on the way that *Queue* is used.

Generic interfaces can be defined in a similar way. It's also easy to define generic classes and interfaces that have two or more type parameters, as is done with the standard interface *Map<K,V>*. A typical example is the definition of a "Pair" that contains two objects, possibly of different types. A simple version of such a class can be defined as:

```
    public class Pair<T,S> {
        public T first;
        public S second;
        public Pair( T a, S b ) {    // Constructor.
                first = a;
                second = b;
        }
    }
```

This class can be used to declare variables and create objects such as:

```
    Pair<String,Color> colorName = new Pair<>("Red", Color.RED);
    Pair<Double,Double> coordinates = new Pair<>(17.3,42.8);
```

Note that in the definition of the constructor in this class, the name "Pair" does not have type parameters. You might have expected "Pair<T,S>". However, the name of the class is "Pair", not "Pair<T,S>", and within the definition of the class, "T" and "S" are used as if they are the names of specific, actual types. Note in any case that type parameters are never added to the names of methods or constructors, only to the names of classes and interfaces.

Record classes can also be generic. For example, a generic record class version of *Pair* could be defined simply as

```
    public record Pair(T a, S b) { }
```

6.5.2 Simple Generic Methods

In addition to generic classes, Java also has generic methods. An example is the method Collections.sort(), which can sort collections of objects of any type. To see how to write generic methods, let's start with a non-generic method for counting the number of times that a given string occurs in an array of strings:

```
/**
Returns the number of times that itemToCount occurs in list.   Items in the
list are tested for equality using itemToCount.equals(), except in the
special case where itemToCount is null.
*/
public static int countOccurrences(String[] list, String itemToCount) {
    int count = 0;
    if (itemToCount == null) {
            for ( String listItem : list )
                    if (listItem == null)
                            count++;
    }
    else {
    for ( String listItem : list )
            if (itemToCount.equals(listItem))
                    count++;
    }
    return count;
}
```

Once again, we have some code that works for type *String*, and we can imagine writing almost identical code to work with other types of objects. By writing a generic method, we get to write a single method definition that will work for objects of any non-primitive type. We need to replace the specific type *String* in the definition of the method with the name of a type parameter, such as *T*. However, if that's the only change we make, the compiler will think that "T" is the name of an actual type, and it will mark it as an undeclared identifier. We need some way of telling the compiler that "T" is a type parameter. That's what the "<T>" does in the definition of the generic class "class Queue<T> { ...". For a generic method, the "<T>" goes just before the name of the return type of the method:

```
public static <T> int countOccurrences(T[] list, T itemToCount) {
    int count = 0;
    if (itemToCount == null) {
        for ( T listItem : list )
            if (listItem == null) count++;
    }
    else {
        for ( T listItem : list )
            if (itemToCount.equals(listItem))
                count++;
    }
    return count;
}
```

The "<T>" marks the method as being generic and specifies the name of the type parameter that will be used in the definition. Of course, the name of the type parameter doesn't have to be "T"; it can be anything. (The "<T>" looks a little strange in that position, I know, but it had to go somewhere and that's just where the designers of Java decided to put it.)

Given the generic method definition, we can apply it to objects of any type. If wordList is a variable of type String[ ] and word is a variable of type *String*, then

```
int ct = countOccurrences( wordList, word );
```

will count the number of times that word occurs in wordList. If palette is a variable of type Color[ ] and color is a variable of type *Color*, then

```
int ct = countOccurrences( palette, color );
```

will count the number of times that color occurs in palette. If numbers is a variable of type Integer[ ], then

```
int ct = countOccurrences( numbers, 17 );
```

will count the number of times that 17 occurs in numbers. This last example uses autoboxing; the 17 is automatically converted to a value of type *Integer*. Note that, since generic programming in Java applies only to objects, we cannot use countOccurrences to count the number of occurrences of 17 in an array of type int[ ].

A generic method can have one or more type parameters, such as the "T" in countOccurrences. Note that when a generic method is used, as in the function call "countOccurrences(wordlist, word)", there is no explicit mention of the type that is sub- stituted for the type parameter. The compiler deduces the type from the types of the actual parameters in the method call. Since wordlist is of type String[ ], the compiler can tell that in "countOccurrences(wordlist, word)", the type that replaces *T* is *String*. This contrasts with the use of generic classes, as in "Queue<String>", where the type parameter is specified explicitly.

The countOccurrences method operates on an array. We could also write a similar method to count occurrences of an object in any collection:

```
public static <T> int countOccurrences(Collection<T> collection, T itemToCount) {
    int count = 0;
    if (itemToCount == null) {
            for ( T item : collection )
                    if (item == null)
                            count++;
    }
    else {
            for ( T item : collection )
                    if (itemToCount.equals(item))
                            count++;
    }
    return count;
}
```

Since *Collection<T>* is itself a generic type, this method is very general. It can operate on an *ArrayList* of *Integers*, a *TreeSet* of *Strings*, a *LinkedList* of *Buttons*, ...

6.5.3 Wildcard Types

There is a limitation on the sort of generic classes and methods that we have looked at so far: The type parameter in our examples, usually named *T*, can be any type at all. This is OK in many cases, but it means that the only things that you can do with *T* are things that can be done with every type, and the only things that you can do with objects of type *T* are things that you can do with every object. With the techniques that we have covered so far, you can't, for example, write a generic method that compares objects with the compareTo() method, since that method is not defined for all objects. The compareTo() method is defined in the *Comparable* interface. What we need is a way of specifying that a generic class or method only applies to objects of type *Comparable* and not to arbitrary objects. With that restriction, we should be free to use compareTo() in the definition of the generic class or method.

There are two different but related syntaxes for putting restrictions on the types that are used in generic programming. One of these is *bounded type parameters*, which are used as formal type parameters in generic class and method definitions; a bounded type parameter would be used in place of the simple type parameter *T* in "class GenericClass<T> ..." or in "public static <T> void genericMethod(...". The second syntax is *wildcard types*, which are used as type parameters in the declarations of variables and of formal parameters in method definitions; a wildcard type could be used in place of the type parameter *String* in the declaration statement "List<String> list;" or in the formal parameter list "void concat(Collection<String> c)". We will look at wildcard types first, and we will return to the topic of bounded types later in this section.

Let's start with a simple example in which a wildcard type is useful. Suppose that *Shape* is a class that defines a method public void draw(), and suppose that *Shape* has subclasses such as *Rect* and *Oval*. Suppose that we want a method that can draw all the shapes in a collection of *Shapes*. We might try:

```
public static void drawAll(Collection<Shape> shapes) {
    for ( Shape s : shapes )
            s.draw();
}
```

This method works fine if we apply it to a variable of type *Collection<Shape>*, or *ArrayList<Shape>*, or any other collection class with type parameter *Shape*. Suppose, however, that you have a list of *Rects* stored in a variable named rectangles of type *Collection<Rect>*. Since *Rects* are *Shapes*, you might expect to be able to call drawAll(rectangles). Unfortu- nately, this will not work; a collection of *Rects* is not considered to be a collection of *Shapes*! The variable rectangles cannot be assigned to the formal parameter shapes. The solution is to replace the type parameter "Shape" in the declaration of shapes with the wildcard type "? extends Shape":

```
public static void drawAll(Collection<? extends Shape> shapes) {
    for ( Shape s : shapes )
            s.draw();
}
```

The wildcard type "? extends Shape" means roughly "any type that is either equal to *Shape* or that is a subclass of *Shape*". When the formal parameter, shapes, is declared to be of type *Collection<? extends Shape>*, it becomes possible to call the drawAll method with an actual parameter of type *Collection<Rect>* since *Rect* is a subclass of *Shape* and therefore matches the wildcard. We could also pass actual parameters to drawAll of type *ArrayList<Rect>* or *Set<Oval>* or *List<Oval>*. And we can still pass variables of type *Collection<Shape>* or *ArrayList<Shape>*, since the class *Shape* itself matches "? extends Shape". We have greatly increased the usefulness of the method by using the wildcard type.

(Although it is not essential, you might be interested in knowing *why* Java does not allow a collection of *Rects* to be used as a collection of *Shapes*, even though every *Rect* is considered to be a *Shape*. Consider the rather silly but legal method that adds an oval to a list of shapes:

```
static void addOval(List<Shape> shapes, Oval oval) {
    shapes.add(oval);
}
```

Supposethatrectanglesisoftype*List<Rect>*.It'sillegaltocalladdOval(rectangles,oval), because of the rule that a list of *Rects* is not a list of *Shapes*. If we dropped that rule, then addOval(rectangles,oval) would be legal, and it would add an *Oval* to a list of *Rects*. This would be bad: Since *Oval* is not a subclass of *Rect*, an *Oval* is not a *Rect*, and a list of *Rects* should never be able to contain an *Oval*. The method call addOval(rectangles,oval) does not make sense and should be illegal.)

As another example, consider the method addAll() from the interface *Collection<T>*. In my description of this method in Subsection 6.1.4, I say that for a collection, coll, of type *Collection<T>*, coll.addAll(coll2) "adds all the objects in coll2 to coll. The parameter, coll2, can be any collection of type *Collection<T>*. However, it can also be more general. For example, if *T* is a class and *S* is a subclass of *T*, then coll2 can be of type *Collection<S>*. This makes sense because any object of type *S* is automatically of type *T* and so can legally be added to coll." If you think for a moment, you'll see that what I'm describing here, a little awkwardly, is a use of wildcard types: We don't want to require coll2 to be a collection of objects of type *T* ; we want to allow collections of any subclass of *T*. To be more specific, let's look at how a similar addAll() method could be added to the generic *Queue* class that was defined earlier in this section:

```
class Queue<T> {
    private LinkedList<T> items = new LinkedList<T>();
    public void enqueue(T item) {
            items.addLast(item);
    }
    public T dequeue() {
```

```
            return items.removeFirst();
        }
        public boolean isEmpty() {
            return (items.size() == 0);
        }
        public void addAll(Collection<? extends T> collection) {
                // Add all the items from the collection to the end of the queue
            for ( T item : collection )
                enqueue(item);
        }
    }
```

Here, *T* is a type parameter in the generic class definition. We are combining wildcard types with generic classes. Inside the generic class definition, "T" is used as if it is a specific, though unknown, type. The wildcard type "? extends T" means some type that is equal to or extends that specific type. When we create a queue of type *Queue<Shape>*, "T" refers to "Shape", and the wildcard type "? extends T" in the class definition means "? extends Shape". This ensures that the addAll method of the queue can be applied to collections of *Rects* and *Ovals* as well as to collections of *Shapes*.

The for-each loop in the definition of addAll iterates through the collection using a variable, item, of type *T*. Now, collection can be of type *Collection<S>*, where *S* is a subclass of *T*. Since item is of type *T*, not *S*, do we have a problem here? No, no problem. As long as *S* is a subclass of *T*, a value of type *S* can be assigned to a variable of type *T*. The restriction on the wildcard type makes everything work nicely.

The addAll method adds all the items from a collection to the queue. Suppose that we wanted to do the opposite: Add all the items that are currently in the queue to a given collection.

An instance method defined as

```
    public void addAllTo(Collection<T> collection)
```

would only work for collections whose base type is exactly the same as *T*. This is too restrictive. We need some sort of wildcard. However, "? extends T" won't work. Suppose we try it:

```
    public void addAllTo(Collection<? extends T> collection) {
            // Remove all items currently on the queue and add them to collection
        while ( ! isEmpty() ) {
```

```
            T item = dequeue();        // Remove an item from the queue.
            collection.add( item );    // Add it to the collection.        ILLEGAL!!
        }
    }
```

The problem is that we can't add an item of type *T* to a collection that might only be able to hold items belonging to some subclass, *S*, of *T*. The containment is going in the wrong direction: An item of type *T* is not necessarily of type *S*. For example, if we have a queue of type *Queue<Shape>*, it doesn't make sense to add items from the queue to a collection of type *Collection<Rect>*, since not every *Shape* is a *Rect*. On the other hand, if we have a *Queue<Rect>*, it would make sense to add items from that queue to a *Collection<Shape>* or indeed to any collection *Collection<S>* where *S* is a superclass of *Rect*.

To express this type of relationship, we need a new kind of type wildcard: "? super T". This wildcard means, roughly, "either *T* itself or any class that is a superclass of *T*." For example, *Collection<? super Rect>* would match the types *Collection<Shape>*, *ArrayList<Object>*, and *Set<Rect>*. This is what we need for our addAllTo method. With this change, our complete generic queue class becomes:

```
    class Queue<T> {
        private LinkedList<T> items = new LinkedList<T>();
        public void enqueue(T item) {
                items.addLast(item);
        }
        public T dequeue() {
                return items.removeFirst();
        }
        public boolean isEmpty() {
                return (items.size() == 0);
        }
        public void addAll(Collection<? extends T> collection) {
                        // Add all the items from the collection to the end of the queue
                for ( T item : collection )
                        enqueue(item);
        }
        public void addAllTo(Collection<? super T> collection) {
```

```
            // Remove all items currently on the queue and add them to collection
        while ( ! isEmpty() ) {
            T item = dequeue();       // Remove an item from the queue.
            collection.add( item );   // Add it to the collection.
        }
    }
}
```

In a wildcard type such as "? extends T", *T* can be an interface instead of a class. Note that the term "extends" (not "implements") is used in the wildcard type, even if *T* is an interface. For example, we have seen that *Runnable* is an interface that defines the method public void run(). Here is a method that runs all the objects in a collection of *Runnables* by executing the run() method from each runnable object:

```
public static runAll( Collection<? extends Runnable> runnables ) {
    for ( Runnable runnable : runnables ) {
        runnable.run();
    }
}
```

Wildcard types are used only as type parameters in parameterized types, such as *Collection<? extends Runnable>*. The place where a wildcard type is most likely to occur, by far, is in a formal parameter list, where the wildcard type is used in the declaration of the type of a formal parameter. However, they can also be used in a few other places. For example, they can be used in the type specification in a variable declaration statement.

One final remark: The wildcard type "<?>" is equivalent to "<? extends Object>". That is, it matches any possible type. For example, the removeAll() method in the generic interface *Collection<T>* is declared as

```
public boolean removeAll( Collection<?> c ) { ...
```

This just means that the removeAll method can be applied to any collection of any type of object.

6.5.4 Bounded Types

Wildcard types don't solve all of our problems. They allow us to generalize method definitions so that they can work with collections of objects of various types, rather than just a single type. However, they do not allow us to restrict the types that are allowed as formal type parameters in a generic class or method definition. Bounded types exist for this purpose.

We start with a small, not very realistic example. Suppose that you would like to create groups of GUI components using a generic class named *ControlGroup*. For example, the parameterized type *ControlGroup<Button>* would represent a group of *Buttons*, while *ControlGroup<Slider>* would represent a group of *Sliders*. The class will include methods that can be called to apply certain operations to all components in the group at once. For example, there will be an instance method of the form

```
public void disableAll() {
    .
    .      // Call c.setDisable(true) for every control, c, in the group.
    .
}
```

The problem is that the setDisable() method is defined in a *Control* object, but not for objects of arbitrary type. It wouldn't make sense to allow types such as *ControlGroup<String>* or *ControlGroup<Integer>*, since *Strings* and *Integers* don't have setDisable() methods. We need some way to restrict the type parameter *T* in *ControlGroup<T>* so that only *Control* and subclasses of *Control* are allowed as actual type parameters. We can do this by using the *bounded type* "T extends Control" instead of a plain "T" in the definition of the class:

```
public class ControlGroup<T extends Control> {
    private ArrayList<T> components; // For storing the components in this group.
    public void disableAll( ) {
        for ( Control c : components ) {
            if (c != null)
                c.setDisable(true);
        }
    }
    public void enableAll( ) {
        for ( Control c : components ) {
            if (c != null)
                c.setDisable(false);
        }
    }
    public void add( T c ) {   // Add a value c, of type T, to the group.
        components.add(c);
```

```
    }
    .
    .        // Additional methods and constructors.
    .
}
```

The restriction "extends Control" on T makes it illegal to create the parameterized types *ControlGroup<String>* and *ControlGroup<Integer>*, since the actual type parameter that replaces "T" is required to be either *Control* itself or a subclass of *Control*. With this restriction, we know—and, more important, the compiler knows—that the objects in the group are of type *Control*, so that the operation c.setDisable() is defined for any c in the group.

In general, a bounded type parameter "T extends SomeType" means roughly "a type, *T*, that is either equal to *SomeType* or is a subclass of *SomeType*; the upshot is that any object of type *T* is also of type *SomeType*, and any operation that is defined for objects of type *SomeType* is defined for objects of type *T*. The type *SomeType* doesn't have to be the name of a class. It can be any name that represents an actual object type. For example, it can be an interface or even a parameterized type.

Bounded types and wildcard types are clearly related. They are, however, used in very different ways. A bounded type can be used only as a formal type parameter in the definition of a generic method, class, or interface. A wildcard type is used most often to declare the type of a formal parameter in a method and cannot be used as a formal type parameter. One other difference, by the way, is that, in contrast to wildcard types, bounded type parameters can only use "extends", never "super".

Bounded type parameters can be used when declaring generic methods. For example, as an alternative to the generic *ControlGroup* class, one could write a free-standing generic static method that can disable any collection of *Controls* as follows:

```
public static <T extends Control> void disableAll(Collection<T> comps) {
    for ( Control c : comps )
        if (c != null)
            c.setDisable(true);
    }
```

Using "<T extends Control>" as the formal type parameter means that the method can only be called for collections whose base type is Control or some subclass of Control, such as Button or Slider.

Note that we don't really need a generic type parameter in this case. We can write an equivalent method using a wildcard type:

```
public static void disableAll(Collection<? extends Control> comps) {
    for ( Control c : comps )
        if (c != null)
            c.setDisable(true);
}
```

In this situation, the version that uses the wildcard type is to be preferred, since the implementation is simpler. However, there are some situations where a generic method with a bounded type parameter cannot be rewritten using a wildcard type. Note that a generic type parameter gives a name, such as *T*, to the unknown type, while a wildcard type does not give a name to the unknown type. The name makes it possible to refer to the unknown type in the body of the method that is being defined. If a generic method definition uses the generic type name more than once or uses it outside the formal parameter list of the method, then the generic type parameter cannot be replaced with a wildcard type.

Let's look at a generic method in which a bounded type parameter is essential. In Subsection 6.2.1, I presented a code segment for inserting a string into a sorted list of strings, in such a way that the modified list is still in sorted order. Here is the same code, but this time in the form of a method definition (and without the comments):

```
static void sortedInsert(List<String> sortedList, String newItem) {
    ListIterator<String> iter = sortedList.listIterator();
    while (iter.hasNext()) {
        String item = iter.next();
        if (newItem.compareTo(item) <= 0) {
            iter.previous();
            break;
        }
    }
    iter.add(newItem);
}
```

This method works fine for lists of strings, but it would be nice to have a generic method that can be applied to lists of other types of objects. The problem, of course, is that the code assumes that the compareTo() method is defined for objects in the list, so the method can only work for lists of objects that implement the *Comparable* interface. We can't simply use a wildcard type to enforce this restriction. Suppose we try to do it, by replacing *List<String>* with *List<? extends Comparable>*:

```
static void sortedInsert(List<? extends Comparable> sortedList, ???? newItem) {
    ListIterator<????> iter = sortedList.listIterator();
...
```

We immediately run into a problem, because we have no name for the unknown type represented by the wildcard. We need a name for that type because the type of newItem and of iter should be the same as the type of the items in the list. The problem is solved if we write a generic method with a bounded type parameter, since then we have a name for the unknown type, and we can write a valid generic method:

```
static <T extends Comparable> void sortedInsert(List<T> sortedList, T newItem) {
    ListIterator<T> iter = sortedList.listIterator();
    while (iter.hasNext()) {
            T item = iter.next();
            if (newItem.compareTo(item) <= 0) {
                    iter.previous();
                    break;
            }
    }
    iter.add(newItem);
}
```

There is still one technicality to cover in this example. *Comparable* is itself a parameterized type, but I have used it here without a type parameter. This is legal but the compiler might give you a warning about using a "raw type." In fact, the objects in the list should implement the parameterized interface *Comparable<T>*, since they are being compared to items of type *T*. This just means that instead of using *Comparable* as the type bound, we should use *Comparable<T>*:

```
static <T extends Comparable<T>> void sortedInsert(List<T> sortedList, ...
```

6.6 INTRODUCTION THE STREAM API

Among its new features, Java 8 introduced a *stream API* , which represents a new way of expressing operations on collections of data. A major motivation for the new approach was to make it possible for the Java compiler to "parallelize" a computation, that is, to break it into pieces that can be run simultaneously on several processors. Doing so can significantly speed up the computation. Chapter 12 will discuss parallel programming in Java using threads. Using threads directly can be difficult and error-prone. The stream API offers the possibility of parallelizing some kinds of computation automatically and safely, and it is not surprising that it has generated a lot of interest on those grounds.

The classes and interfaces that define the stream API are defined in package java. util.stream. *Stream* is an interface in that package that represents streams and defines the basic operations on streams.

A *stream* is simply a sequence of data values. A stream can be created from a *Collection*, from an array, or from a variety of other data sources. The stream API provides a set of operators that operate on streams. (The API is covered in this chapter because it makes extensive use of generic programming and parameterized types.) To perform some computation using the stream API means creating a stream to get the data from some source, and then applying a sequence of stream operations that will produce the result that you want. Once a stream has been used in this way, it cannot be reused. Of course, you can usually make another stream from the same data source if you want to use it in another computation.

Expressing a computation as a sequence of stream operations requires a new kind of thinking, and it takes some getting used to. Let's start with an example. Suppose that stringList is a large ArrayList<String>, where none of the elements are null, and you want to know the average length of the strings in the list. This can be done easily with a for-each loop:

```
int lengthSum = 0;
for ( String str : stringList ) {
    lengthSum = lengthSum + str.length();
}
double average = (double)lengthSum / stringList.size();
```

To do the same thing with the stream API, you could use:

```
int lengthSum = stringList.parallelStream()
                          .mapToInt( str -> str.length() )
                          .sum();
double average = (double)lengthSum / stringList.size();
```

In this version, stringList.parallelStream() creates a stream consisting of all the elements of the list. The fact that it is a "parallelStream" makes it possible to parallelize the computation. The method mapToInt() applies a *map* operation to the stream of strings. That is, it takes each string from the stream and applies a function to it; in this case, the function computes the length of the string, giving a value of type int. The result of the map operation is to produce a new stream, this time a stream of integers, consisting of all the outputs from the function. The final operation, sum(), adds up all the numbers in the stream of integers and returns the result.

The net result is that we've added up the lengths of all the strings in the list. Because of the potential for parallelization, the stream version might be substantially faster than the for loop version. In practice, there is significant overhead involved in setting up and manipulating streams, so the list would have to be fairly large before you would see any speedup. In fact, for small lists, the stream version will almost certainly take longer than the for loop.

The stream API is complex, and I can only give a basic introduction to it here—but hopefully enough to convey some of its spirit.

6.6.1 Generic Functional Interfaces

Many stream operators take parameters, which are often given as lambda expressions. The mapToInt() operator in the above example takes a parameter representing a function from *String* to int. The type for that parameter is given by a parameterized functional interface, ToIntFunction<T>, from package java.util.function. This interface represents the general idea of a function that takes an input of type *T* and outputs an int. If you were to look at the definition of that interface, it would be something like

```
public interface ToIntFunction<T> {
    public int applyAsInt( T x );
}
```

Stream<T> is also a parameterized interface. In the above example, stringList is of type ArrayList<String>, and the stream that is created by stringList.parallelStream() is of type Stream<String>. When the mapToInt() operator is applied to that stream, it expects a parameter of type ToIntFunction<String>. The lambda expression "str -> str.length()" maps a *String* to an int, so it represents a value of the correct type. Fortunately, you don't need to think about all of that to use the stream API: All you need to know is that to convert a stream of strings to a stream of integers using mapToInt, you need to provide a function that maps strings to ints. However, if you want to read the API documentation, you will have to deal with parameter types similar to *ToIntFunction*.

The package java.util.function contains a large number of generic functional interfaces. Many of them, like *ToIntFunction*, are parameterized types, and they are all generic in that they represent very generic functions, with no set meaning. For example, the functional interface *DoubleUnaryOperator* represents the general idea of a function from double to double. This interface is essentially the same as my example *FunctionR2R* from Subsection 4.5.2 (except for the name of the function that it defines, which is often irrelevant).

The interfaces in java.util.function are used to specify parameter types for many stream operators as well as for other built-in functions in the Java API, and you can certainly use them to specify parameter types for your own subroutines as well. I will discuss some of them here. Most of the others are variations on the ones that I cover.

The general term *predicate* refers to a function whose return type is boolean. The functional interface Predicate<T> defines a boolean-valued function test(t) with a parameter of type *T*. This interface is used, for example, as the parameter type for the method removeIf(p), which is defined for any *Collection*. For example, if strList is of type LinkedList<String>, then you can remove all null values from the list simply by saying

```
strList.removeIf( s -> (s == null) );
```

The parameter is a Predicate<String> that tests whether its input, s, is null. The removeIf() method removes all elements from the list for which the value of the predicate is true.

A predicate for testing int values could be represented by the type Predicate<Integer>, but that introduces the overhead of autoboxing every int in a wrapper of type *Integer*. To avoid that overhead, the package java.util.function has the functional interface *IntPredicate*, which defines the boolean-valued function test(n), where n is of type int. Similarly, it defines *DoublePredicate* and *LongPredicate*. This is typical of how the stream API deals with primitive types. For example, it defines *IntStream* to represent a stream of ints as a more efficient alternative to Stream<Integer>.

The functional interface Supplier<T> defines a function, get() with no parameters and a return type of *T*. It represents a source of values of type *T*. There is a companion interface Consumer<T> that defines the void function accept(t) with a parameter of type *T*. There are also specialized versions for primitive types, including *IntSupplier*, *IntConsumer*, *DoubleSupplier* and *DoubleConsumer*. I will give examples of using suppliers and consumers below.

Function<T,R> represents functions from values of type *T* to values of type *R*. This functional interface defines the function apply(t), where t is of type *T* and the return type is *R*. The interface UnaryOperator<T> is essentially Function<T,T>; that is, it represents a function whose input and output types are the same. Note that *DoubleUnaryOperator* is a specialized version of UnaryOperator<Double>, and of course there is also *IntUnaryOperator*.

Finally, I will mention BinaryOperator<T> and its specializations such as *IntBinaryOperator*. The interface BinaryOperator<T> defines the function apply(t1,t2) where t1 and t2 are both of type *T* and the return type is also *T*. Binary operators include things like addition of numbers or concatenation of strings.

6.6.2 Making Streams

To use the stream API, you have to start by creating a stream. There are many ways to make streams.

There are two basic types of streams, *sequential streams* and *parallel streams*. The difference is that operations on parallel streams can, potentially, be parallelized while the values in a sequential stream are always processed sequentially, in a single process, as they would be by a for loop. (It might not be clear why sequential streams should exist, but some operations cannot be safely parallelized.) It is possible to convert a stream from one type to the other type. If stream is a *Stream*, then stream.parallel() represents the same stream of values, but converted to a parallel stream (if it was not already parallel). Similarly, stream.sequential() is a sequential stream with the same values as stream.

We have already seen that if c is any *Collection*, then c.parallelStream() is a stream whose values are the values from the collection. As you might suspect, it is a parallel stream. The method c.stream() creates a sequential stream of the same values. This works for any collection, including lists and sets. You could also get the parallel stream by calling c.stream().parallel().

An array does not have a stream() method, but you can create a stream from an array using a static method in class *Arrays* from package java.util. If A is an array, then

Arrays.stream(A)

is a sequential stream containing the values from the array. (To get a parallel stream, use Arrays.stream(A).parallel().) This works for arrays of objects and for arrays of the primitive types int, double, and long. If A is of type T[ ], where *T* is an object type, then the stream is of type Stream<T>. If A is an array of int, the result is an *IntStream*, and similarly for double and long.

Suppose supplier is of type Supplier<T>. It should be possible to create a stream of values of type *T* by calling supplier.get() over and over. That stream can in fact be created using

Stream.generate(supplier)

The stream is sequential and is effectively infinite. That is, it will continue to produce values forever or until trying to do so produces an error. Similarly, IntStream.generate(s) will create the stream of int values from an *IntSupplier*, and DoubleStream.generate(s) creates a stream of doubles from a *DoubleSupplier*. For example,

DoubleStream.generate(() -> Math.random())

creates an infinite stream of random numbers. In fact, you can get a similar stream of random values from a variable, rand, of type *Random* (see Subsection 5.3.1): rand.doubles() is an infinite stream of random numbers in the range 0 to 1. If you only want a finite number of random numbers, use rand.doubles(count). The *Random* class has other methods for creating streams of random doubles and ints. You will find other methods that create streams in various standard classes.

The *IntStream* interface defines a method for creating a stream containing a given range of integer values. The stream

IntStream.range(start, end)

is a sequential stream containing the values start, start+1, . . . , end-1. Note that end is not included.

Some additional methods for making streams have been introduced in newer versions of Java. For example, in Java 11, for a *Scanner*, input, the method input.tokens() creates a stream consisting of all the strings that would be returned by calling input.next() over and over. And for a *String*, str, that contains multiple lines of text, Java 11 added str.lines() that creates a stream consisting of the lines from the string.

6.6.3 Operations on Streams

Some operations on a stream produce another stream. They are referred to as "intermediate operations" because you will still have to do something with the resulting stream to produce a final result. "Terminal operations" on the other hand apply to a stream and produce a result that is not a stream. The general pattern for working with streams is to create a stream, possibly apply a sequence of intermediate operations to it, and then apply a terminal operation to produce the desired final result. In the example at the beginning of this section, mapToInt() is an intermediate operation that converted the stream of strings into a stream of ints, and sum() is a terminal operation that found the sum of the numbers in the stream of ints.

The two most basic intermediate operations are *filter* and *map*. A filter applies a *Predicate* to a stream, and it creates a new stream consisting of the values from the original stream for which the predicate is true. For example, if we had a boolean-valued function isPrime(n) that tests whether an integer n is prime, then

IntSteam.range(2,1000).filter(n -> isPrime(n))

would create a stream containing all the prime numbers in the range 2 to 1000. (I'm not saying this is a *good* way to produce those numbers!)

A map applies a *Function* to each value in a stream, and creates a stream consisting of the output values. For example, suppose that strList is an ArrayList<String> and we would like a stream consisting of all the non-null strings in the list, converted to lower case:

strList.stream().filter(s -> (s != null)).map(s -> s.toLowerCase())

The specializations mapToInt(), mapToDouble(), and mapToLong() exist to map *Streams* into *IntStreams*, *DoubleStreams*, and *LongStreams*.

Here are a few more intermediate operations on a stream, S, that can be useful: S.limit(n), where n is an integer, creates a stream containing only the first n values from S. (If S has fewer than n values, then S.limit(n) is the same as S.) S.distinct() creates a stream from the values of S by omitting duplicate values, so that all the values in S.distinct() are different. And S.sorted() creates a stream containing the same values as S, but in sorted order; to sort items that do not have a natural ordering, you can provide a *Comparator* as a parameter to sorted(). (Comparators are discussed in Subsection 6.1.6.) Note that S.limit(n) can be especially useful for truncating what would otherwise be an infinite stream, such as a stream generated from a *Supplier*.

To actually get anything done with a stream, you need to apply a terminal operation at the end. The operator forEach(c) applies a *Consumer*, c, to each element of the stream. The result is not a stream, since consumers do not produce values. The effect of S.forEach(c) on a stream S is simply to do something with each value in the stream. For example, we have a whole new way to print all the strings in a list of strings:

stringList.stream().forEach(s -> System.out.println(s));

For parallel streams, the consumer function is not guaranteed to be applied to the values from the stream in the same order that they occur in the stream. If you want that guarantee, you can use forEachOrdered(c) instead of forEach(c).

If we want to print out only some of the strings, say those that have length at least 5, and if we want them in sorted order, we can apply some filters:

```
stringList.stream()
        .filter( s -> (s.length() >= 5) )
        .sorted()
        .forEachOrdered( s -> System.out.println(s) )
```

Some terminal operations output a single value. For example, S.count() returns the number of values in the stream S. And *IntStreams*, *LongStreams*, and *DoubleStreams* have the terminal operation sum(), to compute the sum of all the values in the stream. Suppose, for example, that you would like to test the random number generator by generating 10000 random numbers and counting how many of them are less than 0.5:

```
long half = DoubleStream.generate( Math::random )
                .limit(10000)
                .filter( x -> (x < 0.5) )
                .count();
```

Note that count() returns a long rather than an int. Also note that I've used the method refer- ence Math::random here instead of the equivalent lambda expression "() -> Math.random()" (see Subsection 4.5.4). If you are having trouble reading things like this, keep in mind that the pattern is: Create a stream, apply some intermediate operations, apply a terminal operation. Here, an infinite stream of random numbers is generated by calling Math.random() over and over. The operation limit(10000) truncates that stream to 10000 values, so that in fact only 10000 values are generated. The filter() operation only lets through numbers x such that x < 0.5 is true. And finally, count() returns the number of items in the resulting stream.

A Stream<T> also has terminal operations min(c) and max(c) to return the smallest and largest values in the stream. The parameter, *c*, is of type Comparator<T>; it is used for comparing the values. However, the return type of min() and max() is a little peculiar: The return type is Optional<T>, which represents a value of type *T* that might or might not exist. The problem is that an empty stream does not have a largest or smallest value, so the minimum and maximum of an empty stream do not exist. An *Optional* has a get() method that returns the value of the *Optional*, if there is one; it will throw an exception if the *Optional* is empty. For example, if words is a Collection<String>, you can get the longest string in the collection with

```
String longest = words.parallelStream()
                .max( (s1,s2) -> s1.length() - s2.length() )
                .get();
```

But this will throw an exception if the collection is empty. (The boolean-valued method isPresent() in an *Optional* can be used to test whether the value exists.)

Similarly, *IntStream*, *LongStream*, and *DoubleStream* provide terminal operations min() and max() that return values of type *OptionalInt*, *OptionalLong*, and *OptionalDouble*. Each of these classes also has an average() method that returns an *OptionalDouble*.

The terminal operators allMatch(p) and anyMatch(p) take a predicate as parameter and compute a boolean value. The value of allMatch(p) is true if the predicate, p, is true for every value in the stream to which it is applied. The value of anyMatch(p) is true if there is at least one value in the stream for which p is true. Note that anyMatch() will stop processing, and will return true as its output, if it finds a value that satisfies the predicate. And allMatch() will stop processing if it finds a value that does not match the predicate.

Many terminal operations that compute a single value can be expressed in terms of a more general operation, *reduce*. A reduce operation combines the values from a stream using a *BinaryOperator*. For example, a sum is computed by a reduce operation in which the binary operation is addition. The binary operator should be associative, which means that the order in which the operator is applied doesn't matter. There is no built-in terminal operator to compute the product of the values in a stream, but we can do that directly with reduce. Suppose, for example, that A is an array of double, and we want the product of all the non-zero elements in A:

```
double multiply = Arrays.stream(A).filter( x -> (x != 0) )
                                  .reduce( 1, (x,y) -> x*y );
```

The binary operator here maps a pair of numbers (x,y) to their product x*y. The first parameter to reduce() is an "identity" for the binary operation. That is, it is a value such that 1*x = x for any x. The maximum of a stream of double could be computed with reduce() by using reduce(Double.NEGATIVE INFINITY, Math::max).

The last major terminal operation is collect(c), a very general operation which collects all of the values in the stream into a data structure or a single summary result of some type.

The parameter, c is something called a collector. The collector will ordinarily be given by one of the static functions in the *Collectors* class. This can get very complicated, and I will only give a couple of examples. The function Collectors. toList() returns a *Collector* that can be used with collect() to put all of the values from the stream into a *List*. For example, suppose that A is an array of non-null *Strings*, and we want a list of all the strings in A that begin with the substring "Fred":

```
List<String> freds = Arrays.stream(A)
                      .filter( s -> s.startsWith("Fred") )
                      .collect( Collectors.toList() );
```

That's actually pretty easy! Even more useful are collectors that group the items from a stream according to some criterion. The collector Collectors.groupingBy(f) takes a parameter, f, whose type is specified by the functional interface *Function<T,S>*, representing a function from values of type *T* to values of type *S*. When used with collect(), Collectors.groupingBy(f) operates on a stream of type *Stream<T>*, and it separates the items in the stream into groups, based on the value of the function f when applied to the items. That is, all the items, x, in a given group have the same value for f(x). The result is a *Map<S,List<T>>*. In this map, a key is one of the function values, f(x), and the associated value for that key is a list containing all the items from the stream to which f assigns that function value.

An example will clarify things. Suppose we have an array of people, where each person has a first name and a last name. And suppose that we want to put the people into groups, where each group consists of all the people with a given last name. A person can be represented by an object of type *Person* that contains instance variables named *firstname* and *lastname*. Let's say that population is a variable of type Person[ ]. Then Arrays.stream(population) is a stream of *Persons*, and we can group the people in the stream by last name with the following

code:

```
Map<String, List<Person>> families;
families = Arrays.stream(population)
            .collect(Collectors.groupingBy( person -> person.lastname ));
```

Here, the lambda expression, person -> person.lastname, defines the grouping function. The function takes a *Person* as input and outputs a *String* giving that person's last name. In the resulting *Map*, families, a key is one of the last names from the *Persons* in the array, and the value associated with that last name is a *List* containing all the *Persons* with that last name. We could print out the groups as follows:

```
for ( String lastName : families.keySet() ) {
    System.out.println("People with last name " + lastName + ":");
    for ( Person name : families.get(lastName) ) {
            System.out.println("      " + name.firstname + " " + name.lastname);
    }
    System.out.println();
}
```

Although the explanation is a bit long-winded, the result should be reasonably easy to understand.

6.6.4 An Experiment

Most of the examples of using streams that I have given so far are not very practical. In most cases, a simple for loop would have been just as easy to write and probably more efficient. That's especially true since I've mostly used sequential streams, and most of the examples cannot be efficiently parallelized. (A notable exception is the reduce operation, which is important precisely because it parallelizes well.) Let's look at an example where the stream API is applied to a long computation that might get some real speedup with parallelization. The problem is to compute a Riemann sum. This is something from Calculus, but you don't need to understand anything at all about what it means. Here is a traditional method for computing the desired sum:

```
/**
Use a basic for loop to compute a Riemann sum.
@param f   The function that is to be summed.
@param a   The left endpoint of the interval over which f is summed.
@param b   The right endpoint.
@param n   The number of subdivisions of the interval.
@return    The value computed for the Riemann sum.
*/
private static double riemannSumWithForLoop(
            DoubleUnaryOperator f, double a, double b, int n) {
    double sum = 0;
    double dx = (b - a) / n;
    for (int i = 0; i < n; i++) {
            sum = sum + f.applyAsDouble(a + i*dx);
    }
    return sum * dx;
}
```

The type for the first parameter is a functional interface, so we could call this method, for example, with

```
reimannSumWithForLoop( x -> Math.sin(x), 0, Math.PI, 10000 )
```

How can we apply the stream API to this problem? To imitate the for loop, we can start by generating the integers from 0 to n as a stream, using IntStream.range(0,n). This gives a sequential stream. To enable parallelism, we have to convert it to a parallel stream by applying the .parallel() operation. To compute the values that we want to sum up, we can apply a map operation that maps the stream of ints to a stream of doubles by mapping the integer i to f.applyAsDouble(a+i*dx). Finally, we can apply sum() as the terminal operation. Here is a version of the Riemann sum method that uses a parallel stream:

```
private static double riemannSumWithParallelStream(
            DoubleUnaryOperator f, double a, double b, int n) {
    double dx = (b - a) / n;
    double sum = IntStream.range(0,n)
```

```
                .parallel()
                .mapToDouble( i -> f.applyAsDouble(a + i*dx) )
                .sum();
        return sum * dx;
    }
```

I also wrote a version riemannSumWithSequentialStream(), that leaves out the .parallel() operator. All three versions can be found in the sample program RiemannSumStreamExper- iment.java. The main routine in that program calls each of the three methods, using various values for n. It times how long each method takes to compute the sum, and reports the result. As might be expected, I found that the version that uses a sequential stream is uniformly slower than the other versions. The sequential stream version does essentially the same thing as the for loop version, but with the extra overhead involved with creating and manipulating streams. The situation for parallel streams is more interesting, and the results depend on the machine on which the program is executed. On one old machine with four processors, the for loop version was faster for n = 100,000, but the parallel version was much faster for 1,000,000 items or more. On another machine, the parallel version was faster for 10,000 or more items. Note that there is a limit to how much faster the parallel version can be. On a machine with K processors, the parallel version cannot be more than K times faster than the sequential version, and will probably in reality be somewhat slower than that. I encourage you to try out the sample program on your own computer!

It is even conceivable (or at least this is a goal of the stream API) that you have a machine on which Java can run parallel code on your graphics card, making use of the many processors that it contains. If that happens, you might see a very large speedup.

Chapter 7 INPUT/OUTPUT STREAMS, FILES, AND NETWORKING

Computer programs has utility just when they engage with the external environment in some capacity. This interaction is termed input/output, or I/O (pronounced "eye-oh"). Thus far, this book has focused exclusively on a certain form of interaction: user interaction via either a graphical user interface or a command-line interface. The user represents merely one potential source and one potential recipient of information. We have already seen another form of input/output, since TextIO is capable of reading data from files and writing data to files. Java possesses an input/output architecture that offers significantly greater power and flexibility than TextIO, encompassing several forms of I/O beyond mere file operations. Crucially, in addition to files, it facilitates communication via network connections. In Java, the predominant kind of input/output concerning files and networks is founded on I/O streams, which are objects that facilitate I/O operations analogous to those previously utilized. Standard output (System.out) and standard input (System.in) exemplify I/O streams. It is important to note that I/O streams differ from the streams associated with the stream API discussed in Section 6.6.

Engaging with files and networks necessitates an understanding of exceptions, as discussed in Section 4.3. Numerous subroutines utilized may generate checked exceptions, necessitating obligatory exception management. This often involves invoking the procedure within a try..catch construct capable of handling any exceptions that may arise. Effective network communication necessitates the utilization of threads, which will be addressed in Chapter 12. This chapter will examine the fundamental networking API, with a further discussion on threads and networking in Section 12.4..

7.1 I/O STREAMS, READERS, AND WRITERS

Without the ability to interact with the rest of the world, a program would be useless. The interaction of a program with the rest of the world is referred to as *input/output* or I/O. Historically, one of the hardest parts of programming language design has been coming up with good facilities for doing input and output. A computer can be connected to many different types of input and output devices. If a programming language had to deal with each type of device as a special case, the complexity would be overwhelming. One of the major achievements in the history of programming has been to come up with good abstractions for representing I/O devices. In Java, the main I/O abstractions are called *I/O streams*. Other I/O abstractions, such as "files" and "channels" also exist, but in this section we will look only at streams. Every stream represents either a source of input or a destination to which output can be sent.

7.1.1 Character and Byte Streams

When dealing with input/output, you have to keep in mind that there are two broad categories of data: machine-formatted data and human-readable text. Machine-formatted data is represented in binary form, the same way that data is represented inside the computer, that is, as strings of zeros and ones. Human-readable data is in the form of characters. When you read a number such as 3.141592654, you are reading a sequence of characters and interpreting them as a number. The same number would be represented in the computer as a bit-string that you would find unrecognizable.

To deal with the two broad categories of data representation, Java has two broad categories of streams: *byte streams* for machine-formatted data and *character streams* for human- readable data. There are several predefined classes that represent streams of each type.

An object that outputs data to a byte stream belongs to one of the subclasses of the abstract class *OutputStream*. Objects that read data from a byte stream belong to subclasses of the abstract class *InputStream*. If you write numbers to an *OutputStream*, you won't be able to read the resulting data yourself. But the data can be read back into the computer with an *InputStream*. The writing and reading of the data will be very efficient, since there is no translation involved: the bits that are used to represent the data inside the computer are simply copied to and from the streams.

For reading and writing human-readable character data, the main classes are the abstract classes *Reader* and *Writer*. All character stream classes are subclasses of one of these. If a number is to be written to a *Writer* stream, the computer must translate it into a human- readable sequence of characters that represents that number. Reading a number from a *Reader* stream into a numeric variable also involves a translation, from a character sequence into the appropriate bit string. (Even if the data you are working with consists of characters in the first place, such as words from a text editor, there might still be some translation. Characters are stored in the computer as 16-bit Unicode values. For people who use the English alphabets, character data is generally stored in files in ASCII code, which uses only 8 bits per character. The *Reader* and *Writer* classes take care of this translation, and can also handle non-western alphabets and characters in non-alphabetic written languages such as Chinese.)

Byte streams can be useful for direct machine-to-machine communication, and they can sometimes be useful for storing data in files, especially when large amounts of data need to be stored efficiently, such as in large databases. However, binary data is *fragile* in the sense that its meaning is not self-evident. When faced with a long series of zeros and ones, you have to know what information it is meant to represent and how that information is encoded before you will be able to interpret it. Of course, the same is true to some extent for character data, since characters, like any other kind of data, have to be coded as binary numbers to be stored or processed by a computer. But the binary encoding of character data has been standardized and is well understood, and data expressed in character form can be made meaningful to human readers. The current trend seems to be towards increased use of character data, represented in a way that will make its meaning as self-evident as possible. We'll look at one way this is done in Section 7.5.

I should note that the original version of Java did not have character streams, and that for ASCII-encoded character data, byte streams are largely interchangeable with character streams. In fact, the standard input and output streams, System.in and System.out, are byte streams rather than character streams. However, you should prefer *Readers* and *Writers* rather than *InputStreams* and *OutputStreams* when working with character data, even when working with the standard ASCII character set.

The standard I/O stream classes discussed in this section are defined in the package java.io, along with several supporting classes. You must import the classes from this package if you want to use them in your program. That means either importing individual classes or putting the directive "import java.io.*;" at the beginning of your source file. I/O streams are used for working with files and for doing communication over a network. They can also be used for communication between two concurrently running threads, and there are stream classes for reading and writing data stored in the computer's memory.

(Note: The Java API provides additional support for I/O in the package java.nio and its subpackages, but they are not covered in this textbook. In general, java.nio gives programmers efficient access to more advanced I/O techniques.)

The beauty of the stream abstraction is that it is as easy to write data to a file or to send data over a network as it is to print information on the screen.

The basic I/O classes *Reader*, *Writer*, *InputStream*, and *OutputStream* provide only very primitive I/O operations. For example, the *InputStream* class declares an abstract instance method

public int read() throws IOException

for reading one byte of data, as a number in the range 0 to 255, from an input stream. If the end of the input stream is encountered, the read() method will return the value -1 instead. If some error occurs during the input attempt, an exception of type *IOException* is thrown. Since *IOException* is a checked exception, this means that you can't use the read() method except inside a try statement or in a subroutine that is itself declared with a "throws IOException" clause. (Checked exceptions and mandatory exception handling were covered in Subsection 4.3.3.)

The *InputStream* class also defines methods for reading multiple bytes of data in one step into an array of bytes, which can be a lot more efficient that reading individual bytes. However, *InputStream* provides no convenient methods for reading other types of data, such as int or double, from a stream. This is not a problem because you will rarely use an object of type *InputStream* itself. Instead, you'll use subclasses of *InputStream* that add more convenient input methods to *InputStream's* rather primitive capabilities. Similarly, the *OutputStream* class defines a primitive output method for writing one byte of data to an output stream. The method is defined as:

public void write(int b) throws IOException

The parameter is of type int rather than byte, but the parameter value is type-cast to type byte before it is written; this effectively discards all but the eight low order bits of b. Again, in practice, you will almost always use higher-level output operations defined in some subclass of *OutputStream*.

The *Reader* and *Writer* classes provide the analogous low-level read and write methods. As in the byte stream classes, the parameter of the write(c) method in *Writer* and the return value of the read() method in *Reader* are of type int, but in these character-oriented classes, the I/O operations read and write characters rather than bytes. The return value of read() is -1 if the end of the input stream has been reached. Otherwise, the return value must be type-cast to type char to obtain the character that was read. In practice, you will ordinarily use higher level I/O operations provided by sub-classes of *Reader* and *Writer*, as discussed below.

7.1.2 PrintWriter

One of the neat things about Java's I/O package is that it lets you add capabilities to a stream by "wrapping" it in another stream object that provides those capabilities. The wrapper object is also a stream, so you can read from or write to it—but you can do so using fancier operations than those available for basic streams.

For example, *PrintWriter* is a subclass of *Writer* that provides convenient methods for outputting human-readable character representations of all of Java's basic data types. If you have an object belonging to the *Writer* class, or any of its subclasses, and you would like to use *PrintWriter* methods to output data to that *Writer*, all you have to do is wrap the *Writer* in a *PrintWriter* object. You do this by constructing a new *PrintWriter* object, using the *Writer* as input to the constructor. For example, if charSink is of type *Writer*, then you could say

PrintWriter printableCharSink = new PrintWriter(charSink);

In fact, the parameter to the constructor can also be an *OutputStream* or a *File*, and the constructor will build a *PrintWriter* that can write to that output destination. (Files are covered in the next section.) When you output data to the *PrintWriter* printableCharSink, using the high-level output methods in *PrintWriter*, that data will go to exactly the same place as data written directly to charSink. You've just provided a better interface to the same output destination. For example, this allows you to use *PrintWriter* methods to send data to a file or over a network connection.

For the record, if out is a variable of type *PrintWriter*, then the following methods are defined:

- out.print(x) — prints the value of x, represented in the form of a string of characters, to the output stream; x can be an expression of any type, including both primitive types and object types. An object is converted to string form using its toString() method. A null value is represented by the string "null".
- out.println() — outputs an end-of-line to the output stream.
- out.println(x) — outputs the value of x, followed by an end-of-line; this is equivalent to out.print(x) followed by out.println().
- out.printf(formatString, x1, x2, ...) — does formatted output of x1, x2, ... to the output stream. The first parameter is a string that specifies the format of the output. There can be any number of additional parameters, of any type, but the types of the parameters must match the formatting directives in the format string. Formatted output for the standard output stream, System.out, was introduced in Subsection 2.4.1, and out.printf has the same functionality.
- out.flush() — ensures that characters that have been written with the above methods are actually sent to the output destination. In some cases, notably when writing to a file or to the network, it might be necessary to call this method to force the output to actually appear at the destination.

Note that none of these methods will ever throw an *IOException*. Instead, the *PrintWriter* class includes the method

public boolean checkError()

which will return true if any error has been encountered while writing to the stream. The *PrintWriter* class catches any *IOExceptions* internally, and sets the value of an internal error flag if one occurs. The checkError() method can be used to check the error flag. This allows you to use *PrintWriter* methods without worrying about catching exceptions. On the other hand, to write a fully robust program, you should call checkError() to test for possible errors whenever you use a *PrintWriter*.

7.1.3 Data Streams

When you use a *PrintWriter* to output data to a stream, the data is converted into the sequence of characters that represents the data in human-readable form. Suppose you want to output the data in byte-oriented, machine-formatted form. The java. io package includes a byte- stream class, *DataOutputStream*, that can be used for writing data values to streams in internal, binary-number format. *DataOutputStream* bears the same relationship to *OutputStream* that *PrintWriter* bears to *Writer*. That is, whereas *OutputStream* only has methods for outputting bytes, *DataOutputStream* has methods writeDouble(double x) for outputting values of type double, writeInt(int x) for outputting values of type int, and so on. Furthermore, you can wrap any *OutputStream* in a *DataOutputStream* so that you can use the higher level output methods on it. For example, if byteSink is of type *OutputStream*, you could say

```
DataOutputStream dataSink = new DataOutputStream(byteSink);
```

to wrap byteSink in a *DataOutputStream*.

For input of machine-readable data, such as that created by writing to a *DataOutputStream*, java.io provides the class *DataInputStream*. You can wrap any *InputStream* in a *DataIn- putStream* object to provide it with the ability to read data of various types from the byte- stream. The methods in the *DataInputStream* for reading binary data are called readDouble(), readInt(), and so on. Data written by a *DataOutputStream* is guaranteed to be in a format that can be read by a *DataInputStream*. This is true even if the data stream is created on one type of computer and read on another type of computer. The cross-platform compatibility of binary data is a major aspect of Java's platform independence.

In some circumstances, you might need to read character data from an *InputStream* or write character data to an *OutputStream*. This is not a problem, since characters, like all data, are ultimately represented as binary numbers. However, for character data, it is convenient to use *Reader* and *Writer* instead of *InputStream* and *OutputStream*. To make this possible, you can wrap a byte stream in a character stream. If byteSource is a variable of type *InputStream* and byteSink is of type *OutputStream*, then the statements

```
Reader charSource = new InputStreamReader( byteSource );
Writer charSink   = new OutputStreamWriter( byteSink );
```

create character streams that can be used to read character data from and write character data to the byte streams. In particular, the standard input stream System.

in, which is of type *InputStream* for historical reasons, can be wrapped in a *Reader* to make it easier to read character data from standard input:

Reader charIn = new InputStreamReader(System.in);

As another application, the input and output streams that are associated with a network connection are byte streams rather than character streams, but the byte streams can be wrapped in character streams to make it easy to send and receive character data over the network. We will encounter network I/O in Section 7.4.

There are various ways for characters to be encoded as binary data. A particular encoding is known as a *charset* or *character set* . Charsets have standardized names such as "UTF-16," "UTF-8," and "ISO-8859-1." In UTF-16, characters are encoded as 16-bit UNICODE values; this is the character set that is used internally by Java. UTF-8 is a way of encoding UNICODE characters using 8 bits for common ASCII characters and longer codes for other characters. ISO-8859-1, also known as "Latin-1," is an 8-bit encoding that includes ASCII characters as well as certain accented characters that are used in several European languages. *Readers* and *Writers* use the default charset for the computer on which they are running, unless you specify a different one. That can be done, for example, in a constructor such as

Writer charSink = new OutputStreamWriter(byteSink, "ISO-8859-1");

Certainly, the existence of a variety of charset encodings has made text processing more complicated—unfortunate for us English-speakers but essential for people who use non-Western character sets. Ordinarily, you don't have to worry about this, but it's a good idea to be aware that different charsets exist in case you run into textual data encoded in a non-default way.

7.1.4 Reading Text

Much I/O is done in the form of human-readable characters. In view of this, it is surprising that Java does not provide a standard character input class that can read character data in a manner that is reasonably symmetrical with the character output capabilities of *PrintWriter*. The *Scanner* class, introduced briefly in Subsection 2.4.6 and covered in more detail below, comes pretty close, but *Scanner* is not a subclass of any I/O stream class, which means that it doesn't fit neatly into the I/O stream framework. There is one basic case that is easily handled by the standard class *BufferedReader*, which has a method

public String readLine() throws IOException

that reads one line of text from its input source. If the end of the stream has been reached, the return value is null. When a line of text is read, the end-of-line marker is read from the input stream, but it is not part of the string that is returned. Different input streams use different characters as end-of-line markers, but the readLine method can deal with all the common cases. (Traditionally, Unix computers, including Linux and MacOS, use a line feed character, '\n', to mark an end of line; classic Macintosh used a carriage return character, '\r'; and Windows uses the two-character sequence "\r\n". In general, modern computers can deal correctly with all of these possibilities.)

BufferedReader also defines the instance method lines() which returns a value of type Stream<String> that can be used with the stream API (Section 6.6). A convenient way to process all the lines from a *BufferedReader*, reader, is to use the forEachOrdered() operator on the stream of lines: reader.lines().forEachOrdered(action), where action is a consumer of strings, usually given as a lambda expression.

Line-by-line processing is very common. Any *Reader* can be wrapped in a *BufferedReader* to make it easy to read full lines of text. If reader is of type *Reader*, then a *BufferedReader* wrapper can be created for reader with

```
BufferedReader in = new BufferedReader( reader );
```

This can be combined with the *InputStreamReader* class that was mentioned above to read lines of text from an *InputStream*. For example, we can apply this to System.in:

```
BufferedReader in;   // BufferedReader for reading from standard input.
in = new BufferedReader( new InputStreamReader( System.in ) );
try {
    String line = in.readLine();
    while ( line != null ) {
            processOneLineOfInput( line );
            line = in.readLine();
    }
}
catch (IOException e) {
}
```

This code segment reads and processes lines from standard input until an end-of-stream is encountered. (An end-of-stream is possible even for interactive input. For example, on at least some computers, typing a Control-D generates an end-of-stream on the standard input stream.) The try..catch statement is necessary because the readLine method can throw an exception of type *IOException*, which requires mandatory exception handling; an alternative to try..catch would be to declare that the method that contains the code "throws IOException". Also, remember that *BufferedReader*, *InputStreamReader*, and *IOException* must be imported from the package java.io.

Note that the main purpose of *BufferedReader* is not simply to make it easier to read lines of text. Some I/O devices work most efficiently if data is read or written in large chunks, instead of as individual bytes or characters. A *BufferedReader* reads a chunk of data, and stores it in internal memory. The internal memory is known as a *buffer* . When you read from the BufferedReader, it will take data from the buffer if possible, and it will only go back to its input source for more data when the buffer is emptied. There is also a *BufferedWriter* class, and there are buffered stream classes for byte streams as well.

Previously in this book, we have used the non-standard class *TextIO* for input both from users and from files. The advantage of *TextIO* is that it makes it fairly easy to read data values of any of the primitive types. Disadvantages include the fact that *TextIO* can only read from one input source at a time and that it does not follow the same pattern as Java's built-in input/output classes. (If you like the style of input used by *TextIO*, you might take a look at my TextReader.java, which implements a similar style of input in a more object-oriented way. *TextReader* was used in previous versions of this textbook but is not used in this version.)

7.1.5 The Scanner Class

Since its introduction, Java has been notable for its lack of built-in support for basic input, or at least for its reliance on fairly advanced techniques for the support that it does offer. (This is my opinion, at least.) The *Scanner* class was introduced to make it easier to read basic data types from a character input source. It does not (again, in my opinion) solve the problem completely, but it is a big improvement. The *Scanner* class is in the package java.util. It was introduced in Subsection 2.4.6, but has not seen much use since then in this textbook. From now on, however, most of my examples will use *Scanner* instead of *TextIO*.

Input routines are defined as instance methods in the *Scanner* class, so to use the class, you need to create a *Scanner* object. The constructor specifies the source of the characters that the *Scanner* will read. The scanner acts as a wrapper for the input source. The source can be a *Reader*, an *InputStream*, a *String*, or a *File*, among other possibilities. If a *String* is used as the input source, the *Scanner* will simply read the characters in the string from beginning to end, in the same way that it would process the same sequence of characters from a stream. For example, you can use a *Scanner* to read from standard input by saying:

```
Scanner standardInputScanner = new Scanner( System.in );
```

and if charSource is of type *Reader*, you can create a *Scanner* for reading from charSource with:

```
Scanner scanner = new Scanner( charSource );
```

When processing input, a scanner usually works with *tokens*. A token is a meaningful string of characters that cannot, for the purposes at hand, be further broken down into smaller meaningful pieces. A token can, for example, be an individual word or a string of characters that represents a value of type double. In the case of a scanner, tokens must be separated by "delimiters." By default, the delimiters are whitespace characters such as spaces, tabs, and end- of-line markers. In normal processing, whitespace characters serve simply to separate tokens and are discarded by the scanner. A scanner has instance methods for reading tokens of various types. Suppose that scanner is an object of type *Scanner*. Then we have:

- scanner.next() – reads the next token from the input source and returns it as a *String*.
- scanner.nextInt(), scanner.nextDouble(), and so on – read the next token from the input source and tries to convert it to a value of type int, double, and so on. There are methods for reading values of any of the primitive types.
- scanner.nextLine() – reads an entire line from the input source, up to the next end-of- line, and returns the line as a value of type *String*. The end-of-line marker is read but is not part of the return value. Note that this method is not based on tokens. An entire line is read and returned, including any whitespace characters in the line. The return value can be the empty string.

All of these methods can generate exceptions. If an attempt is made to read past the end of input, an exception of type *NoSuchElementException* is thrown. Methods such as scanner.getInt() will throw an exception of type *InputMismatchException* if the next token in the input does not represent a value of the requested type. The exceptions that can be generated do not require mandatory exception handling.

The *Scanner* class has very nice look-ahead capabilities. You can query a scanner to determine whether more tokens are available and whether the next token is of a given type. If scanner is of type *Scanner* :

- scanner.hasNext() – returns a boolean value that is true if there is at least one more token in the input source.
- scanner.hasNextInt(), scanner.hasNextDouble(), and so on – return a boolean value that is true if there is at least one more token in the input source and that token represents a value of the requested type.
- scanner.hasNextLine() – returns a boolean value that is true if there is at least one more line in the input source.

Although the insistence on defining tokens only in terms of delimiters limits the usability of scanners to some extent, they are easy to use and are suitable for many applications. With so many input classes available–*BufferedReader*, *TextIO*,

Scanner —you might have trouble deciding which one to use! In general, I would recommend using a *Scanner* unless you have some particular reason for preferring *TextIO*-style input. *BufferedReader* can be used as a lightweight alternative when all that you want to do is read entire lines of text from the input source.

(It is possible to change the delimiter that is used by a *Scanner*, but the syntax uses something called "regular expressions." Unfortunately, the syntax for regular expressions is rather complicated, and they are not covered in this book. However, as an example, suppose you want tokens to be words that consist entirely of letters of the English alphabet. In that case, delimiters should include all non-letter characters. If you want a *Scanner*, scnr, to use that kind of delimiter, you can say: scnr.useDelimiter("[^a-zA-Z]+"). After that, tokens returned by scnr.next() will consist entirely of letters. The string "[^a-zA-Z]+" is a regular expression. Regular expressions are an important tool for a working programmer. If you have a chance to learn about them, you should do so.)

7.1.6 Serialized Object I/O

The classes *PrintWriter*, *Scanner*, *DataInputStream*, and *DataOutputStream* allow you to easily input and output all of Java's primitive data types. But what happens when you want to read and write objects? Traditionally, you would have to come up with some way of encoding your object as a sequence of data values belonging to the primitive types, which can then be output as bytes or characters. This is called *serializing* the object. On input, you have to read the serialized data and somehow reconstitute a copy of the original object. For complex objects, this can all be a major chore. However, you can get Java to do a lot of the work for you by using the classes *ObjectInputStream* and *ObjectOutputStream*. These are subclasses of *InputStream* and *OutputStream* that can be used for reading and writing serialized objects.

ObjectInputStream and *ObjectOutputStream* are wrapper classes that can be wrapped around arbitrary *InputStreams* and *OutputStreams*. This makes it possible to do object input and output on any byte stream. The methods for object I/O are readObject(), in *ObjectInputStream*, and writeObject(Object obj), in *ObjectOutputStream*. Both of these methods can throw *IOExceptions*. Note that readObject() returns a value of type *Object*, which generally has to be type-cast to the actual type of the object that was read.

ObjectOutputStream also has methods writeInt(), writeDouble(), and so on, for outputting primitive type values to the stream, and *ObjectInputStream* has corresponding methods for reading primitive type values. These primitive type values can be interspersed with objects in the data. In the file, the primitive types will be represented in their internal binary format.

Object streams are byte streams. The objects are represented in binary, machine-readable form. This is good for efficiency, but it does suffer from the fragility that is often seen in binary data. They suffer from the additional problem that the binary format of Java objects is very specific to Java, so the data in object streams is not easily available to programs written in other programming languages. For these reasons, object streams are appropriate mostly for short-term storage of objects and for transmitting objects over a network connection from one Java program to another. For long-term storage and for communication with non-Java programs, other approaches to object serialization are usually better. (See Section 7.5 for a character-based approach. See Subsection 12.5.1 for an example that uses object streams for network communication.)

ObjectInputStream and *ObjectOutputStream* only work with objects that implement an interface named *Serializable*. Furthermore, all of the instance variables in the object must be serializable. However, there is little work involved in making an object serializable, since the *Serializable* interface does not declare any methods. It exists only as a marker for the compiler, to tell it that the object is meant to be writable and readable. You only need to add the words "implements Serializable" to your class definitions. Many of Java's standard classes are already declared to be serializable.

One warning about using *ObjectOutputStreams*: These streams are optimized to avoid writing the same object more than once. When an object is encountered for a second time, only a reference to the first occurrence is written. Unfortunately, if the object has been modified in the meantime, the new data will not be written. That is, the modified value will not be written correctly to the stream. Because of this, *ObjectOutputStreams* are meant mainly for use with "immutable" objects that can't be changed after they are created. (*Strings* are an example of this.) However, if you do need to write mutable objects to an *ObjectOutputStream*, and if it is possible that you will write the same object more than once, you can ensure that the full, correct version of the object will be written by calling the stream's reset() method before writing the object to the stream.

7.2 FILES

The data and programs in a computer's main memory survive only as long as the power is on. For more permanent storage, computers use *files*, which are collections of data stored on a hard disk, on a USB memory stick, on a CD-ROM, or on some other type of storage device. Files are organized into *directories* (also called *folders*). A directory can hold other directories, as well as files. Both directories and files have names that are used to identify them.

Programs can read data from existing files. They can create new files and can write data to files. In Java, such input and output can be done using I/O streams. Human-readable character data can be read from a file using an object belonging to the class *FileReader*, which is a subclass of *Reader*. Similarly, data can be written to a file in human-readable format through an object of type *FileWriter*, a subclass of *Writer*. For files that store data in machine format, the appropriate I/O classes are *FileInputStream* and *FileOutputStream*. In this section, I will only discuss character-oriented file I/O using the *FileReader* and *FileWriter* classes. However, *FileInputStream* and *FileOutputStream* are used in an exactly parallel fashion. All these classes are defined in the java.io package.

7.2.1 Reading and Writing Files

The *FileReader* class has a constructor which takes the name of a file as a parameter and creates an input stream that can be used for reading from that file. This constructor will throw an exception of type *FileNotFoundException* if the file doesn't exist. For example, suppose you have a file named "data.txt", and you want your program to read data from that file. You could do the following to create an input stream for the file:

```
FileReader data;    // (Declare the variable before the
                    //      try statement, or else the variable
                    //      is local to the try block and you won't
                    //      be able to use it later in the program.)
try {
    data = new FileReader("data.txt");      // create the stream
}
catch (FileNotFoundException e) {
    ... // do something to handle the error---maybe, end the program
}
```

The *FileNotFoundException* class is a subclass of *IOException*, so it would be acceptable to catch *IOExceptions* in the above try...catch statement. More generally, just about any error that can occur during input/output operations can be caught by a catch clause that handles *IOException*.

Once you have successfully created a *FileReader*, you can start reading data from it. But since *FileReaders* have only the primitive input methods inherited from the basic *Reader* class, you will probably want to wrap your *FileReader* in a *Scanner*, in a *BufferedReader*, or in some other wrapper class. (See the previous section for a discussion of *BufferedReader* and *Scanner*.) To create a *BufferedReader* for reading from a file named data.dat, you could say:

```
BufferedReader data;
try {
    data = new BufferedReader( new FileReader("data.dat") );
}
catch (FileNotFoundException e) {
    ... // handle the exception
}
```

Wrapping a *Reader* in a *BufferedReader* lets you easily read lines of text from the file, and the buffering can make the input more efficient.

To use a *Scanner* to read from the file, you can construct the scanner in a similar way. However, it is more common to construct it more directly from an object of type *File* (to be covered below):

```
Scanner in;
try {
    in = new Scanner( new File("data.dat") );
}
catch (FileNotFoundException e) {
    ... // handle the exception
}
```

Working with output files is no more difficult than this. You simply create an object belonging to the class *FileWriter*. You will probably want to wrap this output stream in an object of type *PrintWriter*. For example, suppose you want to write data to a file named "result.dat". Since the constructor for *FileWriter* can throw an exception of type *IOException*, you should use a try..catch statement:

```
PrintWriter result;
try {
        result = new PrintWriter(new FileWriter("result.dat"));
}
catch (IOException e) {
    ... // handle the exception
}
```

However, as with *Scanner*, it is more common to use a constructor that takes a *File* as parameter; this will automatically wrap the File in a FileWriter before creating the PrintWriter:

```
PrintWriter result;
try {
     result = new PrintWriter(new File("result.dat"));
}
catch (IOException e) {
... // handle the exception
}
```

You can even use just a *String* as the parameter to the constructor, and it will be interpreted as a file name (but you should remember that a *String* in the *Scanner* constructor does not name a file; instead the scanner will read characters from the string itself).

If no file named result.dat exists, a new file will be created. If the file already exists, then the current contents of the file will be erased and replaced with the data that your program writes to the file. This will be done without any warning. To avoid overwriting a file that already exists, you can check whether a file of the same name already exists before trying to create the stream, as discussed later in this section. An *IOException* might occur in the *PrintWriter* constructor if, for example, you are trying to create a file on a disk that is "write- protected," meaning that it cannot be modified.

When you are finished with a *PrintWriter*, you should call its flush() method, such as "result.flush()", to make sure that all the output has been sent to its destination. If you forget to do this, you might find that some of the data that you have written to a file output stream has not actually shown up in the file.

After you are finished using a file, it's a good idea to *close* the file, to tell the operating system that you are finished using it. You can close a file by calling the close() method of the associated *PrintWriter*, *BufferedReader*, or *Scanner*. Once a file has been closed, it is no longer possible to read data from it or write data to it, unless you open it again as a new I/O stream. (Note that for most I/O stream classes, including *BufferedReader* the close() method can throw an *IOException*, which must be handled; however, *PrintWriter* and *Scanner* override this method so that it cannot throw such exceptions.) If you forget to close a file, the file will ordinarily be closed automatically when the program terminates or when the file object is garbage collected, but it is better not to depend on this. Note that calling close() should automatically call flush() before the file is closed. (I have seen that fail, but not recently.)

As a complete example, here is a program that will read numbers from a file named data.dat, and will then write out the same numbers in reverse order to another file named result.dat. It is assumed that data.dat contains only real numbers. The input file is read using a *Scanner*. Exception-handling is used to check for problems along the way. Although the application is not a particularly useful one, this program demonstrates the basics of working with files.

```
import java.io.*;
import java.util.ArrayList; import java.util.Scanner;
/**
Reads numbers from a file named data.dat and writes them to a file
named result.dat in reverse order.     The input file should contain
only real numbers.
*/
public class ReverseFileWithScanner {
    public static void main(String[] args) {
            Scanner data;    // For reading the data.
            PrintWriter result;         // Character output stream for writing data.
            ArrayList<Double> numbers;        // An ArrayList for holding the data.
            numbers = new ArrayList<Double>();
            try {     // Create the input stream.
                    data = new Scanner(new File("data.dat"));
            }
            catch (FileNotFoundException e) {
                    System.out.println("Can't find file data.dat!");
                    return;  // End the program by returning from main().
            }
            try {     // Create the output stream.
                    result = new PrintWriter("result.dat");
            }
            catch (FileNotFoundException e) {
                    System.out.println("Can't open file result.dat!");
                    System.out.println("Error: " + e);
                    data.close();       // Close the input file.
                    return;  // End the program.
```

```
        }
        while ( data.hasNextDouble() ) {  // Read until end-of-file.
                double inputNumber = data.nextDouble();
                numbers.add( inputNumber );
        }
        // Output the numbers in reverse order.
        for (int i = numbers.size()-1; i >= 0; i--)
                result.println(numbers.get(i));
        System.out.println("Done!");
        data.close();
        result.close();
    }       // end of main()
} // end class ReverseFileWithScanner
```

Note that this program will simply stop reading data from the file if it encounters anything other than a number in the input. That will not be considered to be an error.

As mentioned at the end of Subsection 4.3.2, the pattern of creating or opening a "resource," using it, and then closing the resource is a very common one, and the pattern is supported by the syntax of the try..catch statement. Files are resources in this sense, as are *Scanner*, *PrintWriter*, and all of Java's I/O streams. All of these things define close() methods, and it is good form to close them when you are finished using them. Since they all implement the *AutoCloseable* interface, they are all resources in the sense required by try..catch. A try..catch statement can be used to automatically close a resource when the try statement ends, which eliminates the need to close it by hand in a finally clause. This assumes that you will open the resource and use it in the same try..catch.

As an example, the sample program ReverseFileWithResources.java is another version of the example we have been looking at. In this case, try..catch statements using the resource pattern are used to read the data from a file and to write the data to a file. My original program opened a file in one try statement and used it in another try statement. The resource pattern requires that it all be done in one try, which requires some reorganization of the code (and can sometimes make it harder to determine the exact cause of an exception). Here is the try..catch statement from the sample program that opens the input file, reads from it, and closes it automatically.

```
try( Scanner data = new Scanner(new File("data.dat")) ) {
            // Read numbers, adding them to the ArrayList.
        while ( data.hasNextDouble() ) {  // Read until end-of-file.
            double inputNumber = data.nextDouble();
            numbers.add( inputNumber );
        }
    }
    catch (FileNotFoundException e) {
            // Can be caused if file does not exist or can't be read.
        System.out.println("Can't open input file data.dat!");
        System.out.println("Error: " + e);
        return;  // Return from main(), since an error has occurred.
    }
```

The resource, data, is constructed on the first line. The syntax requires a declaration of the resource with an initial value, in parentheses after the word "try." It's possible to have several resource declarations, separated by semicolons. They will be closed in the order opposite to the order in which they are declared.

7.2.2 Files and Directories

The subject of file names is actually more complicated than I've let on so far. To fully specify a file, you have to give both the name of the file and the name of the directory where that file is located. A simple file name like "data.dat" or "result.dat" is taken to refer to a file in a directory that is called the *current directory* (also known as the "default directory" or "working directory"). The current directory is not a permanent thing. It can be changed by the user or by a program. Files not in the current directory must be referred to by a *path name*, which includes both the name of the file and information about the directory where it can be found.

To complicate matters even further, there are two types of path names, *absolute path names* and *relative path names*. An absolute path name uniquely identifies one file among all the files available to the computer. It contains full information about which directory the file is in and what the file's name is. A relative path name tells the computer how to locate the file starting from the current directory.

Unfortunately, the syntax for file names and path names varies somewhat from one type of computer to another. Here are some examples:

- data.dat — on any computer, this would be a file named "data.dat" in the current directory.

- /home/eck/java/examples/data.dat — This is an absolute path name in a UNIX operating system, including Linux and MacOS X. It refers to a file named data.dat in a directory named examples, which is in turn in a directory named java, ...
- C:\eck\java\examples\data.dat — An absolute path name on a Windows computer.
- examples/data.dat — a relative path name under UNIX; "examples" is the name of a directory that is contained within the current directory, and data. dat is a file in that directory.The corresponding relative path name for Windows would be examples\data.dat.
- ../examples/data.dat — a relative path name in UNIX that means "go to the directory that contains the current directory, then go into a directory named examples inside that directory, and look there for a file named data. dat." In general, ".." means "go up one directory." The corresponding path on Windows is ..\examples\data.dat.

When working on the command line, it's safe to say that if you stick to using simple file names only, and if the files are stored in the same directory with the program that will use them, then you will be OK. Later in this section, we'll look at a convenient way of letting the user specify a file in a GUI program, which allows you to avoid the issue of path names altogether.

It is possible for a Java program to find out the absolute path names for two important directories, the current directory and the user's home directory. The names of these directories are *system properties*, and they can be read using the function calls:

- System.getProperty("user.dir") — returns the absolute path name of the current directory as a *String*.
- System.getProperty("user.home") — returns the absolute path name of the user's home directory as a *String*.

To avoid some of the problems caused by differences in path names between platforms, Java has the class java.io.File. An object belonging to this class does not actually represent a file! Precisely speaking, an object of type *File* represents a file name rather than a file as such. The file to which the name refers might or might not exist. Directories are treated in the same way as files, so a *File* object can represent a directory just as easily as it can represent a file.

A *File* object has a constructor, "new File(String)", that creates a *File* object from a path name. The name can be a simple name, a relative path, or an absolute path. For example, new File("data.dat") creates a *File* object that refers to a file named data.dat, in the current directory. Another constructor, "new File(File,String)", has two parameters. The first is a *File* object that refers to a directory. The second can be the name of the file in that directory or a relative path from that directory to the file.

- *File* objects contain several useful instance methods. Assuming that file is a variable of type *File*, here are some of the methods that are available:
- file.exists() — This boolean-valued function returns true if the file named by the *File* object already exists. You can use this method if you want to avoid overwriting the contents of an existing file when you create a new output stream. The boolean function file.canRead() returns true if the file exists and the program has permission to read the file. And file.canWrite() is true if the program has permission to write to the file.
- file.isDirectory() — This boolean-valued function returns true if the *File* object refers to a directory. It returns false if it refers to a regular file or if no file with the given name exists.
- file.delete() — Deletes the file, if it exists. Returns a boolean value to indicate whether the file was successfully deleted.
- file.list() — If the File object refers to a directory, this function returns an array of type String[] containing the names of the files in that directory. Otherwise, it returns null. The method file.listFiles() is similar, except that it returns an array of *File* instead of an array of *String*.

Here, for example, is a program that will list the names of all the files in a directory specified by the user. In this example, I have used a *Scanner* to read the user's input:

```
import java.io.File; import java.util.Scanner;

/**

This program lists the files in a directory specified by

the user.      The user is asked to type in a directory name.

If the name entered by the user is not a directory, a

message is printed and the program ends.

*/

public class DirectoryList {

    public static void main(String[] args) {

            String directoryName;    // Directory name entered by the user.

            File directory;          // File object referring to the directory.

            String[] files;          // Array of file names in the directory.
```

```
            Scanner scanner;        // For reading a line of input from the user.
            scanner = new Scanner(System.in); // scanner reads from standard input.
            System.out.print("Enter a directory name: ");
            directoryName = scanner.nextLine().trim();
            directory = new File(directoryName);
            if (directory.isDirectory() == false) {
                  if (directory.exists() == false)
                        System.out.println("There is no such directory!");
                  else
                        System.out.println("That file is not a directory.");
            }
            else {
                  files = directory.list();
                  System.out.println("Files in directory \"" + directory + "\":");
                  for (int i = 0; i < files.length; i++)
                        System.out.println("      " + files[i]);
            }
      } // end main()
   } // end class DirectoryList
```

All the classes that are used for reading data from files and writing data to files have constructors that take a *File* object as a parameter. For example, if file is a variable of type *File*, and you want to read character data from that file, you can create a *FileReader* to do so by saying new FileReader(file).

7.2.3 File Dialog Boxes

In many programs, you want the user to be able to select the file that is going to be used for input or output. If your program lets the user type in the file name, you will just have to assume that the user understands how to work with files and directories. But in a graphical user interface, the user expects to be able to select files using a *file dialog box* , which is a window that a program can open when it wants the user to select a file for input or output.

JavaFX includes a platform-independent technique for using file dialog boxes in the form of a class called *FileChooser*, in package javafx.stage.

A file dialog box shows the user a list of files and sub-directories in some directory, and makes it easy for the user to specify a file in that directory. The user can also navigate easily from one directory to another. The constructor for *FileChooser* has no parameter. Constructing a *FileChooser* object does not make the dialog box appear on the screen. You have to call a method in the object to do that. Often, before showing the dialog box, you will call instance methods in the *FileChooser* object to set some properties of the dialog box. For example, you can set the file name that is shown to the user as a default initial value for the file.

A file dialog box can have an "owner," which is a window. In JavaFX, that means an object of type *Stage*. Until the dialog box is dismissed by the user—either by canceling the dialog or selecting a file—all interaction with the owner window is blocked. The owner can be specified as a parameter to the method that opens the dialog. The owner can be null, which will mean that no window is blocked.

There are two types of file dialog: an *open file dialog* that allows the user to specify an existing file to be opened for reading data into the program; and a *save file dialog* that lets the user specify a file, which might or might not already exist, to be opened for output. A *FileChooser* has two instance methods for showing the two kinds of dialog box on the screen. Suppose that fileDialog is a variable of type *FileChooser*. Then the following methods are available:

- fileDialog.showOpenDialog(window) — shows an open file dialog box on the screen. The parameter specifies the owner of the dialog box. This method does not return until the user has selected a file or canceled the dialog without selecting a file. The method returns a value of type *File*. The return value is null if the user canceled the dialog box. Otherwise, it returns a *File* object representing the selected file.
- fileDialog.showSaveDialog(window) — shows a save file dialog box, with owner equal to window. The parameter and return value are the same as for showOpenDialog(). If the user selects a file that already exists, the system will automatically ask whether the user wants to replace that file. So, you can safely go ahead and save the specified file.
- fileDialog.setTitle(title) — specifies a title to appear in the title bar of the dialog box. The parameter is a string. This method must be called before showing the dialog box.
- fileDialog.setInitialFileName(name) — sets the name that appears as a default name in the input box for the file name. The parameter is a string. If the parameter is null, the input box will be empty; that is also the default. This method must be called before showing the dialog box.

- fileDialog.setInitialDirectory(directory) — sets the directory that is shown in the dialog box when it first appears. The parameter is of type *File*. If the parameter is null, the initial directory will be a system-dependent default (possibly the directory from which the program was run). If the parameter is not null, it must be a *File* object that represents a directory, not a regular file, or an error will occur. This method must be called before showing the dialog box.

A typical program has "Save" and "Open" commands for working with files. When the user selects a file for saving or opening, it can be a good idea to store the selected *File* object in an instance variable. Later, that file can be used to initialize the directory and possibly the file name the next time a file dialog box is created. If editFile is the instance variable that records the selected file, and if it is non-null, then editFile.getName() is a *String* giving the name of the file, and editFile.getParent() is a *File* representing the directory that contains the file.

This leaves open one question: what to do when an error occurs while reading or writing the selected file? The error should be caught, and the user should be informed that an error occurred. In a GUI program, the natural way to do that is with another dialog box that shows an error message to the user and has an "OK" button for dismissing the dialog. Dialog boxes were not covered in Chapter 6, but some common simple dialog boxes can be shown using objects of type *Alert*, from package javafx.scene.control. Here is how to show an error message to the user:

```
Alert errorAlert = new Alert( Alert.AlertType.ERROR, message ); errorAlert.showAndWait();
```

Putting all this together, we can look at a typical subroutine that saves data to a file. The file is selected using a *FileChooser*. In this example, the data is written in text form, using a *PrintWriter* :

```
private void doSave() {
    FileChooser fileDialog = new FileChooser();
    if (editFile == null) {
                // No file is being edited. Set file name to "filename.txt"
                // and set the directory to the user's home directory.
        fileDialog.setInitialFileName("filename.txt");
        fileDialog.setInitialDirectory(
                new File( System.getProperty("user.home")) );
    }
    else {
                // Get the file name and directory for the dialog from
```

```
                    //        the file that is currently being edited.
            fileDialog.setInitialFileName(editFile.getName());
            fileDialog.setInitialDirectory(editFile.getParentFile());
    }
    fileDialog.setTitle("Select File to be Saved");
    File selectedFile = fileDialog.showSaveDialog(mainWindow);
    if ( selectedFile == null )
    return;  // User did not select a file.
// Note: User has selected a file AND, if the file exists, has
//   confirmed that it is OK to erase the exiting file.
PrintWriter out;
try {
    FileWriter stream = new FileWriter(selectedFile);
    out = new PrintWriter( stream );
}
catch (Exception e) {
                    // Most likely, user doesn't have permission to write the file.
            Alert errorAlert = new Alert(Alert.AlertType.ERROR,
                            "Sorry, but an error occurred while\n" +
                                    trying to open the file for output.");
            errorAlert.showAndWait();
            return;
    }
    try {


            .
            .       // WRITE TEXT TO THE FILE, using the PrintWriter
    out.flush(); // (not needed?; it's probably done by out.close(); out.close();
    if (out.checkError())        // (need to check for errors in PrintWriter)
            throw new IOException("Error check failed.");
    editFile = selectedFile;
}
```

```
catch (Exception e)
            Alert errorAlert = new Alert(Alert.AlertType ERROR,
                    "Sorry, but an error occurred while\n" +
                    "trying to write data to the file.");
            errorAlert.showAndWait();
    }
}
```

This general outline can easily be adapted to non-text files by using a different type of output stream.

Reading data from a file is similar, and I won't show the corresponding doOpen() method here. You can find working subroutines for saving and opening text files in the sample program TrivialEdit.java, which lets the user edit small text files. The file subroutines in that program can be adapted to many GUI programs that work with files.

7.3 PROGRAMMING WITH FILES

In this section, we look at several programming examples that work with files, using the techniques that were introduced in Section 7.1 and Section 7.2.

7.3.1 Copying a File

As a first example, we look at a simple command-line program that can make a copy of a file. Copying a file is a pretty common operation, and every operating system already has a command for doing it. However, it is still instructive to look at a Java program that does the same thing. Many file operations are similar to copying a file, except that the data from the input file is processed in some way before it is written to the output file. All such operations can be done by programs with the same general form. Subsection 4.3.6 included a program for copying text files using *TextIO*. The example in this section will work for any file.

Since the program should be able to copy any file, we can't assume that the data in the file is in human-readable form. So, we have to use the byte streams, *InputStream* and *OutputStream*, to operate on the file. The program simply copies all the data from the *InputStream* to the *OutputStream*, one byte at a time. If source is the variable that refers to the *InputStream*, then the function source.read() can be used to read one byte. This function returns the value -1 when all the bytes in the input file have been read. Similarly, if copy refers to the *OutputStream*, then copy.write(b) writes one byte to the output file. So, the heart of the program is a simple while loop. As usual, the I/O operations can throw exceptions, so this must be done in a try..catch statement:

```
while(true) {
    int data = source.read();
    if (data < 0)
            break;
    copy.write(data);
}
```

The file-copy command in an operating system such as UNIX uses command line arguments to specify the names of the files. For example, the user might say "copy original.dat backup.dat" to copy an existing file, original.dat, to a file named backup.dat. Command- line arguments can also be used in Java programs. The command line arguments are stored in the array of strings, args, which is a parameter to the main() routine. The program can retrieve the command-line arguments from this array. For example, if the program is named CopyFile and if the user runs the program with the command

```
java CopyFile work.dat oldwork.dat
```

then in the program, args[0] will be the string "work.dat" and args[1] will be the string "oldwork.dat". The value of args.length tells the program how many command-line arguments were specified by the user.

The program CopyFile.java gets the names of the files from the command-line arguments. It prints an error message and exits if the file names are not specified. To add a little interest, there are two ways to use the program. The command line can simply specify the two file names. In that case, if the output file already exists, the program will print an error message and end. This is to make sure that the user won't accidently overwrite an important file. However, if the command line has three arguments, then the first argument must be "-f" while the second and third arguments are file names. The -f is a *command-line option* , which is meant to modify the behavior of the program. The program interprets the -f to mean that it's OK to overwrite an existing program. (The "f" stands for "force," since it forces the file to be copied in spite of what would otherwise have been considered an error.) You can see in the source code how the command line arguments are interpreted by the program:

```
import java.io.*;
/**
Makes a copy of a file.        The original file and the name of the
copy must be given as command-line arguments.        In addition, the
first command-line argument can be "-f"; if present, the program
```

```
will overwrite an existing file; if not, the program will report
an error and end if the output file already exists.     The number
of bytes that are copied is reported.
*/
public class CopyFile {
    public static void main(String[] args) {
            String sourceName;      // Name of the source file,
                                    //      as specified on the command line.
            String copyName;        // Name of the copy,
                                    //      as specified on the command line.
            InputStream source;     // Stream for reading from the source file.
            OutputStream copy;      // Stream for writing the copy.
            boolean force;          // This is set to true if the "-f" option
                                    //      is specified on the command line.
            int byteCount;          // Number of bytes copied from the source file.
            /* Get file names from the command line and check for the presence of the -f
            option.  If the command line is not one of the two possible legal forms, print
            an error message and end this program. */
            if (args.length == 3 && args[0].equalsIgnoreCase("-f")) {
                    sourceName = args[1];
                    copyName = args[2];
                    force = true;
            }
            else if (args.length == 2) {
                    sourceName = args[0];
                    copyName = args[1];
                    force = false;
            }
            else {
                    System.out.println(
                            "Usage: java CopyFile <source-file> <copy-name>");
                    System.out.println(
```

```
                "       or      java CopyFile -f <source-file> <copy-name>");
        return;
}
/* Create the input stream.        If an error occurs, end the program. */
try {
        source = new FileInputStream(sourceName);
}
catch (FileNotFoundException e) {
        System.out.println("Can't find file \"" + sourceName + "\".");
        return;
}
/* If the output file already exists and the -f option was not specified,
print an error message and end the program. */
File file = new File(copyName);
if (file.exists() && force == false) {
        System.out.println(
                "Output file exists.        Use the -f option to replace it.");
        return;
}
/* Create the output stream.        If an error occurs, end the program. */
try {
        copy = new FileOutputStream(copyName);
}
catch (IOException e) {
        System.out.println("Can't open output file \"" + copyName + "\".");
        return;
}
/* Copy one byte at a time from the input stream to the output stream, ending
when the read() method returns -1 (which is the signal that the end of the
stream has been reached). If any error occurs, print an error
message. Also print a message if the file has been copied successfully. */
byteCount = 0;
```

```
            try {
                        while (true) {
                                    int data = source.read(); \
                                    if (data < 0)
                                                break;
                                    copy.write(data);
                                    byteCount++;
                                    }
                                    source.close();
                                    copy.close();
                                    System.out.println("Successfully copied " + byteCount + "bytes.");
            }
            catch (Exception e) {
                        System.out.println("Error occurred while copying. "
                                    + byteCount + " bytes copied.");
                        System.out.println("Error: " + e);
            }
    }       // end main()
  } // end class CopyFile
```

It is actually quite inefficient to copy one byte at a time. Efficiency could be improved by using alternative versions of the read() and write() methods that read and write multiple bytes (see the API for details). Alternatively, the input and output streams could be wrapped in objects of type *BufferedInputStream* and *BufferedOutputStream* which automatically read data from and write data to files in larger blocks. This would require changing only the two lines in the program that create the streams. For example, the input stream could be created using

```
source = new BufferedInputStream(new FileInputStream(sourceName));
```

The buffered stream would then be used in exactly the same way as the unbuffered stream.

There is also a sample program CopyFileAsResources.java that does the same thing as CopyFile but uses the resource pattern in a try..catch statement to make sure that the streams are closed in all cases. See the discussion at the end of Subsection 4.3.2)

7.3.2 Persistent Data

Once a program ends, any data that was stored in variables and objects in the program is gone. In many cases, it would be useful to have some of that data stick around so that it will be available when the program is run again. The problem is, how to make the data *persistent* between runs of the program? The answer, of course, is to store the data in a file (or, for some applications, in a database—but the data in a database is itself stored in files).

Consider a "phone book" program that allows the user to keep track of a list of names and associated phone numbers. The program would make no sense at all if the user had to create the whole list from scratch each time the program is run. It would make more sense to think of the phone book as a persistent collection of data, and to think of the program as an interface to that collection of data. The program would allow the user to look up names in the phone book and to add new entries. Any changes that are made should be preserved after the program ends.

The sample program PhoneDirectoryFileDemo.java is a very simple implementation of this idea. It is meant only as an example of file use; the phone book that it implements is a "toy" version that is not meant to be taken seriously. This program stores the phone book data in a file named ".phone book demo" in the user's home directory. To find the user's home directory, it uses the System.getProperty() method that was mentioned in Subsection 7.2.2. When the program starts, it checks whether the file already exists. If the file exists, it should contain the user's phone book, which was saved in a previous run of the program; in that case, the data from the file is read and entered into a *TreeMap* named phoneBook that represents the phone book while the program is running. In order to store the phone book in a file, some decision must be made about how the data in the phone book will be represented. For this example, I chose a simple representation in which each line of the file contains one entry consisting of a name and the associated phone number. A percent sign ('%') separates the name from the number. The following code at the beginning of the program will read the phone book data file, if it exists and has the correct format:

```
File userHomeDirectory = new File( System.getProperty("user.home") );
File dataFile = new File( userHomeDirectory, ".phone book data" );
                    // A file named .phone book data in the user's home directory.
if ( ! dataFile.exists() ) {
    System.out.println("No phone book data file found. A new one");
    System.out.println("will be created, if you add any entries.");
    System.out.println("File name:    " + dataFile.getAbsolutePath());
}
```

```
else {
    System.out.println("Reading phone book data...");
    try( Scanner scanner = new Scanner(dataFile) ) {
        while (scanner.hasNextLine()) {
                // Read one line from the file, containing one name/number pair.
            String phoneEntry = scanner.nextLine();
            int separatorPosition = phoneEntry.indexOf('%');
            if (separatorPosition == -1)
                throw new IOException("File is not a phonebook data file.");
            name = phoneEntry.substring(0, separatorPosition);
            number = phoneEntry.substring(separatorPosition+1);
            phoneBook.put(name,number);
        }
    }
    catch (IOException e) {
        System.out.println("Error in phone book data file.");
        System.out.println("File name:    " + dataFile.getAbsolutePath());
        System.out.println("This program cannot continue.");
        System.exit(1);
    }
}
```

The program then lets the user do various things with the phone book, including making modifications. Any changes that are made are made only to the *TreeMap* that holds the data. When the program ends, the phone book data is written to the file (if any changes have been made while the program was running), using the following code:

```
if (changed) {
    System.out.println("Saving phone directory changes to file " +
        dataFile.getAbsolutePath() + " ...");
    PrintWriter out;
    try {
        out = new PrintWriter( new FileWriter(dataFile) );
```

```
        }
        catch (IOException e) {
                System.out.println("ERROR: Can't open data file for output.");
                return;
        }
        for ( Map.Entry<String,String> entry : phoneBook.entrySet() )
                out.println(entry.getKey() + "%" + entry.getValue() );
        out.flush();
        out.close();
        if (out.checkError())
                System.out.println("ERROR: Some error occurred while writing data file.");
        else
                System.out.println("Done.");
}
```

The net effect of this is that all the data, including the changes, will be there the next time the program is run. I've shown you all the file-handling code from the program. If you would like to see the rest of the program, see the source code.

7.3.3 Storing Objects in Files

Whenever data is stored in files, some definite format must be adopted for representing the data. As long as the output routine that writes the data and the input routine that reads the data use the same format, the files will be usable. However, as usual, correctness is not the end of the story. The representation that is used for data in files should also be robust. To see what this means, we will look at several different ways of representing the same data. This example builds on the example SimplePaint2.java from Subsection 3.3.3. (You might want to run it now to remind yourself of what it can do.) In that program, the user can use the mouse to draw simple sketches. Now, we will add file input/output capabilities to that program. This will allow the user to save a sketch to a file and later read the sketch back from the file into the program so that the user can continue to work on the sketch. The basic requirement is that all relevant data about the sketch must be saved in the file, so that the sketch can be exactly restored when the file is read by the program.

The new version of the program can be found in the source code file SimplePaintWith-Files.java. A "File" menu has been added to the new version. It implements "Save" and "Open" commands for writing program data to a file and reading saved data back into the program.

The data for a sketch consists of the background color of the picture and a list of the curves that were drawn by the user. A curve consists of a list of *Point2Ds*. A *Point2D*, pt, has instance methods pt.getX() and pt.getY() that return the coordinates of a point in the xy- plane as values of type double. Each curve can be a different color. Furthermore, a curve can be "symmetric," which means that in addition to the curve itself, the horizontal and vertical reflections of the curve are also drawn. The data for each curve are stored in an object of type *CurveData*, which is defined in the program as:

```
/**
An object of type CurveData represents the data required to redraw one
of the curves that have been sketched by the user.
*/
private static class CurveData {
    Color color;      // The color of the curve.
    boolean symmetric;      // Are horizontal and vertical reflections also drawn?
    ArrayList<Point2D> points;      // The points on the curve.
}
```

Then, a list of type ArrayList<CurveData> is used to hold data for all of the curves that the user has drawn.

Let's think about how the data for a sketch could be saved to a text file. The basic idea is that all data necessary to reconstitute a sketch must be saved to the output file in some definite format. The method that reads the file must follow exactly the same format as it reads the data, and it must use the data to rebuild the data structures that represent the sketch while the program is running.

When writing character data, all of the data has to be expressed, ultimately, in terms of simple data values such as strings and primitive type values. A color, for example, can be expressed in terms of three numbers giving the red, green, and blue components of the color. The first (not very good) idea that comes to mind might be to just dump all the necessary data, in some definite order, into the file. Suppose that out is a *PrintWriter* that is used to write to the file. We could then say:

```
out.println( backgroundColor.getRed() ); // Write background color to file.
out.println( backgroundColor.getGreen() );
out.println( backgroundColor.getBlue() );
out.println( curves.size() );   // Write the number of curves.
for ( CurveData curve : curves ) {      // For each curve, write...
```

```
        out.println( curve.color.getRed() );          // the color of the curve
        out.println( curve.color.getGreen() );
        out.println( curve.color.getBlue() );
        out.println( curve.symmetric ? 0 : 1 ); // the curve's symmetry property
        out.println( curve.points.size() );  // the number of points on curve
        for ( Point2D pt : curve.points ) {  // the coordinates of each point
                out.println( pt.getX() );
                out.println( pt.getY() );
        }
    }
```

This works in the sense that the file-reading method can read the data and rebuild the data structures. Suppose that the input method uses a *Scanner* named scanner to read the data file. Then it could say:

```
        Color newBackgroundColor;        // Read the background Color.
        double red = scanner.nextDouble();
        double green = scanner.nextDouble();
        double blue = scanner.nextDouble();
        newBackgroundColor  =  Color.color(red,green,blue);
        ArrayList<CurveData> newCurves = new ArrayList<>();
        int curveCount = scanner.nextInt();         // The number of curves to be read.
        for (int i = 0; i < curveCount; i++) {
                CurveData curve = new CurveData();
        double r = scanner.nextDouble();  // Read the curve's color.
        double g = scanner.nextDouble();
        double b = scanner.nextDouble(); curve.color = Color.color(r,g,b);
        int symmetryCode = scanner.nextInt(); // Read the curve's symmetry property.
        curve.symmetric = (symmetryCode == 1);
        curveData.points  =  new  ArrayList<>();
        int pointCount = scanner.nextInt();         // The number of points on this curve.
        for (int j = 0; j < pointCount; j++) {
                int x = scanner.nextDouble();       // Read the coordinates of the point.
                int y = scanner.nextDouble();
```

```
            curveData.points.add(new Point2D(x,y));
        }
        newCurves.add(curve);
    }
    curves = newCurves; // Install the new data structures. backgroundColor =
    newBackgroundColor;
```

Note how every piece of data that was written by the output method is read, in the same order, by the input method. While this does work, the data file is just a long string of numbers. It doesn't make much more sense to a human reader than a binary-format file would. Furthermore, it is still fragile in the sense that any small change made to the data representation in the program, such as adding a new property to curves, will render the data file useless (unless you happen to remember exactly which version of the program created the file).

So, I decided to use a more complex, more meaningful data format for the text files created by my program. Instead of just writing numbers, I add words to say what the numbers mean. Here is a short but complete data file for the program; just by looking at it, you can probably tell what is going on:

```
SimplePaintWithFiles 1.0
background 0.4 0.4 0.5
startcurve
    color 1 1 1
    symmetry true
    coords 10 10
    coords 200 250
    coords 300 10
endcurve
startcurve
    color 0 1 1
    symmetry false
    coords 10 400
    coords 590 400
endcurve
```

The first line of the file identifies the program that created the data file; when the user selects a file to be opened, the program can check the first word in the file as a simple test to make sure the file is of the correct type. The first line also contains a version number, 1.0. If the file format changes in a later version of the program, a higher version number would be used; if the program sees a version number of 1.2 in a file, but the program only understands version 1.0, the program can explain to the user that a newer version of the program is needed to read the data file.

The second line of the file specifies the background color of the picture. The three numbers specify the red, green, and blue components of the color. The word "background" at the beginning of the line makes the meaning clear. The remainder of the file consists of data for the curves that appear in the picture. The data for each curve is clearly marked with "startcurve" and "endcurve." The data consists of the color and symmetry properties of the curve and the xy-coordinates of each point on the curve. Again, the meaning is clear. Files in this format can easily be created or edited by hand. In fact, the data file shown above was actually created in a text editor rather than by the program. Furthermore, it's easy to extend the format to allow for additional options. Future versions of the program could add a "thickness" property to the curves to make it possible to have curves with differing line widths. Shapes such as rectangles and ovals could easily be added.

Outputting data in this format is easy. Suppose that out is a *PrintWriter* that is being used to write the sketch data to a file. Then the output is be done with:

```
out.println("SimplePaintWithFiles 1.0"); // Version number.
out.println( "background " + backgroundColor.getRed() + " " +
    backgroundColor.getGreen() + " " + backgroundColor.getBlue() );
for ( CurveData curve : curves ) {
    out.println();
    out.println("startcurve");
    out.println("    color " + curve.color.getRed() + " " +
            curve.color.getGreen() + " " + curve.color.getBlue() );
    out.println( "    symmetry " + curve.symmetric );
    for ( Point2D pt : curve.points )
            out.println( "    coords " + pt.getX() + " " + pt.getY() );
    out.println("endcurve");
}
```

In the program, this code is used in a doSave() method that is similar to the one that is presented in Subsection 7.2.3. The method uses a file dialog box to allow the user to select the output file.

Reading the data is somewhat harder, since the input routine has to deal with all the extra words in the data. In my input routine, I decided to allow some variation in the order in which the data occurs in the file. For example, the background color can be specified at the end of the file, instead of at the beginning. It can even be left out altogether, in which case white will be used as the default background color. This is possible because each item of data is labeled with a word that describes its meaning; the labels can be used to drive the processing of the input. Here is the complete method from SimplePaintWithFiles.java that reads data files created by the doSave() method. It uses a *Scanner* to read items from the file:

```
private void doOpen() {
    FileChooser fileDialog = new FileChooser();
    fileDialog.setTitle("Select File to be Opened");
    fileDialog.setInitialFileName(null);      // No file is initially selected.
    if (editFile == null)
            fileDialog.setInitialDirectory(new File(System.getProperty("user.home")));
    else
            fileDialog.setInitialDirectory(editFile.getParentFile());
    File selectedFile = fileDialog.showOpenDialog(window);
    if (selectedFile == null)
            return;  // User canceled.
    Scanner scanner;
    try {
            scanner = new Scanner( selectedFile );
    }
    catch (Exception e) {
            Alert errorAlert = new Alert(Alert.AlertType.ERROR,
                    "Sorry, but an error occurred\nwhile trying to open the file.");
            errorAlert.showAndWait();
            return;
    }
    try {
            String programName = scanner.next();
            if ( ! programName.equals("SimplePaintWithFiles") )
```

```
            throw new IOException("File is not a SimplePaintWithFiles data file.");
    double version = scanner.nextDouble();
    if (version > 1.0)
            throw new IOException("File requires a newer version of
            SimplePaintWithFiles.");
    Color newBackgroundColor = Color.WHITE;
    ArrayList<CurveData> newCurves = new ArrayList<CurveData>();
    while (scanner.hasNext()) {
            String itemName = scanner.next();
            if (itemName.equalsIgnoreCase("background")) {
                    double red = scanner.nextDouble();
                    double green = scanner.nextDouble();
                    double blue = scanner.nextDouble();
                    newBackgroundColor = Color.color(red,green,blue);
            }
            else if (itemName.equalsIgnoreCase("startcurve")) {
                    CurveData curve = new CurveData();
                    curve.color = Color.BLACK;
                    curve.symmetric = false;
                    curve.points = new ArrayList<Point2D>();
                    itemName = scanner.next();
                    while ( ! itemName.equalsIgnoreCase("endcurve") ) {
                            if (itemName.equalsIgnoreCase("color")) {
                                    double r = scanner.nextDouble();
                                    double g = scanner.nextDouble();
                                    double b = scanner.nextDouble();
                                    curve.color = Color.color(r,g,b);
                            }
                            else if (itemName.equalsIgnoreCase("symmetry")) {
                                    curve.symmetric = scanner.nextBoolean();
                            }
```

```
                        else if (itemName.equalsIgnoreCase("coords")) {
                            double x = scanner.nextDouble();
                            double y = scanner.nextDouble();
                            curve.points.add( new Point2D(x,y) );
                        }
                        else {
                            throw new Exception("Unknown term in
                            input.");
                        }
                        itemName = scanner.next();
                    }
                    newCurves.add(curve);
                }
                else {
                    throw new Exception("Unknown term in input.");
                }
            }
            scanner.close();
            backgroundColor = newBackgroundColor;
            curves = newCurves;
            redraw();
            editFile = selectedFile;
            window.setTitle("SimplePaint: " + editFile.getName());
        }
        catch (Exception e) {
            Alert errorAlert = new Alert(Alert.AlertType.ERROR,
                "Sorry, but an error occurred while\ntrying to read the data:\n"
                    + e);
            errorAlert.showAndWait();
        }
    }
```

The main reason for this long discussion of file formats has been to get you to think about the problem of representing complex data in a form suitable for storing the data in a file. The same problem arises when data must be transmitted over a network. There is no one correct solution to the problem, but some solutions are certainly better than others. In Section 7.5, we will look at one solution to the data representation problem that has become increasingly common.

In addition to being able to save sketch data in text form, SimplePaintWithFiles can also save the picture itself as an image file that could be, for example, printed or put on a web page.

7.4 NETWORKING

As far as a program is concerned, a network is just another possible source of input data, and another place where data can be output. That does oversimplify things, because networks are not as easy to work with as files are. But in Java, you can do network communication using input streams and output streams, just as you can use such streams to communicate with the user or to work with files. Nevertheless, opening a network connection between two computers is a bit tricky, since there are two computers involved and they have to somehow agree to open a connection. And when each computer can send data to the other, synchronizing communication can be a problem. But the fundamentals are the same as for other forms of I/O.

One of the standard Java packages is called java.net. This package includes several classes that can be used for networking. Two different styles of network I/O are supported. One of these, which is fairly high-level, is based on the World Wide Web, and provides the sort of network communication capability that is used by a Web browser when it downloads pages for you to view. The main classes for this style of networking are java.net.URL and java.net.URLConnection. An object of type *URL* is an abstract representation of a *Universal Resource Locator* , which is an address for an HTML document or other resource. A *URLConnection* represents a network connection to such a resource.

The second style of I/O, which is more general and more important, views the network at a lower level. It is based on the idea of a *socket*. A socket is used by a program to establish a connection with another program on a network. Communication over a network involves two sockets, one on each of the computers involved in the communication. Java uses a class called java.net.Socket to represent sockets that are used for network communication. The term "socket" presumably comes from an image of physically plugging a wire into a computer to establish a connection to a network, but it is important to understand that a socket, as the term is used here, is simply an object belonging to the class *Socket*. In particular, a program can have several sockets at the same time, each connecting it to another program running on some other computer on the network—or even running on the same computer.

All these connections use the same physical network connection.

This section gives a brief introduction to these basic networking classes, and shows how they relate to input and output streams.

7.4.1 URLs and URLConnections

The *URL* class is used to represent resources on the World Wide Web. Every resource has an address, which identifies it uniquely and contains enough information for a Web browser to find the resource on the network and retrieve it. The address is called a "url" or "universal resource locator." (URLs can actually refer to resources from other sources besides the web; after all, they are "universal." For example, they can represent files on your computer.)

An object belonging to the *URL* class represents such an address. Once you have a *URL* object, you can use it to open a *URLConnection* to the resource at that address. A url is ordinarily specified as a string, such as "https://math.hws.edu/eck/index.html". There are also *relative url's*. A relative url specifies the location of a resource relative to the location of another url, which is called the *base* or *context* for the relative url. For example, if the context is given by the url https://math.hws.edu/eck/, then the incomplete, relative url "index.html" would really refer to https://math.hws.edu/eck/index.html.

An object of the class *URL* is not simply a string, but it can be constructed from a string representation of a url. A *URL* object can also be constructed from another *URL* object, representing a context, plus a string that specifies a url relative to that context. These constructors have prototypes

public URL(String urlName) throws MalformedURLException

and

public URL(URL context, String relativeName) throws MalformedURLException

Note that these constructors will throw an exception of type *MalformedURLException* if the specified strings don't represent legal url's. The *MalformedURLException* class is a subclass of *IOException*, and it requires mandatory exception handling.

Once you have a valid *URL* object, you can call its openConnection() method to set up a connection. This method returns a *URLConnection*. The *URLConnection* object can, in turn, be used to create an *InputStream* for reading data from the resource represented by the URL. This is done by calling its getInputStream() method. For example:

URL url = new URL(urlAddressString);

URLConnection connection = url.openConnection();

InputStream in = connection.getInputStream();

The openConnection() and getInputStream() methods can both throw exceptions of type *IOException*. Once the *InputStream* has been created, you can read from it in the usual way, including wrapping it in another input stream type, such as *BufferedReader*, or using a *Scanner*. Reading from the stream can, of course, generate exceptions.

One of the other useful instance methods in the *URLConnection* class is getContentType(), which returns a *String* that describes the type of information available from the URL. The return value can be null if the type of information is not yet known or if it is not possible to determine the type. The type might not be available until after the input stream has been created, so you should generally call getContentType() after getInputStream(). The string returned by getContentType() is in a format called a *mime type*. Mime types include "text/plain", "text/html", "image/jpeg", "image/png", and many others. All mime types contain two parts: a general type, such as "text" or "image", and a more specific type within that general category, such as "html" or "png". If you are only interested in text data, for example, you can check whether the string returned by getContentType() starts with "text". (Mime types were first introduced to describe the content of email messages. The name stands for "Multipurpose Internet Mail Extensions." They are now used almost universally to specify the type of information in a file or other resource.)

Let's look at a short example that uses all this to read the data from a URL. This subroutine opens a connection to a specified URL, checks that the type of data at the URL is text, and then copies the text onto the screen. Many of the operations in this subroutine can throw exceptions. They are handled by declaring that the subroutine "throws IOException" and leaving it up to the main program to decide what to do when an error occurs.

```
static void readTextFromURL( String urlString ) throws IOException {

    /* Open a connection to the URL, and get an input stream for reading data from the
    URL. */

    URL url = new URL(urlString);

    URLConnection connection = url.openConnection();

    InputStream urlData = connection.getInputStream();

    /* Check that the content is some type of text. Note: connection.getContentType()
    method should be called after getInputStream(). */

    String contentType = connection.getContentType();

    System.out.println("Stream opened with content type: " + contentType);

    System.out.println();
```

```
        if (contentType == null || contentType.startsWith("text") == false)
                throw new IOException("URL does not seem to refer to a text file.");
        System.out.println("Fetching content from " + urlString + " ...");
        System.out.println();
        /* Copy lines of text from the input stream to the screen, until end-of-file is
        encountered      (or an error occurs). */
        BufferedReader in;         // For reading from the connection's input stream.
        in = new BufferedReader( new InputStreamReader(urlData) );
        while (true) {
                String line = in.readLine();
                if (line == null)
                        break;
                System.out.println(line);
        }
        in.close();
    } // end readTextFromURL()
```

A complete program that uses this subroutine can be found in the file FetchURL.java. When you run the program, you can specify the URL on the command line; if not, you will be prompted to enter the URL. For this program, a URL can begin with "http://" or "https://" for a URL that refers to a resource on the web, with "file://" for a URL that refers to a file on your computer, or with "ftp://" for a URL that uses the "File Transfer Protocol." If it does not start with any of these, then "http://" is added to the start of the URL. Try the program with URL math.hws.edu/javanotes to fetch the front page of this textbook from its website. Try it with some bad inputs to see the various errors that can occur.

7.4.2 TCP/IP and Client/Server

Communication over the Internet is based on a pair of protocols called the *Transmission Control Protocol* and the *Internet Protocol* , which are collectively referred to as *TCP/IP*. (In fact, there is a more basic communication protocol called UDP that can be used instead of TCP in certain applications. UDP is supported in Java, but for this discussion, I'll stick to TCP/IP, which provides reliable two-way communication between networked computers.)

For two programs to communicate using TCP/IP, each program must create a socket, as discussed earlier in this section, and those sockets must be connected. Once such a connection is made, communication takes place using input streams and output streams. Each program has its own input stream and its own output stream. Data written by one program to its output stream is transmitted to the other computer. There, it enters the input stream of the program at the other end of the network connection. When that program reads data from its input stream, it is receiving the data that was transmitted to it over the network.

The hard part, then, is making a network connection in the first place. Two sockets are involved. To get things started, one program must create a socket that will wait passively until a connection request comes in from another socket. The waiting socket is said to be *listening* for a connection. On the other side of the connection-to-be, another program creates a socket that sends out a connection request to the listening socket. When the listening socket receives the connection request, it responds, and the connection is established. Once that is done, each program can obtain an input stream and an output stream for sending data over the connection. Communication takes place through these streams until one program or the other *closes* the connection.

A program that creates a listening socket is sometimes said to be a *server* , and the socket is called a *server socket.* A program that connects to a server is called a *client* , and the socket that it uses to make a connection is called a *client socket* . The idea is that the server is out there somewhere on the network, waiting for a connection request from some client. The server can be thought of as offering some kind of service, and the client gets access to that service by connecting to the server. This is called the *client/server model* of network communication. In many actual applications, a server program can provide connections to several clients at the same time. When a client connects to the listening socket in a server of that type, that socket does not stop listening. Instead, it continues listening for additional client connection requests at the same time that the client is being serviced. But to allow multiple clients to be connected at the same time, it is necessary to use threads.

The *URL* class that was discussed at the beginning of this section uses a client socket behind the scenes to do any necessary network communication. On the other side of that connection is a server program that accepts a connection request from the *URL* object, reads a request from that object for some particular file on the server computer, and responds by transmitting the contents of that file over the network back to the *URL* object. After transmitting the data, the server closes the connection.

A client program has to have some way to specify which computer, among all those on the network, it wants to communicate with. Every computer on the Internet has an *IP address* which identifies it. Many computers can also be referred to by *domain names* such as math.hws.edu or www.whitehouse.gov. Traditional (or *IPv4*)

IP addresses are 32-bit integers. They are usually written in the so-called "dotted decimal" form, such as 64.89.144.237, where each of the four numbers in the address represents an 8-bit integer in the range 0 through 255. A new version of the Internet Protocol, *IPv6* , is being introduced. IPv6 addresses are 128-bit integers and are usually written in hexadecimal form (with some colons and maybe some extra information thrown in). You might see IP addresses of either form.

A computer can have several IP addresses, and can have both IPv4 and IPv6 addresses. Usually, one of these is the *loopback address*, which can be used when a program wants to communicate with another program *on the same computer*. The loopback address has IPv4 address 127.0.0.1 and can also, in general, be referred to using the domain name *localhost*. In addition, there can be one or more IP addresses associated with physical network connections. Your computer probably has some utility for displaying your computer's IP addresses. I have written a small Java program, ShowMyNetwork.java, that does the same thing. When I run ShowMyNetwork on one computer, the output was:

wlo1 : /2603:7080:7f41:f400:441a:459f:2c62:c349%wlo1 /192.168.0.2

lo : /0:0:0:0:0:0:0:1%lo /127.0.0.1

The first thing on each line is a network interface name, which is really meaningful only to the computer's operating system. The same line also contains the IP addresses for that interface. In this example, lo refers to the loopback address, which has IPv4 address 127.0.0.1 as usual. The most important number here is 192.168.0.2, which is the IPv4 address that can be used for communication over the network. (The slashes at the start of each address are not part of the actual address.) The other numbers in the output are IPv6 addresses, but the IPv4 addresses are easier for a human to use.

Now, a single computer might have several programs doing network communication at the same time, or one program communicating with several other computers. To allow for this possibility, a network connection actually has a *port number* in combination with an IP address. A port number is just a 16-bit positive integer. A server does not simply listen for connections—it listens for connections *on a particular port*. A potential client must know both the Internet address (or domain name) of the computer on which the server is running and the port number on which the server is listening. A Web server, for example, generally listens for connections on port 80; other standard Internet services also have standard port numbers. (The standard port numbers are all less than 1024, and are reserved for particular services. If you create your own server programs, you should use port numbers greater than 1024.)

7.4.3 Sockets in Java

To implement TCP/IP connections, the java.net package provides two classes, *ServerSocket* and *Socket*. A *ServerSocket* represents a listening socket that waits for connection requests from clients. A *Socket* represents one endpoint of an actual network connection. A *Socket* can be a client socket that sends a connection request to a server. But a *Socket* can also be created by a server to handle a connection request from a client. This allows the server to create multiple sockets and handle multiple connections. A *ServerSocket* does not itself participate in connections; it just listens for connection requests and creates *Sockets* to handle the actual connections.

When you construct a ServerSocket object, you have to specify the port number on which the server will listen. The specification for the constructor is

public ServerSocket(int port) throws IOException

The port number must be in the range 0 through 65535, and should generally be greater than 1024. The constructor might throw a *SecurityException* if a port number smaller than 1024 is specified. An *IOException* can also occur if, for example, the specified port number is already in use. (A parameter value of 0 in this method tells the server socket to listen on any available port.)

As soon as a *ServerSocket* is created, it starts listening for connection requests. The accept() method in the *ServerSocket* class accepts such a request, establishes a connection with the client, and returns a *Socket* that can be used for communication with the client. The accept() method has the form

public Socket accept() throws IOException

When you call the accept() method, it will not return until a connection request is received (or until some error occurs). The method is said to *block* while waiting for the connection. (While the method is blocked, the program—or more exactly, the thread—that called the method can't do anything else. If there are other threads in the same program, they can proceed.) You can call accept() repeatedly to accept multiple connection requests. The *ServerSocket* will continue listening for connections until it is closed, using its close() method, or until some error occurs, or until the program is terminated in some way.

Suppose that you want a server to listen on port 1728, and that you want it to continue to accept connections as long as the program is running. Suppose that you've written a method provideService(Socket) to handle the communication with one client. Then the basic form of the server program would be:

```
try {
    ServerSocket server = new ServerSocket(1728);
```

```
        while (true) {
                Socket connection = server.accept();
                provideService(connection);
        }
    }
    catch (IOException e) {
        System.out.println("Server shut down with error: " + e);
    }
```

On the client side, a client socket is created using a constructor in the *Socket* class. To connect to a server on a known computer and port, you would use the constructor

```
public Socket(String computer, int port) throws IOException
```

The first parameter can be either an IP number or a domain name. This constructor will block until the connection is established or until an error occurs.

Once you have a connected socket, no matter how it was created, you can use the *Socket* methods getInputStream() and getOutputStream() to obtain streams that can be used for communication over the connection. These methods return objects of type *InputStream* and *OutputStream*, respectively. Keeping all this in mind, here is the outline of a method for working with a client connection:

```
/**
Open a client connection to a specified server computer and
port number on the server, and then do communication through
the connection.
*/
void doClientConnection(String computerName, int serverPort) {
    Socket connection;
    InputStream in;
    OutputStream out;
    try {
            connection = new Socket(computerName,serverPort);
            in = connection.getInputStream();
            out = connection.getOutputStream();
    }
    catch (IOException e) {
```

```
            System.out.println(
                    "Attempt to create connection failed with error: " + e);
            return;
        }
        .
        .   // Use the streams, in and out, to communicate with the server.
        .
        try {
            connection.close();
        }
        catch (IOException e) {
        }
    }   // end doClientConnection()
```

All this makes network communication sound easier than it really is. (And if you think it sounded hard, then it's even harder.) If networks were completely reliable, things would be almost as easy as I've described. The problem, though, is to write robust programs that can deal with network and human error. I won't go into detail. However, what I've covered here should give you the basic ideas of network programming, and it is enough to write some simple network applications. Let's look at a few working examples of client/server programming.

7.4.4 A Trivial Client/Server

The first example consists of two programs. The source code files for the programs are DateClient.java and DateServer.java. One is a simple network client and the other is a matching server. The client makes a connection to the server, reads one line of text from the server, and displays that text on the screen. The text sent by the server consists of the current date and time on the computer where the server is running. In order to open a connection, the client must know the computer on which the server is running and the port on which it is listening.

The server listens on port number 32007. The port number could be anything between 1025 and 65535, as long as the server and the client use the same port. Port numbers between 1 and 1024 are reserved for standard services and should not be used for other servers. The name or IP number of the computer on which the server is running can be specified as a command-line argument. For example, if the server is running on a computer named math.hws.edu, then you could run the client with the command "java DateClient math.hws.edu". If a computer is not specified on the command line, then the user is prompted to enter one. Here is the complete client program:

```
import java.net.*;
import java.util.Scanner; import java.io.*;
/**
This program opens a connection to a computer specified
as the first command-line argument.  If no command-line
argument is given, it prompts the user for a computer
to connect to.          The connection is made to
the port specified by LISTENING PORT.          The program reads one
line of text from the connection and then closes the
connection.  It displays the text that it read on
standard output.      This program is meant to be used with
the server program, DateServer, which sends the current
date and time on the computer where the server is running.
*/
public class DateClient {
    public static final int LISTENING PORT = 32007;
    public static void main(String[] args) {
            String hostName;          // Name of the server computer to connect to.
            Socket connection;        // A socket for communicating with server.
            BufferedReader incoming; // For reading data from the connection.
            /* Get computer name from command line. */
            if (args.length > 0)
                    hostName = args[0];
            else {
                    Scanner stdin = new Scanner(System.in);
                    System.out.print("Enter computer name or IP address: ");
                    hostName = stdin.nextLine();
            }
            /* Make the connection, then read and display a line of text. */
```

```
        try {
                connection = new Socket( hostName, LISTENING PORT );
                incoming = new BufferedReader(
                        new InputStreamReader(connection.getInputStream()) );
                String lineFromServer = incoming.readLine();
                if (lineFromServer == null) {
                                // A null from incoming.readLine() indicates that
                                // end-of-stream was encountered.
                        throw new IOException("Connection was opened, " +
                                "but server did not send any data.");
                }
                System.out.println();
                System.out.println(lineFromServer);
                System.out.println(); incoming.close();
        }
        catch (Exception e) {
                System.out.println("Error:          " + e);
        }
    }       // end main()
} //end class DateClient
```

Note that all the communication with the server is done in a try..catch statement. This will catch the *IOExceptions* that can be generated when the connection is opened or closed and when data is read from the input stream. The connection's input stream is wrapped in a *BufferedReader*, which has a readLine() method that makes it easy to read one line of text. If that method returns null, it probably means that the server closed the connection without sending any data.

In order for this program to run without error, the server program must be running on the computer to which the client tries to connect. By the way, it's possible to run the client and the server program on the same computer. For example, you can open two command windows, start the server in one window and then run the client in the other window. To make things like this easier, most computers will recognize the domain name localhost and the IP number 127.0.0.1 as referring to "this computer." This means that the command "java DateClient localhost" will tell the *DateClient* program to connect to a server running on the same computer. If that command doesn't work, try "java DateClient 127.0.0.1".

The server program that corresponds to the *DateClient* client program is called *DateServer*. The *DateServer* program creates a *ServerSocket* to listen for connection requests on port 32007. After the listening socket is created, the server will enter an infinite loop in which it accepts and processes connections. This will continue until the program is killed in some way—for example by typing a CONTROL-C in the command window where the server is running. When a connection request is received from a client, the server calls a subroutine to handle the connection. In the subroutine, any *Exception* that occurs is caught, so that it will not crash the server. Just because a connection to one client has failed for some reason, it does not mean that the server should be shut down; the error might have been the fault of the client. The connection-handling subroutine creates a *PrintWriter* for sending data over the connection. It writes the current date and time to this stream and then closes the connection. (The standard class java.util.Date is used to obtain the current time. An object of type *Date* represents a particular date and time. The default constructor, "new Date()", creates an object that represents the time when the object is created.) The complete server program is as follows:

```
import java.net.*;
import java.io.*;
import java.util.Date;
/**
This program is a server that takes connection requests on
the port specified by the constant LISTENING PORT.     When a
connection is opened, the program sends the current time to
the connected socket.          The program will continue to receive
and process connections until it is killed (by a CONTROL-C,
for example).          Note that this server processes each connection
as it is received, rather than creating a separate thread
to process the connection.
*/
public class DateServer {
    public static final int LISTENING PORT = 32007;
    public static void main(String[] args) {
            ServerSocket listener; // Listens for incoming connections.
            Socket connection; // For communication with the connecting program.
```

```
        /* Accept and process connections forever, or until some error occurs. (Note
        that errors that occur while communicating with a connected program are
        caught and handled in the sendDate() routine, so they will not crash the
        server.) */
        try {
                listener = new ServerSocket(LISTENING PORT);
                System.out.println("Listening on port " + LISTENING PORT):
                while (true) {
                        // Accept next connection request and handle it.
                connection = listener.accept();
                sendDate(connection);
                }
        }
        catch (Exception e) {
                System.out.println("Sorry, the server has shut down.");
                System.out.println("Error: " + e);
                return;
}
}       // end main()
/**
The parameter, client, is a socket that is already connected to another
program.        Get an output stream for the connection, send the current time,
and close the connection.
*/
private static void sendDate(Socket client) {
        try {
                System.out.println("Connection from " +
                        client.getInetAddress().toString() );
                Date now = new Date();  // The current date and time.
                PrintWriter outgoing;   // Stream for sending data.
                outgoing = new PrintWriter( client.getOutputStream() );
                outgoing.println( now.toString() );
```

```
                outgoing.flush();// Make sure the data is actually sent!
                client.close();
            }
            catch (Exception e){
                System.out.println("Error: " + e);
            }
    } // end sendDate()
} //end class DateServer
```

When you run *DateServer* in a command-line interface, it will sit and wait for connection requests and report them as they are received. To make the *DateServer* service permanently available on a computer, the program would be run as a *daemon*. A daemon is a program that runs continually on a computer, independently of any user. The computer can be configured to start the daemon automatically as soon as the computer boots up. It then runs in the background, even while the computer is being used for other purposes. For example, a computer that makes pages available on the World Wide Web runs a daemon that listens for requests for web pages and responds by transmitting the pages. It's just a souped-up analog of the *DateServer* program! However, the question of how to set up a program as a daemon is not one I want to go into here. For testing purposes, it's easy enough to start the program by hand, and, in any case, my examples are not really robust enough or full-featured enough to be run as serious servers. (By the way, the word "daemon" is just an alternative spelling of "demon" and is usually pronounced the same way.)

Note that after calling outgoing.println() to send a line of data to the client, the server program calls outgoing.flush(). The flush() method is available in every output stream class. Calling it ensures that data that has been written to the stream is actually sent to its destination. You should generally call this function every time you use an output stream to send data over a network connection. If you don't do so, it's possible that the stream will collect data until it has a reasonably large batch of data to send. This is done for efficiency, but it can impose unacceptable delays when the client is waiting for the transmission. It is even possible that some of the data might remain untransmitted when the socket is closed, so it is especially important to call flush() before closing the connection. This is one of those unfortunate cases where different implementations of Java can behave differently. If you fail to flush your output streams, it is possible that your network application will work on some types of computers but not on others.

7.4.5 A Simple Network Chat

In the *DateServer* example, the server transmits information and the client reads it. It's also possible to have two-way communication between client and server. As a first example, we'll look at a client and server that allow a user on each end of the connection to send messages to the other user. The program works in a command-line environment where the users type in their messages. In this example, the server waits for a connection from a single client and then closes down its listener so that no other clients can connect. After the client and server are connected, both ends of the connection work in much the same way. The user on the client end types a message, and it is transmitted to the server, which displays it to the user on that end. Then the user of the server types a message that is transmitted to the client. Then the client user types another message, and so on. This continues until one user or the other enters "quit" when prompted for a message. When that happens, the connection is closed and both programs terminate. The client program and the server program are very similar. The techniques for opening the connections differ, and the client is programmed to send the first message while the server is programmed to receive the first message. The client and server programs can be found in the files CLChatClient.java and CLChatServer.java. (The name "CLChat" stands for "command-line chat.") Here is the source code for the server; the client is similar:

```
import java.net.*;
import java.util.Scanner;
import java.io.*;
/**
This program is one end of a simple command-line interface chat program.
It acts as a server which waits for a connection from the CLChatClient
program.    The port on which the server listens can be specified as a
command-line argument.    If it is not, then the port specified by the
constant DEFAULT PORT is used.    Note that if a port number of zero is
specified, then the server will listen on any available port.
This program only supports one connection.    As soon as a connection is
opened, the listening socket is closed down.    The two ends of the connection
each send a HANDSHAKE string to the other, so that both ends can verify
that the program on the other end is of the right type.  Then the connected
programs alternate sending messages to each other.    The client always sends
```

```
the first message.     The user on either end can close the connection by
entering the string "quit" when prompted for a message.        Note that the first
character of any string sent over the connection must be 0 or 1; this
character is interpreted as a command.
*/
public class CLChatServer {
    /**
    * Port to listen on, if none is specified on the command line.
    */
    static final int DEFAULT PORT = 1728;
    /**
    Handshake string. Each end of the connection sends this     string to the
    other just after the connection is opened.  This is done to confirm that
    the program on the other side of the connection is a CLChat program.
    */
    static final String HANDSHAKE = "CLChat";
    /**
    This character is prepended to every message that is sent.
    */
    static final char MESSAGE = '0';
    /**
    This character is sent to the connected program when the user quits.
    */
    static final char CLOSE = '1';
    public static void main(String[] args) {
            int port;// The port on which the server listens.
            ServerSocket listener;          // Listens for a connection request.
            Socket connection;              // For communication with the client.
            BufferedReader incoming;        // Stream for receiving data from client.
            PrintWriter outgoing;           // Stream for sending data to client.
            String messageOut;              // A message to be sent to the client.
```

```
String messageIn;               // A message received from the client.
Scanner userInput;              // A wrapper for System.in, for reading
                                // lines of input from the user.
/* First, get the port number from the command line,
or use the default port if none is specified. */
if (args.length == 0)
        port = DEFAULT PORT;
else {
        try {
                port= Integer.parseInt(args[0]);
                if (port < 0 || port > 65535)
                        throw new NumberFormatException();
        }
        catch (NumberFormatException e) {
                System.out.println("Illegal port number, " + args[0]);
                return;
        }
}
/* Wait for a connection request. When it arrives, close down the listener. Create
streams for communication and exchange the handshake. */
try {
        listener = new ServerSocket(port);
        System.out.println("Listening on port " + listener.getLocalPort());
        connection = listener.accept();
        listener.close();
        incoming = new BufferedReader(
                new InputStreamReader(connection.getInputStream()) );
        outgoing = new PrintWriter(connection.getOutputStream());
        outgoing.println(HANDSHAKE);   // Send handshake to client.
        outgoing.flush();
        messageIn = incoming.readLine();// Receive handshake from client.
        if (! HANDSHAKE.equals(messageIn) ) {
```

```
                throw new Exception("Connected program is not a CLChat!");
            }
            System.out.println("Connected.    Waiting for the first message.");
        }
        catch (Exception e) {
            System.out.println("An error occurred while opening connection.");
            System.out.println(e.toString());
            return;
        }
        /* Exchange messages with the other end of the connection until one side or the other
        closes the connection. This server program waits for the first message from the
        client. After that, messages alternate strictly back and forth. */
        try {
            userInput = new Scanner(System.in);
            System.out.println("NOTE: Enter 'quit' to end the program.\n");
            while (true) {
                System.out.println("WAITING...");
                messageIn = incoming.readLine();
                if (messageIn.length() > 0) {
                            // The first character of the message is a command. If
                            // the command is CLOSE, then the connection is closed.
                            // Otherwise, remove the command character from the
                            // message and proceed.
                    if (messageIn.charAt(0) == CLOSE) {
                            System.out.println("Connection closed at other end.");
                            connection.close();
                            break;
                    }
                    messageIn = messageIn.substring(1);
                }
                System.out.println("RECEIVED:           " + messageIn);
                System.out.print("SEND: ");
```

```
                messageOut = userInput.nextLine();
                if (messageOut.equalsIgnoreCase("quit")) {
                            // User wants to quit.     Inform the other side
                            // of the connection, then close the connection.
                    outgoing.println(CLOSE);
                    outgoing.flush();// Make sure the data is sent!
                    connection.close();
                    System.out.println("Connection closed.");
                    break;
                }
                outgoing.println(MESSAGE + messageOut);
                outgoing.flush(); // Make sure the data is sent!
                if (outgoing.checkError()) {
                    throw new IOException("Error occurred while transmitting
                    message.");
                }
            }
        }
        catch (Exception e) {
            System.out.println("Sorry, an error has occurred. Connection lost.");
            System.out.println("Error:        " + e);
            System.exit(1);
            }
        } // end main()
    } //end class CLChatServer
```

This program is a little more robust than *DateServer*. For one thing, it uses a *handshake* to make sure that a client who is trying to connect is really a *CLChatClient* program. A handshake is simply information sent between a client and a server as part of setting up a connection, before any actual data is sent. In this case, each side of the connection sends a string to the other side to identify itself. The handshake is part of the *protocol* that I made up for communication between *CLChatClient* and *CLChatServer*. A protocol is a detailed specification of what data and messages can be exchanged over a connection, how they must be represented, and what order they can be sent in. When you design a client/server application, the design of the protocol is an important consideration. Another aspect of the CLChat protocol is that after the handshake, every line of text that is sent over the connection begins with a character that acts as a command. If the character is 0, the rest of the line is a message from one user to the other. If the character is 1, the line indicates that a user has entered the "quit" command, and the connection is to be shut down.

Remember that if you want to try out this program on a single computer, you can use two command-line windows. In one, give the command "java CLChatServer" to start the server. Then, in the other, use the command "java CLChatClient localhost" to connect to the server that is running on the same machine. If the server is not listening on the default port, you can add the port number as a second command line option to the program. If you do not specify the connection information on the command line, you will be asked to enter it.

7.5 A BRIEF INTRODUCTION TO XML

When data is saved to a file or transmitted over a network, it must be represented in some way that will allow the same data to be rebuilt later, when the file is read or the transmission is received. We have seen that there are good reasons to prefer textual, character- based representations in many cases, but there are many ways to represent a given collection of data as text. In this section, we'll take a brief look at one type of character-based data representation that has become increasingly common.

XML (eXtensible Markup Language) is a syntax for creating data representation languages. There are two aspects or levels of XML. On the first level, XML specifies a strict but relatively simple syntax. Any sequence of characters that follows that syntax is a *well-formed* XML document. On the second level, XML provides a way of placing further restrictions on what can appear in a document. This is done by associating a *DTD* (Document Type Definition) with an XML document. A DTD is essentially a list of things that are allowed to appear in the XML document. A well-formed XML document that has an associated DTD and that follows the rules of the DTD is said to be a *valid* XML document. The idea is that XML is a general format for data representation, and a DTD specifies how to use XML to represent a particular kind of data. (There are also alternatives to DTDs, such as *XML schemas*, for defining valid XML documents, but let's ignore them here.)

There is nothing magical about XML. It's certainly not perfect. It's a very verbose language, and some people think it's ugly. On the other hand it's very flexible. It can be used to represent almost any type of data. It was built from the start to support all languages and alphabets. Most important, it has become an accepted standard. There is support in just about any programming language for processing XML documents. There are standard DTDs for describing many different kinds of data. There are many ways to design a data representation language, but XML is one that has happened to come into widespread use. In fact, it has found its way into almost every corner of information technology. For example: There are XML languages for representing mathematical expressions (MathML), musical notation (MusicXML), molecules and chemical reactions (CML), vector graphics (SVG), and many other kinds of information. XML is used by OpenOffice and recent versions of Microsoft Office in the document format for office applications such as word processing, spreadsheets, and presentations. XML site syndication languages (RSS, ATOM) make it possible for web sites, newspapers, and blogs to make a list of recent headlines available in a standard format that can be used by other web sites and by web browsers; the same format is used to publish podcasts. And XML is a common format for the electronic exchange of business information.

My purpose here is not to tell you everything there is to know about XML. I will just explain a few ways in which it can be used in your own programs. In particular, I will not say anything further about DTDs and valid XML. For many purposes, it is sufficient to use well-formed XML documents with no associated DTDs.

7.5.1 Basic XML Syntax

If you know HTML, the language for writing web pages, then XML will look familiar. An XML document looks a lot like an HTML document. HTML is not itself an XML language, since it does not follow all the strict XML syntax rules, but the basic ideas are similar. Here is a short, well-formed XML document:

```
<?xml version="1.0"?>
<simplepaint version="1.0">
    <background red='1' green='0.6' blue='0.2'/>
    <curve>
        <color red='0' green='0' blue='1'/>
        <symmetric>false</symmetric>
        <point x='83' y='96'/>
        <point x='116' y='149'/>
        <point x='159' y='215'/>
        <point x='216' y='294'/>
        <point x='264' y='359'/>
        <point x='309' y='418'/>
        <point x='371' y='499'/>
        <point x='400' y='543'/>
    </curve>
```

```
    <curve>
        <color red='1' green='1' blue='1'/>
        <symmetric>true</symmetric>
        <point x='54' y='305'/>
        <point x='79' y='289'/>
        <point x='128' y='262'/>
        <point x='190' y='236'/>
        <point x='253' y='209'/>
        <point x='341' y='158'/>
    </curve>
</simplepaint>
```

The first line, which is optional, merely identifies this as an XML document. This line can also specify other information, such as the character encoding that was used to encode the characters in the document into binary form. If this document had an associated DTD, it would be specified in a "DOCTYPE" directive on the next line of the file.

Aside from the first line, the document is made up of *elements*, *attributes*, and textual content. An element starts with a *tag* , such as <curve> and ends with a matching *end-tag* such as </curve>. Between the tag and end-tag is the *content* of the element, which can consist of text and nested elements. (In the example, the only textual content is the true or false in the <symmetric> elements.) If an element has no content, then the opening tag and end-tag can be combined into a single *empty tag* , such as <point x='83' y='96'/>, with a "/" before the final ">". This is an abbreviation for <point x='83' y='96'></point>. A tag can include attributes such as the x and y in <point x='83' y='96'/> or the version in <simplepaint version="1.0">. A document can also include a few other things, such as comments, that I will not discuss here.

The author of a well-formed XML document gets to choose the tag names and attribute names, and meaningful names can be chosen to describe the data to a human reader. (For a valid XML document that uses a DTD, it's the author of the DTD who gets to choose the tag names.)

Every well-formed XML document follows a strict syntax. Here are some of the most important syntax rules: Tag names and attribute names in XML are case sensitive. A name must begin with a letter and can contain letters, digits and certain other characters. Spaces and ends-of-line are significant only in textual content. Every tag must either be an empty tag or have a matching end-tag. By "matching" here, I mean that elements must be properly nested; if a tag is inside some element, then the matching end-tag must also be inside that element. A document must have a *root element*, which contains all the other elements. The root element in the above example has tag name simplepaint. Every attribute must have a value, and that value must be enclosed in quotation marks; either single quotes or double quotes can be used for this. The special characters < and &, if they appear in attribute values or textual content, must be written as < and &. "<" and "&" are examples of *entities*. The entities >, ", and ' are also defined, representing >, double quote, and single quote. (Additional entities can be defined in a DTD.)

While this description will not enable you to understand everything that you might encounter in XML documents, it should allow you to design well-formed XML documents to represent data structures used in Java programs.

7.5.2 Working With the DOM

The sample XML file shown above was designed to store information about simple drawings made by the user. The drawings in question are ones that could be made using the sample program SimplePaint2.java from Subsection 3.3.3. We'll look at another version of that program that can save the user's drawing using an XML format for the data file. The new version is SimplePaintWithXML.java. The sample XML document shown earlier in this section can be used with that program. I designed the format of that document to represent all the data needed to reconstruct a picture in SimplePaint2. The document encodes the background color of the picture and a list of curves. Each <curve> element contains the data from one object of type *CurveData*.

It is easy enough to write data in a customized XML format, although we have to be very careful to follow all the syntax rules. Here is how SimplePaintWithXML writes the data for a SimplePaint2 picture to a *PrintWriter*, out. This produces an XML file with the same structure as the example shown above:

```
out.println("<?xml version=\"1.0\"?>");
out.println("<simplepaint version=\"1.0\">");
out.println("      <background red='" + backgroundColor.getRed() + "' green='" +
            backgroundColor.getGreen() + "' blue='" + backgroundColor.getBlue() + "'/>");
for (CurveData c : curves) {
    out.println("    <curve>");
    out.println("    <color red='" + c.color.getRed() + "' green='" +
            c.color.getGreen() + "' blue='" + c.color.getBlue() + "'/>");
    out.println("    <symmetric>" + c.symmetric + "</symmetric>");
```

```
for (Point2D pt : c.points)
        out.println("      <point x='" + pt.getX() + "' y='" + pt.getY() + "'/>");
        out.println("    </curve>");
}
out.println("</simplepaint>");
```

Reading the data back into the program is another matter. To reconstruct the data structure represented by the XML Document, it is necessary to parse the document and extract the data from it. This could be difficult to do by hand. Fortunately, Java has a standard API for parsing and processing XML Documents. (Actually, it has two, but we will only look at one of them.) A well-formed XML document has a certain structure, consisting of elements containing attributes, nested elements, and textual content. It's possible to build a data structure in the computer's memory that corresponds to the structure and content of the document. Of course, there are many ways to do this, but there is one common standard representation known as the *Document Object Model*, or DOM. The DOM specifies how to build data structures to represent XML documents, and it specifies some standard methods for accessing the data in that structure. The data structure is a kind of tree whose structure mirrors the structure of the document. The tree is constructed from *nodes* of various types. There are nodes to represent elements, attributes, and text. (The tree can also contain several other types of node, representing aspects of XML that we can ignore here.) Attributes and text can be processed without directly manipulating the corresponding nodes, so we will be concerned almost entirely with element nodes.

(The sample program XMLDemo.java lets you experiment with XML and the DOM. It has a text area where you can enter an XML document. Initially, the input area contains the sample XML document from this section. When you click a button named "Parse XML Input", the program will attempt to read the XML from the input box and build a DOM representation of that document. If the input is not well-formed XML, an error message is displayed. If it is legal, the program will traverse the DOM representation and display a list of elements, attributes, and textual content that it encounters. The program uses a few techniques for processing XML that I won't discuss here.)

In Java, the DOM representation of an XML document file can be created with just two statements. If selectedFile is a variable of type *File* that represents the XML file, and xmldoc is of type *Document*, then

```
DocumentBuilder docReader
        = DocumentBuilderFactory.newInstance().newDocumentBuilder();
xmldoc = docReader.parse(selectedFile);
```

will open the file, read its contents, and build the DOM representation. The classes *Document- Builder* and *DocumentBuilderFactory* are both defined in the package javax. xml.parsers. The method docReader.parse() does the actual work. It will throw an exception if it can't read the file or if the file does not contain a legal XML document. If it succeeds, then the value returned by docReader.parse() is an object that represents the entire XML document. (This is a very complex task! It has been coded once and for all into a method that can be used very easily in any Java program. We see the benefit of using a standardized syntax.)

The structure of the DOM data structure is defined in the package org.w3c.dom, which contains several data types that represent an XML document as a whole and the individual nodes in a document. The "org.w3c" in the name refers to the World Wide Web Consortium, W3C, which is the standards organization for the Web. DOM, like XML, is a general standard, not just a Java standard. The data types that we need here are *Document*, *Node*, *Element*, and *NodeList*. (They are defined as interfaces rather than classes, but that fact is not relevant here.) We can use methods that are defined in these data types to access the data in the DOM representation of an XML document.

An object of type *Document* represents an entire XML document. The return value of docReader.parse()—xmldoc in the above example—is of type *Document*. We will only need one method from this class: If xmldoc is of type *Document*, then

xmldoc.getDocumentElement()

returns a value of type *Element* that represents the root element of the document. (Recall that this is the top-level element that contains all the other elements.) In the sample XML document from earlier in this section, the root element consists of the tag <simplepaint version="1.0">, the end-tag </simplepaint>, and everything in between. The elements that are nested inside the root element are represented by their own nodes, which are said to be *children* of the root node. An object of type *Element* contains several useful methods. If element is of type *Element*, then we have:

- element.getTagName() — returns a *String* containing the name that is used in the element's tag. For example, the name of a <curve> element is the string "curve".
- element.getAttribute(attrName) — if attrName is the name of an attribute in the element, then this method returns the value of that attribute. For the element, <point x="83" y="42"/>, element.getAttribute("x") would return the string "83". Note that the return value is always a *String*, even if the attribute is supposed to represent a numerical value. If the element has no attribute with the specified name, then the return value is an empty string.

- element.getTextContent() — returns a *String* containing all of the textual content that is contained in the element. Note that this includes text that is contained inside other elements that are nested inside the element.
- element.getChildNodes() — returns a value of type *NodeList* that contains all the *Nodes* that are children of the element. The list includes nodes representing other elements and textual content that are directly nested in the element (as well as some other types of node that I don't care about here). The getChildNodes() method makes it possible to traverse the entire DOM data structure by starting with the root element, looking at children of the root element, children of the children, and so on. (There is a similar method that returns the attributes of the element, but I won't be using it here.)
- element.getElementsByTagName(tagName) — returns a *NodeList* that contains all the nodes representing all elements that are nested inside element and which have the given tag name. Note that this includes elements that are nested to any level, not just elements that are directly contained inside element. The getElementsByTagName() method allows you to reach into the document and pull out specific data that you are interested in.

An object of type *NodeList* represents a list of *Nodes*. Unfortunately, it does not use the API defined for lists in the Java Collection Framework. Instead, a value, nodeList, of type *NodeList* has two methods: nodeList.getLength() returns the number of nodes in the list, and nodeList.item(i) returns the node at position i, where the positions are numbered 0, 1, . . . , nodeList.getLength() - 1. Note that the return value of nodeList.get() is of type *Node*, and it might have to be type-cast to a more specific node type before it is used.

Knowing just this much, you can do the most common types of processing of DOM representations. Let's look at a few code fragments. Suppose that in the course of processing a document you come across an *Element* node that represents the element

<background red='1' green='0.6' blue='0.2'/>

This element might be encountered either while traversing the document with getChildNodes() or in the result of a call to getElementsByTagName("background"). Our goal is to reconstruct the data structure represented by the document, and this element represents part of that data. In this case, the element represents a color, and the red, green, and blue components are given by the attributes of the element. If element is a variable that refers to the node, the color can be obtained by saying:

```
double r = Double.parseDouble( element.getAttribute("red") );
double g = Double.parseDouble( element.getAttribute("green") );
```

```
double b = Double.parseDouble( element.getAttribute("blue") );
Color bgColor = Color.color(r,g,b);
```

Suppose now that element refers to the node that represents the element

```
<symmetric>true</symmetric>
```

In this case, the element represents the value of a boolean variable, and the value is encoded in the textual content of the element. We can recover the value from the element with:

```
String bool = element.getTextContent();
boolean symmetric;
if (bool.equals("true"))
    symmetric = true;
else
    symmetric = false;
```

Next, consider an example that uses a *NodeList*. Suppose we encounter an element that represents a list of *Point2Ds*:

```
<pointlist>
    <point x='17' y='42'/>
    <point x='23' y='8'/>
    <point x='109' y='342'/>
    <point x='18' y='270'/>
</pointlist>
```

Suppose that element refers to the node that represents the <pointlist> element. Our goal is to build the list of type ArrayList<Point2D> that is represented by the element. We can do this by traversing the *NodeList* that contains the child nodes of element:

```
ArrayList<Point2D> points = new ArrayList<>();
NodeList children = element.getChildNodes();
for (int i = 0; i < children.getLength(); i++) {
    Node child = children.item(i);      // One of the child nodes of element.
    if ( child instanceof Element ) {
            Element pointElement = (Element)child;    // One of the <point> elements.
            double x = Double.parseDouble( pointElement.getAttribute("x") );
            double y = Double.parseDouble( pointElement.getAttribute("y") );
```

```
            Point2D pt = new Point2D(x,y); // Create the Point represented by pointElement.
            points.add(pt);   // Add the point to the list of points.
        }
    }
```

All the nested <point> elements are children of the <pointlist> element. The if statement in this code fragment is necessary because an element can have other children in addition to its nested elements. In this example, we only want to process the children that are elements.

All these techniques can be employed to write the file input method for the sample program SimplePaintWithXML.java. When building the data structure represented by an XML file, my approach is to start with a default data structure and then to modify and add to it as I traverse the DOM representation of the file. It's not a trivial process, but I hope that you can follow it:

```
Color newBackground = Color.WHITE;
ArrayList<CurveData> newCurves = new ArrayList<>();
Element rootElement = xmldoc.getDocumentElement();
if ( ! rootElement.getNodeName().equals("simplepaint") )
        throw new Exception("File is not a SimplePaint file.");
String version = rootElement.getAttribute("version");
    try {
        double versionNumber = Double.parseDouble(version);
        if (versionNumber > 1.0)
            throw new Exception("File requires a newer version of SimplePaint.");
    }
    catch (NumberFormatException e) {
    }
    NodeList nodes = rootElement.getChildNodes();
    for (int i = 0; i < nodes.getLength(); i++) {
        if (nodes.item(i) instanceof Element) {
            Element element = (Element)nodes.item(i);
            if (element.getTagName().equals("background")) {
                double r = Double.parseDouble(element.getAttribute("red"));
                double g = Double.parseDouble(element.getAttribute("green"));
```

```
                double b = Double.parseDouble(element.getAttribute("blue"));
                newBackground = Color.color(r,g,b);
    }
    else if (element.getTagName().equals("curve")) {
            CurveData curve = new CurveData();
            curve.color = Color.BLACK;
            curve.points = new ArrayList<>();
            newCurves.add(curve);
            NodeList curveNodes = element.getChildNodes();
            for (int j = 0; j < curveNodes.getLength(); j++) {
                if (curveNodes.item(j) instanceof Element) {
                Element curveElement = (Element)curveNodes.item(j);
                if (curveElement.getTagName().equals("color")) {
                        double r = Double parseDouble(curveElement
                        getAttribute("red"));
                        double g = Double.parseDouble(curveElement
                        getAttribute("green"));
                        double b = Double.parseDouble(curveElement
                        getAttribute("blue"));
                        curve.color = Color.color(r,g,b);
                }
                else if (curveElement.getTagName().equals("point")) {
                        double x = Double.parseDouble(curveElement
                        getAttribute("x"));
                        double y = Double.parseDouble(curveElement
                        getAttribute("y"));
                        curve.points.add(new Point2D(x,y));
                }
                else if (curveElement.getTagName().equals("symmetric")) {
                        String content = curveElement.getTextContent();
                        if (content.equals("true"))
                                curve.symmetric = true;
```

```
                    }
                }
            }
        }
    }
}
backgroundColor = newBackground;
curves = newCurves;
```

You can find the complete source code in SimplePaintWithXML.java.

XML has evolved into a highly significant technology, with certain applications exhibiting considerable complexity. However, there exists a fundamental set of straightforward concepts that can be readily implemented in Java. With a fundamental understanding, you may effectively utilize XML in your Java applications.

INDEX